THE MAZE AND THE WARRIOR

THE MAZE

AND THE

WARRIOR

Symbols in Architecture, Theology, and Music

Craig Wright

Harvard University Press

CAMBRIDGE, MASSACHUSETTS

LONDON, ENGLAND

2001

Publication of this book has been aided by a grant from the
Frederick W. Hilles Publication Fund of Yale University.

Frontispiece: The maze in the nave of the cathedral of Amiens

Book design by Dean Bornstein

Library of Congress Cataloging-in-Publication Data

Wright, Craig M.
  The maze and the warrior : symbols in architecture, theology,
  and music/Craig Wright.
    p. cm.
  Includes biblographical references and index.
  ISBN 0-674-00503-1 (alk. paper)
  1. Labyrinths—Religious aspects—History. 2. Labyrinths—
Religious aspects—Christianity—History. I. Title.
BL325.L3 W75 2001
291.3'7—dc21   00-054118

For Sterling Murray and
in memory of Constance Wright Murray

*En ma fin est mon commencement et
mon commencement ma fin*

Contents

Acknowledgments

Every serious student of the maze will make use of Hermann Kern's monumental book on the subject. I, too, took advantage of his scholarship and erudition, although the recent English version of his work (*Through the Labyrinth*, 2000) did not appear until the present volume was already in press; thus all citations here are to the original German edition (*Labyrinthe*, 1982). Two institutions in particular were helpful during the writing of this book: the Irving Gilmore Music Library at Yale University (Kendall Crilly, music librarian); and the Beinecke Rare Book and Manuscript Library, Yale University (Robert Babcock, curator of medieval manuscripts). The following individuals provided sources, evaluated parts of the manuscript, or stimulated my thinking in a variety of ways: Anne Robertson, John Anderson, Jane Bernstein, Pierre Bizeau, Jenny Bloxam, Philip Bohlman, Mauro Calcagno, Lorenzo Francisco Candelaria, Tova Choate, Thomas Christensen, William Clark, Sherry Dominick, Margot Fassler, Mary Greer, Thomas Greene, Barbara Haggh, Barton Hudson, Michael Huglo, Thomas F. Kelly, Peter Lefferts, Michael Long, Charles McClendon, Robert Morgan, Stephen Murray, Jessie Ann Owens, Alejandro Planchart, Leon Plantinga, Keith Polk, Joshua Rifkin, Kerry Snyder, Pamela Starr, Marica Taconni, Peter Wollny, and Andrew Wright. Bonnie Blackburn and Leofranc Holford-Strevens read all of the text, saving me from myself countless times. Richard Boursy set the musical examples with care, and Dean Bornstein crafted a most pleasing design. Margaretta Fulton of Harvard University Press suggested how my ideas might be shaped into a coherent whole, while senior editor Mary Ellen Geer wisely tempered and arranged my prose. My sincere thanks to you all!

New Haven, Connecticut
1 May 2000

THE MAZE AND THE WARRIOR

Prologue: Maze Mania

Dᴜʀɪɴɢ ᴛʜᴇ 1990s hundreds of labyrinths suddenly appeared in the United States as a "maze mania" swept the country. Most were placed inside or next to churches to facilitate spiritual contemplation. Busy Wall Streeters, for example, could find release from the Stock Exchange by walking the labyrinth at nearby Trinity Church. Elsewhere labyrinths were set in stone in prison yards, painted on gymnasium floors, and mowed into wheat fields. At the Cherry Crest Farm (appropriately located in Paradise, Pennsylvania) one can now walk through a four-acre maize maze (admission $7.00). On the more serious side, labyrinths recently have been endowed with healing powers and visited by groups of AIDS sufferers and by postoperative cancer patients. Focused walking is believed to reduce anxiety and diminish negative thinking. Thus prestigious hospitals in Baltimore, San Francisco, and Chicago have installed mazes as part of their programs of patient rehabilitation. Almost weekly one newspaper or another runs an article with a headline such as "Steps to spirituality," "Labyrinths help worshipers lose selves, find God," "Labyrinths help uncoil meaning on the walk of life," "Believers use labyrinths to prevent getting lost," and "Corn mazes as new cash crop?" On 10 May 1998 the *New York Times* published a front page story entitled "Reviving labyrinths, a path to inner peace." Within the next few days the principal Web site for mazes (*www.grace cathedral.org/labyrinth*) registered no fewer than 15,000 hits from those wishing to learn more. At present 152 other labyrinth Web sites can be accessed through the Internet, and the number grows almost daily. According to the "labyrinth locator" at The World-Wide Labyrinth Project, more than 130 public and private mazes can be visited around the United States. This group aims "to introduce the labyrinth as a spiritual tool to cathedrals, retreat centers, hospitals, prisons, parks, airports, and community spaces worldwide." Competing labyrinth associations, such as The Labyrinth Society (*www.labyrinthproject.com/tls.html*) and The St. Louis Labyrinth Project *(www.labyrinthproject.com)*, intend to do likewise. America has now embraced the maze for spiritual solace, healing, fun, and profit.

But Europe, too, has recently experienced a certain labyrinthine frenzy. In Great Britain 1991 was the Year of the Maze, a culmination of some two decades of renewed interest in this ancient symbol. Perhaps owing to the long history of the English turf maze, most of these new labyrinths were created outdoors. Some were for pure amusement, such as the "Dragon maze" at the Newquay Zoo in Cornwall.[1] Others had a celebratory aim: to commemorate the Silver Jubilee of Queen Elizabeth II (a hedge maze at Springfields Gardens, Lincolnshire) or the five hundredth anniversary of the accession of the Tudor dynasty (a 200,000-brick maze at Kentwell Hall, Suffolk). There have been mazes with musical allusions as well. The sculptor Michael Ayrton created an elliptical maze in response to the theme of "labyrinthine art" that marked the 1984 Bath Festival, where Michael Tippett's opera *The Knot Garden* was produced.[2]

More playful was the Beatles Maze of that same year for the Garden Festival at Liverpool. It was configured in the shape of an apple (for Apple Records), and the goal of the maze-walker was to reach the "yellow submarine" at the center, a visual reminder of the Beatles' hit tune of that name.[3] In Italy the maze serves as an emblem for the Alfa Romeo automobile, where it appears with the motto "It can escape the snarls of traffic" *(Si svincola dalle spire del traffico)*, the conjunction implying that a sporty Alfa can liberate you from the most insoluble maze of all, a Roman rush hour.[4] France is now the home of what is arguably the largest labyrinth ever created: a maze planted in corn on 37 acres of farmland in Reignac-sur-Indre south of Tours. In 1997 more than 80,000 enthusiasts visited this complex of six different patterns drawn from English, African, and Scandinavian designs. Jugglers, conjurers, and magicians led or misled confused families toward the magician's lair in the center.[5] The French government has been inspired to use a replica of the maze at the cathedral of Reims (see Fig. 2.7) as the logo for all historical monuments in that country. What accounts for all this interest in the maze?

My own fascination with labyrinths began quite suddenly. Standing in the nave of the cathedral of Chartres on a sunny afternoon in March 1992, I looked westward to enjoy the extraordinary beauty of the stained glass, as I had on many previous occasions. But this time something was different. The chairs usually placed on the floor of the nave had been removed, and gradually I came to focus on the original, early thirteenth-century pavement. There beneath my feet was a maze. I dimly recalled that there was indeed a maze at Chartres, but up to this moment I had paid no attention to it. What was a maze doing here? How did this seemingly non-religious object come to be placed in what was intended to be the house of the Lord? What function did it serve in the religious services of the distant past? Pursuit of that question carried me not only deeper into the liturgy of Chartres and other churches, but also into the study of theology and, ultimately, anthropology.

Labyrinths have appeared in societies around the globe. The Hohokam Indians near Phoenix, Arizona, played a ball game in a labyrinthine circular enclosure that resembles the maze on which the game of the *pilota* was danced at the medieval cathedral of Auxerre, France. Influence or coincidence? From Italy to Iran, from the Hebrides northwest of England to the New Hebrides northeast of Australia, complex designs, multiple concentric rings, spiral-form patterns, and cerebral-form convolutions abound in locations that seem to be infused with ceremonial significance. They appear painted on walls, carved as graffiti in rocks, cut as chambers in subterranean grottos. Are all of these intricate constructions truly labyrinths?

Some ethnographers would answer yes. But for the purposes of this book, I will employ a more limited definition of a maze. Not only must complexity and confusion be inherent in the pattern, but the design must have a single, clearly defined entrance and a single, equally well-defined center. An intricate, ever-winding path connects the two. The route may contain a series of false turns that momentarily deflect the feet or the eye to one or more dead ends, and these steps must be retraced so as to regain the true path. Those mazes in which a choice, and therefore a wrong turn, is possible are called multicursal mazes; those with only a single path leading directly from entrance to center, no matter how convoluted the path, are unicursal. The former requires logic to solve a puzzle; the latter demands faith to attain a goal. Surprisingly, almost all labyrinths to be seen in the West before the appearance of the Renaissance garden maze are unicursal. The quality by which most of us identify a maze—repeated choice and false turnings—is thus a rather late development. Implicit in both multicursal and unicursal mazes, however, is a goal-oriented challenge, a linear quest, no matter how tortuous the route. The eternal allure of the maze is the seemingly unattainable center.

Mazes which have a path to the center also have something more: someone on that path. Here the image of the warrior of the maze comes into
view. The warrior is part of the myth of the maze. Throughout Western civilization the labyrinth has been not only a visible object, but also an
archetype in which an ancient combat myth was played out. A myth, of
course, expresses some deep-seated desire or fear in human nature that
transcends time and geography. Although not all civilizations tell the tale in
the same way, they all share a core of beliefs. The myth of the maze expresses the eternal hope of salvation—that eternal life will be won for all by
the actions of one savior. This warrior will defeat the forces of evil lurking
in the center of the maze. The central malevolent power may be a bull, the
Minotaur, Khumbaba, Typhon, Satan, or, by metaphorical extension, the
wicked pharaoh of Egypt, the giant Goliath, or the menacing Turk. As for
the hero of the maze, he has assumed many faces over time: those of Theseus, Jason, Gilgamesh, Hercules, Moses, David, Christ, St. Michael, Christian, Tamino, and the Armed Man. The name of this warrior may change,
but he is inseparable from the maze. Every myth needs a hero.

By now the attentive reader will have noticed that the terms "maze" and
"labyrinth" are used here interchangeably. There is no difference between
the two, although they have distinct etymologies. Most Romance languages
(French, Italian, and Spanish, for example) possess only a single word for
this object, one that derives from the Latin *labyrinthus* (distantly related to
the Greek λαβρυς, meaning "double axe"). English speakers are more
fortunate, for since at least the fourteenth century we have also enjoyed
"maze" and, by extension, "amazed" as part of our vocabulary. Although
some twentieth-century observers insist on a distinction between the multicursal maze (involving choice) and a unicursal labyrinth (a one-way
path), the great English writers from Chaucer to Milton to Defoe did no
such thing. For the linguistic richness of the English language, I am profoundly grateful.

Although my own training is in music, this book is not designed primarily for musicologists. Rather, it is intended for those interested in religious studies and spirituality generally. It is framed so as to answer questions that gradually emerged from my experience at Chartres: What did the
maze represent in classical antiquity, and what did it become during its heyday in the medieval cathedrals? What were the special theological implications of the maze? How did these play themselves out in architecture, mu-

sic, dance, and the visual arts? When and why did the maze lose its symbolic resonance? Finally, why was this symbol revived in the twentieth century, and what, if anything, does our New Age maze have in common with its classical and medieval ancestors?

Reading this book, like journeying through a maze, will require patience and perseverance. Sometimes the subject matter may seem dense and obscure. There will be occasional digressions and blind alleys. But as Matthew enjoined, and medieval theologians repeated: "Endure to the end" (10:22 and 24:13). The reader who does so will enjoy, if not the everlasting life promised in the scriptures, at least some greater historical awareness of a timeless symbol.

CHAPTER ONE

The Ancient and Early Christian Maze

THE MAZE IS A SYMBOL in Christian theology and art, but its origins predate Christ, extending far back into the civilizations of the ancient world. It is linked to an old Greek myth that spoke of a hero, Theseus, who descended into a dangerous labyrinth to fight an evil creature and save his people from a horrific end. Later, during the Christian Middle Ages, this pagan hero was transformed into the Savior, and the place of his heroic fight with evil was symbolized by a maze placed near the entry door at many monasteries and cathedrals. As Theseus slew the dreaded Minotaur, so Christ defeated Satan on the day of his resurrection. Thus the church maze and its symbolic meaning grew out of, and remained inextricably tied to, an ancient combat myth.

The story of Theseus, the Minotaur, and the maze at Crete is known to every student of school Latin. It has been passed down to us primarily through the *Metamorphoses* of Ovid (43 B.C.–18 A.D.), an important collection of classical mythology widely read as a Latin primer during the Middle Ages, the Renaissance, and even today. But Ovid was just one of many writers to tell this tale. Plutarch (45–120 A.D.) in the first volume of his *Lives* and Virgil (70–19 B.C.) in his *Aeneid,* as well as many Greek poets and singers extending back to Hesiod and Homer, offer slightly different accounts of all or part of the legend, the gist of which is as follows.[1]

On the island of Crete, in the city of Knossos, there once ruled the powerful king Minos, who had dominion over much of the surrounding lands and islands of the Mediterranean. His wife Pasiphaë, led astray by unnatural affection, had mated with a handsome white bull and produced the hideous Minotaur, a flesh-eating monster with the body of a man and the head of a bull. Advised by certain oracles to hide the queen's beastly adultery, Minos commanded the inventor Daedalus to construct a maze, an edifice of confusion and deceit, from which no one, including the monster, could escape. Minos fed the Minotaur sacrificial victims from among the flower of the youth of Athens, for the Athenians owed Minos tribute. Once every nine years (some accounts say every year), seven young men and seven virgins of Athens were placed in the maze, where, unable to escape, they met a grisly death. Among the third group of fourteen to be sacrificed was Theseus, the son of the Athenian king Aegeus. Alighting on the shores of Crete, the handsome Theseus caught the eye of Ariadne, daughter of Minos, whereupon love compelled her to aid the intended victim. Ariadne supplied the warrior with a ball of pitch and a clew of golden yarn, one end of which was to be fastened to the entrance of the maze, and the rest unwound as he proceeded. Once in the center of the labyrinth, Theseus threw the ball of pitch into the Minotaur's gaping mouth, slew him with his sword, and followed the golden thread back out of the maze. Accompanied by the other youths of Athens, Theseus and Ariadne fled to the island of Delos where they performed a peculiar celebratory dance. In it they recreated, through their steps, the path of the labyrinth, at the center of which was placed a horned altar, a symbol of the bull-headed Minotaur. From Delos the Athenians proceeded to the island of Naxos, where Theseus abandoned Ariadne and then returned to his homeland.

Back on Crete, King Minos was enraged that Theseus had solved the labyrinth and fled with his daughter, so he locked Daedalus and his son, Icarus, in the inventor's own mazy prison. The crafty Daedalus, however, constructed wings for the two, and they flew up and out of the labyrinth. But as "pride goeth before a fall," the impetuous Icarus flew too high. The sun melted the wax that secured his wings, and he plunged to a watery death. Daedalus flew on to the southern Italian town of Cumae, where he built a temple to the Sun-god Apollo, carving on its gates the story of the Cretan maze.

This, in brief, is the tale of Theseus, Daedalus, and the labyrinth at Crete. But what is the relationship between myth and archaeological fact? Was the maze an actual place, or merely an archetype of the imagination?

While Minos appears to have been a genuine historical figure, and his royal palace at Knossos, Crete, an architectural reality, the existence of a labyrinth there is dubious.[2] The palace of the Minoan kings at Knossos, apparently built around 2000 B.C., was unearthed by Sir Arthur Evans early in the twentieth century. Evans uncovered one subterranean prison with markings that suggest a cult of the bull, as well as a mysterious "House of the Double Axe."[3] Yet neither he nor later archaeologists discovered a labyrinth,[4] possibly because sometime before 1600 B.C. the palace was destroyed, apparently by a great earthquake.[5] Perhaps the Cretan maze was only a literary construction, a convenient fabrication around which a storyteller might spin a fanciful yarn. Possibly it was the king's forbidding dungeon, a prison that came to be known as a "labyrinth" because of its twisting and turning corridors. Possibly it was simply an outdoor arena where votaries of Ariadne celebrated a ritual dance with labyrinthine choreography. Possibly, too, the Cretan labyrinth did once exist, but was wholly destroyed by natural forces sometime between 2000 and 1600 B.C.

Although we may never know if a maze did in fact exist at Knossos,[6] one thing is certain: the image of that maze, whether based on myth or on material reality, was forcefully impressed in the imagination of the ancient Greeks. Representations of the Cretan maze appear throughout the pre-Christian world, sometimes on rock carvings, jewelry, or pottery. The people of Knossos, who numbered 100,000 at the peak of Minoan civilization,[7] issued coins stamped with a design of the labyrinth, intending the maze to serve as a symbol of their redoubtable city (Fig. 1.1).[8] In these representations the maze is depicted sometimes as square and sometimes as elliptical. It encompasses a succession of meanders along seven tracks, but offers no possibility of error.

Thus already in the earliest mazes from Crete can be seen an attribute that would hold true for the labyrinth for nearly three thousand years. Almost all mazes in the West prior to the fifteenth century were unicursal.[9] The "one-way" maze was confusing, perhaps frightening, but it did not involve a choice of direction, only perseverance. The path of the maze twisted and turned as it moved inexorably toward the center. There was only a single entrance, which also served as the sole exit. This unicursal Cretan maze, whether found on a Hellenic vase, a Knossan coin, or a Sardinian rock carving, is essentially the same in all its physical particulars, and thus constitutes an archetype. Although no maze has ever been unearthed at Knossos, it is clear that the seven-track pattern of the Cretan labyrinth, as well as the union of that pattern with the myth of Theseus and the Minotaur, had been insinuated in the collective psyche of the civilized Mediterranean world long before the advent of Christ.

The physical attributes of the pre-Christian maze are important. But so, too, are the human responses the Hellenic world associated with it—fear,

FIGURE 1.1 Silver coin from Knossos dating from about 350 B.C.

bravery, tenacity, bewilderment, a sense of evil, and many others. These psychological states are inseparable from the meaning of the maze. Thus the power of the maze derived not only from a bewildering form, but also from the compelling story from which that pattern emerged. The maze achieved its full force only when amplified by the resonant context of the Greek myth. Yet some of the psychological associations inherent in the labyrinth sprang not from Greek, but from Roman sources.

Theseus was a warrior. Indeed, throughout history the hero of the maze is a man of arms. The Roman poet Virgil describes a hero in a labyrinth in his *Aeneid* (Book V, lines 546–591). Here the wandering Aeneas orchestrates a sequence of militaristic games to honor a fallen soldier of Troy.[10] These culminate in a parade in which Ascanius, the son of Aeneas, and other young descendants of Troy create an equestrian ballet. Wearing armor and brandishing lances, they ride in and out, replicating the pattern of the maze at Crete.

> They staged a new set of manoeuvres and counter-manoeuvres, keeping their relative positions, each group, while performing their maze of evo-lutions—a mimic engagement of mounted troops. Now they turn their backs in flight, now wheel and charge with lance in rest, and now ride peacefully, file by file. It was like the fabled Labyrinth constructed in mountainous Crete—a maze of unbroken walls, with thousands of blind alleys, to keep the venturer guessing and trick him, so that the right path into the heart of the maze was a puzzle to find or retrace.[11]

A graphic representation of this Trojan ride survives on an Etruscan wine pitcher, dating from about 625 B.C. but based on an earlier Greek model. Called the Tragliatella pitcher after the area in Italy in which it was discovered, the wine jug depicts youthful riders with lances and shields whose motions recreate the classic form of the seven-track Cretan maze (Fig. 1.2).[12] Within the outermost path of this labyrinth (lower right) is written "Truia," apparently the Etruscan word for Troy.

What was the meaning of the Trojan ride, as depicted on the Tragliatella pitcher and recounted by Virgil, and what was its significance for later centuries? The labyrinth of the Trojan ride emerged from a ritual act in which youthful soldiers honored a fallen hero. As such, the maze was both an object of funereal commemoration and the site of initiation for young warriors who had come of age. Negotiating the intricate path of the maze, while wielding military weapons, was emblematic of bravery and ultimate victory. Later, in the rites of the medieval Christian church, celebratory games played on and around a maze would figure prominently on Easter Sunday, the day of Christ's victory over death.

Yet the symbolic Trojan ride suggested more: as the youthful horsemen processed, they carefully circumscribed a zone into which the uninitiated could not penetrate. The import of the word "Truia" is that these descendants of Troy were recreating Troy itself, the model of the intricate, yet impregnable city of the ancient world.[13] Later, turf and topiary mazes in England and other northern countries would be called "Troy town" as well as "Julian's Bower," evidently because Virgil's Trojan ride was led by Julus or Ascanius, son of Aeneas.[14] The medieval clergy would later replace the impregnable city of Troy with that redoubtable fortress of the Old Testament,

FIGURE 1.2 Etruscan wine jug dating from about 625 B.C. on which is depicted (enhanced below) the Trojan ride and the maze it formed. Written in the outer track of
the maze is the word "Truia" (Troy). The copulating couple to the right is thought to
represent the sacred union of Theseus and Ariadne, following the successful adventure
in the Cretan labyrinth.

Jericho.[15] Stylized gates and towers, as well as labyrinthine geometric patterns, protect the archetypical holy city. Ultimately, in the seventeenth century, Jericho would in turn be replaced by celestial Jerusalem, the city-state
par excellence described in the New Testament Book of Apocalypse. All of
these later resonances spring from the Greek myth of Daedalus and the epic
story of Troy.

FIGURE 1.3 Roman pavement maze dating from the first century A.D., originally in a villa on the Via Cadolini in Cremona, Italy. In the center Theseus and the Minotaur battle to the death.

Crete and Troy were places from which Greek legends arose. But mazes have been found in Roman cities as well.[16] Indeed, remains of Roman pavement labyrinths survive almost everywhere the Roman Empire once extended, in North Africa, Austria, Switzerland, France, Spain, and the British Isles.[17] Most are mosaics made of thousands of small pieces of colored marble or tile. In form these labyrinths are sometimes elliptical, but far more

FIGURE 1.4 Third-century Roman mosaic from a family tomb at Sousse, Tunisia.
At the center, on its back, lies the dying Minotaur. The inscription at the bottom
suggests that anyone caught in the maze will perish.

often square—the square, in turn, often being subdivided into quadrants.[18] Usually the Minotaur can be seen in the center, or perhaps Theseus and the Minotaur engaged in mortal combat (Fig. 1.3). The Roman floor maze was most often placed at the entrance to a patrician's villa, where it served as a "security zone."[19] It protected the master's house from unwanted intruders and evil spirits, for no malevolent force would dare cross a threshold of bestial entrapment. This, too, was evidently the intent of the maze etched on a pillar at the House of Lucretius in Pompeii, where an inscription read: "Labyrinth: Here lives the Minotaur" *(Labyrinthus: Hic habitat Minotaurus)*.[20] Such a greeting must have functioned much like the modern warning "Beware of the Dog."[21]

Tombs, too, were guarded by labyrinths. Placed at the entry to a burial vault, the maze suggested a carefully delimited precinct occupied by shades and demonic spirits, a graphic representation of the Underworld. Crossing into such a "land of the dead" was a perilous act. This, at least, is the clear implication of the inscription in a maze guarding a family tomb at Sousse, Tunisia (Fig. 1.4). The design was accompanied by the words "The man shut in here loses his life" *(Hic inclusus vitam perdit)*. This sense of danger, too, was passed on to the maze of the early Christian church, for only a person of superior faith would step within such a perilous place. And just as Theseus experienced a labyrinthine hell on Crete, so the figure of Christ would undertake the Harrowing of Hell in the maze in the medieval church.

Thus the maze appears to have had many different and sometimes contradictory meanings. To mention just one paradox: the Cretan labyrinth signified a gloomy, tortuous Underworld; yet the maze in the Virgilian Trojan ride served as a metaphor for Troy, the perfect fortress-city. This multivalent quality of the labyrinth accounts, in part, for its power and durability as a symbol through the ages. What is perhaps unique about the maze as both object and archetype is the antithetical nature of so many of its meanings. These can be separated into positive and negative values.

Above all, the maze was a complex work of art, having been designed by Daedalus, an inventor who personified human ingenuity. It was also an arena for trial and ordeal, for confrontation and conquest, for initiatory rites in which the hero undergoes a process of self-discovery. Engaging the maze constituted an exercise of faith and perseverance. In Roman antiquity the labyrinth suggested, in addition, the archetype of the ideal city. Finally, the maze served as a precinct within which evil was contained and into which, paradoxically, no evil spirit would dare to penetrate. In this way it functioned as an amulet against sinister forces. These were several of the positive resonances of the classical maze that would carry over into the Christian Middle Ages.

Yet the maze, like the double-sided axe, had two faces, and for every association *in bono*, there was an opposite one *in malo (in bonam/malam partem)*. The maze was an object of deception, a ruse designed to trick and confound. It was, furthermore, a dark and noisy prison whence there was no escape, a Hades in which the innocent were sacrificed. The perimeter of the maze separated the world of the quick from that of the dead; it differentiated outer from inner space, good from evil. God and Satan are timeless antagonists, and in mythology they are inseparable and reciprocal: for without vice there is no virtue; without a villain there can be no hero. From the time of the first appearance of the maze within the early Christian church, each labyrinth exemplified some, if not all, of these contradictory and complementary meanings.

The Symbolism of the Early Christian Maze

Archaeologists of Hellenic and Roman culture have unearthed labyrinths in a bewildering variety of places. Indoor mazes from this period, however, all have one thing in common: they were located within secular buildings, whether domestic or civic, but not in religious temples. By contrast, all indoor labyrinths from late antiquity and the Middle Ages were situated within Christian churches.[22] Judging from extant archaeological evidence, the medieval labyrinth knew no existence outside a house of worship. Not until the sixteenth century, when the spirit of the Renaissance sought to revivify the traditions of classical antiquity, was a maze again constructed within a civic building or private residence.

The earliest known maze in a Christian sanctuary comes from the floor of the church of St. Reparatus in Orléansville/El Asnam, one hundred miles west of Algiers, Algeria.[23] St. Reparatus was dedicated in 324, the same year that Emperor Constantine commenced building St. Peter's in Rome, and thus it dates from the "heroic" period of North African Christianity.[24] The design of this Algerian maze (Fig. 1.5) belongs to the tradition of the Roman

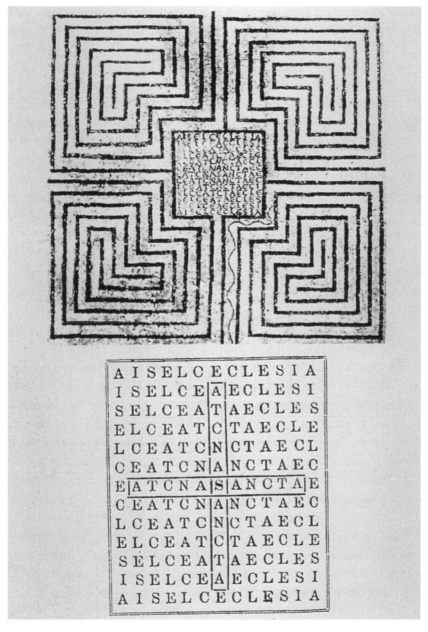

FIGURES 1.5 and 1.6 Fourth-century pavement maze formerly in the church of St. Reparatus in Orléansville/El Asnam, Algeria, presently in the cathedral of Algiers. An enlargement of the center of the maze reveals the words *Sancta Eclesia* formed as a palindrome.

mosaic labyrinth. Indeed, its pattern is similar to the Roman maze found at Sousse, Tunisia (compare Figs. 1.5 and 1.4).

The basilica of St. Reparatus, like the old St. Peter's, was constructed with a semicircular apse on both the east and west ends. The visitor entered at the west portal and was directed around the west apse to the north aisle.[25] On the floor lay the maze, a square labyrinth measuring 2.5 meters on each side and composed of thousands of black and white tiles. An undulating line representing Ariadne's thread leads into the southwest sector, the first of four identical quadratic patterns. The route then proceeds to the southeast sector, and so on in counter-clockwise fashion. At the end a corridor paralleling the initial line of entry leads to the goal, the central square. In the center rests another labyrinth, a verbal rather than a geometric one: the words SANCTA ECLESIA are arranged in a continual palindrome (Fig. 1.6). As SANCTA is read forwards and backwards, up and down, the letters outline a cross. Already in this first Christian labyrinth there is a suggestion that the maze involves a process of reversal—that it is a mirror, an earthly object that reflects a higher spiritual truth. Commencing with the centermost "S" and progressing farther (reading to the left or to the right, then up or down), the text SANCTA ECLESIA, or part of it, will always appear.

Thus the Algerian labyrinth is a maze *in bono.* There is no evil force to conquer, no fearsome Minotaur at the center, only the comfort of the Holy Mother Church *(Sancta ecclesia).* The symbolic journey that this labyrinth proposed to the proselyte of the new Christian religion was strewn with checks and reversals, the snares and perils of the temporal world. Yet it offered the faithful the prospect of infinite reward, symbolized by the central Cross of the Holy Church at the end. Such a maze suggested no return, only a persistent movement toward that ultimate goal. Ariadne's thread appears at the entry to lead in, but not back out.

More symbolism rests in this North African maze, namely a clear west-east axis. The maze was positioned near the west portal, at the people's entrance to the church. (Almost all church mazes found in later medieval sanctuaries would similarly be placed just inside the west door.) Such a location has both physical and symbolic import: physical in the sense that the convert is immediately confronted by the labyrinth, and thus the proposition that adherence to the Christian faith will require an inward effort *(labor intus);* symbolic in the sense that the line of movement through the church progresses from west to east. The new Christian moves from an old world and progresses toward a higher realm. He leaves the terrestrial world at the west door, traverses a zone of initiation and purification (the maze), and advances toward the body and blood of Christ on the altar at the east end of the church.

Not only is the maze approached from the west, but entry into it must be made from a western point. The spiritual pilgrim enters the maze on its west side and proceeds forward with twists and turns, moving sometimes toward the east, sometimes backward to the west, sometimes south, and sometimes north. But the overall course within the labyrinth is west-to-east: just before reaching the center, in this and nearly all church mazes, the line of march again turns eastward. At this point the path becomes parallel with the west-east axis present at the entry into the maze. Thus the first and last steps are taken on a line west to east.

Movement along a west-east axis would become fundamental to the Christian concept of pilgrimage in the Middle Ages. Such an orientation can also be seen in mazes in ecclesiastical manuscripts and in medieval world maps *(mappae mundi)*.[26] In medieval cartography, west (Europe and Africa) is down and east (Asia) is up, contrary to our modern arrangement in which west is to the left and east to the right. For a European, the eye's line of progress—the voyage that the viewer takes—proceeds from a lower western point of entry to a higher eastern terminal. The goal, the Holy City of Jerusalem, is situated in the geographic center.[27] In medieval manuscripts mazes were often positioned adjacent to such world maps.[28] They, too, have their point of entry at the bottom and proceed toward the top, in cartographic terms, from west to east.

Fundamental to the concept of a spiritual march eastward is, of course, the notion of a pilgrimage of the soul from the land of the setting sun to that of the rising sun. The West was a land of the dead, for in the word "occident" is the Latin verb *occidere,* to fall or be slain. West was the direction toward which the beasts of the earth faced.[29] East, contrarily, was the point of the rising sun, the new light, the new fire.[30] "The Lord God planted a garden eastward in Eden," Genesis (2:8) tells us. Eve travels first westward, where she bears the murderous Cain; she then reverses course, moving eastward, and gives birth to Abel, the prototype of the sacrificial Christ. "The Orient is His name," as scripture suggests, and thus the east is associated with Christ himself. "You are facing the East," says St. Ambrose as he prescribes the rite of baptism; "The man who renounces the demon turns to Christ and sees him face to face."[31] Indeed, in Germanic languages the very word "Easter" *(Ostern)* weds the idea of the rising Eastern sun to Christ's ultimate triumph.[32] Thus when faithful Christians had completed the ordeal on the labyrinth at the west end of the church, they had taken an important step away from the zone of the dead and toward a new life in Christ at the eastern high altar.

Mazes in Monastic Manuscripts

The maze surviving from the basilica of St. Reparatus was not the only North African church labyrinth in the ancient world. Another such mosaic once rested in a fifth-century basilica in the city of Tigzirt, just to the east of Algiers.[33] Both mazes stood as symbols of the new Christian religion that spread as the old Roman Empire disintegrated. A gap of nearly seven hundred years, from the fifth to the early twelfth century A.D., separates these two early church labyrinths from those later constructed in sanctuaries in medieval Europe.[34] This void is filled in part by mazes drawn in monastic manuscripts dating as early as the ninth century and emanating from Carolingian France and Germany. The formal patterns created in these manuscript mazes were eventually transferred to the much larger labyrinths installed in the floors of churches in Italy, France, and, far more rarely, Germany, beginning in the twelfth century.

New labyrinthine designs begin to appear in the West around 800 A.D.[35] They were the creation of a monastic culture. Specifically, they were the product of the monastic *scriptorium,* the writing room and intellectual center of the Benedictine communities that monopolized learning during these supposedly "dark" centuries. The monks used the labyrinth for illustrative purposes, creating mazy patterns in many different kinds of books: calendars, astrological charts, geographical tracts, encyclopedias, chronicles, and world histories. The labyrinth was a symbol that could help explain many texts, especially those charting the passing of time. Eventually, having become well known and widely disseminated in manuscript form, these new patterns moved out of the *scriptorium* and into the church.

Surprisingly, it is the old Cretan labyrinth, rather than the quadratic Roman maze, that was the direct ancestor of the new Carolingian designs. Indeed, the Roman type, with its usual rectilinear, quadripartite form in

FIGURE 1.7 A seven-track labyrinth appearing in a treatise of astronomical and computational tables and poems emanating from the monastery of St. Gall, Switzerland, about 850.

which each sector must be traversed in turn, dies out. The often elliptical Cretan-type maze survives but undergoes a gradual process of expansion and refinement. As it changes, it becomes imbued with Christian symbolism.

Christianizing the shape of the maze began during the early ninth century in the eastern part of the Carolingian Empire, in the region of the important monasteries at St. Gall and Reichenau, Switzerland. The elliptical form of the Cretan maze was made round and became fully symmetrical. Eight progressively smaller concentric circles now define seven tracks that work toward the center (Fig. 1.7). The center, too, has become fully circular and is somewhat larger than in its Cretan forebear. Circular mazes such as

FIGURE 1.8 God, the Architect of the Universe, designs with a compass, from a thirteenth-century French *Bible moralisée*.

these were usually drawn with the aid of a compass. In the Middle Ages the compass and the circle it produced were signs of unity and divine perfection, for the circle knows no beginning or end. God, the architect of the world, worked with a compass (Fig. 1.8). Soon, within as few as fifty years, the seven-track circular maze had grown to eleven tracks. This added another element of Christian meaning, for from the time of Augustine and throughout the Middle Ages the number eleven signified sin, dissonance, transition, and incompleteness. It extends beyond the number of the Commandments, yet does not attain that of the Apostles or of the months of the year.[36] Hereafter only rarely would the number of tracks in a labyrinth exceed eleven. The eleven tracks of the maze symbolize the folds of sin that ensnare the soul in this earthly life.

Finally, around the year 900, a clever monk created what would prove to be the ultimate design for the Christian church maze. He was likely working somewhere in the archdiocese of Sens, France, which then extended from the dioceses of Paris and Chartres on the north and west down to those of Auxerre and Nevers in the south. This design is called the "Chartrain type" of labyrinth because it appears on the floor at the cathedral of Chartres—the largest, and many would say the most beautiful, church maze ever created (Fig. 1.9). In fact, however, the eleven-track Chartres-type maze appears in monastic manuscripts some three hundred years before the pattern was set in the pavement of the cathedral of Chartres sometime around 1215. The place of origin of this type of maze was probably not Chartres, but farther to the south in the monasteries at Auxerre, which was a center of Benedictine learning during the second half of the ninth century.[37]

The essential difference between the Chartres-type maze and its monastic predecessors is the superimposition of the figure of the cross (see Fig. 1.9). The cross was incorporated by inserting checks along the east, north, and south axes of the maze, in addition to those already existing on the west end. All full circles were divided into semicircles and quarter-circles, and this in turn necessitated many more reversals of course as the spiritual pilgrim was now checked by the four axes of the cardinal points of the compass. What results is a design that is far more intricate than any previous monastic pattern. Yet it is also aesthetically pleasing, perhaps because the rectilinear lines of the cross provide a welcome counterpoint to the symmetry of the concentric circles. By incorporating the symbolism of the

FIGURE 1.9 The famous labyrinth of the cathedral of Chartres, set on the floor about 1215. Measuring nearly 13 meters across, it is the largest of the surviving church mazes.

cross, in addition to that of the divine circle and the sinful number eleven, the labyrinth in Western Europe had become Christianized in form and meaning.[38] It was a maze both *in bono* and *in malo*.

Evil encompassed by divinely perfect form—this feeling radiates from one of the earliest Chartres-type labyrinths to appear in a manuscript, a

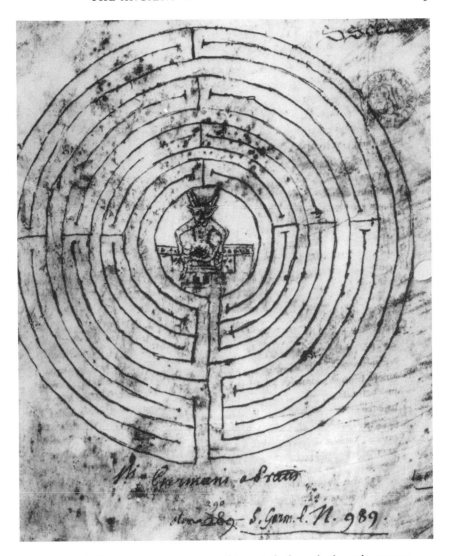

FIGURE 1.10 A Chartres-type maze inserted in a ninth-through-eleventh-century computational book coming from the Parisian abbey of St. Germain des Prés.

computational book from the Parisian monastery of St. Germain des Prés (Fig. 1.10).[39] At the top a text recounts the story of the Cretan labyrinth: the maze was fabricated by Daedalus and is so complex that, once ensnared, it is "impossible to progress from the darkness back to light."[40] The labyrinthine world is a place of sin and error, an *orbis peccati*. To the left a

FIGURE 1.11 The systematic process that creates a labyrinth of the Chartres-type design.

human figure points below to the enclosure made by Daedalus to contain the Minotaur *(Inclausum Dedalus [fecit] Monocentaurum)*. At the center of the maze the monster sits enthroned, his eyes and mouth burning red. Evil lurks deep within the new cruciform design.

How did our diabolically clever French monk—we'll call him Brother Auxerre—create this complex pattern? Using a straight-edge, he drew a line down to set an axis of entry (from the west). Then, placing the point of a compass firmly in what would become the exact center of the maze, he drew a series of 90- and 180-degree arcs. These he connected to form tracks, and thus was made the northern inner sector of the maze (Fig. 1.11A). Brother Auxerre then proceeded similarly to design a southern inner sector (Fig. 1.11B), then a northern outer sector (Fig. 1.11C), which left only the southern outer sector to effect completion (Fig. 1.11D). Thus what appears to be an endlessly confusing configuration can in fact be formed simply by proceeding with a compass from one sector to the next. Moreover, these sectors have a certain similarity. As we shall see in the following chapter, Brother Auxerre's Chartres-type maze is stamped with a perfect, though hidden, symmetry. For the moment it suffices to say that Sector I is mirrored by Sector IV, and Sector II by Sector III.

With the creation of the Chartres-type maze around 900, the evolution of the Christian labyrinth is complete. For the next six hundred years, from the tenth to the sixteenth century, there are only modifications to this fundamental, indeed "classic," church design. Sometimes, as we shall see, the arrangement of semicircles and quarter-circles within the maze appears in a slightly different order. Sometimes the route is shaped, apparently for symbolic purposes, to produce an octagon. Sometimes this octagon has protective "towers" (see Fig. 2.7). But the moral imperative of these Christian labyrinths is always the same: do not deviate from the path of rectitude if you hope to arrive at celestial Jerusalem. Only in the sixteenth century, with the creation of puzzle mazes and the garden labyrinths out of doors, would new labyrinthine forms emerge, and in these the maze-walker would find pleasure and delight in place of spiritual counsel.

CHAPTER TWO

The Maze as Symbol in the Church

THE MAZE WITHIN THE CHURCH had its heyday during the Middle Ages, when symbolism was rampant in the West. Aside from the two North African church labyrinths dating from late antiquity discussed in Chapter 1, the surviving mazes in the West were set in stone during the years 1200–1550 A.D. It is striking that all medieval floor labyrinths are found within churches, not in civic buildings or private residences. This was, of course, a deeply spiritual age, and most surviving medieval architecture—indeed, most medieval art—was religious in nature. Archaeological data suggest, moreover, that church mazes created during the Middle Ages were constructed in only two countries: the lands of modern-day Italy and France. Of course there were once church mazes in other countries, but these have disappeared in the course of time. In Germany, for example, a late-thirteenth-century maze once rested on the floor of St. Severin's in Cologne, but only the center stone of this maze survives today.[1] In England labyrinths were added to churches at Alkborough, Bourn, and Ely in the nineteenth century, late monuments attesting to a Romantic nostalgia for the Middle Ages and the attending "Gothic Revival."[2] There are, however, no authentic medieval church floor mazes in England like the ones that survive in Italy and France. For whatever reason, the English chose to create outdoor mazes in fields and meadows but not indoor mazes within churches.[3] To engage the mazes of the Western Church, consequently, is to enter into those of Italy and France.

Italian Church Mazes

No country preserves a richer cultural patrimony than Italy. But earthquakes, fires, and other disasters, both natural and man-made, have reduced to a mere handful the number of Italian church mazes that survive today, or are known to have once existed. If we know of a half-dozen or so today, however, it is not too wildly speculative to suggest that as many as sixty once graced Italian sanctuaries, applying the standard ten-to-one loss ratio often invoked in medieval studies. Churches in Lucca, Pontremoli, Piacenza, Pavia, Ravenna, and two institutions in Rome are known to have possessed labyrinths.[4] Three of these—those in Rome and Piacenza—disappeared in the nineteenth century, though early drawings by French archaeologists record their shapes and dimensions.

Pavia

What is probably the earliest extant Italian church maze is found on the floor in the choir of San Michele Maggiore in Pavia, just south of Milan.[5] Both choir and maze at San Michele date from the early years of the twelfth century. Although only the top portion of the labyrinth survives *in situ,* a drawing from the late sixteenth century, now in the Vatican Library,[6] reproduces much of the missing material and allows for an almost total reconstruction of the original design. As can be seen in Figure 2.1, this mosaic originally consisted of an elaborate narrative program centering around a Chartres-type labyrinth, one measuring 3.5 meters across. Within the center of the maze the story of Theseus and the Minotaur once again unfolds: Theseus attacks the monster with a club, while the latter wields a sword, at the same time displaying the severed head of his last victim. A semicircular inscription reads: "Theseus entered and slew the double-form monster" *(Theseus intravit monstrumque biforme necavit).*

Surrounding the maze, at the four corners of the central square (proceeding clockwise from the upper right) are a goose (CHANDA?), a flying horse (EQUS), a dragon (DRACO), and a goat (CAPRA), symbols of the bestial nature of the world similar to the "wildman" figures that appear in the margins of medieval books of the hours.[7] On the two flanking borders, the imagery becomes progressively more Christian. To the left we see GOLIA, spear in hand, and DAVID with his slingshot. Goliath's shield declaims: "I am wild and strong and desire to inflict mortal wounds" *(Sum ferus et fortis cupiens dare vulnera mortis).* To which David responds: "The mighty shall be brought down and the humble exalted" *(Sternitur elatus stat mitis ad alta levatus).*[8] David carries a club identical to that of Theseus, thereby making the parallel inescapable: as the classical figure Theseus slew the demonic Minotaur, so the David of the Old Testament destroyed the

FIGURE 2.1 *(top)* The partially preserved pavement maze in the church of San Michele Maggiore in Pavia, Italy. *(bottom)* A sixteenth-century drawing supplies the missing lower part, although the original Chartres-type maze is incorrectly completed as a series of concentric circles.

monstrous Goliath. The inscriptions here seem to be amplifying a passage in a sermon of St. Augustine (d. 430): "Brothers, here you are struggling, on the one side is the devil in the form of Goliath, on the other is Christ typified by David."[9] Old Testament parable gives way to overt Christian symbolism in the incomplete right border with the image of the fish. The letters of the Greek word for fish (ΙΧθΥΣ) formed, according to traditional Christian exegesis, the acronym Jesus/Christ/of God/the Son/Savior.

Finally, at the very top of this labyrinthine mosaic, an enthroned figure appears personifying Annus (the Year), flanked by the names and depictions of the labors of the twelve months; April stands on the right of Annus and May on his left. As we shall see in the discussion of the astrology of the maze (Chapter 4), the labyrinth frequently appears adjacent to calendars and zodiacal charts. In these contexts it symbolizes the endless cycle of earthly time and the spiritual rebirth that comes with the new year, which many Mediterranean cultures reckoned by the arrival of the vernal equinox near April. This maze at Pavia, then, offers a Christian vision of the entire history of the world progressing chronologically from primordial time, to the age of classical mythology, to Old Testament prophecy, and ultimately to Christian revelation.

Piacenza

The labyrinth at the church of San Savino in Piacenza, formally consecrated on 15 August 1107, may have once been as complex and rich in imagery as that at San Michele in nearby Pavia, but nothing of the maze remains today.[10] Yet, as at Pavia, an ANNUS mosaic and a scheme of the months still stand in proximity to the former location of the maze on the floor in the nave of the church. Thus there is reason to believe that this maze at San Savino, too, was a Chartres-type labyrinth dating from the first half of the twelfth century. In 1651 Pietro Maria Campi described it briefly in his *Dell'historia ecclesiastica di Piacenza*,[11] noting that a Minotaur lurked within in the center and that the meaning of the maze was explained through an accompanying text, again in classical hexameters:

> This labyrinth typifies the present world, broad at the entrance but altogether narrow at the return. In this way ensnared by this world, weighed down by sin, one can only return to the doctrine of life with difficulty.

The inspiration here appears to be scriptural: "Because strait is the gate, and narrow is the way, which leadeth unto life and few there be that find it" (Matthew 7:14).[12] Enjoyment of eternal life—presumably the everlasting tree of life promised the faithful at the end of the Book of Apocalypse (22:1–2)—will come only to those who complete the ordeal, progressing not only to the center but also back to the beginning.

Rome

On the floor of the nave of the small church of Santa Maria in Aquiro, near the popular Piazza Navona, once rested a small labyrinth (1.5 meters in diameter) of the Chartres-type design.[13] It was destroyed sometime during the second half of the nineteenth century, but the French archaeologist Julien Durand made a copy of it in 1847, which he reproduced in 1857 (Fig. 2.2, lower right).[14] He describes the labyrinthine courses as made of yellow marble with boundaries of red and green porphyry, and a center disk (*rota*), also of porphyry. Since Santa Maria in Aquiro was dedicated in 1189 and since the maze appeared to both Durand and Barbier de Montault to have been part of the original floor of the church, this lost labyrinth likely dated from around 1200.[15]

A larger pavement labyrinth was formerly on the floor in front of the sacristy in Santa Maria in Trastevere, a Roman basilica just to the south of the Vatican (Fig. 2.2, upper right).[16] This maze was apparently put in place when Pope Innocent II rebuilt the church in the mid-twelfth century. The architectural historian Giovanni Ciampini claimed in 1699 that the maze was identical in shape to that at St. Michael's church in Pavia (see Fig. 2.1) and full of twists and turns.[17] Sometime during the early eighteenth century this labyrinth was improperly repaired; the progressive course of the maze was replaced by a series of nine concentric circles.[18] The original maze (and its imperfect eighteenth-century restoration) measured 3.3 meters, and thus occupied nearly all of the floor of the antechamber before the sacristy.

Pontremoli

Fate is a fickle mistress. The three aforementioned churches in Rome and Piacenza survive, but the mazes they once housed are now destroyed. Yet at Pontremoli (50 miles east of Genoa) the reverse is true. The former Benedictine abbey of St. Peter was wrecked by an Allied aerial bombardment in 1945, but the maze, a single sandstone bas-relief measuring 81 × 55 centimeters, has survived.[19] It is preserved in the Castello Pignaro-Pontremoli

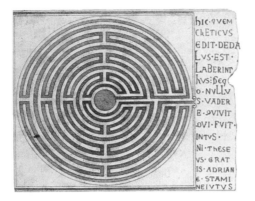

FIGURE 2.2 The mazes at San Martino, Lucca (upper left); Santa Maria in Trastevere, Rome (upper right); San Vitale, Ravenna (lower left); and Santa Maria in Aquiro, Rome (lower right).

and has been described by archaeologists in 1949/50 and again in 1982.[20] Nothing is known about the location of this labyrinth within the church or its date, but given its physical similarities to the maze in bas-relief at nearby Lucca (see below), it, too, may also date from around 1200. While the formal design of the Pontremolian maze is identical to the Chartrain pattern (see Fig. 1.9), the marginal inscription is unique: "Run so that you may obtain" (*Sic currite ut comprehendatis*). This is not a classical hexameter but a prose injunction from the New Testament in which Paul urges his followers to strive so as to obtain the prize: "Know ye not that they which run in a race run all, but one receiveth the prize? So run, that ye may obtain" (1 Corinthians 9:24). The prize, again, is salvation through Christ, as is written in the center of the maze. Instead of the usual depiction of Theseus and the Minotaur, here the letters JHS (Jhesus) appear. Christ alone is the reward for which true Christians quest. At the top of the maze appear two upright horsemen, likely a reference to the armed warriors of the labyrinthine equestrian dance, the Trojan ride.[21]

Lucca

Within the porch at the west end of the cathedral of San Martino at Lucca appears a Chartres-type maze dating from the late twelfth or early thirteenth century (Fig. 2.2, upper left).[22] As at Pontremoli, this maze is cut in bas-relief into a single stone, one set vertically into a pillar that supports a vault of the porch. The entrance to the maze faces the west. Within the same stone and on a tangent to the right of the labyrinth are carved three classical hexameters that encourage the faithful to view the pagan myth of the maze as a metaphor for Christian salvation through divine grace:

> Here is the Cretan labyrinth that Daedalus built. From it no one who entered could escape except Theseus, who succeeded through the grace of Ariadne's thread.

A small representation of Theseus and the Minotaur in combat once stood in the center of this Luccan maze. But as early as 1857 the French antiquarian Julien Durand reported that fingers eager to trace the route of the labyrinth were gradually effacing these classical figures.[23] Now, nearly one hundred and fifty years later, they have wholly disappeared.

Ravenna

The mosaics in the sixth-century churches of Ravenna, once the capital of Latin Christendom, constitute one of the most brilliant displays of religious art in the West.[24] The sacred scenes depicted here, by means of millions of pieces of tinted glass and colored stones, are so vibrant that they seem to have been completed only yesterday. No church has more stunning displays than San Vitale, the mosaics of which collectively constitute a pantheon to the Mystical Lamb of God. Perhaps blinded by the dazzling scenes on the walls and ceiling, the visitor to San Vitale may fail to notice the larger, duller tiles on the floor. But there, immediately to the west of the sanctuary, is a pavement maze measuring 3.4 meters (Fig. 2.2, lower left). The pattern of this labyrinth is not the typical Chartres-type design. Instead of the usual eleven tracks, here there are only seven; and some of the meanders turn 270 degrees rather than the standard 90 or 180 degrees. A succession of 384 small marble triangles point the maze-walker from the center of the labyrinth to the exit and thus to the west. Spiritually prepared, the faithful soul is now worthy to engage the Mystical Lamb of God at the east.

While the labyrinth at San Vitale was once thought to date from the sixth century,[25] it is far more likely that it was newly created during 1538–1539, at which time the floor was elevated and six new mosaics were inlaid.[26] The spirit of this maze, however, situated in proximity to the Mystical Lamb, is very much that of the Middle Ages. Perhaps the present sixteenth-century maze is simply a recreation of a medieval original.

What can we conclude from the disparate, fragmentary evidence surviving for Italian church labyrinths? First, the Italian church maze was mainly a creation of the twelfth century; only the maze at Ravenna undoubtedly comes from a later period. Second, the Italian maze was small in size, ranging from 0.5 meters at Lucca to 3.5 meters at Pavia. Thus on average these Italian labyrinths are a century earlier than, and at most only a third the size of, their later French counterparts. Because of their comparatively small dimensions, the Italian mazes did not serve as sites for formal Christian rituals. Clerical processions did not wend their way through them—at least no chronicle or liturgical manuscript ever makes mention of such a practice. Nor did Italian churchmen dance upon them as in France; the small size of these mazes and the vertical positioning of two of them precluded such use. The faithful traced the route of the maze with the eye or with the finger in hopes of vicariously joining the line of march toward salvation.

Finally, the position of these Italian mazes within the architecture of their respective churches offers little clue as to their significance. One was located in the choir (Pavia), one outside the choir before the sacristy (Santa Maria in Trastevere, Rome), three in the nave or its equivalent (Piacenza, Santa Maria in Aquiro in Rome, and Ravenna), and one in the narthex, or entry hall, to the west of the nave (Lucca). All but one of these mazes (Pontremoli) are apotropaic; their aim is to ward off evil spirits and to show a path around harm's way. The Pontremolian maze, however, like the much earlier labyrinth in Algeria,[27] suggests that Christ, the object of Christian desire, rests at the center. The Piacenzan labyrinth emphasizes the need to run the full course, moving to the center and then back to the beginning.

The maze at Ravenna, on the other hand, suggests that only the egress is of importance; it leads out, but not in. Consequently, Italian mazes not only fail to exhibit a coherent program with regard to placement within the architectural ambitus of the church but also lack a consistent theme as to spiritual meaning. The only near-constant among these labyrinths is that all of them save one (Ravenna) reproduce exactly the Chartres-type pattern (Fig. 1.9), a design strongly stamped with Christological significance.[28] Indeed, the Chartrain pattern is as securely in place in these Italian churches as it would later become in the great cathedrals of France.

French Church Mazes

The true home of the church labyrinth is France, the France of the lofty Gothic cathedrals. Indeed, the grand and geometrically complex labyrinth is a worthy component of the Gothic cathedral, whose design is so heavily dependent on geometric tools, particularly the compass. Unlike the Italian pavement mazes, which are made up of thousands of tiny pieces of colored stone or glass, the French mazes are large labyrinths composed of hundreds of heavy white and black (or dark blue) paving stones measuring approximately 10 × 20 centimeters each. Why did the clergy in medieval France want a maze of such size on the floor of their church? The explanation, as we shall see in Chapter 3, lies in the need for a sizable space within the church to act out Christ's Harrowing of Hell. On average French pavement mazes measure 10 meters in diameter, and they usually consume the entire width of the nave. Because chairs were put in the naves in European churches beginning only in the eighteenth century, in earlier times the maze was immediately exposed for all to see. In fact, the medieval visitor could hardly have escaped the labyrinth and all its symbolism as he passed through the great west door of the church. Even today it is still possible to tread a few of these labyrinths and enter into the spirituality of an earlier age.

The soaring Gothic cathedrals were not the only French churches to house mazes.[29] Some lesser churches had labyrinths of smaller size. These mazes, however, were too diminutive to serve as venues for liturgical rituals. A religious ritual, of course, is merely an acting out of a theological belief in word, song, and gesture. It is the Easter rites that ultimately reveal the theology of the maze—what the church maze meant to the faithful in pre-modern Europe. By the thirteenth century a sacred space—the large pavement maze—had been created in which as many as a hundred clerics could express through dance an important part of the liturgy of Easter Sunday. Consequently, it is these large cathedral mazes, not the smaller peripheral ones, that command our attention.

Circular Mazes in the Archdiocese of Sens

Gothic architecture came into being on the *Île de France,* the core of France that includes Paris more or less at its geographic center. In medieval times the *Île de France* consisted mainly, but not entirely, of lands belonging to two ecclesiastical jurisdictions: the archdiocese of Sens and that of Reims (see Fig. 2.3). All of the large pavement mazes situated within churches in France were found in sanctuaries in just these two ecclesiastical jurisdictions. Those resting within the territory of the archbishop of Sens all appear to have been of the circular Chartrain type, while their counterparts in the lands owing obedience to the archbishop of Reims were, with a single exception, all octagonal in form. Because the mazes in the archdiocese of Sens were generally earlier than those of Reims, we will visit these first.

Chartres

Of the eight dioceses that formed the see of Sens, by far the largest was that of Chartres.[30] So, too, the labyrinth at Chartres was of unusual size—it is the largest church maze ever created. Yet the maze at Chartres deserves pride of place on two additional counts: it is the oldest church pavement maze to survive intact; and its form has come to represent an entire class of labyrinthine design called the Chartres-type maze.[31]

Seen from the surrounding fields of grain, the towers of Notre-Dame of Chartres appear as timeless beacons to the heavens. Yet as is true of all French cathedrals, the church we see today was not the original sanctuary. On this spot were three previous churches extending back to Merovingian times, and all three in turn were destroyed by fire—even churches built principally of stone can burn if the wooden substructure catches fire. The third cathedral at Chartres, an enormous Romanesque building, was almost totally destroyed in 1194.[32] The famous monument we see at Chartres today is, therefore, the fourth Christian sanctuary to occupy this site.

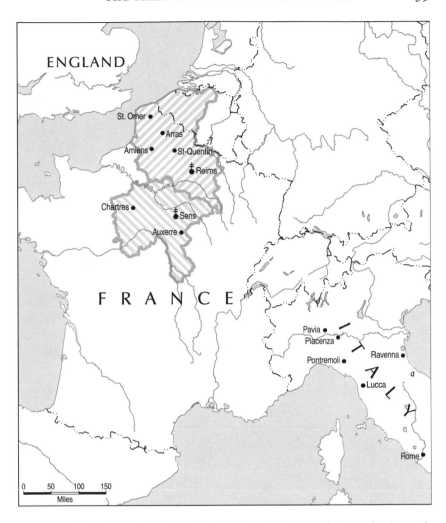

FIGURE 2.3 Map of Italy and France showing the archdioceses of Sens and Reims and the location of churches once possessing pavement mazes.

Most cathedrals took centuries to complete. But the bulk of the present Gothic building at Chartres was constructed in a remarkably short time, fewer than thirty years (1194–c.1221).[33] Much of the decoration—the sculpture, the magnificent stained glass, and the pavement maze—was accomplished during this same period. The aim of the architects was to create a structure of unprecedented height and luminosity. When finished, Notre-Dame of Chartres would be higher, wider, and lighter than all previous

FIGURE 2.4 The maze at the cathedral of Chartres, with the rose window high on the west wall.

churches. While other cathedrals, notably those at Reims, Amiens, and Beauvais, would attempt higher vaulting (sometimes with disastrous results), the nave and choir at Chartres would remain the widest in all of France.[34] It is the exceptionally wide nave that accounts for the great size of the labyrinth (Fig. 2.4).

The maze at Chartres, which was put in place around 1215–1221, measures 12.85 meters in diameter. Its path is formed by 276 slabs of white limestone, each 34 centimeters wide, quarried at nearby Berchères. Separating and defining the eleven bands of the path is a thin (8-cm.) divider of blue-black marble apparently brought from the area of the Meuse River, hundreds of kilometers to the east of Chartres.[35] At the center once rested a brass medallion that was removed at the end of the eighteenth century. Then and now, this central zone is surrounded by six incomplete circles which together form a six-lobed rosette (see Figs. 1.9 and 2.4), a configuration found in no other maze. On the outside of the labyrinth, 113 lunettes compose an equally unique border that runs around the full circumference. As can be seen in Figures 2.4 and 2.5, the labyrinth at Chartres occupies the center pavement of the fourth and fifth bays, extending across nearly the entire width of the nave.

What was sculpted on the brass medallion that once occupied the very center of the labyrinth? In the mid-nineteenth century it was thought that a memorial to the architects of the church had once occupied this central spot, and to prove this theory an excavation was undertaken in 1849. But after digging down some five meters and finding only a few shards of Gallo-Roman tile, both excavation and theory were abandoned.[36] A careful reading of the local histories of Chartres, however, would have revealed the truth: here, as with many medieval Italian church labyrinths and earlier Roman floor mazes, Theseus and the Minotaur occupied the center. The Chartrain historian Charles Challine (1596–1678) describes the maze in the following terms: "There exists in the middle of the nave before and below the pulpit a very beautiful labyrinth or Daedalus *(dédale)* outlined in black marble on the pavement in the center of which can be seen inside a circle the scene of Theseus and the Minotaur."[37] A Chartrain historian writing around 1750 corroborates Challine's description,[38] but he adds that the figures are by then all but defaced. Ultimately, in 1792, the faceless medallion was removed —apparently to be melted down, as were other plaques in Chartres that year, to be made into cannons for the army of the new Republic.[39]

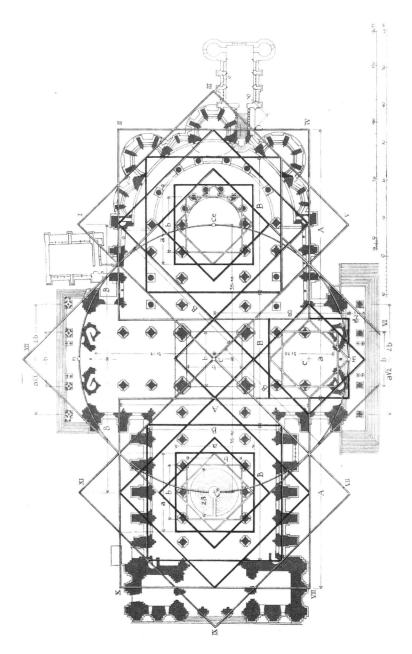

FIGURE 2.5 The floor plan of the cathedral of Chartres, with labyrinth, suggesting
how the present Gothic building may have been designed according to a few basic
geometric processes. The high altar and the maze serve as complementary epicenters.

Surrounding the area where the medallion lay is a six-lobed rosette (see Figs. 1.9 and 2.4). While such a rosette is unique to the labyrinth at Chartres, its meaning, too, has a venerable history:

The motif [of the six-lobed rosette] belongs to an old and widespread family of stellar symbols, the origins of which reach back into antiquity. Eight- or six-lobed rosettes, as symbols of the stellar nature of God, are a common occurrence in Sumerian, Babylonian, Jewish, and Roman art. The motif was quickly absorbed into the Christian cult, as a reference to the celestial nature of the new god, and subsequently became so closely associated with the cross of Christ as to be practically interchangeable with it.[40]

The rosette within the labyrinth of Chartres was thus meant to be a Christian amulet capable of warding off, or at least containing within it, the evil that lurked at the very center of the maze (the Minotaur). It symbolized the apotropaic powers of Christ no less than the cross stamped upon the tracks of the maze.

A mention of the stellar symbolism of the rosette in the labyrinth suggests, in turn, a possible link between it and the great rose window high at the west end of the church. The west rose at Chartres was put in place in 1215 and is exactly coeval with the maze (see Fig. 2.4).[41] Both rose and maze are approximately the same size, a diameter of 13.36 meters for the former and 12.85 meters for the latter.[42] Moreover, the center of the rose is about 32 meters above the floor at the west door, almost the same distance as the center of the maze from that same place of entry.[43] Thus something akin to an isosceles triangle unites these two circular figurations.[44] If it were possible to put hinges on the west wall, the rose would fold down over the labyrinth.[45]

As Christ is signified by the rosette in the center of the maze, so too he resides in the west rose. The theme of this radiant glass is the Last Judgment as foretold in the Book of Apocalypse.[46] At the center sits Christ enthroned, surrounded by the four creatures of the Apocalypse, the twelve disciples, and a host of angels sounding the trumpet of the Last Judgment. In the outer lobes St. Michael does battle with Satan for control of the destiny of the dead, and the elect rise from Hell to the bosom of Abraham where they will await the end of all time. The west rose foretells the events to occur at the very end of Christian world history. The maze on the floor below, however, reveals an earlier part of this eschatological narrative: the labyrinth symbolizes the inferno from which Christ must escape prior to his resurrection.

Although the maze at Chartres has a geometric similarity to the west rose in terms of the spatial plan of the church, it enjoys a more fundamental affinity with the high altar. Many historians—most creditable, some disreputable—have taken measurements at Chartres with the goal of divining the overarching design of the cathedral.[47] All agree on one critical point: the center of the maze and the high altar are the two principal points of reference within the west and east ends of the building. The plan of the Gothic church was apparently laid out as follows. After the fire of 1194, both the west facade and the apsidal crypt at the east end were still in place. These extremities established the western and eastern ends of the new church. A midpoint was fixed between these two boundaries, and a large circle (or two isosceles triangles forming a square, if one wishes) swung out from this central point (see Fig. 2.5). The circle in turn defined the extremities of the north and south porches of the transept as well as the midpoints of the west and east ends (nave and choir) of the church. At these midpoints the labyrinth and high altar, respectively, would be placed, but not until some twenty years later, about 1215, when the basic plan had been realized in stone and mortar. In this way sacred spaces for Christian ritual (a maze and an altar) were set *a posteriori* upon a rational geometric base. The maze is not fundamental to the structure of the church; it is ornamental. At Chartres, function followed form.

Ultimately, the meaning of the labyrinth at the cathedral of Chartres is the same as that of the other labyrinths in the archdiocese of Sens. Like the rose on the west facade, the labyrinth is a beautifully intricate ornament that expresses a fundamental tenet of Christian faith: as Christ suffered and sacrificed for others, so humankind must struggle through this hellish world to achieve everlasting life. If the maze seems more mysterious than the rose—its meaning more hidden—that is because it is constructed of geometric symbols rather than lifelike figures set in colored glass.

In truth, the meaning of the maze at Chartres relates as much to theology as it does to architecture. The Chartrain maze does not serve as a memorial to the architects who built the church, as is true for the mazes at Reims and Amiens.[48] What architectural significance it possesses rests exclusively in the fact that this grand and complex design provides an appropriate visual counterweight to the high altar at the east end. The maze and the altar function as visual epicenters for the nave and the choir, respectively. The choir was the clergy's portion of the church, a sacred precinct in which hope of an everlasting communion with Christ was dispensed at the high altar. The nave, by contrast, belonged to the people and was of this world. Work-crews shaped up in its side aisles, goods were bought and sold there, and at vigils of high feasts a flood of pilgrims slept on the floor.[49] If a spot had to be found in the church for Hell, as came to be required by the newly emerging doctrine of Purgatory, then the nave was the place. If a theological need could be satisfied by a design that gave greater visual symmetry to the building, both God and man would be better served. Thus during the critical years 1215–1221 architecture and theology worked in tandem at Chartres, and the labyrinthine Hell was placed in the midst of the people.

Sens

In Gallo-Roman times Sens was a more important commercial center than Paris, and the archbishop of Sens was of greater ecclesiastical authority than the bishop of Paris. We will not be concerned with Paris, because neither Notre-Dame nor any other Parisian church housed a maze. But Sens and its neighboring cathedral town of Auxerre did. Unfortunately, these two labyrinths were destroyed prior to the French Revolution, and no drawing of them survived.

At least that was the case until I came upon a depiction of the maze at Sens during the summer of 1996 (Fig. 2.6).[50] Indeed, two mazes may have been discovered at once, because the labyrinth at Auxerre was said to have been "of the same sort" *(de la même manière)* as that at Sens.[51] As it turns out, the maze at Sens was a Chartres-type maze with one important deviation: the place at which the spiritual pilgrim entered and began the 90-degree and 180-degree turns, and, accordingly, the spot at which he exited, is different. In all other ways, however, the paths of the labyrinths at Chartres and Sens unfold in a similar manner (compare Figs. 1.9 and 2.6).

As can be seen in Figure 2.6, the drawing of the labyrinth at Sens was made in the second half of the eighteenth century, probably between 1768 and 1789. Immediately below the maze rests an inscription:

FIGURE 2.6 An eighteenth-century drawing of the now-destroyed pavement maze at the cathedral of Sens. The inscription at the bottom tells of its location and history.

"This labyrinth was formerly in the nave of the metropolitan church of Sens, under the organ tribune; this work, which was not without merit, was of lead set long ago within the tombstones with which the floor was paved. The canons of the chapter had it destroyed in 1768 when they had the floor paved evenly."[52]

The description continues at the very bottom of the page (not shown):

> This labyrinth was thirty feet in diameter. An entire hour was said to be needed to traverse its circuits, and one took 2,000 steps following all the detours without doubling back over the same spot. It occupied all of the width of the nave. The design was ingeniously created. [A] letter [writer] of 1758 says that he does not know for what it was used.[53]

While the first of these descriptions rings true, the second, at least at first blush, seems in several ways preposterous. Undoubtedly the maze at Sens was situated beneath the last double bay of the nave, below the organ *buffet* just inside the west door. The floor surrounding the maze at Sens was encrusted with tombstones. Thus in 1768, as the archives confirm, the canons determined to "tidy away" all such medieval impediments, engaging one "Corbel, sculpteur marbrier à Paris" to repave the church in marble at a total cost of 15,491 *livres*.[54] The second notice begins plausibly enough: the diameter of the labyrinth was "trente pieds"—something slightly less than ten meters[55]—and hence about two meters smaller than its northern neighbor at Chartres. It would, therefore, have indeed occupied most of the width of the nave, as the notice reports. Yet the second inscription also relates that an hour was needed to run the course of the labyrinth (presumably both forward and backward). In fact, proceeding on foot, much less time would have been needed. Even moving at a very leisurely pace, a dedicated walker can traverse "round trip" the slightly larger mazes at Chartres and St. Quentin in less than fifteen minutes. That such a journey required 2,000 steps likewise borders on the incredible. Fewer than 700 steps would be needed, even for a person with the smallest stride.

Only one explanation can account for these seemingly fantastic numbers: one hour and 2,000 small steps were needed to "parcourir les circuits" at Sens because the pilgrim was not always standing but often on his knees. By comparison, the maze in the cathedral of Arras was said to require an hour to negotiate, but the feat was accomplished "on bended knee" (*à genoux*) while reciting pious prayers.[56] Creeping around the maze—crawling or walking and then kneeling to pray—was evidently an eighteenth-century practice at Sens as well.

As to the date and function of the labyrinth at Sens: a capitular decree of 1413 permits the clergy to perform an Easter ceremony upon the maze "as is the tradition."[57] Undoubtedly that tradition extended back into the thirteenth century and possibly earlier,[58] for it was tied to the ancient liturgy of Easter Sunday. After the clergy of Sens celebrated Vespers in the choir, they processed to the baptistry attached to the north side of the church. The line of march proceeded across the maze and out the west door, likely through the *portail Saint-Jean* marked by an elaborate sculptural program depicting the life of this saintly shepherd. En route to the baptistry the clergy chanted the responsory *These are the New Lambs (Isti sunt agni novelli)*, which celebrates the martyrs whom Christ liberates from Purgatory. During the processional return to the cathedral the clergy again crossed the labyrinth; now the canons and their subalterns sang the psalm *When Israel came out of Egypt (In exitu Israel de Egypto)*, commemorating Moses' rescue of the chosen people from the bondage of the Pharaoh. At some point that afternoon the clergy and townsfolk engaged in a labyrinthine dance, as we shall see in Chapter 5. There would be variations on this theme, but the tradition persisted for some three hundred years, into the sixteenth century.

Auxerre

A procession across the maze and to the baptistry also marked Easter Sunday at the cathedral of Auxerre. Sens and Auxerre, only 60 kilometers apart (see Fig. 2.3), have tightly linked liturgical histories as well as some fundamental architectural similarities.[59] Both cathedrals are dedicated to St. Étienne, and both have a baptistry under the usual patronym of St. John near the north transept.[60] Moreover, both once had a labyrinth in the nave of the church immediately beneath the organ.

The fame of the maze at Auxerre is inversely proportional to our knowledge of it. While the peculiar dance of the "pilota" at Auxerre (described in Chapter 5) has fired the imagination of almost all who have written about the maze, the labyrinth on which this bizarre ceremony was performed remains mostly an object of speculation. Because the Easter ritual of the "pilota" can be traced back to at least 1396, the maze in the nave was certainly just as old. Most likely it dated from the early- or mid-fourteenth century, given the architectural history of the building.[61]

Only one description of the maze of Auxerre survives, a fleeting mention offered in 1726 by Abbé Jean Lebeuf as part of his singular description of the dance of the maze and the organ that accompanied it. The Abbé's run-on sentence reads as follows:

This instrument [the organ] was within arm's reach of the participants, since they carried out their roles almost directly under the organ case, at that place in the nave where before 1690 one saw on the pavement a type of labyrinth in the form of many interlocking circles, just as there is still one today in the nave of the church of Sens.[62]

Lebeuf knew of what he spoke. He was born in Auxerre in 1687, and if he had no memory of the labyrinth from his childhood, he conversed with those who did. We may confidently conclude that the labyrinth of Auxerre was of the circular type as at Chartres and Sens (see Fig. 2.6), but somewhat smaller than its northern neighbors—the nave of Auxerre measures little more than 10 meters from pillar to pillar. The maze nonetheless must have filled nearly the entire width of this modest expanse, because the ceremony of the "pilota" required that the full residential chapter, which included six dignitaries and fifty canons, dance on and around it.[63] As Lebeuf suggests, the maze at Auxerre enjoyed proximity to the organ of the church, which was then situated on the wall of the nave near the north transept.[64] The position of the maze, therefore, was more toward the middle of the nave, as at Chartres, than toward the very western end, as at Sens. Ultimately, the fate of the labyrinth at Auxerre was linked to the tombstones of the cathedral. It was removed in 1690 as part of a general repaving intended to rid the church of an almost 500-year accumulation of sepulchral debris and other musty remnants of the Middle Ages.[65]

Octagonal Mazes of the Archdiocese of Reims

To the kings of France the city of Reims (160 kilometers east of Paris) was arguably the most important in their realm, for it was in the cathedral of Reims that the French monarchy formally began. On Christmas Day in the year 496, Saint Rémi, bishop of Reims, baptized Clovis, making him the first Christian king of the Francs.[66] During the early-Capetian era the crown of France was placed on the royal pate by the archbishop of Sens. In the late twelfth century, however, that honor was usurped by the Archbishop of Reims, and henceforth Reims became the cathedral in which nearly all French kings were crowned. The Archbishop of Reims was now "first peer" of the realm,[67] and he counted as suffragans the bishops of

Cambrai, Châlons, Soissons, Beauvais, Laon, Noyon, Amiens, Thérouanne, Arras, and Senlis. Within these bishoprics the cathedrals at Amiens and Arras once possessed large pavement mazes, as did Reims itself, and also the gigantic collegiate church of St. Quentin, which sat within the diocese of Noyon, as well as the monastery of St. Bertin, in St. Omer in the diocese of Thérouanne. In addition, rumors that mazes were once found at the cathedrals of Noyon and Laon are still bruited about, but no evidence survives to support this claim. What we can say with certainty is that there were once at least five mazes in this ecclesiastical jurisdiction—those at Arras, Amiens, St. Quentin, St. Omer, and Reims—and that only one of them, the maze at St. Quentin, survives today in its original state.

Though lamentably little of these northern French mazes remains, they once possessed a unique characteristic. With one exception (St. Omer), all were octagonal in shape: an eleven-track pattern was set within an octagon, and in one instance (Reims) the octagon was fitted with octagonal "towers" protruding from its oblique sides (see Fig. 2.7). The octagonal shape, of course, lent an additional Christian meaning to the maze, for in medieval number symbolism the number eight denoted baptism and rebirth through Christ.[68] Given the historical ties to baptism at the cathedral of Reims, it is not surprising to find the labyrinth there in octagonal form. But it is something of a shock to discover that at Reims, and at Amiens as well, Christian symbolism had to share pride of place with a pagan theme. At these churches the labyrinths were conceived not only as serpentine symbols of Christian victory but also as memorials to the ingenuity of the many Daedaluses who created the giant cathedrals.

Reims

The cathedral of Reims has been designated by the United Nations as "a monument belonging to the cultural heritage of the world."[69] Work on the present Gothic structure commenced in 1211 and was completed about 1290, at which time a large labyrinth was set in the pavement. Unlike the maze at Amiens, which can be precisely dated to the year 1288, the exact time of origin of the Reims maze is not known. The date most often suggested is "about 1290,"[70] though some have linked the completion of the labyrinth specifically to the coronation of King Philippe le Bel at Reims on 6 January 1286.[71] The maze remained in place until shortly before the Revolution, by which time the constant play of children on the meandering

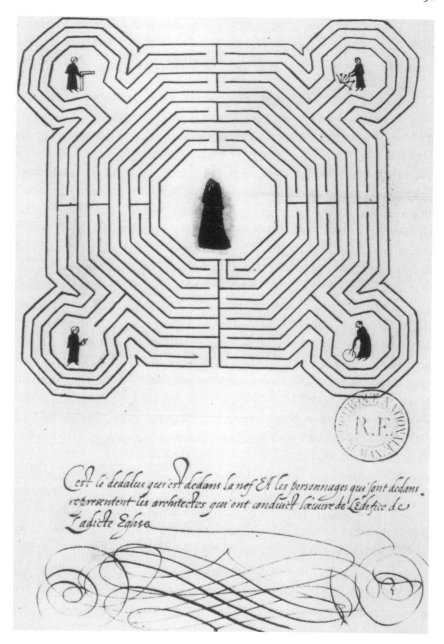

C'est le dedalus qui est dedans la nef Et les personnages qui sont dedans representent les architectes qui ont conduict lœuvre de Ledifice de ladicte Eglise

FIGURE 2.7 Jacques Cellier's sixteenth-century drawing of the now-destroyed pavement maze at Reims with the architects of the cathedral depicted in the four corners.

path had become a nuisance to the canons wishing to celebrate the divine
office in peace. In August 1778 canon Jean Jacquemart offered the chapter
one thousand francs for its removal, and the following year the labyrinthine
playground disappeared.[72]

Despite this irreparable loss, a drawing of the maze at Reims does survive, as well as several eyewitness descriptions.[73] Sometime between 1583
and 1587 an architect of the city, Jacques Cellier, made several sketches of the
interior of the church, including one of the labyrinth (Fig. 2.7).[74] Some fifty
years later canon Pierre Cocquault described the maze and transcribed the
inscriptions that surrounded the figures in the four octagonal "towers."
From Cellier's drawing and Cocquault's description it is possible to reconstruct the essentials of the maze and assay its meaning.

Cellier's floor plan of Reims places the labyrinth in the seventh and
eighth bays of the nave (a modern rendering is shown in Fig. 2.8). Cocquault confirms this, adding that "the Daedalus is made of black marble
and of twelve lines [drawn] in the track equidistant from all sides and
twelve inches separate from each other. It is 34 feet square in its entirety."[75]
Thus the maze at Reims was a black marble path set on a white stone background with a total width of approximately 10.20 meters. Cocquault then
goes on say that a round medallion lay in the center within which was an
effigy of the person who designed, or made possible, the labyrinth (celuy
qui l'a faict).[76] Cellier also suggests that this figure, as well as the four
smaller ones at the corners, represented the architects who built the cathedral, as can be seen in the note he added at the bottom of his drawing (Fig.
2.7): "Here is the Daedalus which is in the nave and the figures which are in
it represent the architects who directed the work of the construction of said
church." Cocquault orients the four smaller effigies and gives the text of the
inscription that surrounded each one, as best he could read them given the
deteriorated condition of the leaden letters:

Northeast	Southeast
The image of Jean le Loup who	The image of Jean d'Orbais,
was master of the works of this	master of these works who
church for a period of sixteen	began the upper stories of
years and who began its portals.	the chevet of the church.[77]

Center
(inscription not legible)

Northwest	Southwest
The image of Gaucher de Reims,	The image of Bernard de Soissons,
who was master of the works	who made five vaults and worked
for a period of eight years	on the O [west rose], master of
and who worked on the arches	the works for a period of
and the portals.	thirty-five years.

Each of the four architects holds a tool of the trade or is engaged in the act of design. Jean le Loup stands with a square; Jean d'Orbais uses a compass to plot out the round point at the east end; Gaucher de Reims uses his fingers to give orders of construction; while Bernard de Soissons, the creator of five vaults and the great west rose, rotates a compass to construct a circle.

Much has been made of these inscriptions and even of the tools held by the architects: the maze at Reims has been seized upon by historians of art as a Rosetta Stone capable of revealing the chronology of the cathedral itself. Indeed, the cathedral of Reims has become the most analyzed building in Western Europe, in part because of the tantalizing information provided by the maze. During the last century at least fifteen architectural historians have attempted to explain the sequence of the construction of the cathedral, each trying to harmonize his theory with the information provided by the maze.[78]

What can be concluded from so many divergent opinions, other than the obvious fact that architectural analysis is an art and not a science? Is it possible to unravel the tangled thread of interpretation simply by following the maze in and out? If a sequence of architects can be extracted from the maze itself, does it accurately reflect the order in which the architects worked — the order in which they built the various parts of the church? In other words, are the figures in the maze descriptive of the history of the cathedral or merely commemorative decorations?

Figure 2.9 traces the path of the labyrinth at Reims. During a journey to the center thirty-one segments come into play, each requiring either a quarter-turn (90 degrees) or a half-turn (180 degrees). The maze-walker enters from the west and covers the outer perimeter of the north sector (segments 1–4), crosses over into the south sector (5) and passes through its outer and middle portions (6–15) before switching back to the north (16) to tread its middle and inner portions (17–26), and ultimately reverses (27) back to the south for a final circuit of its inner part (28–31). Accordingly, in proceed-

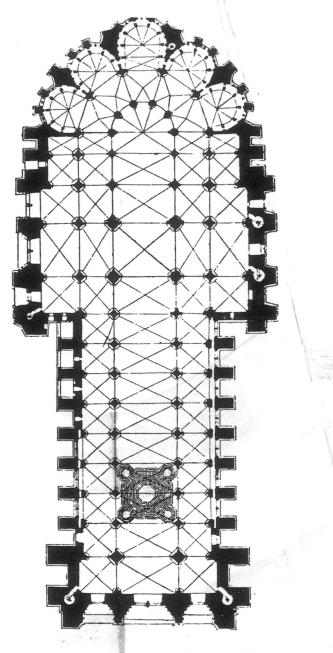

FIGURE 2.8 A modern rendering of Jacques Cellier's
floor plan of the cathedral of Reims showing the maze
in the seventh and eighth bays of the nave.

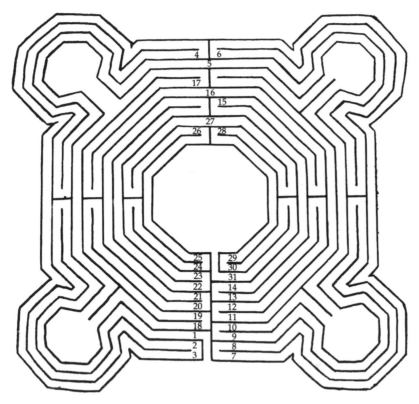

FIGURE 2.9 Path of the maze at Reims (derived from Cellier's floor plan), showing the order in which the tracks (and architects) are encountered. Note how the numbers form a retrograding pattern, or mirror image.

ing toward the center one meets in order the architects Bernard de Soissons and Jean d'Orbais (10) and then Jean le Loup and Gaucher de Reims (18) before encountering the unknown central figure. However, a far more compelling reading of the maze—one that conforms with the traditional theological imperative of the labyrinth—would commence in the center and work outward, away from the demonic and toward the divine. This would suggest that the architect in the center is not the last master, but the first, the one who designed the labyrinth and perhaps the building.[79] The labyrinth, then, implies the following sequence of architects: the original, unnamed master builder in the center, then Gaucher de Reims, Jean le Loup, Jean d'Orbais, and Bernard de Soissons. At least this interpretation is concordant with an archival entry of 1287 that establishes Bernard de Soissons as the last in a long line of master builders.[80] Thus, if the maze does indeed hold a history of the construction of the cathedral of Reims, it suggests that the architects began by working on the west and north portals, built and vaulted the eastern portion of the nave and then the choir, and ended with the western vaults of the nave and the west rose.

Despite the conflicting opinions of architectural historians about the sequence of construction of the cathedral of Reims, one fact is undeniable: the lost labyrinth occupied a critical spot in the design of the building. The cathedral was conceived outward from the center-most point of the crossing of the transept. The length of the choir and chevet, the width of the transept and the length of the nave were set by "squaring out" from the square and diagonal of the crossing.[81] Once the vessel was completed, strategic points in the design were assigned important devotional functions. The high altar (the altar of St. Nicaise) was placed beneath the crossing; the altar of the Holy Cross was placed one double square to the east in the "second" choir;[82] the crucifix of the rood screen was set one double square to the west in the nave; and the epicenter of the maze was placed two double squares to the west in the nave (see Fig. 2.8). Once again, as at Chartres, geometry determined the overall form as well as the essential points of the cathedral. Only after the structure was complete, or major portions of it finished in turn, was greater visual emphasis as well as sacred meaning given to these critical spots. In the case of Reims, these points were adorned with two altars, a crucifix, and, finally, a maze.

In the course of time the labyrinth at Reims came to have both sacred and profane significance, resonating with Christian as well as classical meaning. True, the maze was built as a monument to the skill of generations of master builders who had designed this architectural wonder. It was called the "Daedalus" by the people of the day because the architects whose effigies rested therein were considered worthy successors to the great inventor of Greek mythology. Some have even claimed that the bodies of at least two of the architects were once interred beneath the maze, making it not merely a commemorative decoration but a functioning mausoleum.

Yet this memorial, as we have seen, was more than a symbol of a timeless Greek myth, for it projected Christian meaning as well. King Clovis had been baptized at Reims in 496. Baptism and spiritual rebirth, of course, are integral themes in the liturgy surrounding the maze on Easter Sunday, when the labyrinth served in many churches as a venue for celebratory dances. Progressing through the twists and turns of the sinful world prepared the soul for a higher realm of spiritual awareness, just as the regenerative waters of baptism led the soul away from a sinful old world to be reborn in the spirit of Christ. Both the maze and the baptismal font were places of initiation and purification, preliminary steps along a spiritual journey to everlasting life.[83] For this reason both were usually placed in the least sanctified end of the church, the west end. Indeed, many baptistries were situated entirely outside the church.

From the moment they were first constructed in Rome, Milan, Ravenna, and in southern France, baptistries and baptismal fonts had been octagonal in shape. The fathers of the church had regarded the number eight as a symbol for regeneration (Ambrose) and glorious resurrection (Augustine).[84] Eight was the traditional number of Christ.[85] Sunday, "the eighth day," following six days of creation and the seventh day of rest, was a symbol of the Lord's return.[86] An octagonal figure suggested completion and perfection, as well as the waters of spiritual renewal. The octagonal shape of the maze at Reims is thus a vestige of an ancient symbolic design. More recently, it has also come to assume a special contemporary symbolism, for the French government has chosen the Reims pattern to serve as a logo for all historical sites throughout France.

In the Middle Ages the maze at Reims likewise had a twofold meaning: one old, one more recent; one pagan, one Christian. True to the classical tradition, it honored the constructive genius of the architect; and, simultaneously faithful to Christian doctrine, it recalled the purgation of baptism, a ritual of purification that every soul had to pass through if it was to progress toward celestial Jerusalem. In the course of time, Christian symbolism was further stamped upon the maze at Reims by means of sacred ritual, specifically the liturgy of Easter Sunday, the holiest of holy days. By the mid-fourteenth century at the latest, the Easter rites of Reims demanded that the clergy arrange themselves in a long line extending from the great west door to the entry of the choir on the east, where the Lord hung on the cross of the rood screen.[87] In their midst was the labyrinth. So disposed, the archbishop and his servants sang of the Israelites' exit from hellish Egypt (the psalm *When Israel Went out of Egypt*) and of Christ's ultimate victory (the antiphon *Christ Rising*). Looking down this clerical line

FIGURE 2.10 The maze in the nave of the cathedral of Amiens. The present labyrinth is an exact reproduction of the thirteenth-century original.

from east to west, the faithful could visualize the Lord's two great ordeals, his suffering on the cross and his trial in the hellish maze.

Amiens

The spirit of the legendary Daedalus must have hovered high above the cathedral city of Amiens. At least the town masons must have felt an affinity to the first man to fly as they clambered high in the vaults of the tallest of all medieval churches. As the cathedral soared skyward, one of the canons of the church, the *trouvère* poet Richard de Fournival, composed a poetic flight of fancy, paying homage to Daedalus and the maze in his song "I had the urge to love" *(Talent avoie d'amer)*.[88] And on earth the labyrinth itself was set into the pavement of the nave and became known as "La Maison Daedalus."[89] Here, too, the maze was the home of Daedalus, one he shared with the memory of the master builders who constructed the cathedral.

If the meaning of the maze at Reims is something of an enigma wrapped in a labyrinth, the meaning of the maze at the cathedral of Amiens is perfectly clear. The labyrinth at Amiens is the second largest of the pavement mazes after that at Chartres. It spans 12.14 meters and consumes the entire width of the fourth and fifth bays of the nave (Fig. 2.10). At the center is an octagonal medallion surrounded by an inscription that tells of the construction of the church:[90]

> In the year of grace 1220
> the construction of this
> church first began.
> Blessed Evrard was at that time
> bishop of this diocese.
> The king of France was then Louis
> the son of Philip the wise.
> He who directed the work
> was called master Robert,
> surnamed Luzarches.
> Master Thomas de Cormont
> came after him,
> and after him his son,
> Renaud, who had placed here
> this inscription in the year
> of the incarnation, 1288.[91]

Thus the cathedral of Amiens was begun in 1220 and completed in 1288, at which time the labyrinth and its inscription were set in place. Within this octagonal central medallion were laid effigies of the four individuals mentioned above, Bishop Evrard de Fouilly (1211–1222) and master builders Robert de Luzarches, Thomas de Cormont, and his son Renaud. Each carries a symbol of his profession: the bishop a crosier, and the architects, respectively, a rule, a square, and a compass. Bishop Evrard was buried a few meters from the labyrinth, and many other important personages were entombed in the nave as well. In this way the nave began to assume a funeral and commemorative function. The fourth and fifth bays in particular came to be seen as a hallowed precinct, for here, deep within the twisting corridors of the house of Daedalus, was a memorial plaque honoring those who built the church.

At first glance the maze at Amiens appears to be identical, or at least very similar, to that at Reims (compare Figs. 2.7 and 2.10). Yet closer inspection reveals that the labyrinth at Amiens is somewhat different from the one at Reims. In fact, the Amiens maze follows exactly the same course of meanderings as does the labyrinth at Chartres. As we shall soon see, the design at Amiens is only superficially different from the circular one at Chartres. This maze is simply the Chartrain pattern shaped as an octagon.

Once set on the floor of the nave by Regnaud de Cormont in 1288, the labyrinth remained in place at Amiens until the 1820s, when "it was removed to make the old pavement more polite," as John Ruskin observed.[92] Not only was the labyrinth displaced at this time, but so too were all the medieval tombs and funereal inscriptions resting in the nave. Almost immediately, however, local historians began to decry this destruction. Some of the more substantial episcopal sarcophagi were restored, and eventually, during the years 1894–1897, an exact replica of the labyrinth was put in place. Thus for all but seventy of the last seven hundred years, the people of Amiens have experienced a labyrinth in the heart of their religious center. So important is the labyrinth to the communal psyche at Amiens that recently the city fathers constructed a large, though incomplete, maze of stones set in turf in the central "parc-sportif" (Parc St.-Pierre), much to the delight of children of all ages who trace its path.

St. Quentin

The collegiate church of St. Quentin, 170 kilometers north of Paris, is a cathedral in all but title. It is a gigantic structure, indeed in volume the fourth largest sanctuary in all of France.[93] The magnitude of the church can be explained by its history. From the time of Saint Louis (ruled 1226–1270) to the Revolution, St. Quentin was supported and maintained by the kings of France, who had the hereditary right to appoint the clergy of the church.[94] If St. Quentin was the architectural equal of the cathedrals at Amiens and Reims, it owed this magnificence solely to a line of royal patrons that can be traced back to Saint Louis and, more distantly, to a relative of Emperor Charlemagne.

The labyrinth at St. Quentin is one of only two large pavement mazes to survive from medieval times (see Fig. 7.7).[95] It measures 10.66 meters from side to side and occupies the last two bays of the very west end of the church. Although it replicates the octagonal pattern at Amiens in all particulars, the present labyrinth at St. Quentin may be more than two centuries younger. The Gothic nave at St. Quentin is a late medieval structure that was not completed until 1451. Apparently, the maze within it dates from 1495, the year in which the present pavement was laid.[96] It is also possible, however, that the existing maze may be a reconstruction of a thirteenth-century original belonging to the earlier church on this site.[97] Whatever its status—original or five-centuries-old replica—the labyrinth at St. Quentin is constructed of approximately 700 small black slabs, bordered by white stones of equal size. Proceeding at a leisurely pace, the spiritual pilgrim requires about fifteen minutes to walk its anfractuous path to the center and back to the entrance. Today the collegiate church of St. Quentin sits on high in majestic solitude, never disturbed by the tourists who visit Amiens and overrun Chartres. One can experience the labyrinth at St. Quentin in quiet contemplation, for usually no one but the solitary meanderer of the maze has entered the church.

Arras

Nothing remains of the labyrinth that once rested in the cathedral of Arras, a town north of Amiens whose fortunes have steadily declined since the fifteenth century. Both labyrinth and cathedral were destroyed in the aftermath of the French Revolution, and no drawing of the maze survives. A de-

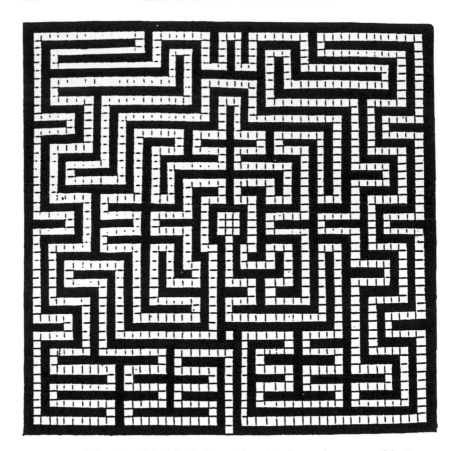

FIGURE 2.11 A drawing of the labyrinth once found in the south transept of the Benedictine abbey of St. Bertin, in St. Omer, France. The design has been corrected, according to the copy of the original maze now in Ghent, to reflect a single path to the center.

piction of this maze did, however, once exist and was known to the architectural historian Emanuel Wallet. In an article published in 1843, Wallet
offers the following information about this lost labyrinth.[98]

The maze at Arras was situated in the nave near the west end of the
church. Its eleven tracks were configured in a fashion identical to the mazes
at Amiens and St. Quentin, and thus it, too, was octagonal in shape. Measuring 10.56 meters in width, it was only slightly smaller than its counterpart at St. Quentin (10.66 meters), but larger than the maze at Reims (10.20
meters). The paving stones forming the field of this labyrinth were arranged in sixty-four bands, nine for the center octagon and fifty-five for the

outline of the tracks. These smallish stones were yellow and blue-black in color, the former composing the background and the latter the tracks of the path. Wallet reports that prior to the destruction of this maze in 1795, the devout souls of Arras followed its course on their knees, reciting pious prayers as they proceeded. This spiritual journey required an hour from beginning to end.

St. Omer

The maze once found at the now-destroyed church of St. Bertin in the town St. Omer (Fig. 2.11) is an anomaly on several counts. It was placed on the floor of a monastery, not a cathedral or a collegiate church, and thus, as nearly as can be determined, was the only monastic pavement labyrinth of any size. In contrast to all other French floor mazes, the labyrinth at St. Omer was not found in the nave of the church, but rather in the south transept. Most important, its form is unlike that of any other maze. The perimeter is square. Yet this labyrinth is not divided into simple quadrants as is the Roman-influenced church maze in Algiers, the only other square church labyrinth presently known. Instead, one enters and, proceeding through a seemingly endless series of right-angle turns, traverses portions of the maze in sequence, first those closest to the center and then, having returned to a point very near the entrance, around the outer zones until the center is finally attained. When the monastery of St. Bertin was destroyed in the late eighteenth century, this labyrinth was lost with it.[99] In more recent times, the same design was inlaid on the floor of the present cathedral of St. Omer, immediately before the high altar.[100]

Although the maze at St. Omer was a victim of eighteenth-century anti-clerical fervor, a description of it, fortunately, was included in the above-mentioned study by Emanuel Wallet. The labyrinth was set in place about 1350; measuring 10.85 meters across, it occupied most of the floor of the newly finished south transept. No fewer than 2,401 white or blue-black stones were used to fashion the intricate pattern. The creator set out a large square with a side of forty-nine stones, but one row of stones was used to indicate the north-south and east-west axis. What resulted, then, was a square of forty-eight rows which was divided by the axes into four quadrants, each containing 24^2 stones.

Not only does this maze display mathematical perfection, but a striking icon is visible as well. The creator has erected a large cross in the upper portion, which seems to grow out of the center of the maze. Whatever Christian symbolism may have been lost by substituting a square for an octagon or a circle is thus more than compensated for by the sign of the Lord's sacrifice. For a viewer familiar with the teachings of the church, this particular arrangement—a cross atop the epicenter of a labyrinth—may have possessed additional symbolism.

Traditional theology held that, after the Fall, Adam and his soul resided in Hell. This Hell was directly beneath Golgotha and the place of the Holy Cross, the absolute center of the world.[101] When Christ undertook the Harrowing of Hell to rescue Adam and the other elect, he descended into Hell and left there a sign of his triumph:

> The saints besought Him to leave the sign of victory, the holy Cross, *apud inferos,* lest His evil servants should prevail to keep back any one accused whom the Lord absolved. The Lord set up His Cross *in medio inferni,* and it will remain there for ever. Then we all went out thence with the Lord, leaving Satan and *Infernum* in Tartarus.[102]

Albrecht Dürer must have known of this account, for in his famous woodcut *Christ's Descent into Limbo* (see Fig. 3.1), he, like the creator of the maze at St. Bertin, places a cross in the middle of the inferno. The labyrinth at St. Omer reveals to the faithful a sign of the Lord's power standing tall in Satan's den at the epicenter of the earth.

The Hidden Symmetry of the Church Maze

The maze was thus a decorative ornament, not a structural component of the architecture of the church. It did not influence, but merely gave added meaning to, the master plan of the building wrought *a priori* by means of geometry. Never, for example, did the size or location of the labyrinth determine the width of the central vessel or the position of the pillars that supported it. On the contrary, in most cases the size of the pavement maze was set by the width of the nave: the larger the expanse across from pillar to pillar, the larger the labyrinth. Like the steeple atop the central crossing, the maze was an optional element of architectural design added *a posteriori* to the completed sanctuary. Many important cathedral churches, Notre-Dame of Paris to name one, had no maze.[103]

If the labyrinth was neither structural nor necessary, it must have been symbolic. Indeed, as we have seen, it signified the ingenuity of the architect, and, by means of the cross, the octagon, and the rosette, it reminded the people of fundamental articles of Christian faith—specifically, salvation, purification and rebirth, and the celestial origins of Christ. But there is a further symbolic element inherent in nearly all of these church mazes, be they Italian or French: the symmetrical construction of the maze.

Look again at the maze once found on the floor at St. Bertin in St. Omer (Fig. 2.11). Focus on the center and the cross above it. Notice that the top left side is an exact mirror image of the top right: one set of twists and turns is duplicated by another. For the maze-walker moving within a labyrinth, however, none of this symmetry is apparent. No carefully crafted sequence of turns is felt experientially but, on the contrary, only disorder and confusion—"amazement" in the literal sense of the word. The beauty of the rhythm nested within the maze becomes apparent only when one stands above the labyrinth, on a different plane, and can apprehend the configuration in its entirety. Only then does the meaning of the maze as a symbol of divine creation become evident.

How many other church pavement mazes have a similar sort of symmetry? All of them save one. The exception is the labyrinth at St. Vitale in Ravenna, which is the youngest of the surviving pavement labyrinths, originating in the Renaissance (1538–1539; see Fig 2.2, lower left). Medieval church mazes, by contrast, possess a rhythmic beauty that is immanent in each of them but is by no means immediately apparent to the eye. They suggest that, while life on this earth may be full of unfathomable confusion, the higher realm of paradise is ruled by divine order. The church maze is simply one more manifestation of humankind's eternal desire to comprehend the divine and mirror its perfection by means of symmetrical configurations.[104]

Reflect upon all of the circular and octagonal mazes illustrated in this chapter, including the design for a pavement maze found in the notebook of the early thirteenth-century church architect Villard de Honnecourt (Fig. 2.12).[105] At first glance they all appear rather different. The maze at Ravenna (Fig. 2.2, lower left) is indeed different. The others, however, have much in common: eleven tracks, thirty-one segments from entrance to center, and a succession of checks that creates a cross running along the west-east and north-south axes.

FIGURE 2.12 A mirror image of the maze at Chartres entered in the drawing book of architect Villard de Honnecourt about 1230.

The cross stamped on the church maze determines its form. It provides a succession of barriers that prevent the wanderer from traversing more than a quarter (90 degrees) or a half (180 degrees) of a full circle. The checks thus divide the maze into segments of quarter or half traverses, and these segments in turn form a rhythm that can be expressed by a sequence using the letters "Q" and "H." Tracing with the finger the pattern of the maze at Chartres (Fig. 1.9) or its mirror image (Fig. 2.12), for example, will quickly show what is meant by the letter sequences that follow:

Chartres-type Pattern

QQHHQQHQHQHQQHQ**H**QHQQHQHQHQQHHQQ CENTER QQHHQQHQHQHQQHQ**H**QHQQHQHQHQQHHQQ

Reims/Sens-type Pattern

QQHQHQHQQHHQQHQ**H**QHQQHHQQHQHQHQQ CENTER QQHQHQHQQHHQQHQ**H**QHQQHHQQHQHQHQQ

Tracking through the twists and turns of these church mazes, we come to see that, despite their superficial differences, there are only two rhythmic patterns. The maze at Chartres—duplicated at Amiens, St. Quentin, Lucca, Pontremoli, Pavia (and as nearly as we can determine at Rome, Piacenza, and Arras)—constitutes a basic type, the so-called Chartrain pattern. The labyrinth drawn by Villard de Honnecourt, who visited Chartres around 1230, is simply a mirror image of this Chartrain design and thus its rhythm is identical to it. The mazes at Reims and Sens (and presumably at Auxerre as well) constitute a slightly discrepant group. Their pattern is different, but only because the point at which the maze-walker engages the first segment is not the same. One enters the first segment of these mazes at the third track and not the fifth, as in the Chartrain type; and consequently one departs the final segment from the third and not the fifth track from the center of the maze. The symmetry is obvious.

Despite this minor difference between the two designs, these mazes are linked by an important common factor: each forms a double retrograde. Of course, every trip in a unicursal maze involves a single retrograde, a journey to the center and back; the wanderer must retrace his steps exactly. But the church maze is more ingeniously organized. Progressing to the center, the maze-walker encounters thirty-one segments. (It may be sheer coincidence that in Jewish and medieval Christian cabalistic speculation, the number of God is 31.)[106] Notice that the sixteenth segment (the underlined

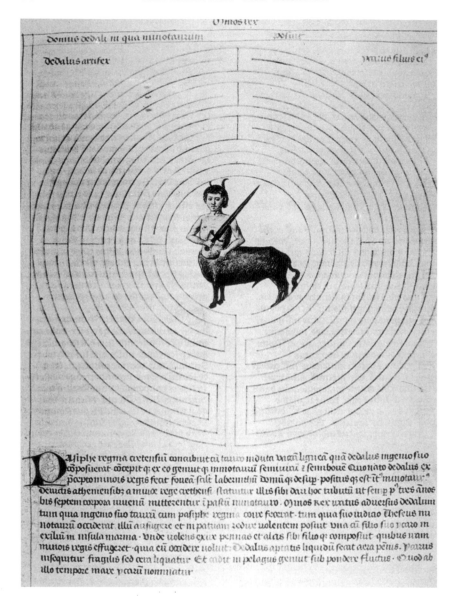

FIGURE 2.13 A fifteenth-century copy of the original twelfth-century *Liber floridus* which recounts the myth of the labyrinth: "Pasiphaë, queen of Crete, disguised as a wooden cow by the ingenious Daedalus, mated with the bull . . ." The maze, with the Minotaur in the center, is called the House of Daedalus (*Domus Dedali*).

"H") constitutes a midpoint, and when one moves from that center point in either direction, the pattern replicates itself. Once in the center of the maze, the retrograding design must be repeated before the exit is reached. Thus there are two retrogrades within each full transit of these church labyrinths, regardless of whether the maze is of the Chartrain or the Reims/Sens type.

Moving further back in time, the fourth-century Algerian maze also embodies a pleasing, though different, recursive rhythm (see Figs. 1.5 and 1.6). Within the first quadrant (southwest), the maze-walker works his way to the center and then exits by means of a mirror image of the path of entrance. The same course is followed in the remaining three quadrants. When the center of the labyrinth is finally reached, the spiritual pilgrim encounters a palindrome extolling the Holy Church: SANCTA ECLESIA.

Although symmetry can be identified in mazes since the dawn of the Mediterranean world, not all mazes possess a beautifully repeating rhythm. Many labyrinths found in medieval manuscripts, for example, do not. Consider the often-copied maze that appears in Lambert of St. Omer's *Liber floridus* (1121), which serves there as an illustration of the house of Daedalus (Fig. 2.13). There are twenty-five segments in this labyrinth and no symmetry whatsoever; the succession of quarter, half, and full turns has no rhythmic reason to it.

The *Liber floridus* tells a pagan tale and offers a pagan illustration, and that is precisely the point: irrationality can flourish within this and similar mazes because they lack the cross. The axes of the cross dictate the artful sequence of quarter- and half-turning segments. It is the cross that creates the perfect symmetry; it forces the turns that create the mirror images. Rationality, order, and perfection are caused by this most fundamental of Christian symbols. The message that the creators of the Chartrain and Reims/Sens-type mazes wished to convey was twofold: first, inherent in every true maze is the process of a miraculous reversal; and second, divine perfection can be wrought from chaos only with the aid of the cross.

The mirror *(speculum)* was, of course, a favorite symbol among medieval intellectuals, who used it as a metaphor by which to understand the universe. Theologians taught the importance of such signs as necessary to the knowledge of God. In so doing, they drew on Platonic philosophy as well as scripture.[107] At no time in the history of the West were there more treatises entitled *Speculum* than during the years 1150–1350.[108] Then all the

FIGURE 2.14 Palindromic Bull's Head with Double Axe and sacral knots from the late Minoan Age.

knowledge in the world seemed to be reflected, however darkly, through a looking glass.

It is possible, finally, that the image of a mirror or palindrome, although most consistently expressed in the medieval church maze, is primordial with the labyrinth. Many of the first mazes associated with Crete are formed, in one way or another, in palindromic shapes.[109] And although no maze was ever found within the remnants of King Minos's palace, a Hall of the Double Axe and a Bull's Head Sanctuary have been identified.[110] The Minotaur of Crete, with its human body and bull's head, also appears as a palindrome when viewed frontally (Fig. 2.14). Mirror image, in this case, can symbolize both the divine and the demonic.

Domus Dei/Domus Daedali

The architects of the great Gothic cathedrals rejoiced in hiding doctrine behind symbol, in ingeniously disguising meaning behind appearance. Every
part of the church was given its symbolic significance. Cathedrals were not
simply places of worship, but sermons in stone. The nave, the choir, the
aisles, the pillars, the altar—all had their figurative meanings and invited
worshipers to contemplate things unseen and spiritual.[III] Could the abstract pattern of the labyrinth have been any different?

The "unseen and spiritual" force reflected in the maze was nothing less
than the intellect of God. God had always been difficult to see; here was a
way to glimpse the divine. To grasp the sublimity of the celestial cause, one
need only contemplate the terrestrial effect. The earthly object, moreover,
suggested demonic potential as well as divine perfection. But evil was part
of a larger plan, and celestial perfection extended all around. Although the
pavement labyrinth was ingenious, it was insignificant when compared
with the magnificent structure in which it was confined, a building of celestial proportions and infinite beauty. The house of the Lord *(domus Dei)*
consumed the house of Daedalus *(domus Daedali)*. In the great Gothic
cathedrals in particular, Christian architecture was shown to be vastly superior to pagan artifice, the earthly inventor a mere shadow of the supreme
architect.

CHAPTER THREE

The Theology of the Maze

A MYTH IS A TIMELESS TALE, an eternal truth that speaks at different moments in different ways to different cultures. In the many civilizations of the ancient Mediterranean world—Egyptian, Hellenic, Etruscan, and Roman—the labyrinth and the story surrounding it had various meanings depending on time and place.[1] It was an ingenious, complex work of art, yet also a gloomy, tortuous prison without means of escape. It was a carefully circumscribed "security zone" into which the uninitiated might penetrate only upon pain of death, yet also a metaphor for the ideal fortified city of the ancient world. Then, at the height of the Roman empire, a new cult from the Near East, Christianity, began to grow in the midst of these same Mediterranean cultures. Not surprisingly, the proponents of the youthful religion endowed the labyrinth with fresh meaning. Just as they adapted the temples and festivals of pagan Rome to serve the cultic needs of Christianity, so too the fathers of the Church took the ancient symbol of the labyrinth and gave it a specifically Christian interpretation. For more than a thousand years, from the time of the patristic fathers until the Renaissance, the maze was used to promote the beliefs of the Western Church.

The Maze Made Christian

As Rome's empire slowly turned Christian, one of the city's first bishops, Hippolytus (c.175–c.235), wrapped the maze in purely Christian garb. His Gnostic branch of Christianity saw the labyrinth as a complex design symbolizing a spiritual arena full of sin and error within which the human soul must wander. The Savior descends and brings special wisdom (Gnosis), which frees the soul and leads it out of the labyrinth.[2]

73

So, too, St. Ambrose (c.340–397), bishop of Milan, believed that the errant soul had need of divine guidance. When commenting on Psalm 118,
verse 59 ("I have thought on my ways, and turned my feet unto thy testi-
monies"), Ambrose invokes the metaphor of the maze. Humankind,
though tainted with original sin and caught in the deceptive labyrinth of
life's journey, has the capacity to correct the error of its ways, to follow the
path of moral rectitude, and, consequently, to enjoy the possibility of for-
giveness. In his own words: "Some frequently leave the communal road, re-
ceding into a labyrinth of error, and are punished for it; and only after
much toil do they strive to regain the path they relinquished."[3] In Ambrose's
labyrinth, humankind can exercise its free will to stay on the straight and
narrow road or to deviate, to sin or not to sin.[4]

But what did the Christian maze look like? Prudentius (348–c.405) describes its topography. In fact, for Prudentius there are two forms of the
maze, the multicursal and the unicursal. The former is a deceitful construct
of misleading byways that nurture confusing heresies, while the latter offers
a simple model for orthodoxy. Prudentius sets the metaphor of the maze of
many choices in opposition to the single-path labyrinth as a way of framing the doctrinal argument in favor of one true God. Heathens who sacrifice chickens and cocks to a multiplicity of pagan gods, for example, "are
prisoners in a labyrinth of multilateral error."[5] Only with great difficulty
can we discern the narrow road to salvation amidst the twisting path:

> So many cross-roads meet us, which have been trodden smooth by the
> misguided straining of the faithless; so many side-roads join together,
> where tracks intertwine on this hand and that; and if, wandering at ran-
> dom, a man follows them, leaving the straight path, he will plunge into
> the snare of a hidden pitfall.[6]

Although the multicursal maze may not have been visible in the physical
world until the fifteenth century,[7] as a theological construct it was already
well formed here in the fourth century.[8] In the traditional single-path maze,
God is the beacon; within the multicursal maze, Satan leads the way:

> On the manifold way the guide is the devil, who on the left hand splits it
> into the confusion of a hundred paths . . . Do you not see how it is but
> one way, that wanders in many windings under a guide who will not let
> you go to the Lord of salvation, but shows you the road to death along
> byways . . . Depart ye afar, and enter into your own darkness, whither that

guide calls you, who goes before you over tangled ways from the road, in the night of hell!⁹

Stones are placed along the route, both markers of the true path and obstacles to our vanity:

> Behold, a stone is set to trip us up, that vanity may strike against it, a guide-post to the wary, but to the unwary a stumbling-block; the one it lays low, the other it directs. The blind man groping on with uncertain step runs into that which stands in his way. The torch of faith alone is to be carried before our feet, that our steps may be straight [Psalm 118:105].¹⁰

Christ guides the faithful along this rocky, labyrinthine path—this is the doctrine that gains ascendancy in the works of Gregory of Nyssa and St. Jerome. Gregory (c.331–c.396), one of the four great fathers of the Eastern Church, wrote his *Catechetical Oration* to defend Christianity against pagans and Jews. In it he suggests that Christ, like Theseus, has entered the maze from outside, achieved victory, and escaped from this prison of death:

> Those who wander, caught in a labyrinth, do not know how to find the way out; but if they meet someone who knows this maze well, they undertake to follow him to the end, through the complicated and misleading turns of the edifice. They would not have escaped had they not followed their guide step by step. Reflect: the labyrinth of life would be similarly inextricable for man if he did not follow the same path that led Him who once entered back outside. . . . This labyrinth symbolizes for me the inextricable prison of death, where unhappy mankind was once imprisoned.¹¹

Most important, for Gregory the journey out of the labyrinth begins in the baptistry: "Those who will have harmonized their life with the purification of baptism march toward their essential being."¹² The march through the labyrinth of life starts in the baptistry. In the course of time the maze and the baptismal font will come to serve as axes along which the liturgy of the church will be played out during the service of Easter Sunday. But let us stay on the straight and narrow path of theology.

The wayward soul must be tethered to Christ. The lifeline, according to St. Jerome (345–c.420), is Ariadne's thread, now transformed into the thread of Christ (*filum Christi*). Christ will lead humanity through a worldly abyss worthy of the great Dante.

> We pass from obscurity to greater obscurity, and like Moses we are enveloped in a cloud and darkness; abyss calls to abyss with the sound of the cataracts of God, and, circling in circuits, the spirit goes forth and returns in its own circles. We suffer labyrinthine errors, and we guide our blind footsteps by the thread of Christ.[13]

This, in brief, is the essence of patristic thought regarding the labyrinth. At its core is a surprisingly uniform doctrine. The labyrinth instantiates the uncertainty and confusion of this life. The route is full of moral difficulty, bewildering twists and turns experienced by humans stained by original sin. Death and eternal damnation await those who deviate from the straight and narrow. To navigate the tortuous route, a divine guide will be needed, who will effect a spiritual rebirth. The Theseus of the ancient Greek myth passes the thread to the Messiah of the Christian pageant.[14] Henceforth Christ will serve as guide through the hellish labyrinth of earthly life.

This Christianizing of the myth of Theseus, Ariadne, and the maze was intensified during the high Middle Ages, when many Western theologians sought to marry the teachings of the church to the precepts of classical philosophy.[15] Now every particular in the story of the labyrinth is given an *interpretatio christiana*. For example, in the eleventh century a monk drew a maze in a commentary on Virgil's *Aeneid*. Around the serpentine path of this labyrinth he inserted a Latin poem which equates not only Christ with Theseus, but Satan with the Minotaur:

> Behold the Minotaur consumes all things which are enveloped in the labyrinth; this labyrinth is the mark of the inferno, the sign of Zabulum [Satan].[16]

By the early fourteenth century the push to sanctify all things classical had extended to Ovid's great collection of mythology, his *Metamorphoses*. The entire tale of Daedalus's maze was now dressed in the garb of Christian allegory by a French man-of-letters, Pierre Bersuire.[17]

> Said in allegorical terms the Minotaur represents the Devil, Hell, and death which indeed from time immemorial devour humankind, for death truly devours bodies. . . . The Minotaur was the Devil whom God

expelled from Heaven and enclosed in an infernal labyrinth, or one of this world, where he consumed the spirits of many thousands of humans. However the fate of the human condition was such that successively the Athenians were fed to these minotaurs by Minos; that is, Adam and all humankind were dispatched by Lucifer. Because, as Ecclesiasticus [21:3] says, "the teeth of the lion are used to kill the souls of humankind," such animals were confined from the very beginning in a labyrinth of diverse twists and turns and a profundity of diverse difficulties. Thus anyone who entered therein labored in vain to go back out. So firmly did death, the Devil, and Hell detain humankind, that none returned from these snares. For as Wisdom [2:1] says, "No one is known to have come back from the abyss." But just as Theseus was the son of King Aegeus, so Christ, the son of God the Father, was sent by fate to an earthly death which he accepted and had the courage to descend to these minotaurs. Certainly he did not remain there because by means of the thread of divinity and the pitch of humanity he conquered these monsters, namely death, Devil, and Hell, and whence through the resurrection, free and victorious, he went out and returned. Having assumed the vessel of the body, He led away with him to the paradisiacal homeland Ariadne, daughter of Minos, human nature, the daughter of Adam, who lay in Limbo. And thus it is said in the hymn "The victor comes back from the abyss. . . . Amen I say to you, thou shalt by no means come out thence" [Matt. 5:26]. What then can such [a sinner] as Daedalus do but put on wings of contemplation so as to fly up to the bounty of Paradise, and through contemplation may pass over the vicissitudes of the worldly sea, and thus may exit from this labyrinth of the world and of sin, and fly free from the dominion of Minos, that is the Devil. For just as is said in Psalm 12 [10:2], "In the Lord put I my trust: how say ye to my soul, Flee as a bird to your mountain."[18]

Here every part of the myth of the labyrinth is given Christian significance. The Athenian tribute children represent all humanity, ensnared in an infernal prison and about to be devoured by death (Minotaur/Satan). As did Theseus, the son of an Athenian king, so now Christ, the son of the Father, subjects himself to death and rescues the entrapped. Christ does not tarry in the hellish labyrinth but, victorious over death and the Devil, he rises up to Paradise, bringing out Adam and other true believers with him. The moral: if you wish to escape the labyrinth of this world you must put on wings of spiritual contemplation and, like a bird, fly toward the mountain of the Lord.

As myth becomes Christian parable, the labyrinth is situated in a landscape with three tiers: inferno, earth, and Paradise above. What is most
striking, the labyrinth is now associated with the lower portion of this topography, not earth but Hell. Christ subjects himself to death on this earth,
descends into the labyrinthine Underworld to rescue those awaiting for-
giveness from venial sins, and leads them to celestial Paradise. The parable
of the maze now teaches a fundamental Christian tenet: Christ's death and
resurrection are necessary to remove the stain of original sin. The labyrinth
has become a symbol vital to the drama of the resurrection, and it owes this
status in large measure to the development of the late medieval doctrine of
Purgatory.

The Maze as Symbol of Purgatory

The doctrine of Purgatory emerged as a response to a basic question in
Christian thinking: What happens to the soul between the moment of
death and the time of the Last Judgment? For nearly a thousand years, theologians wrestled with this issue. Most agreed that persons dying as martyrs for Christ went directly to Heaven, while those guilty of mortal sin descended to Hell to suffer eternal pain.[19] For Christians burdened by venial
sins, however, various patristic fathers posited differing forms and durations of postmortem penance in a zone that would ultimately be called Purgatory. As time progressed, a series of witnesses for Christ gave lurid testimony to the nature of the punishment the repentant sinner might expect
to receive therein. The dreams of these visionaries—of Furseus, Drythelm,
and Charles the Fat, among others[20]—helped feed the popular imagination
as to the nature of purgatorial pain. The vision of Charles the Fat (d. 888),
recorded sometime around the year 900 in the area of Reims, is especially
instructive, for it shows how the route of a spiritual journey might be
mapped directly upon the topography of the Cretan labyrinth. Here the
seer is Charles III, Holy Roman Emperor, who sits resting on his bed at the
moment of his supernatural experience:

> There came a tremendous voice to me, saying, "Charles, in a little while
> your spirit shall leave you for some time." Immediately I was carried away
> in spirit, and he who carried me away was most glorious to see. In his
> hand he held a ball of thread emitting a beam of the purest light, such as

comets shed when they appear. He began to unwind it and said to me, "Take the thread of this brilliant ball and wind and tie it firmly on the thumb of your right hand, for by it you will be led through the inextricable punishments of the infernal regions." Saying this, he went before me, quickly unrolling the thread of the brilliant ball, and led me into very deep and fiery valleys that were full of pits boiling with pitch and brimstone and lead and wax and grease. . . .

While I was fearfully listening to this, the blackest demons came flying around me with fiery claws trying to snatch away the thread of life, which I held in my hand, and to draw it to them; but repelled by the rays of the ball they were unable to touch it. Next running behind me, they tried to grip me in their claws and cast me head-first into those sulphurous pits; but my guide, who carried the ball, threw a thread of light over my shoulders, and doubling it drew me strongly after him.[21]

The thread that had been Ariadne's is now the lifeline of salvation; the guide is no longer Theseus, but Christ; the path of the maze runs through the sulphurous pits of Hell. In later visionary journeys—those of Thurkill, Alberic of Settefrati, and the Knight Owen in St. Patrick's Purgatory—the landscape of Hell is described in increasingly horrific terms, as if each new spiritual pilgrim steps forward as a witness to yet greater torments and misery.

Ultimately, by the late twelfth century, a consistent doctrine of Purgatory had evolved, one that posited answers to the following: Where was this zone of purgation? Who must abide there and for how long? What might be the nature of the punishment?[22] The majority of theologians situated Purgatory in the upper reaches of the Underworld, an antechamber to Hell. Here the souls of those who die in a state of grace, yet not free from all imperfection, make atonement for forgivable sins. The instrument of postmortem punishment is fire. A condition of purgation will continue until the Last Judgment, when Christ will once again descend, defeat the forces of evil, and deliver those who have been purged of sin. In the fullness of time, then, the purified shall be redeemed and led back by the Savior. By 1200 the doctrine of Purgatory had become a central component of Christian theology.

Not coincidentally, it was precisely at this time that the labyrinth—the symbol of imprisonment within a demonic zone—began to appear for the first time on the floors of French and Italian churches. The Christianized maze of the Chartrain type had existed since at least 900, copied again and again in ecclesiastical manuscripts.[23] Yet only now, during the twelfth and thirteenth centuries, was it brought into the church and its dimensions greatly enlarged. Purgatory had extended the Christian narrative, which began with the Incarnation and ended with the Last Judgment. The story of how and where the individual might gain salvation in this ethical tale had become longer and more vivid. A zone both for visualizing and dramatizing Purgatory had to be identified within the architectural ambitus of the church. That zone was the maze.

The Maze as Stage for the Harrowing of Hell

The doctrine of Purgatory added force to the drama of Christ's descent into Hell. For if there were no temporary zone of penance and expiation—if all souls went either directly to eternal bliss in Heaven or to eternal damnation in Hell at the moment of earthly death, as certain heretics believed—then who would be left in Hell for Christ to rescue? Although Christ's mission to Hell is not described in the Bible, a passage in Matthew (12:40) certainly adumbrates it: "For as Jonas was three days and three nights in the whale's belly, so shall the Son of man be three days and three nights in the heart of the earth." By the fourth century the concept of a katabasis by Christ was already accepted as dogma in what was later to be called the Apostles' Creed:[24]

> I believe in God the Father, the Almighty, creator of heaven and earth. And in Jesus Christ, his only son, our Lord, who was conceived by the Holy Ghost, born of the Virgin Mary, suffered under Pontius Pilate, crucified, dead and buried, descended into Hell, the third day rose again from the dead . . .

Yet it is principally through the apocryphal Gospel of Nicodemus, most of which was written sometime during the second or third century, that we learn, with a wealth of detail, of Christ's journey into the Underworld. Between his death and resurrection the Savior descends into Hell to rescue all righteous souls who had not themselves been baptized because they were born prior to his coming. Now arise the prophets who had foretold Christ's advent, as well as Adam and Eve, the aged Simeon, and John the Baptist.

The Savior attacks (harries) Hell, and thereby breaks Satan's power to hold the just. The narrative of Nicodemus reads like an eyewitness account of someone who has personally seen, as well as benefited from, Christ's arrival and victory over Satan:

> We, then, were in Hades with all who have died since the beginning of the world. And at the hour of midnight there rose upon the darkness there something like the light of the sun and shone, and light fell upon us all, and we saw one another. And immediately our father Abraham, along with the patriarchs and the prophets, was filled with joy, and they said to one another: This shining comes from a great light. The prophet Isaiah, who was present there, said: This shining comes from the Father and the Son and the Holy Spirit. This I prophesied when I was still living: "The land of Zabulon and the land of Nephthalim, the people that walked in darkness saw a great light" (Isaiah 9:1–2). . . .
>
> And while they were all so joyful, Satan the heir of darkness came and said to Hades: O insatiable devourer of all, listen to my words. This is one of the race of the Jews, Jesus by name, who calls himself the Son of God. But he is (only) a man, and at our instigation the Jews crucified him. And now that he is dead, be prepared that we may secure him here. For I know that he is (only) a man, and I heard him saying: "My soul is very sorrowful, even to death" (Matthew 26:38). . . .
>
> While Satan and Hades were speaking thus to one another, a loud voice like thunder sounded: "Lift up your gates, O rulers, and be lifted up, O everlasting doors, and the King of glory shall come in" (Psalm 23:7). When Hades heard this, he said to Satan: Go out, if you can, and withstand him. So Satan went out. Then Hades said to his demons: Make fast well and strongly the gates of brass and the bars of iron, and hold my locks, and stand upright and watch every point. For if he comes in, woe will seize us.
>
> When the forefathers heard that, they all began to mock him, saying: O all-devouring and insatiable one, open, that the King of glory may come in. The prophet David said: Do you not know, blind one, that when I lived in the world, I prophesied that word, "Lift up your gates, O rulers"? (Psalm 23:7). Isaiah said: I foresaw this by the Holy Spirit and wrote: "The dead shall arise, and those who are in the tombs shall be raised up, and those who are under the earth shall rejoice" (26:19). O death, where is thy sting? (I Corinthians 15:55, referring to Isaiah 25:8).
>
> Again the voice sounded: Lift up the gates. When Hades heard the voice the second time, he answered as if he did not know it and said:

"Who is this King of glory?" (Psalm 24:10). The angels of the Lord said: "The Lord strong and mighty, the Lord mighty in battle" (Psalm 23:8). And immediately at this answer the gates of brass were broken in pieces and the bars of iron were crushed and all the dead who were bound were loosed from their chains, and we with them. And the King of glory entered in like a man, and all the dark places of Hades were illumined. . . .

Then the King of glory seized the chief ruler Satan by the head and handed him over to the angels, saying: Bind with iron fetters his hands and his feet and his neck and his mouth. Then he gave him to Hades and said: Take him and hold him fast until my second coming. . . .

While Hades was thus speaking with Satan, the King of glory stretched out his right hand, and took hold of our forefather Adam and raised him up. . . . Likewise also all the prophets and the saints said: We give thee thanks, O Christ, Savior of the world, because thou hast brought up our life from destruction. When they had said this, the Savior blessed Adam with the sign of the cross on his forehead. And he did this also to the patriarchs and prophets and martyrs and forefathers, and he took them and leaped up out of Hades. And as he went the holy fathers sang praises, following him and saying: "Blessed be he who comes in the name of the Lord. Alleluia" (Psalm 118:26). To him be the glory of all the saints.

Thus he went into paradise holding our forefather Adam by the hand, and he handed him over and all the righteous to Michael the archangel.[25]

The story of a conquering god who descends into the land of the dead and does battle with the forces of evil is not unique to Christianity.[26] Indeed, it was a prominent theme in Babylonian, Persian, and Egyptian spiritual lore, as well as Greek mythology.[27] Yet Nicodemus's vivid, dramatic account of Christ's trial in the Underworld captured the imagination of theologians and laymen alike for more than a thousand years.[28]

Artists, in both East and West, naturally seized upon the exciting tale of the Harrowing of Hell as a subject worthy of depiction.[29] In manuscript illuminations, frescoes, engravings, and stained glass they portrayed Christ in mortal combat with the forces of evil.[30] Perhaps the most graphic treatment of Christ's Harrowing of Hell can be seen in a woodblock that Albrecht Dürer fashioned in 1510 as part of a cycle of the Lord's Passion (Fig. 3.1). Here Christ, having broken down the gates of Hell, does battle with dragons and flying demons as he reaches to pull St. John the Baptist from the infernal pit. Already freed are Eve and Adam, who represent all humanity. Adam holds in his right hand the instrument of his destruction (an

FIGURE 3.1 The end point of Christ's infernal journey, the Harrowing of Hell as depicted in a woodcut by Albrecht Dürer (1510).

apple) and in his left that of his liberation (the cross). Securely planted in the center of the scene is the archetype of the cross, just as Christ's standard stood in the center of the labyrinth at St. Omer (see Fig. 2.11).[31]

This hellish tale was not merely visually provocative; it was full of dramatic confrontation as well. Thus by the fourteenth century Christ's Harrowing of Hell had taken center stage in Ireland, England, France, Germany, and Italy.[32] When presented in the vernacular and out of doors for the general populace, the sacred drama was called a mystery play. When performed in Latin inside the church, however, the Harrowing belonged to a genre of medieval theater called liturgical drama.

Early on Easter morning, at the end of Matins, the clergy processed in silence from their choir stalls westward to a chapel in the nave designated to serve as Limbo. There they gathered in darkness, except for a single light, which represented the imminent radiance of the Redeemer. Soon arrived the figure of Christ (the local bishop, abbot, or a priest), attended by an angelic choir (choirboys). Pounding on the brass doors of Hell with his cross, Christ compels the princes of darkness to open the gates, then shatters these portals. Hades flees, but Satan engages Christ in a verbal sparring match, and is placed in chains. As Christ leads the exemplary ancients (represented by the adult clergy) up and out of Limbo, they sing a song of deliverance, *Cum rex glorie Christus infernum bellatus*:

> When Christ the king of glory, ready to engage in battle, entered the Underworld, the angelic chorus commanded that the gates of the princes be lifted. The host of saints, who were held captive in death, cried out in lamentation: "You have come, desired one, for whom we have waited in the darkness that you might this night lead the enchained out of bondage. We called to you with our sighs. We sought you with lengthy laments. You are made the hope of the desolate, the great consolation in torment."[33]

The newly liberated captives, sometimes clutching palm branches as signs of victory,[34] then process eastward toward the rood screen to venerate the cross. In many churches across Europe the excitement of the moment inspired exuberant display, as the clergy symbolically danced their way toward Paradise.[35] In France, at least in the great cathedrals with floor mazes, this dance was moved to the afternoon of Easter and centered on the labyrinth, as we shall see in Chapter 5.

The most intensely dramatic moment of the Harrowing of Hell occurs when Christ and Satan meet face to face. Hell, of course, is a place associated with noise, indeed cacophony.[36] But now the discord becomes shattering as the two powerful adversaries engage in a clamorous dispute. Christ shouts at Satan, calling him a wicked fiend; Satan, in turn, mocks Christ for having suffered the same indignities as all of humankind.[37] In the vernacular mystery plays, this verbal confrontation is called an *estrif* or *débat*,[38] and in Latin ecclesiastical documents it is referred to as a *verberatio*.[39] At the cathedral of Chartres such a *verberatio* occurred in association with the Easter dance, which was acted out on the floor of the nave of the cathedral where the maze was situated.[40] Here the maze served as a stage for, if not a morality play, then a morality dance, a dance of death in which damnation and salvation are paired.

Regardless of whether Christ's trial in Hell was played out in the form of a liturgical drama or expressed as a celebratory dance on the maze, the themes of this spiritual progress are the same: the clergy moves from east (Paradise) to west (Hell) and then reverses course; within Hell a spirited, noisy debate (a *verberatio*) transpires between Christ and Satan in which Christ is victorious; the cross, the instrument through which salvation is achieved, is carried to the center of Hell, where it will stand until the end of time as a warning to Satan. This cross marks the end of the line in Christ's journey, and now his return begins. Medieval theologians often spoke of Christ's life as a round-trip *transitus*, a coming and going from Paradise to Hell and back.[41] Thus the Lord's journey can be conceptualized not only as a horizontal movement east-west-east, but also vertically, as empyrean-abyss-empyrean. Either way, it was seen as a linear progression with two distinct features: a point of reversal is found at the center, and the places of beginning and end are the same, conditions also inherent in the labyrinth of the church.

With the doctrine of Purgatory fully established by the late Middle Ages, a new stop was now in place on Christ's round-trip journey. That station, of course, was Hell—Hell, Purgatory, and Limbo taken collectively. In truth, this terminal was not wholly new, but one that had been only dimly lit, or at least not fully described by the theologians. Now burning more brightly, Hell became the terminus on Christ's itinerary leading from Heaven to the abyss and back. The length of this recursive journey had been extended into the netherworld, and the labyrinth was part of this extension.

By means of this symbol Hell became a more separate and distinct realm, detached from the complementary dominions of earth and Paradise. The maze suggested a code of ethical conduct for this present world by making more apparent—indeed, by making visible on the floor of the church—a zone of penance and punishment. It helped humans understand circumstances in this world by clarifying the next.

The Maze as Metaphor for the Sinful World

Purgatory and Christ's Harrowing of Hell were medieval theological constructs that came to demand expression in the form of theater and dance. They developed within the established Church of Rome and culminated in liturgical drama and the dance of the maze during the thirteenth, fourteenth, and fifteenth centuries. With the winds of reform blowing across northern Europe in the sixteenth century, however, a less institutionalized, more personal religious spirit was borne aloft.[42] This new pietism affected how people perceived the labyrinth as symbol. The emphasis now begins to shift away from the He to the I, from Christ to the Christian, from Hell back to earth.

Erasmus of Rotterdam's *Trusty Weapon of the Christian Soldier (Enchiridion Militis Christiani)* was the most influential work of pre-Reformation theology.[43] First printed in 1503, it appeared in eight Latin editions between 1514 and 1518, and was soon translated into English, Czech, German, Dutch, Spanish, French, Portuguese, Italian, and Polish.[44] For Erasmus the labyrinth functions, as it had earlier with the patristic fathers, as a metaphor for the sinful world. The faithful will need a guiding thread, a set of rules, to chart a course through a life of temptation.

> We shall try to pass on briefly certain rules with the help of which you can easily extricate yourself from the labyrinthine errors of this world, and, using these rules like the thread of Daedalus, find your way into the clear light of spiritual living.[45]

Steeped in classical literature, Erasmus knew well the myth of Daedalus and the Cretan maze. So, too, he knew the patristic maze as metaphor for the sinful world, as well as the medieval pavement maze as symbol of the place of Christ's Harrowing of Hell. Erasmus composed his *Trusty Weapon of the*

Handbüchlin Fol. XVI

Anfang des handbüchlinſz
eins chꝛſtenlichen Ritters.

Erasmus Roterdam
entbüt seim friind Johanni german/
ein hoffman syn grůß.

FIGURE 3.2 Woodcut from the 1520 German edition of Erasmus of Rotterdam's *Trusty Weapon of the Christian Soldier*, printed in Basel by Adam Petrus. The Christian knight remains steadfast in the face of earthly vanities.

FIGURE 3.3 The faithful soldier of Christ rides through the perilous maze of this
world in Albrecht Dürer's great *Knight, Death, and the Devil* (1513).

Christian Soldier while residing at the Benedictine monastery of St. Bertin,
in St. Omer, a church that possessed a pavement labyrinth with the cross at
the center (see Fig. 2.11).

The soldier of Christ will need weapons to combat the sins of this world. Thus Erasmus calls his *Trusty Weapon* a *gladiolus* ("small blade"), a dagger to be used against the world, flesh, and the Devil. It is a spiritual weapon for all occasions, smaller and more portable than the weighty Bible. Daily this little book will protect the layman as he proceeds along the path of life. To visualize the teachings of the *Trusty Weapon,* consider the title page of the German edition of 1520 (Fig. 3.2).[46] In the center stands the Christian soldier wearing the armor of spiritual virtue. He is assailed from above by the arrows of the fallen angels, and tempted below, on the right by the deathly figure of Avarice, who holds out a pot of gold, and on the left by the buxom enticements of Lust, who prefers a laurel wreath (the vain pride of worldly fame). The warrior, however, remains steadfast, looking neither left nor right. He stands victorious, with the serpentine Satan trampled below. In his right hand the soldier brandishes the *Gladium Spiritus,* a sword that has pierced a heart, demonstrating that he possesses a spiritual soul. The sword of the spirit is the word of God (Ephesians 6:17). In his left hand the warrior holds a book, signifying his knowledge of the gospel. Prayer based on knowledge of the scriptures, Erasmus argues, will give potency to the soldier's spiritual weaponry. Thus Erasmus is merely a squire to the Christian knight, helping to dress his pious reader with a set of rules for daily conduct. These injunctions form the combatant's armor and allow the warrior to stride forth fearlessly no matter where the foe resides. As for the enemy, he lurks in the labyrinth of sin.

During the years 1520–1521 Albrecht Dürer traveled through the Low Countries, selling his art, studying the paintings of others, and all the while writing in his journal. When false news of an assassination of Martin Luther reached him, Dürer, a reformist sympathizer, penned in his log an impassioned cry to his fellow reformer Erasmus of Rotterdam: "Hark, thou Knight of Christ *(du Ritter Christi),* ride forth at the side of Christ our Lord, protect the truth, obtain the crown of the Martyrs."[47] Dürer viewed Erasmus, author of the *Trusty Weapon of the Christian Soldier,* as a true knight of Christ plodding his way along the labyrinth of life. As Erwin Panofsky has pointed out, Dürer's outburst provides a clue to the meaning of one of his greatest works, *Ritter, Tod, und Teufel.*

Knight, Death, and the Devil (Fig. 3.3), or simply *The Knight* as Dürer himself called it, is a line engraving on copper created by the artist in 1513.

Here the Christian soldier is not the beautiful, youthful knight of many a church altarpiece, but a more commonplace, world-weary figure, Everyman. Fully outfitted with sword and armor, he rides a magnificent steed alongside of which trots a dog, the timeless symbol of fidelity. Knight, horse, and dog all look straight ahead, their purpose and "directionality"— their faith—emphasized by full side profiles. Death approaches from the front, a cadaverous, half-rotten form who holds an hourglass, a reminder of the fleeting nature of human time. From behind steals the Devil, a hideous phantasmagory. The path is rocky and strewn with reptiles, indications of its difficulty and danger. A human skull suggests the inevitable fate of all. As Panofsky has emphasized, the Christian Knight marches through "the cold, dark and perilous maze of the world."[48] Yet he proceeds resolutely, even stoically, his gaze fixed on the narrow path that leads to his ultimate destination, celestial Jerusalem seen far above in the distance.

The cathedral builders of the Middle Ages could not very well construct a symbolic path of life through the middle of the church and strew it with lizards and skulls. Yet their need to express the devouring march of time and the tortuous route of this world was no less intense than Dürer's. The visual metaphor they chose was different, yet eminently practical within the church. Borrowing an icon from the ancient world, they inlaid on the floor of the nave a circular (sometimes octagonal, rarely square) symbol, the maze. Circular form had distinct advantages over the visual metaphor of the linear route. A circular maze was self-contained and delimiting. It embodied perfection because it had no beginning or end. It created sacred space, a zone which both circumscribed and confined the forces of evil. For medieval theologians the maze symbolized the defining moment in the life of Christ, his battle with Satan. Erasmus saw it as a metaphor full of moral implications for everyday life. Yet even he perpetuated a mood of spiritual warfare. The labyrinth objectified a fundamental axiom: every true believer (Christian warrior) would have need of protection (the Lord's armor) as he proceeded through this sinful world (the maze).

While Erasmus and his fellow Catholic reformers had a fondness for the spiritual soldier, Protestant theologians preferred the image of the solitary pilgrim.[49] Thus in John Amos Comenius's *Labyrinth of the World and the Paradise of the Heart* (1631) the hero of the maze is a pilgrim.[50] To help his reader visualize this earthly life, Comenius offers a labyrinth as his fron-

FIGURE 3.4 A vision of the confusing maze of this earthly world which serves as the frontispiece to John Amos Comenius's *Labyrinth of the World and the Paradise of the Heart* (1631).

tispiece (Fig. 3.4). This labyrinthine world is a circular city in which the streets form tracks resembling those of a maze. Along these routes lie the offices of the various "estates" or occupations of the world—tradesmen, clergy, soldiers, magistrates, justices, rulers, and the like. The tower to the east (on the left) is the gate of life; the one to the west is the castle of Lady Fortune, who presides over a large wheel which determines who may enter her realm.

As the pilgrim sets forth in this labyrinthine world, his goal is to find a calling for his life's work and, implicitly, a system of values. Ultimately, in Comenius's account, he meets nothing but confusion, delusion, vanity, and folly: the tradesmen are dishonest, the scholars pedantic, the clerics venal, the soldiers brutal, and the justices unjust. Reaching the center of the labyrinth, the errant soul falls to the ground and laments:

> Oh, that I had never been born, never passed through the gate of life! For after the many vanities of the world; nothing but darkness and horror are my part! O God, God, God! God, if Thou art a God, have mercy on wretched me![51]

Suddenly a voice calls out, "Return! . . . Return whence thou camest, to the house of your heart, and shut the door behind you!"[52] It is the voice of God urging the pilgrim not to seek vain glory in this world, but to reverse course and find contrition within his own heart.

> Where have you been, my son? Where did you tarry so long? Where have you been wandering? What have you been seeking in the world? Satisfaction? Where should you have sought it but in God? And where else to seek God but in His temple? And where else the temple of the living God but the living temple which He had prepared for himself, your own heart? I have watched you my son, in your stray wanderings; but I wished to see you astray no longer, and have brought you to yourself by leading you into yourself.[53]

There would be other, later visions of the world as a labyrinth of sin and error,[54] but Comenius sums up the Protestant view: the route out of the maze will be found only by looking inward, through a personal search for God within the Christian heart.

The Maze as Religious Emblem: 1539–1866

Erasmus had intended his *Trusty Weapon of the Christian Soldier* to be a *vade mecum*, a small, portable book to which every devout soul might have recourse as he travels through the maze of life. True to the militant spirit of the work, Erasmus characterized his *Trusty Weapon* as a dagger to be used against the evils of this world. Soon after Erasmus, however, a less pointed companion appeared in Western Europe, the emblem book. It, too, employed the maze as a symbol of Christian teaching.

Although little known today, emblem books enjoyed astonishing favor in sixteenth- and seventeenth-century Europe. They were pocket volumes, usually no more than 8 by 10 centimeters, designed for personal edification and private meditation. Opening the typical book to any given page, the

XXXV.

EN uolupté facilement on entre:
  Mais on en sort à grand difficulté.
Par trop uouloir obeyr à son uentre,
L'on en est pire en toute faculté.
Ce beau propos auons pour resulté,
Du Labyrinthe, auquel facilement
L'on peult entrer:mais si parfondement
On est dedans,l'yssue est difficile.
En uain plaisir aussi semblablement,
L'on entre tost:mais sortir n'est facile.
                                    F

FIGURE 3.5 Facing pages in Guillaume de La Perrière's *The Theater of Fine Devices* (1539), with the emblem of the maze and a poem explaining its symbolism.

reader found a particular moral or spiritual theme presented by means of three separate but mutually reinforcing modes: first by a motto (usually in Latin), next by an emblem or symbol (always in pictorial form), and finally by an explanation of the emblem (usually in verse). The motto reduced the sometimes complex principle to an epigraph, the emblem transformed it into a succinct visual image (an anaglyph), while the verse allowed for more leisurely contemplation. Between 1531 and 1616 no fewer than seven hundred different emblem books were published in Western Europe.[55]

In Guillaume de La Perrière's *Theater of Fine Devices* (*Le theatre des bons engins;* Lyon, 1539) the maze is a complicated construct, having seventeen tracks instead of the usual eleven found in the classic Chartres-type church maze (Fig. 3.5).[56] The imprint of the cross is still present, but no demonic element lurks in the center. Instead, the central figure is simply a man in a contemporary costume—a human, but certainly not a militant soldier. Along the outer circuit are four protrusions reminiscent of the four "towers" of the labyrinth at Reims (see Fig. 2.7). Within each appears one of the four elements: earth, water, wind, and fire. La Perrière's poem offers a traditional interpretation of this maze. To summarize: it is easy to enter into a life of voluptuousness and vain pleasure, but difficult to get out; if one follows base instincts, the other critical faculties decline. But what do the four elements from Greek philosophy signify? Mozart, to anticipate a bit, offers an answer. As the hero Tamino enters the labyrinthine Temple of Trial in *The Magic Flute,* the libretto reads:

> Whoever walks along this path so full of troubles
> Is purified by fire, water, air, and earth.
> If he can conquer the fear of death,
> He will soar from earth up to heaven!

Thus the labyrinth and the four elements consort to form an earthly zone of trial and purification.

More than fifty years after La Perrière issued his *Le theatre des bons engins,* Thomas Combe rendered it in English (London, c.1593).[57] A new, cruder woodcut was fashioned for the emblem of the maze and a somewhat different poem appended. A guide is now needed in the maze:

> *The way to pleasure is so plaine,*
> *To tread the path few can refraine.*
> A labyrinth is framed with such art,
> The outmost entrance is both plaine and wide:
> But being entred, you shall find each part,
> With such odde crooked turnes on every side,
> And blind by-ways, you shall not for your hart
> Come out againe without a perfect guide:
> So to vaine pleasures it is ease to go,
> But to returne againe it is not so.

If the "perfect guide" is Christ, Combe does not name him.

But Christ was still at the heart of the traditional Catholic labyrinth, as evidenced by Herman Hugo's *Pious Longings Made Emblematic* (*Pia Desideria Emblematis;* Antwerp, 1624).[58] Intending to inflame the soul with a love for Jesus, this Jesuit didactic manual went through no fewer than forty-two Latin editions between 1624 and 1757, in addition to others in French, German, and English.[59] As did medieval theologians before him, Hugo turns to the exploits of classical heroes as a way of explaining the meaning of the maze. The labyrinth is a construct full of error and deception, a worthy

Vtinam dirigantur viæ meæ ad custodiendas iustificationes tuas! Psal. 118.

17.

FIGURE 3.6 The emblem of the maze with pilgrims treading thereon in Herman Hugo's *Pious Longings Made Emblematic* (1624). The caption draws from Psalm 118:5: "O that my ways were directed to keep thy statutes."

challenge to Theseus or any brave soul. The deserving Christian must show the resolution of Hercules when faced with the choice between Virtue and Vice, and the determination of Leander, who swam the Hellespont for the love of Hero. Biblical allusions also appear. Just as the people of Israel were guided out of Egypt by a glorious cloud (Exodus 13:21) and the wise men to Bethlehem by a miraculous star (Matthew 2:2), so the wandering soul should be guided by divine light.

With the poetic explanation of the meaning of the labyrinth completed, Hugo now calls upon the authority of venerable fathers of the Catholic Church, patristic and scholastic writers whose views support and encourage his own poetic interpretation. Augustine steps forward because the good bishop of Hippo speaks to the essence of a labyrinthine experience:

> O winding paths! Grief to the bold soul who hopes to possess something that is better if it retreats from you! Turned one way and back, on its back, on its sides, and on its stomach, and all things are harsh, and you alone are rest.[60]

All devout souls must imitate the steps of Christ:

> This is the order. Some precede, others follow. Those who precede offer themselves as a model to those who follow. Surely they follow somebody! If they follow nobody, they wander. Therefore, even those follow somebody: Christ himself. And you see that their steps were ordered through the apostle Paul, when he said, "Be imitators of Christ, just as I."[61]

In the labyrinthine world of the Jesuits, Christ is still the leader, the eternal Redeemer of the maze.

Given this highly orthodox view of the labyrinth, Hugo's accompanying emblem comes as something of a shock, for it offers a radically new vision of the maze (Fig. 3.6). At the center stands a pilgrim, identified by his hat and staff. He walks along a rock-strewn path on either side of which lie deep ravines. Two unfortunate souls have already fallen into these pits of damnation. Another pilgrim, staff in hand, follows blindly behind his faithful Fido. The goal is the tower of the heavenly city, high and far away. Once the exit gate of the labyrinth has been traversed, the traveler still must climb the narrow, rocky road to the celestial kingdom. Here, too, two other aspirants have come to grief. Distant ships at sea also navigate toward the tower's beckoning light. In a similar way, a radiant angel directs the steps of the central pilgrim by a guiding thread, the life-line of faith.

Thus by 1624 the pilgrim had replaced the soldier at the center of the maze. No longer does a hero battle demons in the inner circle of Hell. In fact, there is no sense of journeying to the center and back, only a movement outward from the center toward a distant goal. Perhaps building on the scriptural imperative "endure to the end" (Matthew 10:22; 24:13; and Mark 13:13), this scene suggests that life is a long, steady climb. Although Hugo's explanation of the maze is strongly Catholic, his emblem seems to have reformist sympathies. Pilgrims of many denominations would soon follow his lead.[62]

Hugo's *Pious Longings Made Emblematic* was originally intended for Catholics, but it became a favorite with Protestants as well. Puritans, Calvinists, and Lutherans kept Hugo's emblems but modified his text to conform to their own doctrinal requirements. For example, in a German edition printed in Augsburg in 1710, the image of the pilgrim on the maze is still present, but allusions to the myth of classical antiquity have been removed, as have all quotations from the Catholic fathers. Most important, there is no mention of Christ, only the God of the Psalter.

> O that my ways were directed
> to keep thy statutes [Protestant Psalm 119:5]
> Within the deceptive maze
> Fraught with twists and turns
> I will go without fear
> And await the help
> Which your word promises. . . .
> Life is a labyrinth
> And that you walk safely in it
> You must, without wavering,
> Wait for God in blind faith
> In pure love
> And without hypocrisy.[63]

The peaceful pilgrim was not to be confined to the emblem book, for around 1680 he appears painted on the wall of a Lutheran church in Stetten, Baden-Württemberg (Fig. 3.7).[64] This quiescent soul seeks divine guidance, and counsel comes from above as the word of God (symbolized by the sword). The epigram that surrounds the maze is more psalmodic than mes-

FIGURE 3.7 Labyrinthine emblem on the wall of a Lutheran Church in Württemberg. The German inscription reads: "I hold fast to God's word; there lies my staff and my refuge."

sianic, more pastoral than militant: "I hold fast to God's word; there lies my staff and my refuge" (Ich halte fest an Gottes Wort; Das ist mein Stab und starcker Hort).

English Protestants, too, removed the militant warrior while retaining the image of the labyrinth. In 1635 Francis Quarles published what he simply called Emblemes, a volume that was to become the best-seller of all English emblem books.[65] Although not acknowledging the fact, Quarles blithely drew most of his emblematic designs from the Jesuit Hugo's book of 1624.[66] Quarles's engraver, William Simpson, even managed to get the earlier image of the labyrinth reversed exactly! Quarles's debt to Hugo, however, did not extend much beyond the pictorial. Gone are the classical references and the patristic authority. Gone, too, is any reference to Christ. What appears instead is a newly styled poem to explain the beloved emblem. The verse of the labyrinth is fashioned as a lament coming from the mouth of a pilgrim, who wanders about all amazed.

> The world's a lab'rinth, whole anfractuous wayes
> Are all compos'd of rubs and crook'd meanders:
> No resting here; He's hurried back that stayes
> A thought; and he that goes unguided wanders:
> Her way is dark, her path untrod unev'n
> So hard's the way from earth; so hard's the way to Heav'n.

> This gyring lab'rinth is betrench'd about
> On either hand with streams of sulph'rous fire,
> Streams closely sliding, erring in and out,
> But seeming pleasant to the fond descrier
> Where if his footsteps trust their own invention,
> He falls without redresse, and sinks beyond dimension.

> Where shall I seek a Guide? where shall I meet
> Some lucky hand to lead my trembl'ing paces?
> What trusty Lantern will direct my feet
> To scape the danger of these dang'rous places?
> What hopes have I to passe without a Guide?
> Where one gets safely through, a thousand fall beside.

> An unrequested Starre did gently slide
> Before the Wisemen to a greater Light;
> Back-sliding, Isr'el found a double Guide;
> A pillar, and a Cloud; by day, by night:

> Yet in my desp'rate dangers, which be farre
> More great then theirs, I have nor Pillar, Cloud, nor Starre. . . .

> Great God, that are the flowing Spring of Light,
> Enrich mine eyes with thye refulgent Ray:
> Thou art my Path; direct my steps aright;
> I have no other Light, no other Way:
> I'll trust my God, and him alone pursue;
> His Law shall be my Path; his Heav'nly Light my Clue.

Quarles concludes with a valediction which celebrates labyrinthine contradiction:

> Pilgrime, trudge on: What makes thy soul complain
> Crownes thy complaint. The way to rest is pain:
> The road to resolution lies by doubt:
> The near way home's the farthest way about.

There is little here in the spirit of a Catholic holy war for Christ—no spiritual armor, no victory over Satan. In this Puritan maze, persistence supplants militancy, quest replaces conquest. The soul awaits God's direction while dutifully trudging toward a fate that is perhaps preordained.[67]

Quarles's *Emblemes* was reissued in London nearly every decade until 1777,[68] and then more sporadically until 1866. In 1816 an American edition appeared (reprinted in 1854 and 1864), with the irrepressible pilgrim still circling the maze.[69] By then, however, the emblem book was read as much for its literary worth as for its religious teachings. In the nineteenth century those few mazes that appeared in print were mainly reproductions of ancient ones published in archaeological journals. Curiosity had replaced spirituality. The fractious quality of religious life in post-Reformation Europe had diversified the meaning of this symbol. The later Enlightenment ridiculed medieval symbols, regardless of their meaning or denominational affiliation. Thus, with its meaning fragmented and its logical integrity challenged by the rationalists of the Enlightenment, the maze disappeared as an alluring religious symbol. Not until the arrival of the "New Age" spiritualists of the twentieth century would it regain its power of attraction.

CHAPTER FOUR

The Warrior, the Lamb, and Astrology

Wʜᴀᴛ ᴅᴏᴇꜱ ᴛʜᴇ ʟᴀᴍʙ have to do with the maze? In a word, both are symbols of sacrifice and cyclical renewal. Among Christians the lamb is the sign of the victorious Redeemer and his sacrifice, a holy act that in medieval times was commemorated on and around the maze at Vespers on Easter Sunday. When the clergy danced and chanted on the labyrinth, they sang of the paschal victim, the paschal lamb. Moreover, as is true of the labyrinth itself, the sign of the lamb was a symbol common to many cultures and religions. Babylonians, Greeks, Jews, Christians, and, later, Muslims afforded it special significance in their festivals and cosmology. Finally, the lamb has exceptional resonance for music, for it was in the chant *Agnus dei* (Lamb of God) of the Mass, and in other pieces containing the words "Agnus dei," that the idea of recursive movement—going and coming—was played out through an exacting musical process called retrograde motion.

The Warrior/Lamb of Apocalypse

The lamb had served as a symbol of Christ even before his coming.[1] The prophet Isaiah (53:6–12) announces that a servant of the Lord, the Messiah, will come forth for all humanity "brought as a lamb to the slaughter . . . [to] bear their iniquities" and remove the stain of their sin. This passage not only portends the advent of Christ, but also looks backward, for the salvific power of the blood of the lamb is a theme that had existed since the time of Moses. The blood of the Passover lamb, sent by God and offered to God, saves the people of Israel from destruction (Exodus 12:1–11).

Old Testament prophecy reaches a climax in New Testament gospel. The evangelist John records the joyful exclamation of John the Baptist, who sees the Messiah at the River Jordan: "Behold the lamb of God, who taketh away the sins of the world" (1:29), and it is this text that becomes the basis of the *Agnus dei* of the Mass. Similarly, the apostle Peter urges the newly converted to fear God during the pilgrimage of life because the precious blood of the immaculate lamb has been spilled to ransom humanity, as preordained from the beginning of the world (I Peter 1:19–20). Paul, too, speaks of "the God of peace, that brought again from the dead our Lord Jesus, that great shepherd of the sheep, through the blood of the everlasting covenant" (Hebrews 13:20). Here the apostle invokes the image of Christ returning from death as well as that of the Savior who is the shepherd: Christ is both sacrificial lamb and keeper of the flock. This is the central paradox of the Christian religion: Christ wages war with the Devil and is victorious through the submissive act of self-sacrifice.

The vision of the all-powerful lamb reaches a frenzy of mystical intensity in the Book of Apocalypse (Revelation), where the author John sees the ovine image no fewer than twenty-eight times. The lamb stands before the throne of Glory, the equal of God. He has been sacrificed, yet remains upright and triumphant (5:6–14). He possesses the power to break the seven seals of the mysterious book and thereby to unleash vengeance upon the earth (6:1–12). The just and the elect surround him, washing their white robes in his blood (7:9–14). Atop Mount Zion he stands, adored by 144,000 virgins and elect who sing his heavenly song (14:1–4). The lamb conquers the beast and the wicked kings, for he is the king of kings (17:15). He ascends to a union with celestial Jerusalem within which he is the temple and the light (21:9 and 22–23). The apocalyptic image of the lamb, then, is what the Christian Middle Ages would call the Mystical Lamb of God, a redemptive creature, adored in heaven by those who have benefited from the spilling of his blood.

Given the fantastic, indeed phantasmagorical, vision of the warrior/lamb in the Book of Apocalypse, it is not surprising that this image became a powerful icon in Christian art, most specifically in medieval manuscript painting. A stunning set of illustrations adorns the so-called St. Sever Apocalypse, a manuscript compiled for a Cluniac monastery in southwestern France during the eleventh century.[2] Once the Mystical Lamb has loosened the seals of the book, the horrific combat between good and evil commences (Fig. 4.1). The eyes of the bellicose lamb look down upon two soldiers of Christ who wield oversized swords. The first has decapitated the false prophet; the second has done likewise to the beast, and has also con-

FIGURE 4.1 Here in the St. Sever Apocalypse the warriors of the Mystical Lamb slaughter the false prophet, the beast, and the dragon, and thereby conquer the Devil.

quered the Devil and brought down the dragon. As if the fate of these demonic creatures were not fully obvious, the illustrator adds explanatory texts: "Here the false prophet is killed by the warring lamb and his army" *(Hic occiditur pseudopropheta pugnante agno et exercitu ei[us]);* and "Here the beast is killed and the Devil and the dragon are conquered" *(Hic occi-ditur bestia diabolus quoque et draco vincuntur).*

An equally militant lamb appears in an early fifteenth-century illus-trated Apocalypse from the Low Countries (Fig. 4.2).[3] Here Christ sits in majesty; his sacrificial symbol (the lamb) stands to his right, now married to the community of celestial Jerusalem. Below unfolds the Parousia, the fi-nal return of the Lord. The day of wrath *(Dies irae)* has begun. Leading the army on a white horse is the figure of Christ, his eyes aflame. He fights with the shield of the Cross before him. The double-edged sword in his mouth suggests Christ's dual nature as victim and avenger as well as the moral con-sequence of the double-edged sword: "He that killeth with the sword must be killed with the sword" (Apocalypse 13:10). Christ, wearing a white robe splattered with the blood of the lamb, conquers the Devil and consigns him to the flames of the mouth of Hell. The lamb's authority derives from sac-rifice and leads to ultimate dominion.

"Lamb of God Who Taketh Away the Sins of the World"

The contradictory nature of the Savior—victorious warrior and sacrificial lamb—is also incorporated into the prayers and chants of the medieval Christian liturgy. At Vespers on Easter Sunday—the very moment at which the maze came into play[4]—the clergy rejoiced in singing the hymn *At the Banquet of the Lamb (Ad caenam agni).* The opening stanzas invite those who have passed through the Red Sea and been admitted to the lamb's table to sing in honor of Christ, whose blood has revivified them. It then continues:

> Protect us at this hour of
> Paschal Vespers, from the
> Devastating angel; deliver us from
> The cruel realm of the Pharaoh.
>
> Now our Passover is Christ,
> The lamb slaughtered for us,
> The unleavened of purity
> His flesh was offered.

FIGURE 4.2 With eyes ablaze and white robe dripping with blood, the vengeful Christ fights the battle of Armageddon in an illuminated fifteenth-century Book of Apocalypse.

Oh true and worthy victim
Through whom Tartarus was broken,
The captive people were ransomed
And the rewards of life returned.

Christ arises from the tomb.
He returns victorious from the pit,
Urging the tyrant with a chain
And unlocking paradise.

We beseech you, author of all things:
During this paschal joy,
From every onrush of death
Defend your people.[5]

A famous medieval Easter chant, *Salve festa dies,* concludes with a vision of both the lamb *(agnus)* rescuing the flock from the mouth of the wolf, as well as the warrior *(belliger)* safely returning his flock to heaven.[6] This processional hymn is still sung around the world today on Easter Sunday as *Hail Thee, Festival Day.*

The Mystical Lamb of God, of course, was not only honored at Easter, but also celebrated daily in the Catholic Mass. Since the eighth century, the threefold petition "Lamb of God who taketh away the sins of the world, have mercy upon us" has been sung together by clergy and populace at every Mass, as accompaniment to the breaking of the bread.[7] The ritual of the Eucharist is the culmination and spiritual end point of the Mass. Standing before the altar, the banquet table of the lamb, the celebrating priest breaks the bread and prepares the wine. It is here—as these symbols of Christ's body and blood are passed to those about to engage in a mystical communion with the Lord—that the *Agnus dei* is sung. And it is in the music of the *Agnus dei* that the lamb's ceaseless renewal, death and rebirth, will come to be symbolized through retrograde motion.

Backward Movement as a Sign of the Warrior/Lamb

Musicians as well as theologians knew that the course of Christ's life was a recursive journey, a coming and going, a *descensus* and *ascensus*. They symbolized this transit through several musical processes, the most important

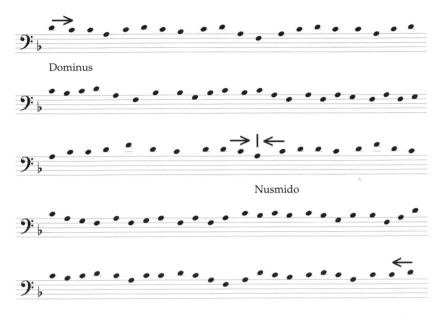

Dominus

Nusmido

EXAMPLE 4.1 Tenor voice (without rhythm and without accompanying upper voice) of two-voice clausula *Dominus-Nusmido* (Florence, Biblioteca Medicea Laurenziana, MS Pluteus 29.1, fols. 150–150v). The piece was composed in Paris c. 1200.

of which was retrograde motion. The first extant piece in the history of music to use retrograde motion appears in a setting for the gradual of the Christmas Mass treating the theme of revelation: "The Lord has made known his salvation: his righteousness hath he openly shewed in the sight of the heathen" (Psalms 97:2).[8] Here a two-voice piece is built on a phrase of Gregorian chant that is placed in the tenor, the lower of the two voices. The music sets only a single word: "The Lord" *(Dominus)*. This musical lord is made to go first forward to a stopping point at the end of the chant, and then backward, taking each note in turn en route back to the beginning. Not only does the music of the tenor constitute an exact retrograde, but in the text the composer has attempted to fashion a verbal retrograde as well, transforming "Dominus" into "Nusmido" (Example 4.1).[9]

The warrior/lamb likewise goes backward and forward in the music of Guillaume Dufay (c.1400–1474). In 1431 Dufay composed a four-voice motet, *Balm and Pure Wax (Balsamus et munda cera)*, to accompany a special Easter ceremony celebrated by Pope Eugenius IV. In this year Eugenius blessed and distributed to the members of his curia small figures called

"Agnus dei," each made of balm and pure wax and stamped with an image of the Mystical Lamb of God. These waxen effigies were to be carried by the faithful as talismans against ills and evils of every sort.[10] The blessing which the pope pronounced upon them suggests the therapeutic powers attributed to these amulets:

> Lord God ruler of all sanctified things, whose goodness is felt endlessly, who willed that Abraham, the father of our faith, prepared to sacrifice his son Isaac according to your command, consummate the sacrifice of him by means of the ram stuck by the horns [Genesis 22:8–13]; and who commanded that Moses, your servant and law-giver, offer a holocaust with lambs of no blemish [Exodus 12:3–8; and 29:15–31]; we humbly beseech you, that exhorted by means of our voice you deign to bless and sanctify through the invocation of your holy name these waxen images, fabricated with the figure of the most innocent Lamb, that by means of touch and use the faithful are inspired toward your praise. May the crash of hail, the tumult of tornadoes, raging tempests, wild winds, thunderous battles be pacified; and may evil spirits tremble and flee before the standard of the cross which has been carved in them [the Agnus dei], and before which every knee genuflects and every tongue confesses, because Jesus Christ devoured death through the gibbet of the cross and reigns in the glory of God the Father. For he himself is just like a sheep led to the slaughter. He offered a holy sacrifice of his body through death to you, Father. In order to lead back the lost sheep, led away by the Devil's deception, he returned. He brought it back, carrying it on his shoulders to the flock of his celestial homeland. . . . Amen.[11]

When Pope Eugenius IV distributed the waxen Agnus dei figures during Easter Week of 1431, he did so at Santa Maria in Trastevere, a Roman church that had possessed a pavement maze since at least 1200 (see Fig. 2.2, upper right, and the accompanying description). Indeed, the labyrinth was situated before the door of the sacristy, where the Agnus dei were stored prior to distribution. When the moment came to transport the images on a platter from the sacristy to the pope waiting at the high altar, the clergy did so by crossing the maze and chanting in an increasingly loud voice *These are the New Lambs (Isti sunt agni novelli)*. As we have seen, *These are the New Lambs* was also sung in several French cathedrals at Vespers on Easter Sunday as the clergy processed across the maze in transit to or from the baptismal font.[12] The text of the chant reads:

These are the new lambs of God who sang alleluia, even as they came to the fountain, they are filled with purity, alleluia, alleluia. In the sight of the lamb they are dressed in white garb and hold palms in their hands.

Once again, the spiritual source for these words is the Book of Apocalypse, for these new lambs are the martyrs whose robes have been washed white through the blood of Christ (Apocalypse 7:14). Dufay took the chant *These are the New Lambs* and built his motet *Balm and Pure Wax* upon it. Twice in the motet the chant proceeds forward and then, note for note, goes backward to symbolize the recursive Easter journey of Christ. When the motet had been sung and the Agnus dei figures distributed to the papal curia, the pontifical Mass concluded with the singing of the *Agnus dei,* now set in three-voice polyphony, again by Dufay. Here, too, the chant of the *Agnus dei* is sung first forward and then backward.

Thus symbol is heaped upon symbol: the Chartres-type maze with its double retrogrades to signify the coming and going of Christ, the waxen Agnus dei to symbolize the therapeutic powers of the Mystical Lamb, and the retrograding chant to suggest that, as with spiritual renewal through Christ, the end of all things is also the beginning. Dufay's compositions represent the first of more than a dozen surviving pieces to convey the image of the Mystical Lamb of God by means of retrograde motion. The practice began in the Middle Ages and would end in the eighteenth century with the music of Bach.

"Ego sum Alpha et Omega"

The words "I am the Alpha et Omega" are spoken by the Lamb/Lord in the Book of Apocalypse. They refer, of course, to the first and last letters of the Greek alphabet and mean that the son of the Father is the beginning and end of all things. Like most concepts in the New Testament, this theme is adumbrated in the Old, specifically through the words of the Prophet Isaiah (48:12): "Thus saith the Lord the King of Israel, and his redeemer the Lord of hosts; I am the first, and I am the last; and besides me there is no other." But throughout the New Testament Book of Apocalypse, this phrase sounds like a clarion call, appearing in one form or another six times, first at the beginning and then the end (1:8; 1:11; 1:17; 2:8; 21:6; and 22:13). It encapsulates God's all-embracing plan for the world: "'I am the Alpha and Omega,' says God the Lord, 'who is and who was and who is to come, the Almighty'" (1:8). Just as the first step within the unicursal maze is also the last, so the Lord is the first and last moment in cyclical time.

The central moment in God's great chronological design is, of course, Easter. The mystery of paschaltide is expressed in two sacramental rites, those of baptism and the Eucharist.[13] The ritual of baptism recalls Christ's own immersion in the River Jordan (John 1:29–34); through baptism the catechumen dies and is reborn to a new life in Christ. Converts to Christianity were traditionally baptized only during the vigil of Easter. Similarly, on Easter Sunday—and before modern times only on Easter Sunday—the faithful received the communion of the Holy Eucharist, thereby sharing in Christ's death and resurrection. Death, rebirth, return, and renewal—these are the themes of Easter.

Easter must occur on the first Sunday after the first full moon after the vernal equinox, so said the fathers of the Council of Nicaea in 325.[14] The sense that "the beginning was the end" or "the end was the beginning" was keenly felt by the early Christians, for in their calendrical reckonings many placed the conception of Christ and his crucifixion on the same day, 25 March.[15] This was, of course, only an abstraction—Easter is a movable feast dependent upon celestial events—but it suggests how firmly entrenched in the ancient mind was the notion that life and death, origin and destiny, were ceaseless, cyclical processes.

Medieval poets and theologians spoke of Easter as a "time of regression," a time of going back to the beginning, of death and rebirth.[16] The association of Easter and historical reversal encouraged the growth of poetic conceits involving antitheses (life and death) or paradoxes (a lamb who redeems the sheep; a conqueror who is slaughtered). A popular medieval chant offers a succession of such contraposita:

> Within one bosom you nurture
> Lion and the lamb, great and small
> Son and progenitor,
> About to die but live eternally
> For both are the same
> The end and the beginning.[17]

Christ is sent by the Father to earth and there endures pain and deprivation. Yet he descends still further after his earthly death to bring about the Harrowing of Hell. Hell constitutes one terminus in the course of his divine mission. Christ conquers Satan, binds him in chains, and reverses his path.[18] Leading the elect from Purgatory, he returns to Paradise. The authors of the Latin Church were sensitive to the spiritual imperative of Christ's return and the doctrine of a miraculous reversal. In their hymns, sequences, and sermons they found a multitude of ways to express the recursive nature of the Lord's journey by means of verbs formed with the prefix "re": *reddo, redimo, redio, reduco, refero, regresso, remeo, reverto* (to restore, deliver, go back, lead back, bring back, step back, return, turn back).[19]

Singing of return and spiritual renewal was thus the ritual of Easter Sunday. At the medieval cathedral of Reims, for example, the clergy left their stalls before Mass and processed to the door of the church at the north portal. From there they made a circuit around the canons' cloister, all the while chanting the lengthy antiphon *I am the Alpha and the Omega.*[20] Here lines from Apocalypse are combined with a gospel account of the Crucifixion (John 19–20). Finally, Christ speaks for himself:

> I am the Alpha and Omega, first and most recent, beginning and end; I was before the beginning of the world and will be for all eternity. My hands which made you were pierced through with nails; on your behalf I have been struck with scourges, crowned with thorns; on the Cross I asked for water and they brought vinegar; they put salt for my food and a lance in my side: dead and buried, I arose, look, I am with you!—because I am the one true God and there is no other except me, Alleluia.[21]

"My End Is My Beginning and My Beginning My End"

One of the clerics of Reims who participated year after year in this procession across the maze was the famous poet and musician Guillaume de Machaut (c.1300–1377). Machaut had strong ties to the city of Reims. He was a canon of the cathedral from 1333 until his death in 1377, and was buried in the church.[22] Machaut knew the antiphon *I am the Alpha and Omega* and of its origins in the Book of Apocalypse. It is likely that he was also familiar with a widespread French translation of Apocalypse, which reads in part:

Je sui li premier et li dariains Commencement et fin. Cil [sunt] boneürez
qui lavent lur estoles ou sanc de l'agniel, Ke lur poer soit en [l']arbre de
vie et qu'il entrent par les portes enz la cité (22:14)[23]

(I am the first and the last Beginning and end. Blessed are they who wash
their mantles in the blood of the lamb, that they may have the right to the
tree of life and enter through the gates into the city.)

Among Machaut's approximately 120 musical-poetic creations is a rondeau, *Ma fin est mon commencement et mon commencement ma fin,* a piece
famous in the history of music because of its unique structure: it forms a
double retrograde. The music of the upper voice is to be sung against itself,
starting at the end; the beginning and end proceed against each other until
the beginning has become the end and vice versa. Simultaneously, a third
voice, the contratenor, written to last only half as long as the upper voices,
must be performed in reverse when the midpoint of the piece is reached
(the music is given as Example A.1 in Appendix A). Using numbers to represent measures, the flow of the piece can be represented as follows:

Superius: 1   5   10 15 20 25 30 35 40
Tenor: 40 35 30 25 20 15 10   5   1

Contratenor: 1   5   10 15 20 15 10   5   1

Ma fin est mon commencement	A	My end is my beginning
Et mon commencement ma fin	B	and my beginning my end.
Et teneüre vraiëment.	a	This much is clear.
Ma fin est mon commencement.	A	My end is my beginning.
Mes tiers chans iij fois seulement	a	My third voice sings three times only
Se retrograde et einsi fin.	b	in retrograde, and then is done.
Ma fin est mon commencement	A	My end is my beginning
Et mon commencement ma fin.	B	and my beginning my end.

As the poem suggests, the complete course of the music in retrograde is to
be performed, from beginning to end, three times; meanwhile the text is
sung following the poetic form of a rondeau: AB(1)aAab(2)AB(3). In this
way a directive contained in the poetic text is executed through a musical
process.

This is how Machaut's inventive composition works, but what does it
mean? Perhaps because the poem is in the form of a rondeau—a common
vehicle for vernacular love poetry in the Middle Ages—most musicologists

have viewed *Ma fin est mon commencement* as a secular amusement, something of a clever musical game.[24] On the contrary, its meaning is deadly serious.

Inherent in every labyrinth, as we have seen, is recursive motion. The maze at Reims, like most church mazes, involves not only a journey to the center and back, but also a hidden retrograde in each leg of the trip.[25] Recursive motion was also evident in some ancient spiritual writings that literary scholars have found to be labyrinthine in construction. The most important of these is Boethius's *The Consolation of Philosophy* (c.520) in which the author accuses Philosophy of exploiting the tension inherent in the maze, of creating either a bewildering labyrinth or a perfectly divine circle:[26]

> Doest thou mocke mee, making with thy reasons an inextricable labyrinth that now thou maist go in where thou meanest to goe out againe, and after goe out, where thou camest in, or does thou frame a wonderful circle of the simplicity of God.[27]

Recursive motion, Boethius tells us, recycles endlessly. This is a divine law.

> Each thing a certain course and lawes obeyes,
> Striving to turne backe to his proper place;
> Nor any settled order can be found,
> But that, which doth within it selfe embrace
> The births and ends of all things in a round.[28]

For a thousand years *The Consolation of Philosophy* was digested by Western intellectuals. Dante devoured it; Chaucer translated it into English; and Queen Elizabeth I did likewise, chewing through it at the rate of one page every half hour, as one report has it.[29] A French translation was prepared in the area of Reims, shortly after Machaut's death (1377). To illustrate the idea of a maze, a crude facsimile of the pavement labyrinth at Reims cathedral was added to it.[30]

Machaut knew of Boethius's *The Consolation of Philosophy*,[31] for he modeled his didactic poem *Remede de Fortune* (c.1340) on it.[32] Likewise, Machaut knew of the story of Theseus and the maze, for he refers to the myth in his poem *Le Jugement du roy de Navarre* (c.1350).[33] In addition, Machaut was familiar with several large pavement labyrinths in northern France, not only the one in his own church but also those at Arras, Amiens, and St. Quentin, where he had held canonries at various times.[34] Surely, he

was witness to the games of tennis and other Easter Sunday revels that tran-
spired at Reims, as well as the processions that went across the maze on
Easter afternoon.[35] Ultimately, Machaut was buried in the nave of the cathedral of Reims—his bones, at his request, placed only a few meters to the east
of the labyrinth.[36] In life he had declared that origin and destiny were inseparable; in death he was united with a symbol that said the same.

But the motto "In my end is my beginning" did not die with Machaut. It
became something of an epitaph for the ages, a cry for salvation and a plea
for the answer to the mystery of life. Marie de Guise, a French princess who
married King James V of Scotland in 1538, adopted it as her device.[37] So, too,
did her daughter, who succeeded to the throne as Mary Queen of Scots
(1542–1587) and had the motto literally emblazoned upon it.[38] Queen Mary
was eventually taken prisoner and executed by order of Queen Elizabeth I
of England. During her long captivity, Mary passed the hours embroider-
ing *En ma fin est mon commencement* on various royal insignia.[39] In this way
the Catholic queen declared that her escape from her earthly prison would
begin with her end.

In more recent times a modern Machaut, the poet T. S. Eliot (1888–1965),
made use of the motto as a refrain in his poem *East Coker*.[40] Here the poet
muses on biological time (the short span between birth and death) and on
historical time (the passing of the centuries).

> In my beginning is my end. In succession
> Houses rise and fall, crumble, are extended,
> Are removed, destroyed, restored, or in their place
> Is an open field, or a factory, or a by-pass.
> Old stone to new building, old timber to new fires,
> Old fires to ashes, and ashes to the earth. (lines 1–6)

East Coker proceeds like a journey through a gallery of images, beginning
with Eliot's ancestral home of that name, descending to a dark land of the
dead, and finally ascending through a spiritual rebirth to a place of brilliant
light. Eliot commenced the poem on Good Friday, 1940, with a picture of
the crucified Christ strongly in his mind's eye:

> The dripping blood our only drink,
> The bloody flesh our only food:
> In spite of which we like to think

That we are sound, substantial flesh and blood—
Again, in spite of that, we call this Friday good. (lines 167–171)

Like the apostolic Christ who is lamb and shepherd, victim and victor, Eliot's Savior is also a paradoxical redeemer, a "wounded surgeon," a "dying nurse." The poet's dark, labyrinthine world, too, is full of contradictory meaning, of winter lightning, still dancing, agony and ecstasy, death and birth, and an end at the beginning. Humanity's fate is full of such reversals and antitheses ("To be restored, our sickness must grow worse"). Our destiny, as we set forth in the maze of life, is to return to our point of departure. No matter if we proceed in a circle or along a linear retrograde, the end point is always the beginning ("Home is where one starts from"). This is the sentiment of both Machaut's *Ma fin est mon commencement* and Eliot's *East Coker*. Machaut amplified his meaning through the process of musical retrograde; Eliot did so by means of a verbal reversal. The last line of Eliot's poem, "In my end is my beginning," is an anagram of the first, "In my beginning is my end."

The Symbol of the Lamb among the Israelites

The festival of Easter, of course, has its counterpart in the Jewish ritual of Passover. Indeed, Christ celebrated "Pesach," the proper Hebrew name for the festival, immediately before his death, and the early Jewish Christians continued to do so for more than a century thereafter.[41] Here again the new religion patterned itself upon the old. Events inscribed in the Old Testament were said to have occurred as prefigurations of, and preparations for, the divine acts recorded in the New.

No symbol was more central to both religions than the sacrificial lamb. When Christians wished to justify the offering of the symbolic body and blood of Christ during the Mass, they did so by invoking stories of sacrifice told in the Old Testament, namely those of Abel (Genesis 4:1–15) and Abraham (Genesis 22:10–13).[42] Abel offered the firstling of his flock to God, which the Lord accepted; his brother Cain, a farmer, brought forth the fruits of the land, which were less pleasing to the Lord. "By faith Abel offered unto God a more excellent sacrifice than Cain" (Hebrews 11:4). The jealous Cain slew the innocent shepherd Abel.

Abraham was willing to sacrifice even more to God—Isaac, his only son. But Abraham's lineage was saved through the miraculous appearance, and sacrifice, of a ram:

> And Abraham stretched forth his hand, and took the knife to slay his son. And the angel of the Lord called unto him out of heaven, and said, "Abraham, Abraham:" and he said "Here am I." And he said, "Lay not thine hand upon the lad, neither do thou any thing unto him: for now I know that thou fearest God, seeing thou hast not withheld thy son, thine only son from me." And Abraham lifted up his eyes and looked, and behold behind him a ram caught in a thicket by his horns: and Abraham went and took the ram, and offered him up for a burnt offering in the stead of his son. (Genesis 22:10–13)

The story of Abraham and Isaac has special relevance to Jewish religious practices, for the horns of the ram survived the sacrificial burning, becoming the prototype for the shofar.[43] With the shofar came symbolic music to the people of Israel, and thus it enjoyed a privileged place in Jewish services. In the centuries after the destruction of the Temple, the shofar was the only musical instrument allowed in the synagogue, all others being banned until the coming of the Messiah.[44] Even today its sounds announce and terminate all festivals in the Jewish religion as well as commemorations of the state of Israel. Like the sign of the lamb, the shofar signals beginnings and endings.

As the Book of Genesis gives way to that of Exodus, so the story of Abraham yields to that of Moses, the prophet who leads the Israelites out of the hostile land of Egypt. Central to the salvation of God's chosen people is Passover, a spring festival celebrated by the Jews to commemorate their liberation. Passover, along with Sukkot and Shavuot, is one of the three "pilgrimage festivals" of the Jewish religion. Christians celebrated this moment, too, at Easter Vespers when they chanted the pilgrimage psalm (113) *When Israel went out of Egypt* (*In exitu Israel de Egypto*), and at some churches they did so while processing from the baptistry across the maze.[45] As is well known, the Passover Seder concludes with the petition "Next year in Jerusalem," an implicit recognition that the spiritual pilgrimage of the Jewish people is not yet complete. The Hebrew soul in search of deliverance has the same goal as the eighteenth-century Christian on the maze who treads along "the path of Jerusalem" heading toward the celestial city.[46]

. . .

Divine command required that the Israelites select a he-lamb of the first year without blemish, and sacrifice it on the eve of the fourteenth day of the first month, the spring month of Nisan (Exodus 12:1–11). The blood of the lamb was sprinkled on the lintel and jambs of the doors of the dwellings of the Israelites, so that the Lord should "pass-over" them when he went forth to destroy the first-born of the Egyptians (Exodus 12:22–23). Drained of its life-giving blood, the lamb was roasted and consumed by the followers of Moses, who were directed to be ready, with loins girded and pilgrimage staff at hand, for the Exodus from the Pharaoh's hell was to follow.

The deliverance of Israel from bondage and death was, like Easter, commemorated after the vernal equinox, in the first month of Nisan. Not coincidentally, the Islamic festival of the Hajj—requiring, among other things, a pilgrimage to Mecca, the stoning of Satan, and the slaughter of sheep— also occurs in conjunction with the spring moon.[47] Thus each of the West's three great religions celebrates in its own way the idea of deliverance and spiritual rebirth in connection with this celestial moment.

According to Hebrew tradition, the first Passover was preordained by Moses at the command of God. Moses' injunction, however, is recognized as being nothing more than a historicizing of a timeless ritual, for the sacrifice of the spring lamb appears to go back even earlier, when the Israelites were a semi-nomadic pastoral people.[48] Like many Semitic and Arab tribes, they moved seasonally with their flocks and in the spring offered up a firstling in petition for a year of prosperity. They were also stargazers, reckoning the events of their lives by the turning of the heavens. When much later, in medieval France, the clergy at Chartres and Auxerre danced around the maze each spring, singing of the sacrificial lamb, they merely perpetuated a paschal celebration that had already existed for many thousands of years.

The Symbol of the Ram in Greek Mythology

If a genderless lamb was a redemptive symbol with Christians, a male or female sheep with Muslims, and a firstling he-lamb with the Israelites, the male ram was a sacred sign with the ancient Greeks. In the myth of Jason's quest for the Golden Fleece, the ram assumes divine powers. As always in

Greek mythology, the full story must be teased out of a tangle of legends that come down to us from antiquity.[49]

Long ago a Greek king named Athamas offered his son Phrixus as a sacrifice to the god of the harvest. As Phrixus awaits his fate on the altar, a wondrous ram with fleece of pure gold appears and spirits him safely away to the distant isle of Colchis, ruled by King Æetes. At Colchis Phrixus sacrifices the ram, and gratefully offers its golden fleece to Æetes. The spirit of the ram then ascends into the sky to form the constellation Aries.[50]

Soon the warrior Jason, a kinsman of Phrixus, is charged to return the now sacred Golden Fleece to its homeland. He gathers the greatest heroes of Greece, among them Hercules and Orpheus, and sets sail in the ship *Argo*. Overcoming countless perils, the adventurers reach Colchis where Medea, the daughter of Æetes, helps Jason win a fierce battle against demonic dragons and fire-breathing bulls, and thereby reclaim the Golden Fleece. Jason leads Medea and the Argonauts safely back to Greece, but ultimately he condemns her to a life of exile. The Golden Fleece is returned to its homeland.

The similarities between this story of Jason and the myth of Theseus in the Cretan maze are obvious: A young warrior defies death and, aided by the daughter of an aged king, defeats the forces of evil, only later to abandon the maiden who made possible his victory.[51] A parallel also can be drawn to the life of Christ, for this myth speaks of a redemptive ram who returns to the heavens. The ram with the golden fleece has saved humankind and, by right of sacrifice, can now rise to the light of heavenly glory. Positioned for all time as the constellation Aries, this celestial configuration would come to constitute the zodiacal sign of the Lamb/Ram and, later, the stellar symbol of Christ.

The Astrology of the Maze

Much has been written about the maze and astrology.[52] One writer has claimed that the position of the labyrinth in the cathedral of Chartres was determined by a grand scheme based on the ratio of the height of the south tower (which he calls the lunar tower) to that of the north (called the solar tower).[53] Another sees the positioning of the maze at Chartres as the lodestar in a configuration connecting many Marian churches in northern

France, one that is said to duplicate the zodiacal sign of Virgo.[54] Similarly at
Amiens, tradition has it that the west-east crossing in the central plate in
the labyrinth (see Fig. 2.10) is so placed as to mark the rays of the rising and
setting sun on the summer solstice.[55] A skeptical voice might reply that at
Chartres the north tower was not constructed until three hundred years after the maze was in place, and that at Amiens no rays can enter the church
along an exact west-east axis at any time of the year because of the mass of
masonry that forms the southwest wall. Other claims for the "archeoastro-
nomical" significance of the maze seem as unfounded as they are irrepressible.[56] Granted, the position of the maze in churches along a west-east axis
is a reflection of a solar event—placement of the altar at the east end; the
spiritual pilgrim enters and progresses, however circuitously, in the direction of the rising sun. But the church labyrinth was not an instrument of
solar measurement, like Stonehenge and similar astronomical monuments.
Nor was it an accurate gauge of astronomical time, as was the meridian
placed on the floor in many Italian and French churches from the sixteenth
century onward.[57]

Indeed, the maze was not an object used to set the seasons, but rather a
symbol that came into play once the seasons, specifically the Easter season,
had been determined by other means. As mentioned previously, the Council of Nicaea enjoined Christians to celebrate Easter on the first Sunday after the full moon following the vernal equinox.[58] Passover, too, had historically been reckoned by the spring equinox and the full moon coming
thereafter. The new celestial year began with that first spring month, called
Nisan (Exodus 12:2): "In Nisan the world was created; in Nisan the Patriarchs were born; on Passover Isaac was born; on New Year Sarah, Rachel
and Hannah were visited; on New Year Joseph went forth from prison; on
New Year the bondage of our ancestors ceased in Egypt; and in Nisan they
will be redeemed in time to come."[59] Following this line of Jewish salvation
history, the world begins and ends in the month coming after the vernal
equinox.[60]

As with Easter and Passover, all the great religious festivals of the ancient
world were seasonal and were based on the cyclical experiences of life. They
celebrated the eternal round-dance of death and rebirth, prophecy and
consummation, conditions inherent in the natural world. Celestial events
determined the time of these rituals. The ancients gradually came to con-
ceptualize the annual movements of the heavens by means of the twelve

signs of the zodiac, twelve constellations each representing the outline of an animal or an inanimate object.[61] The zodiac initially came into being as a device for measuring time; only later was it used for divination.[62] The appearance in the early night sky of one of the zodiacal symbols signified the proper moment to sacrifice a lamb, plant a crop, or, even as late as Chaucer's time, undertake a pilgrimage.[63]

Babylonians, Greeks, Romans, Jews, Christians, and many Muslims followed the signs of the zodiac through the heavens.[64] Yet the course of the zodiac was, in truth, something of an abstraction: a particular constellation forming one of the twelve signs might appear in the night sky in a somewhat different place depending upon the longitude and latitude of the viewer, and even the historical time in which he lived.[65] The theory of the system, however, was that each of the twelve signs occupied exactly 30 degrees within a full circumference of 360 degrees in a band around the equator. As the sun set in the western sky each evening, it would do so into, or "under," one of these twelve constellations. Pursuing its annual march north and south, the sun would enter, reside in, and then gradually exit these signs at the rate of roughly one a month.

Whether called *Ku* by the Babylonians, κριος by the Greeks, Ammon by the Egyptians, *Arios* by the Romans, *Teli* by the Jews, or *al-hamal* later by the Muslims,[66] first among the zodiacal symbols was the Ram (the Lamb with the Muslims). Ancient astronomical theory held that the signs of the zodiac were placed in the heavens according to the historical epoch over which they held dominion. The earth was created when the sun was within the boundary of Aries, and thus this sign was first.[67] It was the symbol of rebirth and vernal regeneration. It was the sign from which the others departed and would return, as the Roman astronomer Manilius wrote around the year 10 A.D.:

> First Aries shining in his golden fleece
> Wonders to see the back of Taurus rise,
> Taurus who calls, with lowered head, the Twins,
> Whom Cancer follows; Leo follows him,
> Then Virgo; Libra next, day equalling night,
> Draws on the Scorpion with its blazing star,
> Whose tail the Half-horse aims at with his bow,
> Ever about to loose his arrow swift.
> Then comes the narrow curve of Capricorn,

> And after him Aquarius pours from his urn
> Waters the following Fishes greedily use,
> Which Aries touches, last of all the signs.[68]

Aries is the first and last sign. It was under Aries "whan God first maked man,"[69] and with the return of Aries man will return to a state of prelapsarian bliss with the angels.[70]

The Christian symbolism here is obvious. Eagerly the fathers of the Church embraced the revivifying Lamb/Ram of the zodiac. Sometimes medieval theologians equated the sign of the backward-moving Crab (Cancer) with Christ, because under this constellation the sun reached its apex in Europe and then, like Christ, began a retrograde journey.[71] Sometimes Christ was signified by the scale of Libra, because on the Day of Judgment the Lord would hold all souls in a balance.[72] Most often, however, Aries symbolized the Savior, who was conceived and crucified under the constellation of the Lamb.

Zeno, eighth bishop of Verona (d. c.380), was the first to employ the twelve ancient zodiacal signs as Christian images, transforming them into a Christian allegory of good versus evil.[73] In a baptismal sermon to the neophytes, he urges his converts to see in Aries the sacrificial Christ whose body supplies sustenance for the faithful. Arrayed against the Lamb are the venomous Scorpio, the deceptive Cancer, the duplicitous two-horned Capricorn, and the dangerous arrows of Sagittarius. Virgo, the Virgin Mary, holds Libra, the scale, to weigh all souls at the Last Judgment. Through the purifying waters of baptism, brought by Aquarius, heathen and Jew alike will be cleansed and reconciled "as one people of Christ marked by a single sign" (*in unum populum Christi uno signo signati).*[74]

For Zeno the sign of the Lamb enjoys pride of place. This position is confirmed by later theologians such as Isidore of Seville, the Venerable Bede, and Hirenicus:

> Christian faith recognizes among the signs
> First the lamb, who reigns with shining majesty
> On high, together with the Father for all eternity.[75]

Medieval zodiologions—books in which the author names, describes, and ascribes meaning to the twelve signs of the zodiac—offer a variety of explanations as to the significance of Aries, but at the core of each is the image of a paschal holocaust. There are many of these, but two can stand for all:

> Aries is correctly placed first, since it holds the beginning of the zodiac. This ram is proved by ecclesiastical truth to designate the completion of certain things, for in the Old Testament, this animal is usually offered as a holocaust to the Lord. Although there it signifies Christ offered as a holocaust to the Father through his suffering on the Cross, nevertheless it can fittingly designate those who consecrate their very selves through devotion to the Lord. [ninth-century monastic source widely disseminated in northern Europe][76]

> In April the sign is of Aries because Abraham offered a ram to God as a holocaust in place of his son Isaac. The reason: the sign of Aries is placed in April because this animal is noteworthy for its horns, just as the sun, from this time, begins to train the force of its rays to melt the earth, frozen up to that point by the season of winter and stiffness, or else because it shines upon the right side of the sky from this equinox through the entire summer up until the following equinox . . . The figure: Aries, which is usually offered, represents Christ, who proffered his very self through his suffering on the Cross as a holocaust and even those who insinuate themselves to God from their voices by slaughtering a living victim. [twelfth-century German source][77]

Poets, painters, and musicians were quick to exploit the symbolic meaning of the equinoctial Lamb/Ram.[78] No painter incorporated more symbolic detail per square inch than Jan van Eyck. When creating his *Mystical Lamb* (1432) for St. Bavo's church at Ghent, he worked the letters Alpha and Omega into the floor tiles to suggest that Christ was the beginning and end of all things. A few years later, in his *Annunciation* (c.1435), van Eyck again imparted significance to the floor; now the angel Gabriel, the herald of the coming Christ, stands on a tile depicting the zodiacal sign of Aries, while the Virgin Mary is above the sign of Virgo.[79]

Another artist from Ghent, the composer Jacob Obrecht (c.1457–1505), symbolically equated Christ and Aries in the medium of sacred music. In the *Agnus dei* of his *Missa Graecorum* (c.1485) he asks the tenors to sing the chant backward, the last note becoming the first, thereby again signifying the sacrificial lamb's recursive journey. The order to the tenors to effect this retrograde reads: "Let Aries be turned toward Pisces" (*Aries vertatur in pisces).*[80] Instead of exiting Aries and proceeding into Taurus, the Son (sun) marches backward into Pisces. Obrecht might have chosen any object in a sequence, or any one of the other twelve signs in the zodiac, to prescribe retrograde motion, but he selected the stellar sign of Christ.

The planets, too, were cosmic signifiers. The ancient world knew five planets, in addition to the sun and moon: Mercury, Venus, Mars, Jupiter, and Saturn.[81] To be sure, the constellations occupy one celestial zone, fixed objects in the sky which appear to circulate daily only because of the earth's rotation. Yet the planets fill another space, moving through the heavens along repeating paths of various durations, set by the length of time needed by each to revolve around the sun. For the earth-bound observer, the planets seem to move forward, stand still, and sometimes move backward. What was actually an elliptical journey around the sun might appear as a linear retrogression.[82] Medieval astronomers often commented on the "retrograding" quality of the planets. Said one: "A planet is like a vicious mule that sometimes goes backward, sometimes forward, and sometimes doesn't move at all."[83]

Each of the planets governed two of the zodiacal signs. Aries was ruled by the red planet Mars, the Roman equivalent of the Greek Ares (Ἀρης). In Roman and Greek theology, Mars and his counterpart Ares were male warrior gods. War-dances in honor of Mars were held in ancient Rome during the month of March. Indeed, in the Latin *Mars-Martius* lies the origin of the name for our spring month of March; so, too, we derive the word "martial" from *Mars-Martis.* During the reign of Caesar Augustus, the god Mars was given an important new title, *Ultor* (Avenger), to commemorate his role in the defeat of those who had conspired against Julius Caesar.[84] In Islamic astrology the warrior Mars is often depicted riding the Lamb, sometimes carrying a sword and a severed head.[85]

The martial attributes of Mars were known to all writers from antiquity through the Middle Ages.[86] In Dante's *Divine Comedy* (c.1300) the planetary attributes are in turn given spiritual significance as the pilgrim ascends higher and higher into the cosmos. Arriving on the fifth planet, Mars, the poet has a vision of Christ, the victorious warrior of the Cross:

> As leads the galaxy from pole to pole,
> Distinguish'd into greater lights and less,
> Its pathway, which the wisest fail to spell;

> So thickly studded, in the depth of Mars,
> Those rays described the venerable sign,
> That quadrants in the round conjoining frame.
> Here memory mocks the toil of genius. Christ
> Beam'd on that cross; and pattern fails me now.
> But whoso takes his cross, and follows Christ,
> Will pardon me for that I leave untold,
> When in the flecker'd dawning he shall spy
> The Glitterance of Christ. . . .
> So from the lights, which there appear'd to me,
> Gather'd along the cross a melody,
> That, indistinctly heard, with ravishment
> Possess'd me. Yet I mark'd it was a hymn
> Of lofty praises; for there came to me
> "Arise," and "Conquer."[87]

Following this moment of musical ecstasy commemorating the Christian soldier, Dante sees the souls of many renowned warriors who reside on the planet Mars, among them Joshua, Judas Maccabeus, Charlemagne, Roland, and Godfrey of Bouillon (c.1060–1100), the hero of the First Crusade.[88] If the zodiacal sign of the Mystical Lamb is Aries, the planetary symbol of *Christus victor* is Mars. In astrological terms, the vengeful powers of Aries derive from his hereditary ties to the House of Mars. The Savior's crucifixion is merely a prelude to God's inevitable wrath.

Throughout the ancient world, people saw the sun make its annual circuit and knew it came under the sign of Aries at the spring equinox; they saw the planet Mars pass into Aries. Successive civilizations had celebrated this celestial event in various ways: the Greeks by a circle dance commemorating Theseus, the Romans by a war-dance honoring Mars, and the Christians by a liturgical dance around the maze, celebrating the victory of the Savior to the strains of *Praises to the Easter Victim (Victimae paschali laudes)*. From the dawn of European civilization, the celestial signs of the Lamb and the Warrior had presided over these rituals.

Of what relevance is all this to the maze? Recall that two Italian church mazes, those at Pavia and Piacenza, were flanked by the figure of Annus (symbol of the year) and by depictions of the human labors associated with the twelve months (see Fig. 2.1).[89] Remember, too, that a maze can be seen

FIGURE 4.3 A twelfth-century Chartres-type maze, with a demonic Minotaur at the center, appears above Priscian's description of the turning of the heavens.

in a cosmological volume (c.900–1100) from the monastery of St. Germain des Prés in Paris (see Fig. 1.10). In the Middle Ages, mazes were often drawn in such computus books: volumes containing tables, charts, graphs, and poems that track the movements of the planets and stars, the constellations and the zodiacal signs.[90] Before the advent of mechanical clocks in the fourteenth century, the signs of the zodiac made sense of the seemingly endless stream of time. The maze told of earthly time, the zodiac of the ceaseless turning of the heavens.

A maze joined to the zodiacal signs is illustrated in Figure 4.3, a page from a twelfth-century manuscript coming from the Benedictine monastery of Mouzon near Reims, France.[91] Here, much worn by the passage of time, is a labyrinth of the Chartrain type. Around the outer circumference runs a four-line epigraph beginning: "The Minotaur resides in the deep hole of this labyrinth; may the first virtue of God drive away this image of death from our hours" (Hic laberintheo residet minotaurus in alveo[?]; quam mortis formam nostris depellat ab horis virtus prima dei).[92] Leering from within the center of the maze is a demonic figure. Is this the Minotaur or the Devil? Whatever his name, the beast plays two incompatible musical instruments, a psaltery and a drum, creating the cacophony of Hell. Around him runs an inscription: "May the Lord remove such monsters from the homeland" (Talia deus monstra/Patria depellat ab ista). Below the maze is a well-known poem, called the Epitome, attributed to Priscian (Versus Prisciani de astrologia: Ad boree partes).[93] It lists, in order, the primary northern constellations, then those of the zodiac that move around the equator and begin with Aries, and finally the southern ones. Priscian's verse was to be memorized by schoolboys so that they could follow the annual turning of the heavens.[94] On subsequent pages of this computus book are tables for determining when Easter will fall and how much light and darkness will occur in each hour of each day in each month of the year.[95] Time can be measured. But time, like the demonic Minotaur in the center of the maze, devours all living creatures. Our time on this earth is finite; only the infinite heavens are timeless.

In sum, the maze is an enduring symbol that contains a multitude of meanings. We have seen that it epitomizes complex design and does honor to the master builder, as in the mazes at the cathedrals of Reims and Amiens. In traditional Christian theology, the labyrinth serves as a metaphor for the sinful world, a zone of trial and tribulation within which the righteous soul must struggle. In the celestial orbit, in proximity to the constellations and the planets, the maze assumes yet another significance. It is a symbol of terrestrial time, the sum of human experience on earth. The firmament reveals the whole sphere of God's completeness; the labyrinth suggests the futility of human effort. When the twelve zodiacal signs are found at the beginning of a book of hours or at the door of a cathedral, as at Amiens and Chartres for example, they symbolize a cosmic chronology under the dominion of the Lord.[96] Christ is the Lord of all time. He is the beginning and end. His sign returns annually in the heavens. Around him wander the planets, sometimes going forward and sometimes backward. Below, the spiritual pilgrim wanders the maze, sometimes progressing and sometimes retrograding, gradually devoured by time, gradually moving back to point of origin. Both planet and pilgrim move according to a grand, ever-recursive design, and they will do so until that final moment when all celestial motion stops. For then, as is foretold in the Book of Apocalypse (10:6), "there shall be time no longer."

CHAPTER FIVE

The Dance of the Maze

ALL ANCIENT CIVILIZATIONS, eastern and western, made use of dance to sanctify religious rites. This is as true of ancient Hebrew and Hindu ritual as it is of Greek and early Christian. King David danced and leaped unashamed around the Ark of God when he first brought it into Jerusalem (2 Samuel 6:14–16). The Indian god Shiva, King of the Dance, traditionally turns within a flaming circle, thereby signifying the continually recycling world; here the spiritual message is similar to that of the early Christian ring-dance that celebrates the God who knows no beginning or end. Indeed, dance had its origins in sacred ceremonies. It animates religious rituals, embellishes them, and renders them more imposing and more joyful. It sanctifies a finite zone, creating sacred space, and thus makes religious expression more intense. Only in modern times, and then only in a few western religions, has dance been removed from the sanctuary. When in August 1997 Pope John Paul II celebrated Mass in Notre-Dame of Paris to the sound of drums and the swaying of the faithful, some were scandalized by what appeared to be a timid surrender to modern urges. In fact, the pontiff, consciously or not, was reverting to a custom that can be traced back to the dawn of Christianity, and indeed to the beginning of human time.

The Warrior and the Dance of the Maze

In his *Iliad,* written around 700 B.C., Homer describes the "dancing floor" that Daedalus constructed for Ariadne on the island of Crete next to the labyrinth.[1] It was here that Ariadne taught Theseus the dance of life and death that signified the maze. Homer envisages this floor emblazoned upon the great shield of the warrior Achilles, the hero of the siege of Troy. Depicted around the shield are Ariadne and other youths, with men and

129

women alternating in a row. They have formed a chain by joining hands, and as they dance in a circular motion they produce a labyrinthine pattern that initiates Theseus to the twists and turns of the maze. The leader moves forward along one path until he reaches the center and then turns back in the opposite direction. At that moment the dancers toward the front of the line are moving backward while those farther back are still moving forward. In this way the dance begins to outline a labyrinthine pattern of parallel tracks. The girls wear garlands; the young men carry golden-hilted daggers.[2]

Many centuries after the Homeric account, additional descriptions of the dance of the maze begin to surface. They are nested in the narratives of mythographers who relate the tale of Daedalus and his Cretan labyrinth— how Theseus killed the deadly Minotaur and fled with his Athenian comrades to Delos, where they celebrated their triumph through song and dance.[3] These versions, therefore, do not speak of an initiation dance on Crete, as did Homer, but rather of a victory dance on Delos. Traditionally named the "Crane dance" after the complicated flight patterns of the crane,[4] this celebratory ritual, too, produced a complex design.[5] The account of Plutarch (first century A.D.) suggests how the Athenians gave thanks for their salvation:

> Now Theseus, in his return from Crete, put in at Delos, and having sacrificed to the god of the island . . . danced with the young Athenians a dance that, in memory of him, they say is still preserved among the inhabitants of Delos, consisting in certain measured turnings and returnings, imitative of the windings and twistings of the labyrinth. And this dance, as Dicaearchus writes, is called among the Delians the Crane. This he danced around the Ceratonian Altar, so called from its consisting of horns taken from the left side of the head. They say also that he instituted games in Delos, where he was the first that began the custom of giving a palm to the victors.[6]

Pollux, a lexicographer of the second century A.D., adds the following details:

> The Crane was danced in a group, dancer after dancer in a line, the dance leader [moving in turn] in both directions. Theseus danced the Crane first, during which he and the rescued youths reproduced the way out of the labyrinth as he danced around the altar of Delos.[7]

FIGURE 5.1 The so-called François Vase painted by Kleitias c.570 B.C. The top band of
the vase (enlarged at the top of the photograph) shows a chain of dancing youths and
maidens, hand in hand. It likely represents the dance that Theseus led on Delos after
the rescue of the Athenian hostages from the labyrinth of Crete.

The famous François Vase, painted by Kleitias around 570 B.C., is believed to depict Theseus leading the dance on Delos. Twelve young dancers, alternating men and women, follow his steps (Fig. 5.1).[8] A dance of the sort described by Plutarch and Pollux—with the dancers holding hands and moving backward and forward—could still be seen on Easter Day at Delos as late as 1903.[9]

In addition to Ariadne's labyrinthine dance on Crete, described by Homer, and that of Theseus on Delos, a third maze dance was known in the ancient world, namely the Trojan ride. As mentioned previously, this dance was an equestrian ballet first said to have been performed on Sicily by the descendants of Aeneas.[10] According to Virgil, this horse-dance formed the concluding part of funeral games to honor a fallen hero.[11] The youthful descendants of Troy rode out to execute a complex sequence of maneuvers which replicated the pattern of the maze at Crete. Wielding military weapons, they negotiated the intricate path of the labyrinth; their dance was emblematic of bravery and ultimate victory. Later, in imperial Rome, the Trojan ride was one of the military spectacles encouraged by Emperors Augustus and Nero.[12]

Given the importance of maze dances in the ancient Mediterranean world—and in light of the absence of any remains of an actual labyrinth at Knossos on Crete—one hypothesis immediately comes to mind: the origin of the maze rests not in any ur-labyrinth on Crete, but rather in the maze-like pattern danced there and elsewhere.[13] Perhaps the intricate design stamped upon the ground in the course of a jubilant victory dance created the archetype of the labyrinth. Whatever the truth, it is certain that the earliest references to the dance of the maze appear in connection with the shield of the warrior Achilles, the victory celebration of Theseus on Delos, and the cavalry ride of the youthful descendants of Troy. Thus in the "prehistory" of the labyrinth there existed already an indissoluble link between the warrior and the dance of the maze.

Origins of the Christian Easter Dance

With the spread of Christianity in the second and third centuries A.D., the dance of the maze was gradually transformed into a Christian salvation drama: Christ replaces Theseus, Satan substitutes for the infernal Minotaur, and the elect whom Christ redeems from Hell supplant the rescued Athenians. The transition from pagan to Christian ritual is evident in the third-century apocryphal Acts of St. John. On the night before his death, Jesus gathers his followers and bids them to join hands in a circle. The Lord leads the singing. Dancing around their savior, the disciples respond "Amen" and "Glory to the Father" to Christ's exhortations. The ring-dance is called the *choreia*, a Greek term that had already been employed to describe the maze dance of antiquity and would continue to be used into the sixteenth century to denote a labyrinthine church dance called *chorea* in Latin.[14] To quote the Acts of St. John directly:

> Glory be to you Father
> And going round in a circle we answered him:
> Amen. . . .
> One ogdoad [the eight] sings together with us.
> Twelve is the number dancing on high.
> Ah, it is possible for the whole world to dance!
> He who dances not knows not what comes to pass
> Amen. . . .
> Listen, and respond to my choral dance.
> Behold yourself in me as I speak, and seeing what I do,
> Keep silent about my mysteries.
> You who are dancing, know that this human suffering
> Which I am about to bear is yours. . . .
> Acknowledge suffering and you will have no suffering.
> I myself shall teach you what you do not know.
> I am your God, not the God of the betrayer.
> I wish to set holy souls in rhythm with me.[15]

The dance initiates the convert to the mysteries of redemption. In the circular whirl the neophyte joins ecstatically with the rhythms of the new song, and his soul is wedded to that of Jesus.

Obviously there are cosmic overtones to this Christian ring-dance as well. Greek philosophy had taught that the circle, or ring, was the most perfect and eternal form, one without beginning or end. Naturally Christian beliefs of late antiquity were strongly influenced by neo-Platonic thought. Thus the eight who "sing together with us" were to be understood as the earth and the seven planets of Ptolemaic cosmology, and the twelve "dancing on high" as the twelve signs of the zodiac.[16] These same cosmic elements

—the seven planets and twelve constellations—again dance in a passage from the apocryphal Acts of St. Thomas in which Wisdom appears as the bride of Christ the King.

> The maiden (Sophia) is the daughter of light.
> The proud glance of Kings rests upon her.
> Ravishing is her beauty. . . .
> She is surrounded by the seven bridal attendants
> Chosen by herself.
> Her handmaidens are also seven,
> Dancing a ring-dance before her,
> Twelve is the number of her servants,
> And they are her subjects.[17]
> Toward the bridegroom they direct their gaze and attention,
> So that they might be illuminated by the sight of him.[18]

For Christian warriors willing to hold up the shield of spiritual virtue and stand shoulder to shoulder with Christ against Satan, the reward was a place in the line of the elect in the eternal round-dance of Paradise—this according to Gregory of Nazianzus (c.329–c.389):

> How terrible for the soldiers of salvation to be subject to the soldiers of death! Defended by the shield of faith we should rightly stand firm against the wiliness of the Devil: and having triumphed with Christ and fought in the company of the Martyrs we shall hear that great sound: "Come hither, oh you who have been honoured by my Father! Receive the kingdom promised as your inheritance, the domain of all who joyfully dance the perpetual choral dance."[19]

We have seen that the maze was charged with astronomical significance throughout the Middle Ages. In manuscripts it was often placed next to calendrical lists and zodiacal charts.[20] So too, the cosmic overtones of the Easter round-dance continued to resonate in the Latin West into the twelfth century and well beyond, as we learn from the theologian Honorius Augustodunensis (c.1075–c.1156).

> The choir of musicians had its origin in the ring-dance of antiquity before the false gods, so that one might believe that they, ensnared by their delusions, both praised their gods with their voices and served them with their bodies. But in their ring-dances they thought of the rotation of the

firmament; in the clasping of their hands the union of the elements; in the sounds of song the harmony of the planets; in the gestures of the body the movements of the celestial bodies; in the clapping of hands and the stamping of feet the sound of thunder; something which the faithful imitate, converting all to the true service of God. For we can read how the people passed through the Red Sea and then danced ring-dances. . . . From that time and until now ring-dances have been performed to the accompaniment of music, while the heavenly bodies are said to revolve to sweet music.[21]

Thus the dances of the victorious Christians, no less than those of the newly liberated Israelites, were heard as hymns of thanksgiving resounding with the earthly equivalent of celestial harmony.

Not surprisingly, the pleasing image of a celestial dance fired the imagination of artists working in various media. Among the more famous representations of the angelic dance are Dante's poetic description of "the circuit of their joyous ring" in Canto VIII of his *Paradise*, Luca della Robbia's sculpture for the organ loft at the cathedral of Florence (Fig. 5.2), and Fra Angelico's fresco of the Last Judgment for the convent of San Marco in the same city. As late as the seventeenth century, the vision of a cosmic dance still burned brightly. In Milton's *Paradise Lost* the angels, learning that God has created a son, dance joyfully around the throne of the Lord. The labyrinthine pattern they create, like the church maze, seems irregular yet is most perfectly formed.

> That day, as other solemn days, they spent
> In song and dance about the sacred hill,
> Mystical dance, which yonder starry sphere
> Of planets and of fixed in all her wheels
> Resembles nearest, mazes intricate,
> Eccentric, intervolved, yet regular
> Than most, when most regular they seem:
> And in their motions harmony divine
> So smooths her charming tones, that God's own ear
> Listens delighted . . .[22]

The image of the celestial dance was not confined to Milton's lofty verse, but sifted down into popular culture as well. From the fifteenth century to the present day the English have sung *The Coventry Carol*, a haunting mix of Christian gospel and Anglo-Irish folk ballad.

FIGURE 5.2 A round-dance of wingless cherubs dancing in Paradise, from the fifteenth-century cantoria of the cathedral of Florence by Luca della Robbia.

> Tomorrow shall be my dancing day,
> I would my true love did so chance
> To see the legend of my play
> To call my true love to my dance.
>   (refrain)
> Sing, O my love, O my love, my love, my love;
> This have I done for my true love.

It is the voice of Christ which speaks to the Christian community ("my true love"). The Lord recounts the events of his earthly life, beginning with baptism and proceeding to the crucifixion. The "legend of my play" concludes with Christ's descent into Hell and final ascent to Paradise, a journey undertaken so that all might join him in the universal dance.

> Then down to hell I took my way
> For my true love's deliverance,
> And rose again on the third day,
> Up to my true love and the dance.
> (refrain)
>
> Then up to heaven I did ascend,
> Where now I dwell in sure substance
> On the right hand of God, that man
> May come unto the general dance.
> (refrain)[23]

And as late as the eighteenth century, English folkloric tradition held that the sun danced on Easter morning to celebrate the Resurrection: "To this pool the people used to come on Easter morning to see the sun dance and play in the water and the angels who were at the Resurrection playing backwards and forwards before the sun."[24]

Such an important article of Christian faith—the dance of the elect with Jesus at the center—naturally came to be imitated here on earth. The moment of earthly mimesis was Easter Sunday. As early as the mid-third century A.D. Gregory Thaumaturgus writes: "Today Christ, the sun of justice, shone a clear light upon us and illuminated the minds of the faithful. Today Adam is resurrected and performs a ring dance with the angels, raised up to heaven."[25]

But Satan, too, knew the steps. Only a thin line separated an exuberant imitation of the angels from a wanton dance of the Devil, as St. Ambrose (d. 397) suggests:

> Scripture enjoins us to sing loud to music (Psalms 47:1). It also enjoins us to dance wisely, since God said to Ezekiel (6:11), "clap your hands and stamp your feet." The revealed mysteries of the Resurrection have nothing to do with shameless dancing.[26]

According to St. Basil (d. 379), when Lent ended all hell broke loose, or at least the lewd gestures of Satan:

Casting aside the yoke of service under Christ and the veil of virtue from their heads [at the end of Lent], despising God and His Angels, they [the women] shamelessly attract the attention of every man. With unkempt hair, clothed in bodices and hopping about, they dance with lustful eyes and loud laughter; as if seized by a kind of frenzy they excite the lust of the youths. They execute ring-dances in the churches of the Martyrs and at their graves, instead of in the public buildings, transforming the Holy places into the scene of the lewdness. With harlots' songs they pollute the air and sully the degraded earth with their feet in shameful postures.[27]

The end of Lent, the arrival of Easter, and the advent of spring proved to be a powerful syzygy for clergy and populace, male and female, alike. Later we shall return to the place of women as participants in the dance of Easter.[28] For the moment it suffices to say that the jubilant celebration of Christ's victory was expressed through dance and through the Latin songs that served as accompaniment to that dance. On Easter the quick and the saved of the dead were able to join symbolically and dance their way to Paradise.

Dancing on the Maze

In the course of time the Easter dance came to be directed to and confined within the labyrinths that were set within the nave of the church, at least at several of the great cathedrals of northern France. We do not know exactly where or when this first occurred. What can be said with certainty is that all of the extant references relating to the use of the labyrinth in the church prior to the seventeenth century pertain to the ceremony of the Easter dance and no other.

These documents are few in number, and with good reason. The labyrinth had its origins among the heroes and gods of pagan antiquity, primitive forces which the early Christian fathers sought to transform or suppress. Moreover, as the comments of countless reformers show, dancing within the church often degenerated into boisterous, even indecent behavior. Lay persons who led the dance in church (*ducere choream*) were usually stigmatized along with practitioners of other dubious professions—actors, mimes, prostitutes, and gamblers.[29] Even so, all such undesirables appeared sporadically, sanctioned or not, within the walls of the church. Understandably, the canons of the cathedrals and their notaries who kept the chapter acts of the church were not quick to record this side of ecclesiastical life, where a division between profane and sacred was not always clearly enforced. In sum, the Easter dance of the labyrinth belongs to that category of experience that Michael Camille has dubbed "art on the edge."[30] The dance of the labyrinth was on the margin of acceptable religious practice, and the less said about it the better.

The Dance of the Maze at the Cathedral of Auxerre

Why Auxerre? With the great cathedrals at Chartres, Amiens, and Reims looming majestically before us, why focus on the comparatively small cathedral of St. Etienne at Auxerre? To put it simply, the preponderance of historical evidence draws us here. Isolated as Auxerre may seem today, in the early Middle Ages the town was an important center of monastic learning and the site at which the standard Chartres-type maze likely originated.[31] Auxerre, too, was the place where the earliest conciliar decrees against dancing in the church were issued, specifically in the years 573 and 603[32]—if dance was proscribed here, it surely must have been practiced. But most important, it is from the cathedral of Auxerre that we receive the fullest description of the dance of the maze, indeed the most complete account of any ecclesiastical dance in the premodern Western world. Not only does this document describe the dance of the maze at Auxerre, it also, like a Rosetta stone, suggests a plausible interpretation of the far more fragmentary accounts surviving from Sens and Chartres, and perhaps Reims and Amiens as well.

Discovered in the early eighteenth century by a priest of Auxerrois origin, this early eyewitness account reads as follows:

> Having received the *pilota* [a leather ball] from the newest canon, the dean, or someone in his place, in former times wearing an amice on his head and the other clergy likewise, began antiphonally the sequence appropriate for the feast of Easter, *Victimae paschali laudes.* Then taking the ball in his left hand, he danced to the meter of the sequence as it was sung, while the others linked hand in hand did the dance around the maze (*circa Daedalum*). And all the while the pilota was delivered or thrown by the ringed dean alternately to each and every one of the dancers whenever they whirled into view. There was sport, and the meter of the dance was set by the organ. Following this dance, the singing of the sequence and the jumping having concluded, the chorus proceeded

to a meal. There all of the canons of the chapter, the chaplains and officers, as well as certain of the more noble citizens of the town sat on
benches in a circle. To each of them was served sweets, fruit tarts, and
game of all sorts: boar, venison, and rabbit; and white and red wine was
offered in moderation, each cup being refilled no more than one or two
times. During this an appropriate sermon was read from the bishop's seat
or the pulpit. Thereafter, following the ringing of the larger bells from the
towers, they proceeded to Vespers.[33]

Tantalizing as this description may be, it is both incomplete and ambiguous. Further explanation is needed.

Each year, from at least 1396 until 1538, the canons and chaplains of the
cathedral of Auxerre gathered in the early afternoon of Easter Sunday
around the maze situated in the nave of their church. Joining hands to form
a ring-dance, or *chorea,* they chanted antiphonally the sequence *Praises to
the Easter Victim (Victimae paschali laudes)* as they danced on the labyrinth.
At the center of it all was the dean, the leader of the chapter. We may assume, because he was surrounded "garland-like" by the others, that the
dean proceeded through the tracks of the maze to the center and back. The
remaining clergy joined hands and, singing and jumping for joy, danced
around the maze. (Here Latinists may argue whether *circa* means "around"
or "within" the maze.) Most likely, they danced in a chain-line through the
maze, led by the dean. As they progressed, moving in swirling circular patterns, they created a giant sphere. Possibly additional clerics danced around
the outer circumference, encircling the maze in a ring. Whatever the case,
as the dean danced he threw a large leather ball (the *pilota*) back and forth
to those surrounding him. Apparently he was allowed to handle the ball
only with his left hand, a sinister challenge. And how, we might ask, were
the dancing clergy to catch the *pilota* and return it if their hands were linked
to those of their neighbors—by using their feet or head? Herein likely lay
the sport of the dance, as well as the occasion for disarray and impropriety.
Yet some sort of regular cadence was imposed on the proceedings, both by
the singing of the sequence and by the strains of the organ that accompanied the chant. As we have seen, the organ at Auxerre was situated high
above the singers in the first bay on the north wall of the nave.[34] When the
music of the organ had stopped, and the singing and the jumping ceased,
the participants repaired to the chapter house, where they enjoyed a sumptuous repast. Later in the afternoon, when summoned by the bells of the

church, the clergy returned to the church to celebrate the office of Vespers and again pass over the labyrinth.

Because the dance on the maze at Auxerre was a venerable ritual, its particulars were vigilantly maintained by the dean and chapter. Each year the most recently received canon of the church was required to provide a large ball and pay for the lavish meal that followed the dance. Beginning with Easter 1396, a succession of canons tried to negotiate with the chapter in order to reduce this financial burden.[35] From these disputes, recorded in the chapter acts of the church, we learn several details of the ceremony. In 1412, for instance, the size of the ball was adjusted so as to reduce its cost; the chapter allowed for a ball that was somewhat smaller in circumference but not so small that it could be grasped by a single hand (an early precedent for our present basketball rule against palming!).[36] Eventually, doubts about the liturgical propriety of dancing and ball playing began to surface. In 1471 the newly received canon Gerard Royer, doctor of theology, aligned his religious scruples with his economic self-interest and refused to provide both ball and meal.[37] To lend a voice of authority to his refusal, he cited the then two-centuries-old *Rationale divinorum officium* (c.1280) of the church liturgist Guillaume Durand, which stipulated that, although such ball games were widespread, the church would be a better place without them.[38] To no avail did canon Royer plead: the chapter and local governors simply overruled him and, finding a second-hand ball around the church, proceeded with the ceremony.

Sixty years later a more serious attack was launched against the traditional round-dance on the maze at Auxerre. Once again a canon refused to present the *pilota,* but this time his protest was carried to the local court, the *bailliage d'Auxerre.* Despite the pleading of the chapter that the ceremony should be maintained, because of the amusement it provided for the magistrates and citizens of the town, on 22 August 1531 the dance of the maze was condemned and the canons were ordered to transform it into something more edifying, namely a *Salve* service in honor of the Virgin.[39] The losers appealed to the court of the Parliament of Paris, where the case caused something of a sensation. It even reached the ears of King François I, who opined unofficially that "the ceremony was good and praiseworthy and shouldn't be changed or abolished without good reason, but if any abuses or deformities had crept in, these should be removed so that it might be maintained honestly."[40]

The affair dragged on. The court of Paris dispatched councilor François Disque to Auxerre to observe the ritual on Easter (28 March) 1535, and he in turn reported his findings to a commission consisting of no fewer than four councilors of Parliament, four canons of Notre-Dame of Paris, four doctors of theology of the Sorbonne, and four procurators representing the two contending parties! Finally, on 7 June 1538, the court of Paris rendered its verdict. The opinion of the lower court was upheld: the ceremony would be reformed. No more would the *pilota* be presented or food and drink served. Dance and ball were laid to rest.

An essential element of the round-dance at Auxerre was the *pilota*, but what did it symbolize? Several interpretations of the meaning of the ball have been offered, some more tightly bound to the traditional meanings of the labyrinth than others.[41] One theory holds that the *pilota* represents the ball of pitch that Theseus stuffed into the mouth of the Minotaur prior to the kill—the canons were hurling a symbol of an ancient Greek myth.[42] A more folkloric explanation sees in the spherical ball the orb of the rising sun, which was thought to dance on the horizon early on Easter morning.[43] Since the dawn of Christianity, Christ has been termed the Sun of Justice (*Sol justitiae*) and the Sun of the Resurrection (*Sol resurrectionis*).[44] Most likely, however, the *pilota* was a symbol of the cosmic harmony attendant upon a hero's return to his rightful place in heaven.[45] Since at least the twelfth century the clasping of hands and the rotation of the ring-dance were taken to be signs of cyclical and eternal perfection, celestial elements brought to earth.[46] Much earlier, in the fourth century, Marius Victorinus described Theseus's dance on Delos as an imitation of celestial motions: the first gesture of the dance, moving to the right, imitates the motion of the heavens turning east to west; the second, moving to the left, from west to east, replicates the orbits of the planets; while in the third all the dancers remain stationary, like the earth at the center of the ancient universe.[47]

Thus the flying *pilota* symbolized several things: the instrument of salvation derived from the Greek myth, the rising sun from folkloric legend, and the harmony of spheres from classical philosophy. But all were overwhelmed by the music of the dance. That is to say, the text of the Easter sequence *Praises to the Easter Victim* was so overtly Christian in its meaning that all other resonances became of secondary importance. A fourteenth-century missal of the liturgical usage of Auxerre provides both the text and

EXAMPLE 5.1 *Victime paschali laudes* of the usage of the cathedral of Auxerre (Paris, Bibliothèque nationale, MS fonds latin 17312, fol. 199). The spelling is that of the original fourteenth-century manuscript.

the music (Example 5.1). Picture a hundred clerics dancing, leaping, and swirling as they sang:

> Christians, sing forth praises to the Easter victim,
> The lamb redeems the sheep.
> The innocent Christ has redeemed the sinners to the Father.
> Life and death have been joined in a wondrous battle.
> The leader of life rules, living though dead.
> Tell us, Mary [Magdalene], what did you see along the way?
> "I saw the tomb of the living Christ, and the glory of the resurrection.
> To this testify the angels, his clothes and shroud.
> Christ, my hope, has risen, he goes before us in Galilee."
> Believe in the one true Mary, rather than the lying crowd of Jews.
> We know that Christ has risen from the dead, you our King and Conqueror, have mercy upon us. Amen.

Christ the pascal lamb is victorious. He defeats death and redeems his flock. Indeed, *Praises to the Easter Victim* speaks as much to the Harrowing of Hell as it does to the Lord's resurrection. It embraces many of the spiritual themes emphasized in this book, themes of paradox and reversal: the sacrificial lamb who redeems the sheep, the hero who descends and returns, the warrior who conquers by dying, mourning turned to joy.

Praises to the Easter Victim is a venerable chant, one composed in the eleventh century by an obscure Swiss monk named Wipo. It is not difficult to sing. Although the phrases of text and music are of irregular length, the melody moves mostly by step, without taxing leaps or chromatic inflections. It sits comfortably in the middle of the male vocal range. Like most medieval chant, this paean to the paschal lamb was designed to be easily accessible to the entire clerical community.

Indeed, the clergy of Auxerre would have known *Praises to the Easter Victim* by heart. They would have sung it many times during the Easter dance, because, as sequences go, it is very short. Many repetitions would have been needed to accompany the elaborate dance on the maze as the symbolic warrior proceeded to the center and back. What is more, the choir had already sung *Praises to the Easter Victim* earlier that same day, at the end of Easter Matins.[48] They would do so again, after the festal meal following the dance on the maze, when the clergy returned to the cathedral for Vespers.[49] Here at this evening service *Praises to the Easter Victim* sounded forth prior to the

procession that went from the chancel to the baptismal font, during which
the line of march crossed the maze in the nave. Returning from the font,
and again traversing the labyrinth, the clerics sang the psalm *When Israel
came out from Egypt* (Psalm 113) commemorating the exodus of the Israelites from the hell of Egypt.[50] As if that were not enough, *Praises to the
Easter Victim* was heard each and every evening during the Vespers procession to the font on the four ferial days following Easter.[51] Could the clergy
at Auxerre really have danced, sung this chant, and played catch with a large
ball all at once? Certainly.

The Dance of the Maze at the Cathedral of Sens

Easter Vespers at the cathedral of Sens was similar to that at nearby Auxerre.
The clergy departed the chancel in procession, chanting the responsory
These are the New Lambs (Isti sunt agni novelli), celebrating the newly elect
as they enter into Heaven. Crossing the labyrinth at the west end of the
church, the clerics headed out the door and around to the north side of the
cathedral where the baptistry of St. Jean was situated. Upon their return
they again crossed the maze, this time chanting the psalm *When Israel came
out from Egypt,* signifying Moses' redemption of the people of Israel from
the clutches of the Pharaoh.

Before Vespers the clergy at Sens, like their brethren at Auxerre, danced
on the maze. We know this from a single document, dated Wednesday, 14
April 1413—a petition by the lesser clergy to the chapter of canons to allow
"according to custom" that on the following Easter Sunday "they may play
freely the game on the labyrinth during the ceremony."[52] By "the game" we
may understand the tossing of the *pilota,* and by "the ceremony" the liturgical dance itself. We do not know how far back in time this ritual extended,
only that in 1413 it was executed "according to custom"; the maze at Sens
was one of the earliest ones in France, possibly dating from the late twelfth
century.[53]

At some point during the fifteenth century the labyrinthine dance at
Sens was transferred from the church to the cloister, the outdoor square
that bordered the nave on the south side. Once again, we are informed on
the matter because of a scandalous condition: women are participating.
The potential for much evil (*multa mala*) exists, a capitular decree of 1517
declares, because people of both sexes are dancing. The dance must be suppressed and replaced by a more decorous procession within the church.

Because it was the ancient tradition in the church of Sens, to promote a praiseworthy custom, that male ecclesiastics, those beneficed and wearing the habit of the metropolitan church of Sens, as well as the archbishop, if he be present, after the midday meal on Easter, gathered in the courtyard of the cloister, and there dancing a round-dance—not jumping as in other peculiar dances—they sang hymns of the resurrection of Christ and other Latin texts in praise of God. But because a large number of people of both sexes ran to join in the said round-dance, where perhaps much evil might be perpetrated, it seemed to the lords, dean, and chapter of said church of Sens, after mature, slow, and diligent deliberation, in order to remove a danger to souls, that custom should be wholly abolished. And in place of this dance, venerable and discreet men, lords Louis la Hure, archdeacon of Provins, and Robert de Fonte, canon of the church of Sens, offered the sum of five hundred *livres* of Tours . . . with the condition that, on said Easter, from six thirty to seven [in the evening], the canons will be held to sound the four great bells of the church, and that at precisely seven the choir will exit from the chancel, the cantor beginning the antiphon *Salvator mundi* . . .[54]

Later remarks by two canons of Sens further describe the Easter dance and suggest why it was suppressed:

This dance, or *carrole,* took place in the cloister in the evening of Easter. The archbishop attended with all the clergy of the church, marching two by two and turning around the square, followed by some of the more notable citizens two by two. And when the *carrole* was completed, they went to a meal provided by the most recently received canon. These canons often offered large sums for the fabric of the church and for the poor in order to palliate and avoid the insolences of some individuals, because a ritual that had been introduced in good faith had been transformed into ridicule, and people often exceeded the boundaries of modesty.[55]

Do you know of the ecclesiastical dance that was practiced here a long time ago in the evening of Easter and that they called the *cazzole* [*carrole*]? It was done around the well of the cloister, and the dignitaries of the chapter, the archbishop at the head, each lead a choirboy by the hand.[56]

This last detail is circumstantially confirmed by the Jesuit priest Claude-François Ménestier, who says in his *Des Ballets anciens et modernes* (1682):

"I have seen, in several churches, on Easter, canons take the hands of the choirboys and, while singing hymns of joy, dance in the church."[57]

Thus the ancient dance at Sens, which had existed first indoors on the maze and then outdoors in the episcopal courtyard, was terminated in 1517, just as it would be twenty years later at Auxerre. In its place was instituted a solemn ecclesiastical procession within the walls of the church, one that would endure at Sens until the Revolution.[58]

The suppression of the Easter dance at Sens and Auxerre had the effect in pre-Reformation France of removing from the church an extravagant medieval ritual. At Sens the canons cited the fact that women had crept into the ring of the dance as a pretext for their action. Yet, wanted or not, women had been dancing in Christian churches since at least the fourth century, as the earlier complaint of St. Basil suggests and many conciliar decrees affirm. The Council of Chalon-sur-Saône (639) censured wanton feminine dancing and singing, and the Council of Rome (826) did likewise, fearing pagan acts and gestures by the women. The Council of Paris (1215) issued an outright ban on women dancing within any sacred precincts, including cemeteries, while the Council of Basel (1435) sought to bring an end to an even more blasphemous offense, clerics dancing with other clerics dressed as women.[59] Perhaps the addition of the ladies of Sens to the Easter dance caused the ritual to be moved from the maze to the less sacrosanct confines of the cloister, where the mixed company (clerics, choirboys, and women) might circle the cloistral well. Perhaps too, as was true in Besançon, the ceremony returned to the nave of the cathedral in times of inclement weather, and the clergy again danced around the maze.[60]

The Dance of the Maze at the Cathedral of Chartres?

Sometimes supposition is more satisfying to the spirit than documentable fact—an intriguing allusion allows the historical imagination to roam more freely. This is the case of the dance of the maze at the cathedral of Chartres where, in contrast to Auxerre and Sens, the evidence is more suggestive than incontrovertible.

At Chartres, once again, the only hint as to how the maze was used prior to the seventeenth century comes in regard to the paschal liturgy, specifically that of Vespers on Easter Sunday. Easter Week, beginning on Easter Sunday, was a joyful season, one that bordered on the riotous. Depending upon the customs of the church, ball games, court tennis, and the throwing of the *pilota* might be enjoyed as the clergy "cut loose" following the severity of the Lenten season, just as they disported themselves at the Feast of Fools after Christmas.[61] Needless to say, the authorities of the church inveighed, usually in vain, against such unseemly behavior.[62] At Chartres, the paschal victim was quickly forgotten in favor of the paschal vice of dicing. On the afternoon of Easter Sunday each canon was allotted five sous with which to gamble in the chamberlain's counting house, at least until the mid-fourteenth century when a more dour element took control of the affairs of the church. In 1354, 1363, and again in 1366, the chapter of canons repeatedly decreed (thereby proving how deeply rooted was this ancient tradition) that henceforth five sous were to be allocated to each canon only if he attended a sermon on the subject of Christ's resurrection, to be offered from the pulpit in the nave of the church, immediately next to the maze (see Fig. 8.3).[63]

Other special rituals were practiced on the afternoon of Easter Sunday as well. First of all, during the chanting of Vespers the younger clerics climbed down from their choir stalls, removed their purple vestments in favor of white surplices, and returned to stand as a group in the middle of the aisle. Now the subcantor (the leader of the chorus) intoned the great responsory *This is the Day the Lord Hath Made* (*Haec dies quam fecit dominus*); the younger clergy, standing in the center, sang and danced the verse *Now the Jews Say* (*Dicunt nunc Judei*), recalling the Jews' incredulous response to the events at the tomb. The term used to describe the central group of singers and dancers is *chorea*, which, as we have seen, had been used since antiquity to denote a ring-dance.[64] Soon the Chartrain procession departed the chancel and headed for the baptistry in the south aisle of the crypt, where orations were said. Returning from the font to the choir, the clergy chanted the lengthy antiphon *I am the Alpha and Omega* (*Ego sum alpha et omega*), recalling that all life begins and ends in the Lord. This same agenda—Vespers in the chancel, procession to the font in the crypt, return to the chancel for Compline—continued at Chartres each afternoon throughout the succeeding days of Easter Week.[65] All this is firmly established in the rites of Chartres by at least the twelfth century.[66]

By 1215, of course, a maze had been placed on the floor of the cathedral nave.[67] Whether the clergy henceforth engaged the labyrinth at this moment on Easter Sunday is a matter of speculation, but a capitular decree of 1452 appears to say as much. It seems that the dancing and, indeed, shouting of the lower clergy on Easter afternoon was getting out of hand, in the choir as well as the nave, and that greater decorum was thought necessary. The document begins with a synopsis in French ("Proscription against dancing and any verbal confrontation on Easter and Easter Week)," and then continues in Latin:

> The chapter declared, just as it had declared previously, that henceforth no chaplains or other members of the choir and the habit of the cathedral of Chartres are permitted, while the service is being danced [*servicio faciendo in chorea*], as it is customarily done on Easter and during Easter week in the nave and choir or elsewhere, to shout against one another [*verberare*] owing to the insolence and opprobrium which traditionally result therefrom and will result in the future.[68]

Clearly, what annoyed the more conservative canons was the raucous *verberatio,* the reenactment of the shouting match between Christ and Satan. As mentioned earlier, a din of chaos and confusion was a necessary backdrop to the dramatic Harrowing of Hell performed on Easter.[69] The clergy at Chartres recreated Hell, or at least the sounds thereof, and then danced their way out.

Church authorities and the civil courts suppressed the Easter dance at Sens and Auxerre in the early sixteenth century. At Chartres, however, the dance seems to have survived somewhat longer. Drawing on late-sixteenth-century sources, the Chartrain historian Sébastien Rouillard says the following about this Easter ritual in his *Parthénia* (1609):

> Standing before the high altar the subcantor awaits the second choir composed of canons, singing-men, and chaplains of the church in the lowest holy orders, such as acolytes and subdeacons, each of whom holds in his hand a large white candle, and they sing as a partial choir. Then, after the entire choir is assembled, it goes to the baptismal font, which is, as I have said in the crypt of the church.
>
> In procession, the subcantor along with all those holding the said white candles guard the middle, with the canons and other priests surrounding them on both sides ...
>
> The archives of the church attribute several meanings to this ceremony. One says that it represents the state of the children of Israel during their captivity. Another holds it is an allusion to the Passover of Moses who must display a staff in his right hand. And finally [another contends] that these white robes and white candles represent the ancient

solemnity of the children who are baptized at Easter who are presented in church dressed in white attire as a sign of their purity, candor, and innocence.

All these reasons seem to me plausible, yet nevertheless, I would like to add a stronger and more seminal one, one that serves in the long run to explain the point of this mystery. That is to say, without going into great detail, all of this ceremony represents the Fathers who were in Limbo, [and] by the triumph of the Cross at the glorious resurrection of the son of God celebrated on that day and on which they sing the chant correctly named *Haec dies,* we transform ourselves from mourning into joy through him . . .

Then the subcantor, dressed in white and holding a white staff, goes before the high altar with the *chorea.* There they reenact the dance of shaking and fear [*qui représente le bransle et doubte*] that those who were first in Limbo had when they saw come toward them the Savior—something they could scarcely believe despite the ardor of their faith.

Finally, after the station has been made in the chancel, the entire choir goes in procession to the crypt, those dressed in liberated white always in the middle, the canons [in higher orders] on the two sides, in order to demonstrate that it was in this fashion that God led away from Limbo the captive people.[70]

Thus it was that the clergy of Chartres acted out the deliverance of the elect from Limbo, the clergy in the lower orders representing the liberated souls. The point of reference for the white vestments worn by those emancipated by Christ was surely the Book of Apocalypse: "These are they which came out of great tribulation, and have washed their robes, and made them white in the blood of the Lamb" (7:14). Appropriately attired in purified white, this youthful *chorea* probably stopped in station and danced on the maze; at the very least, they did so while passing over it. The key word here is *bransle,* which during the sixteenth century was both a dance step and a dance of somewhat ill-defined character.[71] With only a bit of imagination we can see the liberated captives shaking and quaking on the maze in a circular dance as the procession moves through the nave, the more senior canons holding in check the younger dancers in the center.

How long the dance from Limbo persisted at Chartres is not known, but certainly not into the seventeenth century. The mid-seventeenth-century Chartrain historian Charles Challine speaks in the past tense of the ceremony reported by Rouillard ("was observed in this church during Easter week"), giving no hint that the tradition continued. The only paschal ceremony that Challine thinks worthy of note is the following:

> Easter Monday, at five o'clock in the evening, the cantor, choirboys, and the full complement of polyphonic singers go up into the exterior galleries [in the two towers] on either side of the front of the church and sing motets in polyphony, which can be heard a great distance, then passing into the bell towers, they carillon, and then dine together at the expense of the canons, an ancient custom of this church that is called "the paschal lamb."[72]

In mid-seventeenth-century Chartres, these motets were evidently all that remained of the ritual liberation from Limbo.

The Music of the Dance

"They sang hymns of the resurrection of Christ and other Latin texts in praise of God"—this was the music of the Easter dance at Sens and presumably elsewhere.[73] Does any of this dance music survive? Indeed, it can be found in a famous music book compiled in Paris around 1250.[74] One unit of the manuscript begins with an illumination depicting clerics caught, so to speak, in the act of dancing (Fig. 5.3); thereafter come the music and texts for sixty dances. No collection before the appearance of printed dance music in the sixteenth century is as large.[75] Exactly half of these sixty dances (the first thirty) are for Easter, a clear sign of the importance of the Easter dance to medieval dancing generally. Another manuscript, this one now preserved in Tours and also dating from the thirteenth century, contains eleven of these same Easter dances as well as five additional ones.[76] In sum, the known repertoire of Easter dances consists of at least thirty-five pieces.

How can we be sure this is dance music? If the introductory illumination depicting a clerical ring-dance is not evidence enough (Fig. 5.3), the musical-poetic structure of the pieces proves the point. It generates a musical form called "the ring song" (*cantilena rotunda*), so named "because, like a circle, it turns back on itself."[77] Medieval music theorists classified the *cantilena rotunda*, along with the purely instrumental *ductia* and *estampie*, among the principal forms of medieval dance music.[78]

FIGURE 5.3 Clerics hold hands as they execute a round-dance. The illumination precedes a group of thirty Easter dances preserved in a thirteenth-century French music book.

To hear an Easter round-dance, let us consider *Let Resound the Temperate Voice* (*Fidelium sonet vox sobria;* Example 5.2). It is composed of only two short musical phrases (a and b). As the text unfolds, a textual refrain continually appears. (The letters a and b are capitalized to show when the music is carrying the textual refrain.)

Fi - de - li - um   so - net vox so - bri - a   Con - ver - te-re, Sy - on, in gau - di - a.

Sit o - mni - um   u - na le - ti - ti - a,   Quos u - ni - ca, re - de - mit gra - ti - a.

Con - ver - te-re, Sy - on, in gau - di - a.   Te li - be - rat pas - cha - lis hos - ti - a.

EXAMPLE 5.2 Easter round-dance *Fidelium sonet vox sobria* (Florence, Biblioteca Medicea Laurenziana, MS Pluteus 29.1, fol. 465; the rhythm is conjectural).

(first strophe)		(second strophe)	
Let resound the temperate voice of the faithful,	a	Christ is armed for the battle,	
Convert, O Zion, to joy,	A	*Convert, O Zion, to joy,*	
Let all unite in a single joy,	a	He has smashed the enemy gates	
Whom the one grace redeemed:	b	While Egypt holds the mantle:	
Convert, O Zion, to joy	A	*Convert, O Zion, to joy,*	
The paschal host frees you.	B	*The paschal host frees you.*	
(third strophe)		(fourth strophe)	
A younger daughter gains the dowry,	a	For the supreme victory of the daughter	
Convert, O Zion, to joy,	A	*Convert, O Zion, to joy,*	
A younger (son) gains the prizes of the older,	a	May there be praise and glory to God the Father,	
Because Jacob suppressed the blessing:	b	Who reigns for all time:	
Convert, O Zion, to joy,	A	*Convert, O Zion, to joy,*	
The paschal host frees you.	B	*The paschal host frees you.*	

In *Let Resound the Temperate Voice,* the structure of each strophe is aAabAB. The form is "circular" in the sense that the two musical phrases (a and b) are continually recycled.[79]

Now let us imagine a performance. As was typical of medieval song, the verses of the text were undoubtedly sung by a leader, perhaps by the dean who represented Christ in the center of the ring. To his singing the dancers circling around responded with the refrain (given in italics in the strophes shown above). Indeed, one might be tempted to assign a choreography to the ring-dance of the maze following the description of Marius Victorinus[80]—turning to the right for the first line of the verse, to the left for the second, and standing still for the refrain. Possibly the singing of verse and refrain was coordinated in some way with the quarter and half turns in the path through the maze. Possibly the dancers on the perimeter of the maze proceeded 180 degrees to the right for the first musical phrase ("a") and 180 degrees to the left for the second ("b")—that way at the end each dancer would be returned to the position he or she had occupied at the beginning.

Such thoughts, of course, are no more than pure speculation. What is certain is that the texts of these Latin ring-dances were fully harmonious with the maze and its symbolism on Easter Sunday. *Let Resound the Temperate Voice* speaks of Christ the warrior armed for battle. He has smashed Satan's gates, a direct reference to his thunderous entry at the commencement of the Harrowing of Hell. Other dances also allude to Christ's titanic struggle with the prince of evil ("Who is this king of glory, a Lord powerful and potent, mighty in battle")[81] and to the weapons brandished by the Savior ("The weapon which he embraced he displayed to all").[82] He is a warrior, yet a lamb as well ("The lamb of innocence did battle with the tyrant of iniquity").[83] All of the faithful will share in the triumph ("His followers, the catholic flock, share his victory").[84] Leading the elect out of the Inferno, the Redeemer follows a recursive path ("Christ reverts from the Underworld; the victor returns from the battle").[85] As they moved through the maze singing lines from the dramatic Harrowing of Hell, the medieval dancers expressed the kinetic equivalent of the play itself.[86]

Other Easter round-dances borrowed not from liturgical drama, but from the canonical liturgy of Easter Sunday. For example, the round-dance *On this Day of the Lord* (*In hac die Dei*) is simply an elaboration of the Vespers processional chant *Dicant nunc Judei*, with the words "Tell us now, ye Jews" changed to "Tell us now, ye Hebrews."[87] It is to this chant that the *chorea* at Chartres danced; and it is to this round-dance that the *chorea* at Besançon would dance into the eighteenth century.[88] Most significantly, the striking anti-Semitic line "The true testimony of Mary [Magdalene] is to be believed more than the lying crowd of Jews" from the Easter sequence

Praises to the Easter Victim is quoted as the refrain in yet another dance, *Let the Voice of Joy Resound* (*Decet vox letitie*).[89] The clergy at Sens, Chartres, and elsewhere may not have literally danced to *Praises to the Easter Victim*, as they did on the maze at Auxerre, but they alluded to the Savior and mocked the disbelieving Jews through these and similar Latin round-dances. With regard to Christians and Jews, these dance tunes and their texts drive home an important point: what really divided the religions, despite all the fables and prejudices of each, was a simple dispute about a historical fact—whether Jesus experienced a bodily resurrection.

Maze Dances Sacred and Pagan

The popularity of these thirty-five Easter maze dances was enduring and universal. Some spread beyond French-speaking lands, to Spain and to the British Isles, for example, extending even to churches that had no maze.[90] Some dances were supplied with additional voices so as to create two- and three-part polyphonic works.[91] A few remained favorites in French churches for centuries. For example, *Let Resound the Temperate Voice,* given above, was sung at the collegiate church of Mary Magdalene in Besançon (eastern France) into the fifteenth century;[92] and the aforementioned *On this Day of the Lord* was similarly sung there on Easter afternoon until 1738 —a period of some five hundred years.[93] The canons and chaplains of Besançon joined hands as they executed the *chorea;* they danced outdoors in the cloister if the weather was clement but inside in the middle of the nave if it was not.[94] No labyrinth is known in the nave of this church, but the dance was celebrated there nonetheless. In churches that had no maze the choreography was presumably only that of a round-dance; in those that did, a snaking line-dance through the labyrinth was always possible.

To be sure, at some moments and places in history these Easter dances were performed on a maze and at others they were not. The Easter dance, which had existed since the dawn of Christianity, predated the entry of the maze into the church. Even after the advent of pavement mazes in the great French cathedrals, the joyous dance of the elect was celebrated elsewhere without benefit of a labyrinth. The church maze was an independent architectural ornament loaded with religious symbolism, just as the Easter dance was an autonomous ritual lending voice and kinetic energy to the most profound of Christian beliefs. But symbol and ritual need not necessarily be joined.

Nor need maze and church be joined. We know, for example, that there was dancing and feasting at Eastertide on at least one turf maze in England, although that maze was well outside of any church or church cloister.[95] What music might the dancers of the English maze have sung outdoors on a bright spring morning? Perhaps the famous canon *Sumer is icumen in*,[96] the first round to carry an English text. Yet it also sports an alternative Latin verse that alludes to the Harrowing of Hell,[97] and its *pes* (repeating bass line) derives from a chant sung at the evening service on Easter Sunday.[98] Did *Sumer is icumen in* begin life as a clerical round-dance on an English turf maze?

Similarly, in southern Italy and on the island of Corsica, clergy and populace joined in maze dances outdoors in the spring to commemorate Christ's resurrection as well as the commencement of a period of agricultural renewal. These dancers did not tread upon a pre-existing maze. Rather, their feet created *ex tempore* a labyrinth in the dirt as they spiraled around in vernal jubilation. A reflection of a timeless Mediterranean tradition, these maze dances continued into the nineteenth century.[99]

In France, too, the ancient dance of the maze had a life well outside the confines of the church and, indeed, outside the calendrical boundaries of Eastertide. As late as 1838 a folklorist reported that in certain parts of southern France a dance called "the Cretan dance of the Greeks" ("la *danse candiote* des Grecs")[100] could still be seen on feast days and especially during Mardi-gras. The twisting line of dancers was said to create the labyrinth shown in Figure 5.4. A youth representing Theseus led the way:

> A young man, directed by a fife and drum, leads the dance, holding in his left hand the end of a handkerchief or a ribbon, the other end of which is held by a young lady. All the other dancers are similarly linked by a handkerchief or a ribbon. The leader holds another in his right hand, that he shakes every which way, making it follow the various movements he imposes on the chain. The longer the line of persons, the more pleasure results from all of the turns and detours to which they are subjected by the leader. Sometimes the leader runs back against the line, turning suddenly and successively to the right and to the left, he forces the chain to make all the turns and detours that represent and perfectly imitate the contour of the labyrinth. Then—what is most striking—while all the dancers raise their arms without breaking the chain, the leader, whom

FIGURE 5.4 A contemporary sketch approximating the maze formed by the dancers of the Dance of Crete (*Danse candiote*) as performed in nineteenth-century France.

one calls Theseus, goes back and forth in silence, as with a look of fear, followed by the person who holds the handkerchief; and, after many attempts, he finally exits with great joy, jumping into the arms of the last two persons of the chain, shaking his handkerchief free, the thread which had served him as a guide throughout this Daedalus.

The final configuration imitates perfectly the ball [*peloton*] that Theseus used to exit the labyrinth: the person who forms the last ring of the chain stops and no longer moves; the head of the line turns around with everyone else remaining in the dance, and everyone stops himself in turn when he arrives at this center. Thus in this manner the chain forms nothing more henceforth than a great ball [*peloton*] which turns from time to time in a wheel as against itself.[101]

Thus the myth of the Cretan maze and the victory dance of Theseus were recreated in French custom into the middle of the nineteenth century. The maze that was formed through this folkloric ritual was obviously not an architectural labyrinth but rather a human configuration generated by the dancers themselves, just as was once done in ancient Greece, we suppose. No allusion to the Savior or the Harrowing of Hell was signified here. Surviving from pre-Christian times, this primitive dance was spiritually and physically remote from the church and the labyrinth within it.[102]

But earlier, during the Middle Ages, dance and labyrinth had been united in several of the great French cathedrals, and we should consider how this came about. As we have seen, the maze—whether at Chartres, Sens, or Auxerre—was an object with strong pagan associations. The dance of the maze, too, had begun life in Homeric times and continued to exist in France as a pagan ritual for nearly three millennia, without any specific calendrical position. During the early centuries of Christianity the faithful commenced the practice of dancing joyfully to celebrate the Savior's resurrection. Just as the pagan labyrinth was Christianized rather early on by the patristic fathers, so later the dance of the labyrinth came to be sanctified on the floor of the Christian shrine. As this ancient Greek ritual became Christianized, it received a place within the calendar of the church, namely, in the liturgy of Easter Sunday. The medieval church fathers knew of the historical link between the maze and the victory dance. They knew that the labyrinth and the dance were traditional partners. They felt a need to defuse the potentially explosive tension between pagan exuberance and Christian solemnity that naturally surfaced at the end of the long penitential season of Lent. Thus they seized upon the circuitous twists of this primeval dance as a way of adding one further layer of salvific symbolism to Christian doctrine: the dancing warrior Theseus had presaged long ago the deliverance of souls from Limbo, the resurrection of Christ, and the regeneration of humankind. By reinterpreting an ancient Greek "rescue drama" as a specifically Christian dance of liberation, the medieval clergy suggested even more strongly to the faithful that, hellish as the maze of life may appear, it might not be inextricable after all.

Would anyone care to dance the Limbo?[103]

CHAPTER SIX

Symbolizing the Christian Warrior

THE MAZE WAS A SYMBOL that conveyed an astonishing wealth of meanings, as the preceding chapters have shown. As with any symbol, the potency of this sign was directly proportional to the number of its implied meanings. Adding to the allure of the maze was the fact that its significance could change according to the context in which it appeared. Placed on a Cretan coin, a labyrinth alluded to the Greek myth; on a pavement in a Roman villa, it marked a line of defense or protection; in a Gothic cathedral, it suggested both death and eternal life. Even the position of the viewer affected the psychological force of the labyrinth: seen as a whole from above, the maze resonated with divine perfection; but experienced from within, it baffled and frightened the spiritual pilgrim.

The symbol of the maze demonstrates convincingly that meaning in the physical world need not always be expressed in narrative or chronological order. Thoughts that might otherwise come in linear sequence can, by invoking a symbol, cascade simultaneously upon the mind, and thereby gain added force. Such a symbolic use of words is at the very heart of poetry. In that art a symbol has the power simultaneously to augment and synthesize, to amass in a single image a multitude of associations. So, too, does an icon, or logo, function in the visible world. The white dove of peace and the black swastika of the Nazis are potent symbols of the twentieth century. Each comes freighted with a host of associations, for good or for ill.

Music is the most symbolic of the arts, or at any rate the least literal. Except when the composer is setting a text, or is tied to a prescriptive "program" (as in nineteenth-century programmatic music), the listener's imagination is allowed to roam free. The sounds themselves are the symbols, and their exact meaning is left for each individual to decide. No one interpretation is privileged. Nevertheless, throughout history every composer has had an expressive intent—has suggested in the most general terms what the listener should experience in his or her music. That is the very nature of musical communication.

Not surprisingly, the means by which composers have suggested musical meaning have changed over the centuries. Beginning in the High Renaissance, composers gradually developed a system whereby a variety of expressive gestures could stimulate specific responses on the part of the listener. This was possible because, at first, the expressive gestures were closely tied to a specific phrase of text. If the words of a motet or madrigal said "and he ascended on high," the music would rise in pitch and become lighter in texture. Conversely, if the text read "and he fell into the flaming pits of Hell," the music would descend, become denser in texture, and likely would be filled with painful dissonance. In the course of time, these localized, imitative gestures continued to communicate meaning even when a text was no longer present. Composers from Vivaldi to Bach, Beethoven, and Tchaikovsky all used this method of expression in purely instrumental music.

This kind of music, in which meaning is suggested at every moment by an array of commonly understood expressive gestures, might well be called mimetic or, perhaps, onomatopoeic music. Once the conventional devices, or codes, are established, music sounds out its meaning. The listener may know nothing of the subject matter of a composition, but he or she can intuit its general significance—happy or sad, bellicose or pacific—simply by following the expressive gestures. We hear Beethoven's Symphony No. 3 as heroic, even without knowing that its title is *Eroica*.

Early music, however, did not work this way. Most music written before 1530—to pick a date somewhat arbitrarily—expresses meaning in a wholly different fashion. It does so by means of a different kind of symbolism, a symbolism that is all but lost to modern listeners.

To prove the point, listen to any three religious works composed before 1530. One might celebrate the tender compassion of the Virgin Mary, another might mourn the dead, and the last might commemorate a militant warrior, such as St. Michael. The music for all three compositions will sound the same: an indistinguishable stream of polyphony, however beautiful. The tender, mournful, or bellicose content of the respective pieces will not seem to be communicated through the music. Even trained musicologists will be unable to identify the subject matter or spiritual message of the individual works unless they happen to know these particular compositions. But surely this music had distinctive meaning for the composers who wrote it in the late Middle Ages. Surely a motet for the Virgin was intended to convey different sentiments than a motet for St. Michael. If we do not hear the distinction today, it is because we do not understand the language of musical communication in early music. To do so, we must attune our ears to these earlier auditory symbols, just as we sensitize our minds to the meaning of earlier visual signs such as the maze.

Symbolism in Early Music

Symbolism was a primary means of artistic communication in the West from the Middle Ages to the beginning of the Enlightenment in the seventeenth century.[1] It was most intensely expressed, in music no less than the visual arts, during the late Middle Ages and early Renaissance. Many of the great musicians of the time—Guillaume Dufay (c.1400–1474) and Josquin Desprez (c.1455–1521), to name just two—enjoyed the same ecclesiastical and courtly patrons as the great symbolic painters—Jan van Eyck (c.1390–1441) and Hans Memling (c.1433–1494) among them. But music, of course, is a unique mode of expression involving sounds and silences passing in time. The physical objects employed by the artists as symbols in their paintings—lilies, crosses, anchors, and palm branches, for example—could not enter into music. But composers of early music devised many other ways to project the theme of a religious composition. They met the challenge of symbolizing through sound in ways that range from the naive to the esoteric.

The most overt musical symbolism appeared in "symbolic scores," music manuscripts in which the layout on the page suggested the composer's intent.[2] The musical lines (staves) of a love song might be disposed to form a heart; a circular canon (round) might be written in notation that curved in a circle back to the beginning; or a funeral dirge might be composed entirely in black notes. More than one composition, as we shall see, was set down on the page in the shape of a maze.[3] Needless to say, only the performers who sang or played from such labyrinthine scores could enjoy the symbolism written on the page. This music had to be seen to be understood.

But musical symbolism could also be communicated in more subtle ways, namely by means of number. Notes within a motet could be arranged in groups of thirty, for example, to represent Judas's betrayal of Christ for thirty pieces of silver.[4] A large rhythmic pattern of 6:4:2:3 might be created to suggest the proportions of the biblical Temple of Solomon (60 by 40 by 20 by 30 cubits).[5] Jacob Obrecht composed his *Missa Sub tuum presidium* in precisely 888 measures, probably to symbolize Christ—8, and by extension 888, being the Lord's traditional number.[6] Number symbolism, of course, was not limited to music. The octagonal labyrinths at Reims and Amiens, for example, each incorporate eleven tracks to suggest human struggle and eight sides to signify the perfection of Christ.[7]

Finally, composers conveyed meaning in early music by symbolic musical processes. An unusual or striking technical procedure appears in a composition in order to amplify the meaning of the text. A portion of the Mass that speaks of the son born of the father ("Et ex patre natum"), for example, might suddenly burst into a canon, with a second voice duplicating exactly the pitches of the first, to symbolize that the son emerges from, yet is identical to, the father.[8] Similarly, a composition treating the subject of the wheel of Fortune might modulate progressively through many keys to suggest the turning motion of a wheel.[9] Symbolic communication such as this was commonly understood by the intelligentsia of the church and court. Indeed, such an art was premised on a shared set of symbolic conventions, musical practices that disappeared with the advent of early modern Europe.

Important to the maze and the warrior within it is the symbolic process of reversal. As we saw in Chapter 2, the most perfect form of the medieval church labyrinth possesses a beautiful, double-retrograding rhythm. Similarly, Christ's journey from Heaven to Hell and back involved a recursive progress, a miraculous reversal, as medieval theologians often emphasized.[10] Two early motets reveal how retrograde motion might be used for symbolic purposes in music.

In the Anglo-Norman motet *Queen of Mercy (Regne de pité)*,[11] dating from the mid-fourteenth century, four voices sing of the virtues of the bountiful Virgin Mary and contrast her with the barren woman Eve. The tenor part is only half as long as the others, but the last line of text, "You are the reverse of Eve in sound and meaning" *(Tu es Eva la besturné de vois et d'entendement)*, reveals that the tenor is to be sung as a retrograde, moving from the first notes to the end and then backward to the beginning. Here both text and music delight in a spiritual palindrome: Eve is the opposite of Mary, just as "Eva" is the reverse of "Ave," the first word of the angelic salutation of Gabriel, "Hail, Mary full of grace."

Two hundred years later, the composer Jacobus Clemens non Papa (c.1510–1555) also made use of this symbolic process in his five-voice motet *Thou Art Entirely Beautiful (Tota pulchra es)*, written in honor of St. Margaret. The text recalls the story of how Satan, in the form of a dragon, consumed Margaret and how she was able to burst free from the belly of the beast by means of the cross that she clutched in her right hand.[12] The moment of her escape is signified in the music by a biblical quote: "Go backwards, Satan," or "Get behind me, Satan" ("Vade retro Satanas"), the words by which Christ commanded the Devil to retreat (Luke 4:8). From this point on the tenor chants its litany-like petition to Margaret in exact retrograde motion. Reverse motion functions as the musical equivalent of a spiritual reversal along the path of the maze or a reverse turn in a Christian wheel of Fortune.

Thus retrograde motion was used in early music to symbolize at least three theological reversals: Margaret's successful opposition to Satan, Mary's reversal of Eve, and, most important, the Lord's recursive journey from Paradise to Hell and back. As we shall see, musical retrograde is one of several symbolic processes that reveal the true meaning of the Armed Man, another warrior who goes forward and then backward.[13]

Graphic representations, number symbolism, and symbolic processes were important tools in the composer's workshop. But none of these devices was as widely, or effectively, used as *cantus firmus* technique. To put it simply, a *cantus firmus* is a pre-existing melody around which the other voices in a polyphonic piece are composed. Usually this melody is all or a portion of an old Gregorian chant, a melody that came heavily laden with symbolic meaning because each chant had a special place in the Christian liturgy. Most were sung before or after a reading of scripture. Many were chanted as the clergy stood before a statue of one saint or another, or before a stained glass window commemorating a particular event in the life of Christ, for example. The brightness of the candles, the liturgical colors in the vestments of the clergy, the smell of the incense—these too lent visual and olfactory associations to the symbolism of the text.

Although the meaning of any given Gregorian chant rests with the text, the words, paradoxically, need not always be present in order for the meaning of the chant to be expressed. Many of the most beloved chants could be stripped of their texts, and the melodies alone would still communicate the original spiritual theme. So closely associated was an individual melody with a particular phrase of sacred text that the singing of a few notes would be all that was necessary for the faithful to recall the intended message; the opening notes of *The Star Spangled Banner* or the theme from *Star Wars* have a similar effect in the secular world of today. Thus in the Middle Ages melodies such as *Salve regina* or *Pange lingua* functioned as musical symbols that could be invoked in many different religious contexts. The notes themselves served as musical icons of specific Christian themes—the intercession of Mary or the descent of the Holy Spirit in the case of the two above-named chants. Composers built polyphonic compositions around these traditional chants *(cantus firmi)*, placing the melody prominently in the tenor voice. As clearly as the trumpet of the Day of Judgment, these melodies symbolically sounded God's message.

At first only sacred Gregorian chants were employed as *cantus firmi*. By the mid-fifteenth century, however, secular tunes with vernacular texts were made to serve the same purpose. Strange as it may seem, sacred Masses were built on such popular songs as *If my Face Blushes (Se la face ay pale)*, *Goodbye, my Love (Adieu mes amours)*, *Desperate Fortune (Fortuna desperata)*, and *The Armed Man (L'Homme armé)*. When placed in an ecclesiastical context and surrounded by a host of religious artifacts, popular tunes miraculously became sacred signifiers.

The Armed Man Tune

Along the vast expanse of early music history, one group of works stands out with exceptional prominence. It is a collection of more than thirty-five *cantus firmus* Masses, nearly all written between 1450 and 1585, that incorporate a tune with a French text beginning *L'Homme armé*—in English, *The Armed Man*.[14] This group of Masses constitutes "the most famous musical tradition of this age."[15] Masses incorporating the Armed Man tune outnumber those employing any other *cantus firmus* nearly ten to one. Indeed, no other melody in the history of music has been borrowed as often—settings of *Greensleeves* or *God Save the King (America)*, for example, pale in

EXAMPLE 6.1 The popular tune *L'Homme armé* (Naples, Biblioteca nazionale, MS VI.E.40, fol. 58v).

numerical importance. Even in the twentieth century, half a dozen composers have set the tune as a means of establishing a musical dialogue with the distant past.[16]

Why this extraordinary interest in this one French song? Did it allude to contemporary historical events, such as the Crusades? Did it have some hidden spiritual meaning connected to the maze? Pursuit of these questions will lead us to still more Christian heroes. But let's start at the beginning, with the Armed Man and his tune (Example 6.1).

> The armed man, the armed man, should be feared.[17]
> Everywhere the cry has gone out,
> Everyone should arm himself
> With a breastplate of iron.
> The armed man, the armed man, should be feared.[18]
>
> L'homme, l'homme, l'homme armé, l'homme armé
> L'homme armé doibt on doubter, doibt on doubter
> On a fait partout crier

Que chascun se viegne armer[19]
D'un haubregon de fer
L'homme, l'homme, l'homme armé, l'homme armé
L'homme armé doibt on doubter.

Clearly, this is a war cry, a call to arms. Yet the brevity of the text leaves much to the imagination. Who is the Armed Man that has necessitated, or is making, this call to arms? The ordinary citizen is urged to take up arms in the presence of a warrior, but against whom? Is this warrior friend or foe? Are we to arm ourselves and join with the Armed Man, or gird ourselves to fight against him? Is the tune a secular song or a chant from the church?

With its French text, catchy rhythms, rounded structure (ABA'), and clear-cut tonality, the Armed Man tune is certainly of secular origin. Perhaps it originated as a folk song that first passed among the people as an unwritten melody, part of popular oral tradition.[20] Perhaps it served as a call to arms, one played from a watchtower at the approach of the enemy.[21] Perhaps it was the product of a skilled composer working at a secular court and writing so as to emulate the style of popular music.[22]

Whether popular or courtly in origin, the Armed Man tune soon became a favorite with musicians everywhere in Europe, appearing in keyboard and dance music as well as in vocal medleys.[23] But most important, during the fifteenth and sixteenth centuries, the tune provided a musical scaffold (a *cantus firmus*) upon which skilled polyphonists composed at least three dozen sacred Masses.[24] Thus not only was the Armed Man melody widely popular, it was equally at home in profane and sacred musical contexts. Like the maze itself, it resonated with both worldly and religious overtones.

Sanctifying the Mundane in Late Medieval Art

When the Armed Man tune was sung or played in the secular world, in a tavern or inn, for example, its meaning was presumably clear to all. This was a song about soldiering. Similarly, when it was sung in church or chapel as part of the ceremony of the Mass, the meaning was equally clear to every worshiper. Yet those profane and sacred meanings may not have been the same. Indeed, they could not have been the same. Over the centuries, ecclesiastical authorities had been vigilant to keep secular musicians out of the sacrosanct confines of the church. Minstrels and *jongleurs,* for example, were banned because they belonged to an undesirable class of public entertainers that included dancers, acrobats, actors, and prostitutes.[25] Yet while the secular musician was barred from the church, a secular tune might be sanctioned, but only if it were transformed, its meaning changed and sanctified in some way, so as to project a tenet of Christian doctrine. The tune thereby ceased to be a secular object and became a sacred symbol.

At no time in the history of the Western Church was religious symbolism more widespread than at the end of the Middle Ages.[26] In this profoundly spiritual period, every article of Christian faith was transformed into a visible object. Christ's power to defend and protect was transferred, in the popular mind, to the amulet of the cross that warded off evil spirits. Mary's capacity to intercede before her son could be seen and felt in the beads of the rosary, the cult of which emerged in the early fifteenth century. Saints came to be associated with specific objects that symbolized their role as helpmates of Christ. St. Peter had his keys, St. Lawrence his grill, and St. Catherine her wheel. By these signs the faithful came to know them. An altarpiece depicting the annunciation might symbolize the virginity of Mary by a lily, her purity by a water basin, the word of God by an open book, and Christ's escape from the snares of Satan by a mousetrap.[27] Yes, even the humble mousetrap could signify Christ's ultimate victory on the Cross, for according to Augustine, Satan is caught by the bait of Christ's blood—"the Cross of the Lord was the Devil's mousetrap *(muscipulum).*"[28] Thus every object in the physical world, no matter how trivial, could be made to stand for some saintly attribute or spiritual concept. These quotidian artifacts signified the meaning of the Christian story. They, rather than abstract doctrine, told the people what to believe. Seeing was believing.

An altarpiece, by definition, must be put at the altar of the church. Before it the priest celebrates the most holy of Christian mysteries, the transubstantiation of bread and wine into the body and blood of Christ. In this sacrament, common commodities—bread and wine—are sanctified. The same is true of the medieval religious painting. When the altarpiece was put in place in the church, the objects depicted therein became sacred symbols because they amplified the Christian message. The plain brass bowl signified that Mary was to be the sacred vessel of the coming Christ. The cruciform mousetrap foretold Satan's defeat. The ultimate destiny of these artifacts was no different from that of the maze, for the labyrinth had once been a mundane object on the floor of the Roman villa and then became, during the course of the Middle Ages, a sacred symbol within the Christian sanctuary. Because the medieval church was a catholic house of all-embracing reinterpretation, secular articles such as these—a maze, a mousetrap, and a popular tune—came to be welcome there as newly converted Christian symbols.

Toward the Identity of the Armed Man

In the Christian Middle Ages all art was functional art—this is the great lesson Johan Huizinga has taught us.[29] All art had a purpose. There was, moveover, no distinction between "high art" and "low art." An altarpiece stood at the altar of a church, not in an art gallery. The same great hands that created what we call a masterpiece also painted the ducal flag pole. Similarly, a polyphonic Mass was sung before an altar in the sanctuary or in a side-chapel of the church, not in a concert hall as is often done today. Medieval composers did not create music for the sake of music—autonomous, mysterious works for generations yet unborn to contemplate. That would come only with nineteenth-century Romanticism. Instead, they wrote with an expectation of immediate realization—a performance—within some precisely defined societal activity. Music was created for immediate enjoyment, to dance to after dinner; or to serve some pressing spiritual need, to sing as part of a religious service.

If meaning in pre-modern art can be assessed by determining the function of an object, then to determine the symbolism of the Armed Man it is only necessary to identify the liturgical function of the Armed Man Mass. Two documents from sixteenth-century Germany do just that. One reveals that the Armed Man Mass was appropriate for the feast of a great Christian warrior, St. Michael (September 29),[30] while another calls the Armed Man Mass a "Missa Dominicalis"—literally a Mass of the Lord, a Mass of Christ, but at the same time, speaking in terms of liturgical ceremony, a Mass for Sunday, the Lord's Day.[31] The Armed Man, it would seem, is more than one warrior. Depending on the context, he is Christ, St. Michael, and, as we shall see, every Christian soldier.

The Armor of Spiritual Virtue

In the age of chivalry, few symbols were more pervasive than a knight's armor, for this period was as deeply militaristic as it was spiritual. For more than five hundred years, roughly 1050 to 1571, soldiers of the Latin church embarked on, or swore to embark on, crusades to reclaim the Holy Land. The collective virtues of the brave, pious warrior formed a behavioral code against which the conduct of all men was to be measured. When sculpted on the portals of the medieval cathedral—as at Chartres, Amiens, and Reims, for example—the Christian knight appears in full armor, with sword, breastplate, helmet, and shield. Here at each church he personifies the allegorical figure Fortitude.[32] When Fortitude speaks,[33] he does so by quoting a famous scriptural passage from the letters of St. Paul (Ephesians 6:11–17):

> Put on the whole armour of God, that ye may be able to stand against the wiles of the devil. For we wrestle not against flesh and blood, but against principalities, against powers, against the rulers of the darkness of this world, against spiritual wickedness in high places. Wherefore take unto you the whole armour of God, that ye may be able to withstand in the evil day, and having done all, to stand. Stand therefore, having your loins girt about with truth, and having on the breastplate of righteousness; and your feet shod with the preparation of the gospel of peace; Above all, taking the shield of faith, wherewith ye shall be able to quench all the fiery darts of the wicked. And take the helmet of salvation, and the sword of the Spirit, which is the word of God.[34]

St. Paul's courageous Christian, clothed with the armor of spiritual virtue, was a powerful image in the Latin West for more than sixteen hundred years. Visions of the biblical "breastplate of righteousness," "shield of faith," and "helmet of salvation" were shared by St. Jerome and other patristic fathers.[35] Gregory of Nyssa (c.331–c.396) imagines an army following in step beyond its general, the Redeemer, as it marches out of the labyrinth.[36] In a tenth-century English *Descent into Hell*, Christ himself says that John the Baptist supplied him with spiritual armor so that he might triumph in the battle of the Cross: "I have endured much since you came to me before, when you entrusted to me sword and armour, helmet and battledress."[37]

FIGURE 6.1 "Grace shows Pilgrim his sacred armor" in a fifteenth-century illumination from Guillaume de Deguileville's *The Pilgrimage of Human Life* (c.1331).

Later, in William Langland's *Piers Plowman* (c.1360) Christ is again depicted wearing the helmet and breastplate, this time as signs of his earthly humanity. His breastplate *(haberioun)* is identical to the iron breastplate (the *haubregon de fer*) required of all citizens in the Armed Man tune.

> This Iesus of his gentrice wole Iuste in Piers armes
> In his helme and in his haberioun, *humana natura.*[38]

Similarly, the mystical theologian Henry Suso (c.1295–1366) urges all Christians to take up divine armor in his *Clock of Wisdom* (*Horologium Sapientiae*): "Put on as a giant the dress of war. Take to yourself my armor. An arms-bearer should follow his lord."[39] In a related work, called *Little Book of Eternal Wisdom* (*Büchlein der ewigen Weisheit),* Suso assumes the voice of Christ and commands the faithful to enter the knightly arena dressed for battle:

Away with faint-heartedness and enter with me the lists of knightly
steadfastness. Indulgence is not fitting for the servant when the lord is
practicing warlike boldness. I shall clothe you with my armor because all
my suffering has to be endured by you as far as you are able.[40]

Sometimes Christ is the Armed Man, and sometimes he is the purveyor
of arms. Sometimes, too, the armor once worn by Christ is given to the pilgrim, who thereby becomes a Christian soldier. The pilgrim steps forward
in Guillaume de Deguileville's *The Pilgrimage of Human Life* (*Le Pèlerinage
de la vie humaine*, c.1331), a work whose popularity in the late Middle Ages
approached that of the Bible.[41] As he sets out on his journey through life,
Pilgrim is given a set of armor by the allegorical figure Grace (Fig. 6.1). This
is no ordinary armor, but divine armor sent down from heaven with the
power to effect miraculous reversals:

> "These arms will defend you," says Grace, "and you will vanquish all your
> enemies." First, she provides him with a coat of mail, a gambeson, to
> which she gives the allegorical name Patience. "Jesus wore this gambeson
> when he was hung on the cross for you ... Those who wear it find profit
> in what others see as misfortune and adversity. Storms make their grain
> grow, tempests fill their barns, and plagues fill their cellars. They make a
> soft bed of great hardship and they make of trouble a great delight. They
> take pleasure in poverty and find solace in adversity."[42]

Next, Grace offers an iron breastplate, an hauberk, which is called Fortitude: "It was made in ancient times for doing battle against Death and
against all her army—that is, against pain and torment and all their hor-
rors." It was not forged by the smiths of this earth, but rather in Heaven
from the nails of the Cross, and it is tempered with the blood of Christ. This
breastplate, like that in *Piers Plowman,* is also identical to the *haubregon de
fer* in the Armed Man tune ("Everyone should arm himself with a breastplate of iron"). Finally, Grace gives Pilgrim a helmet with visor called Tem-
perance to guard the eye from folly and vanity, a throat-guard (*gorget*)
called Sobriety to ward off the sin of gluttony, gloves called Continence, and
a sword named Justice.

Strictly speaking, the armor provided by Grace is neither knightly armor
nor the armor of the Christian soldier embarking on a crusade. It is, rather,
metaphorical armor to be worn daily by the ordinary citizen—the pilgrim,

A more Vnequal match can hardly be
Christian must fight an Angell but you see
The Valiant man by handling sword & shield
Doth make him tho a dragon quit the field

FIGURE 6.2 Christian and the dragon Apollyon in mortal combat as depicted in John Bunyan's *Pilgrim's Progress* in the fifth edition of 1682.

or soldier, of life. It repels the evils and temptations of this sinful world. It wards off death. It girds the faithful soldier during the march toward the celestial kingdom and everlasting life. This armor is the armor of the Lord. If the maze is a symbol of the confusing trials and travails of this world, the armor of spiritual virtue is a metaphor for the protection Christ provides the faithful soldier during this treacherous journey. The soul must be armed for the trial of the maze.[43]

The power of Guillaume de Deguileville's allegorical fiction endured for centuries. The Renaissance poet Edmund Spenser borrowed from it, as did his later countryman John Bunyan.[44] In fact, Bunyan's enormously popular *Pilgrim's Progress* (1678) was modeled directly upon an early English translation of Deguileville's *The Pilgrimage of Human Life.* Thus it is not surprising to find Bunyan's Pilgrim, now appropriately named Christian, escorted to an armory by three virtues, namely Piety, Prudence, and Charity. Here he, too, puts on the armor of spiritual virtue:

> The next day they took him into the Armory, where they showed him all manner of Furniture, which their Lord had provided for Pilgrims, as Sword, Shield, Helmet, Breast-plate, All-Prayer, and Shoes that would not wear out. And there was here enough of this to harness out as many men for the service of their Lord as there be stars in the Heaven.[45]

Next the three virtues show Christian the weapons used by ancient warriors against the forces of evil: the Rod of Moses, the Hammer and Nail of Joel, the Trumpets of Gideon, the Jaw-bone of Samson, the Sling and Stone with which David slew Goliath, and finally "the Sword also with which their Lord will kill the Man of Sin, in the day that he shall rise up to the prey."

Now dressed in Christ's armor, Christian continues his pilgrimage, only to encounter the hideous dragon, Apollyon, sent by Beelzebub (Satan). They engage in mortal combat (Fig. 6.2). Just when the dragon appears to have won, Christian gives a deadly thrust and snatches victory from the jaws of defeat. At this crucial moment, as with the resurrection of Christ, a miraculous reversal occurs. Christian exalts: "Rejoyce not against me, O mine enemy! when I fall, I shall arise" (Micah 7:8).[46] His triumph now complete, Christian offers a hymn of thanksgiving to St. Michael and to the Lord's double-edged sword.

Great Beelzebub, the Captain of this Fiend,
Design'd my ruin, therefore to this end
He sent him harnest out, and he with rage
That Hellish was, did fiercely me engage:
But blessed Michael helped me, and I
By dint of Sword did quickly make him flye;
Therefore to him let me give lasting praise,
And thank, and bless his holy name always.[47]

The armory is becoming crowded with warriors. Christ was the first and last knight to wear the armor of spiritual virtue. Through faith and fortitude, the Lord triumphed on the Cross. He will wield the sword of justice in the last great battle. In the course of the Middle Ages *Christus Victor* became the hero of the West's great drama of salvation, superseding Theseus and Aeneas from classical mythology, and Moses and David from Hebrew scripture. Theseus entered into the labyrinth and defeated the Minotaur; Aeneas descended into Hades and returned victorious; Moses did battle with the army of the Pharaoh, and David with Goliath. St. Michael was a squire to both Christ and Christian. But there are other warriors important to this primeval combat myth. With the dawn of the Renaissance and its renewed interest in classical literature, brave Jason and mighty Hercules now come forward as paladins of Christ. They, too, take up the armor of spiritual virtue and march forth beside the Armed Man.

CHAPTER SEVEN

Sounds and Symbols of an Armed Man

THE CHRISTIAN ARMED MAN marched forward and backward through the maze of life into the seventeenth century. Sometimes his name was Christ, sometimes St. Michael, and sometimes simply Christian. Yet no matter what his station, his armor of spiritual virtue guaranteed victory. Evil changed to good, want to abundance, tempests to tranquillity, and death to eternal life—these divine reversals came to pass simply by donning in good faith the Lord's metaphorical armor. In music such reversals could be symbolized by means of retrograde motion: a predetermined melody *(cantus firmus)* in a Mass or motet would be made to move forward and then backward. When that melody is the Armed Man tune, the Christian warrior appears to rise up from ages past and make his round-trip journey before our eyes.

Guillaume Dufay's Mass for Warrior and Lamb

Sometime during the late 1450s or early 1460s—we can't be sure precisely when—the French composer Guillaume Dufay wrote the first polyphonic Mass incorporating the Armed Man tune, his *Missa L'Homme armé.*[1] Here the specter of the Armed Man rises from the tenor voice. He appears in long notes once in the *Kyrie,* twice in the *Gloria,* three times in the *Credo,* twice in the *Sanctus,* and three times in the *Agnus dei.* The symbolism of the Mystical Lamb reaches its climax in the final movement of the Mass, the three-fold petition *Agnus dei.* In the first supplication, "Lamb of God who taketh away the sins of the world," the Armed Man marches straight ahead in the tenor. In the second "Lamb of God," he falls silent. But in the third and final supplication, the Armed Man proceeds backward and then forward, again in the tenor. The recursive motion is effected by means of a brief di-

rective to the singers: "Rule: Let the crab go forward fully but go backward
from the middle" *(Canon: Cancer eat plenus sed redeat medius)*. Since a crab
goes backward, the tenors are first to sing the tune backward and, once that
is accomplished, then forward.

For Dufay, this contrapuntal *tour de force*—writing good counterpoint
against a melody going backward—was both the musical and symbolic
high point of the Mass. For the modern listener, however, this climactic
moment sounds decidedly anti-climactic. The compelling Armed Man
tune, by moving backward, has lost its force, like a soldier who charges
backward. Rather, in this retrograde version the music sounds like a non-
sensical abstraction. This one moment of musical retrograde underscores
the fundamental difference between the medieval way of communicating
through symbol and the more modern method of musical expression by
means of mimetic gesture. What was for Dufay a crowning moment of
symbolic communication goes unheard by the modern listener unless
alerted in advance to the retrograde motion and its meaning. The listener
of Dufay's time, however, being familiar with the tune and all of its attendant symbolism, would have recognized the retrograde motion and experienced all the subliminal associations the composer intended: to the Mystical Lamb, to Christ the Alpha and Omega of all things, to the Lord's
round-trip journey, and perhaps to the recursive maze.

Statistical evidence proves the composer's symbolic intent. Of the more
than two hundred extant compositions by Guillaume Dufay, only three incorporate retrograde motion, and the subject of each is the Mystical Lamb
of God. For Dufay, the Mystical Lamb went forward and backward.

How would Dufay have come to know of the symbolism of the retrograding warrior/lamb? The sacrificial lamb who returned annually to its
point of origin was a primordial theme, one played out in Christian circles
through the Easter ritual on the maze. As a cleric of the archdiocese of
Reims, Dufay would have known of the mazes at Reims and at nearby St.
Quentin; as the leader of the papal singers resident at Santa Maria in Trastevere in Rome, he would have been familiar with that labyrinth as well.[2] But
most telling, Dufay read about the retrograding hero in his personal library,
which included a copy of Guillaume de Deguileville's *Pilgrimage of the Soul*
(*Pèlerinage de l'ame*, 1355).[3] As in Deguileville's earlier *Pilgrimage of Human
Life*,[4] we again meet Pilgrim, the wandering soul who represents all of humanity. Here Pilgrim proceeds in a dream-like vision from earth to Purga-

tory to Heaven and back to earth. Toward the end of the poem, we see the zodiacal signs that symbolize Christ. Among them is Cancer, the formation that appears in the heavens at the moment of the summer solstice, when the sun reaches its apogee in the northern hemisphere and begins to move backward in its annual circular journey.[5] Deguileville states that the crab is a Christological symbol because Christ made three important "round trip" journeys: one when he came down to earth and then ultimately returned to Heaven, another when he went from life to death and then back to eternal life, and yet another when he descended into Hell and returned.[6] Thus not only Aries but also Cancer might serve as the celestial sign of Christ.

> This sign is called Cancer
> Symbolizing the returns and
> Reversals that it makes.
> Three times Christ came back
> And returned whence he had come.
> He descended into Hell
> And when he accomplished his aim
> He soon after returned.
> He also went from life to death,
> But returned in three days
> Making a very joyous return.
> He also came to earth
> For the humankind he loved,
> And escaped by his death
> From which he also returned
> To Heaven whence he had come
> Where he was joyfully received.
> These are the three glorious returns.[7]

Since Deguileville's book was in Dufay's library, he must have known about this stellar symbolism. When he wished to instruct the Armed Man to go backward in the *Agnus dei* of his Armed Man Mass, as we have seen, he did so by reference to the sign of Cancer: "Let the crab [or Christ] go forward fully but go backward from the middle."

The Armed Man, St. Michael, and the Apocalypse

There are many heros of the maze, be it the maze of Greek mythology, the labyrinth on the floor of a Christian church, or the metaphorical maze of life. This is not surprising, for the characters in every true myth are protean figures that, over the course of centuries, assume many different forms. But no matter what the name of the hero is, all versions of the story of the maze have a common theme: combat between good and evil. And no description of battle is more extreme, more vivid, indeed more bizarre, than the phantasmagorical account of the war between the godly and the demonic in the Book of Apocalypse (Revelation).[8] Here a vision of the final great battle preliminary to the end of all time unfolds in a vast panorama. The savior who leads the charge is not the evangelist's merciful shepherd but Christ the avenging warrior, a man of arms, who brings death and destruction (Apocalypse 14:14–20). As the Last Judgment approaches, the army of the Lord crushes the Devil and his earthly minions. Only then can the just enjoy the fruits of divine promise.

During the fiscal year 1462–1463, a notary at the cathedral of Cambrai in northern France recorded a payment of four *livres* to the scribe Symon Mellet for having copied "the Mass of Regis written upon the Armed Man" *(le messe Regis sus l'ome armé).*[9] Johannes Regis (c.1430–1496) was a protégé of Guillaume Dufay, and his Armed Man Mass is the first of several to brim with apocalyptic imagery.[10] The archangel Michael looms here as well, for not only is the Armed Man tune used as a *cantus firmus* but so too are chants and texts honoring St. Michael. Sometimes words in praise of Michael are set upon the Armed Man tune. Principal among these is "While John saw the sacred mystery, the archangel Michael blew the trumpet" *(Dum sacrum mysterium cerneret Johannes, archangelus Michael tuba cecinit),* a text which conflates images of the warrior Michael and the trumpet of the Last Judgment. Putting the text of one *cantus firmus* on the melody of another conveys the spiritual message of two chants in the space of one. Thus Regis saturates the air with symbolic references not only by often using two *cantus firmi* simultaneously—the Armed Man melody and a chant for St. Michael —but also by assigning a double meaning to the Armed Man tune. Sometimes the Armed Man is Christ, and sometimes he is St. Michael.

The archangel Michael had long occupied an important place in West-

FIGURE 7.1 An illuminated Apocalypse prepared for King Edward I of England c.1285. As the Mystical Lamb breaks the fifth seal, Michael gives white robes of martyrdom to those arising from Purgatory.

ern theology.[11] The name *mīkā'el* in Hebrew means "He who is like God," and Michael was seen as a protector of the Israelites during the Babylonian Captivity (Daniel 12:1). In the Old Testament Michael disputes with the Devil for the disposition of the body of Moses (Jude 9), a prefiguration of his role as guardian of the souls of the elect. Ultimately, in the Book of Apocalypse (12:7–9) he leads the celestial soldiers to victory over the dragon (Satan) and his imps. Apocryphal books of both the Old and New Testament, as well as church fathers such as Augustine and John Chrysostom, attribute other actions to Michael: he descends into Hell to retrieve the souls of those who are to sit on the right hand of God the Father; he chains Satan in Hell at Christ's command; he holds the book in which the names of the elect are recorded; and he weighs the souls of all humanity on the Day of Judgment.

Each of these images of the warrior Michael, militant champion of the church, is depicted countless times in the sculpture, stained glass, altarpieces, and manuscript illuminations of the Middle Ages and beyond.[12] A late thirteenth-century illuminated Apocalypse shows Michael providing white robes to the newly liberated as the Mystical Lamb unseals the book (Fig. 7.1). In the Rohan Master's illumination of the Office of the Dead (c.1425) the angel Michael, sword in hand, contends with the Devil to save a human soul teetering between the land of the dead and Christ's throne (Fig. 7.2). Similarly, in an altarpiece painted by Josse Lieferinxe around 1480, Michael slays the dragon while holding the scales of the Last Judgment (Fig. 7.3); his power derives from the sign of the cross emblazoned on his iron breastplate.

Michael's triumph in battle is an allegory of Christ's triumph on the cross.[13] Wearing the Lord's armor, the archangel defeats the forces of evil; his instrument of victory is the warrior's sword. Nailed to the cross, Christ conquers Satan and frees humankind from sin; his instrument of triumph is the wood of the cross. Consequently, churches in Northern Europe began to include the story of Michael's victory in the liturgy of Easter Sunday. Easter was said to encapsulate the entire history of the world: "On that day the world was created, Adam was given life, the lamb was sacrificed for Isaac, the sons of Israel passed through the Red Sea, Christ was made incarnate and sacrificed, and Michael was victorious over the Devil."[14] In the Middle Ages the visual arts, liturgy, and music worked together to amplify common themes. A Mass honoring St. Michael, such as Regis's Armed Man Mass, would have been entirely appropriate on Easter Sunday or on any other Sunday (the Lord's day) which honored Christ the Savior.

Christ, of course, is the lord of champions. But he combines humility with fortitude, as we see in the *Sanctus* of Regis's Armed Man Mass. While the alto sings the Armed Man tune, the tenor chants "Hosanna" to the melody of the famous antiphon *Pueri Hebreorum portantes*.[15] Proclaimed universally at the procession before Mass on Palm Sunday, this chant invokes another powerful image: Christ entering Jerusalem astride the back of a humble donkey as the Hebrew children strew his path with palms, a traditional symbol of victory. This was the Lord's most triumphant moment on earth, and it preceded by a week his culminating spiritual conquest on Easter Sunday.[16]

Thus the Armed Man Mass of Johannes Regis emphasizes the theme of Christian victory: Christ's triumph of Easter week, as well as St. Michael's combat with the Prince of Darkness. To create a vision of these Christian

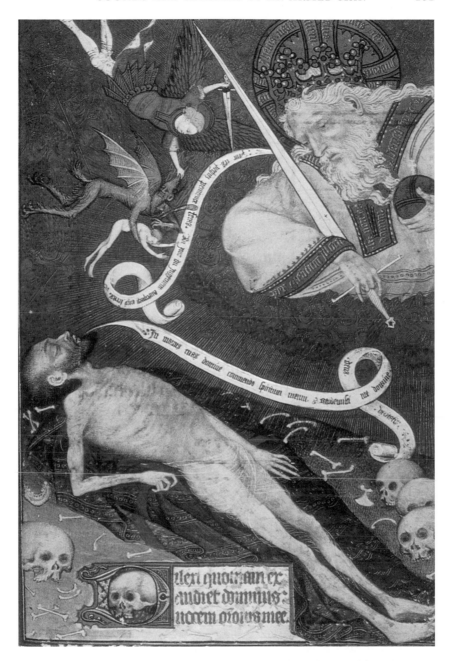

FIGURE 7.2 Manuscript painting of the Last Judgment from the early fifteenth-century Rohan Hours. St. Michael wars with the Devil for control of a soul, while Christ (identified as Jesus Nazarenus Rex Judeorum) looks with compassion upon the dead man.

FIGURE 7.3 St. Michael slays the dragon while balancing the scales of justice. Painting on wood by Josse Lieferinxe, c.1480.

FIGURE 7.4 John sees the Apocalypse as painted by Hans Memling (1479), part of a fifteenth-century altarpiece for the Hospital of St. John, Bruges.

battles in word and music, Regis puts into play a host of verbal references and musical allusions—passages from Apocalypse, the Armed Man tune, chants from the office of St. Michael, and the famous Palm Sunday antiphon *Pueri Hebreorum portantes*—that reinforce and redefine one another in new and unexpected ways. In the *Gloria,* for example, Christ the Mystical Lamb opens the book of the seven seals while Michael leads the angelic host. In the *Sanctus* John sees the Apocalypse, Michael plays the trumpet of the Last Judgment, and Christ enters Jerusalem. Regis's Armed Man Mass is thus not unlike Hans Memling's *The Last Judgment* (1475–1479), in which Christian art reinforces Christian dogma (Fig. 7.4). In a single tableau John foresees the fate of all things (bottom part of the painting), the four horsemen bring destruction to the earth (middle), St. Michael and his warrior angels harass the dragon and throw down the rebel angels (above right), while the Mystical Lamb of God leaps nimbly to the knee of the Lord to open the Book of the Seven Seals (above left). Whereas Memling captures John's eschatological vision in paint on canvas, Regis does so in pitches and words. For the spiritually attuned listener of the fifteenth century, this collection of symbolic sounds and verbal associations created a vivid picture of the ultimate end of the world.

The Apocalyptic Vision of the Naples Armed Man Masses

Duke Charles the Bold of Burgundy was the personification of the headstrong warrior.[17] Ultimately, he lost his life, and most of the Burgundian territories, at the battle of Nancy (1477). But Charles was also a music lover, and among the music he enjoyed was a set of six Armed Man Masses composed or collected at his court and then sent to the King of Naples in Italy.[18] No composer's name appears in the collection, but most believe it is the work of Antoine Busnois (c.1440–1492), a composer Duke Charles had personally chosen for his court.[19]

What makes this collection of Armed Man Masses unique in the annals of music history is the fact that the six were fashioned so as to form an interlocking set.[20] Each of the first five Masses highlights one word, image, and musical segment from the Armed Man tune, and the sixth Mass once again rejoins them. The themes of the Masses, with their French and Latin signifiers, are as follows:

Mass I: "man" ("homme" = "homo")
Mass II: "armed" ("armé" = "armatus")
Mass III: "to be feared" ("doibt on doubter" = "timende")
Mass IV: "to cry to all" ("crier" = "clamando")
Mass V: "breastplate" ("haubregon de fer" = "lorica")
Mass VI: all of the above

The sixth and final Mass serves as a culmination of the preceding five as the limbs of the Armed Man are reincorporated. By breaking the *cantus firmus* into smaller units in the first five Masses, the composer is able to work with a short melody that can easily be subjected to a series of symbolic musical processes. Precisely how these processes are to unfold is revealed by a canon (a set of verbal instructions) that precedes each Mass. Like most instructional canons in music, these are puzzles or brain teasers. Fortunately, the composer has supplied a solution *(resolutio)* for each. Table B.1 in Appendix B shows the distribution of music, the canons, and the text of each *Kyrie* of each of the six Armed Man Masses.

As the verbal canons unfold, the tenor voice becomes personified as the Armed Man. Like a ghost from the dead, his figure rises up by means of the ingenuity of the instructions. His movements, up or down, backward or forward, dictate the motion and actions of the tenor voice. If the Armed Man goes backward, the music of the Armed Man tune proceeds in retrograde motion; if he jumps up four steps, the music is transposed up four scale degrees; if he moves without pauses, all of the rests in the tune are to be ignored, and so forth.

The canons of the Naples Masses are not only recondite, they are also erudite. The canon to Mass VI, for example, borrows from the opening of Virgil's *Aeneid*.[21] For readers of classical literature, Aeneas was the ideal man of arms, the personification of manliness of body and wisdom of mind.[22] Like Christ, Aeneas descended into the Underworld (*Aeneid*, Book VI), a journey that would be allegorized by medieval theologians as a heroic Christian quest.[23] Later, during the Renaissance, Aeneas would serve as a stand-in for the Church or for the Pope, depending on the context.[24] Here in these anonymous Masses, Christ is now equated with Aeneas: a man of arms who conquers by means of spiritual armor.[25]

Whereas the texts of the canons embrace the style and vocabulary of classical Latin, those of the *Kyrie* are written in the common liturgical Latin

FIGURE 7.5 Christ gives strength (the sacramental bread and wine) to the Armed
Man. In the background an army can be seen marching toward the door at the left
named "[Jerusa]lem."

of the medieval Church. Biblical kings march by, each presaging Christ as savior of humankind. From the Old Testament appear Moses and David. Moses leads the Israelites from bondage in Egypt (Exodus 14:1–31), the trumpet of the Lord gathers his followers at the foot of Mount Sinai (Exodus 19:16–20), and David defeats Goliath and the Philistines (1 Samuel 17). Moses' victory over the Pharaoh (*Kyrie* III) and David's defeat of Goliath (*Kyrie* V) were viewed by medieval Christian exegetes as prefigurations of Christ's greater victory over Satan. As Moses led his people from captivity and David saved his from the threat of oppression, so Christ will deliver his faithful from the clutches of the Devil.

But Christ's victory is a miraculous paradox: He wages war with Satan, and is victorious, through the submissive act of sacrifice. He is transfixed on the Cross (*Kyrie* I). He routs the ancient tempter and gives the palms of victory to those in the celestial kingdom (*Kyrie* II). His act of sacrifice provides the helmet, the shield, and the breastplate by which the Christians can deflect the forces of evil (*Kyrie* V). He spills his blood to redeem all humanity (*Kyrie* VI). A contemporary manuscript painting (Fig. 7.5) brings this divine transformation to life. Christ presents sacramental symbols of his body and blood (bread and wine) to an Armed Man. This soldier will become part of a vast host fighting its way along the difficult, winding road to celestial Jerusalem (written above the door), a shining city brilliantly described in the Book of Apocalypse.

Everywhere the spirit of Apocalypse hovers over the Naples Armed Man Masses. Christ appears as a savior, but also as the avenger of sins (*Kyrie* III). This is the wrathful divinity who, splattered with his own blood, wreaks vengeance by pressing out the grapes of wrath (see Fig. 4.2). He is man, God, armorer, and avenger in the ultimate court of the millennium. Everywhere the trumpet sounds (canon IV and *Kyrie* IV), first that of Moses and then the trumpet of the Last Judgment. As is well known, the trumpet of the Last Judgment is the primary musical icon in the Book of Apocalypse. Nineteen times the trumpet sounds in John's visionary account, more than in any other book of the Bible.

The seer John declares that on earth and in heaven no one but the Mystical Lamb of God is capable of opening the book of the seven seals and revealing its terrors (Apocalypse 5:6–8). A text added to the *Gloria* of Armed Man Mass VI says as much: "Lord God, lamb of God, Son of the Father who revealed the seven seals of the book." As the seals in turn are broken, a succession of disasters—warfare, famine, death, pestilence, and earthquakes—descend upon the land. The destruction of this world has begun.

The ancient spiritual conundrum "In my end is my beginning" sounds forth in these Masses as well. It first appears at the end of the canon of Mass II with the words "the end corresponds to the beginning" *(respondent ultima primis),* instructing the tenor voice to reproduce here at the end the phrase of music that it had sung at the beginning. Similarly, the end of the canon to Mass V includes the injunction: "You who are singing, give an ending that is the same as the beginning" *(principio finem da qui modularis eundem),* and again the tenor concludes by returning to the opening music. Finally, in the *Kyrie* of Mass VI God is described as the beginning, end, and founder of the immense world. This is not a musical instruction, but rather an allusion to a phrase that appears six times in the Book of Apocalypse. Christ himself is the beginning and end of all things. He is the Alpha and the Omega, and through him we end our temporal life (the Alpha) and begin our spiritual life in the world beyond (the Omega).

In all, the Armed Man marches forward and then backward eight times in these Naples Masses. The composer orders these reversals by a variety of Latin terms, among them "retrograditur," "vice versa," "cantando revertere," and "reboat." These injunctions are the musical equivalents of the words describing the great Christian reversal on the day of resurrection, when the Lord "goes back, leads back, brings back, steps back, returns, and turns back."[26] The intent here is symbolic rather than rhetorical. The music does not try to persuade the listener by growing suddenly loud, dense, or dissonant to suggest apocalyptic battles. Rather, it expresses its meaning by means of a controlled and fully rational process, the manipulation *a priori* of a tune fraught with symbolic meaning. The informed listener hears the end of the music become the beginning in an implicitly infinite process of musical renewal, just as Christ personifies endless spiritual renewal: "I am the beginning and the end, He who was once dead and is now alive" (Apocalypse 2:8).

Josquin's Music for the Armed Man and for Hercules

Josquin Desprez (c.1455–1521) is one of the finest composers who ever walked this earth.[27] His music has all the technical wizardry of Bach coupled with the grace and formal perfection of Mozart. He was capable of writing rhetorical, mimetic music of the newer style of the High Renaissance, though at the same time his Masses and motets radiate with medieval symbolism.

It is symbolism that rules his two Armed Man Masses. One is called *Armed Man Mass on Musical Pitches (Missa L'Homme armé super voces musicales)* because the Armed Man tune is made to begin on a successively higher scale each time it appears. Again, the Armed Man moves in retrograde motion, first in the *Gloria* with the words "He who taketh away the sins of the world," and then in the *Credo* where the text proceeds "And he was made flesh." The "he" who goes forward and backward in both *Gloria* and *Credo* is, of course, Christ. Retrograde motion does not appear in the *Agnus dei*. Yet in two manuscripts preserving this work in the library of the Sistine Chapel in Rome, the *Agnus dei* is decorated with a historiated initial showing the Armed Man, sword in hand, slaying Satan in the form of a dragon (Fig. 7.6).[28] Normally such a scene is placed at the beginning of a Mass so as to signal at the outset its spiritual theme.[29] But here the artist felt the appropriate place to celebrate the victory of the Armed Man would be in the midst of this final hymn to the Mystical Lamb, thereby signaling that Christ is both warrior and lamb.

The warrior/lamb also goes forward and backward in Josquin's *L'Homme armé sexti toni*—a Mass in the sixth mode, something akin to our F major scale.[30] Here the climax comes in the third and final petition of the *Agnus dei*, where the composer inserts an additional alto and soprano part, thereby increasing the total number of voices from four to six. Modern ears will hear this final plea to the Mystical Lamb as a heavenly cascade of sweet parallel thirds and sixths; the receptive soul has ascended to God's peaceable kingdom. Yet only the most historically informed listeners will perceive the medieval symbolism hidden within. The tenor sings part B of the Armed Man tune (see p. 165), while the bass starts at the end of part A and sings in retrograde motion. The Armed Man is moving forward and backward simultaneously, just as the dancers do on the maze on Easter Sunday. When the exact midpoint of the section is reached, the roles are reversed: the tenor sings part B in retrograde, the bass presents A in its original form, and all the while the altos and sopranos sing pairs of musical canons—a contrapuntal construction worthy of both Daedalus and Bach![31]

Where did Josquin learn of the symbolism of the recursive warrior/lamb? Possibly he found it in the maze placed in the garden of the château

FIGURE 7.6 The Armed Man slays the dragon at the beginning of the *Agnus dei* of Josquin Desprez's *Missa L'Homme armé super voces musicales.*

of Baugé belonging to his first patron, King René of Anjou.[32] Possibly he found it in the garden mazes at Belriguardo maintained by another patron, Ercole d'Este, duke of Ferrara.[33] Yet most likely, Josquin first experienced this doctrinal symbol on the maze at St. Quentin in his native Vermandois, France, where, it is said, he had been a choirboy.[34]

FIGURE 7.7 Labyrinth at the royal collegiate church of St. Quentin in St. Quentin.

The collegiate church of St. Quentin is one of the largest Gothic struc-
tures in France, its choir being longer than those at the more famous cathedrals of Paris and Chartres.[35] St. Quentin remains today one of just two
churches in northern Europe to preserve a pavement labyrinth from the
Middle Ages (Fig. 7.7). This maze was put in place in 1495, but it may represent a replica of an earlier labyrinth on that site.[36] Thus we cannot be certain that Josquin trod this maze as a choirboy, since the labyrinth may not
have been completed at the time of his initial sojourn there, presumably
around 1465–1470. But he surely saw it on later visits to the church when
journeying, as he often did, from Paris to his home town of Condé-sur-
l'Escaut.[37] Similarly, Josquin would have known of the Harrowing of Hell
from scenes of the life of Christ sculpted on the front of the rood screen at
St. Quentin between 1316 and 1342. The tenth of these scenes depicted "the
descent of our Lord into Hell" and carried the inscription: "In spirit the
body of Christ the warrior, nobly ordered from the tomb, went into the infernal shadows."[38]

Josquin's veneration of warriors was not limited to Christ the Armed Man,
for he composed another Mass that honors both the classical hero Hercules
and, simultaneously, Josquin's last patron, Ercole d'Este, duke of Ferrara.
    Ercole d'Este, who ruled the Italian city-state of Ferrara from 1471 to
1505, was obsessed with his namesake, the pagan demi-god Hercules. By
means of painting, sculpture, drama, and music, Ercole sought to represent
himself as a modern-day strong man.[39] For example, between 1502 and 1504
he issued a silver coin with his own likeness on the front and an image of
Hercules on the reverse.[40] At court he dressed in the armor of a military
leader (Fig. 7.8). And from his chapel master Josquin Desprez he commissioned a four-voice Mass with a double meaning: that the hero of this music is both a classical champion and his contemporary reincarnation. Ercole
is Hercules.
    The core of Josquin's *Missa Hercules dux Ferrarie* is the *Credo*, and here
the *cantus firmus* appears twelve times,[41] perhaps an allusion to the twelve
labors of Hercules.[42] At the exact midpoint of the movement, immediately
after the words "whose reign will be without end," the tenor suddenly starts
to move backward. The tenor part proceeds in retrograde motion, note for
note, until it has reached the point at which it had begun, the text "And he
was made flesh." Thus the doctrine that the Lord is the beginning and end

FIGURE 7.8 Dosso Dossi, portrait of Duke Ercole I d'Este (ruled 1471–1505) as an
Armed Man.

of all things causes the music to regress toward the beginning, to the commencement of the account of Christ's life on earth. As we have come to expect, retrograde motion also appears in the *Agnus dei,* where Hercules goes
forward and then backward. Once again, statistics demonstrate intent: in
the more than 150 compositions of Josquin Desprez, retrograde motion is
found in only three works: this Mass for Hercules and his two Armed Man
Masses. By means of musical symbolism, Josquin suggests that Hercules

and the Armed Man are fellow knights in armor. But how did the pagan hero Hercules come to be a soldier of Christ?

Like the maze itself, the mythological Hercules became Christianized in the course of the Middle Ages and early Renaissance.[43] Originally a simple tale of a simple strong man, the story of Hercules' twelve labors acquired over time a moral significance, each adventure becoming an allegory for a triumph of good over evil.[44] When standing at the crossroads of life (in the fable Hercules at the Crossroads), he opts for the narrow, high, and rocky path of Virtue, instead of the low, flat road of Vice, which leads to indolence and inescapable death.[45] Hercules' route can be seen as a Christian path, one charted in Christ's sermon on the mount: "Enter ye in at the strait gate: for wide is the gate, and broad is the way, that leadeth to destruction, and many there be which go in thereat: Because strait is the gate, and narrow is the way, which leadeth unto life, and few there be that find it" (Matthew 7:13–14). Thus Renaissance artists often depict Hercules contemplating the alternative routes of Christian Virtue and worldly Vice bifurcating before him as if in a dream (Fig. 7.9). In such illustrations Hercules is dressed in the chain-mail and armor of a man-of-arms, the armor of Christian rectitude. He symbolizes Fortitude and wears a breastplate, the traditional symbol of this cardinal virtue. In classical mythology, Hercules had no need of armor; his strength was insuperable. Now Christianized, he is engaged in the great spiritual battle of right against wrong. He has traded his club and lion's skin for the spiritual armor of the Lord, which will protect him as he follows the narrow, rocky path of Virtue along the dangerous road of life.

Like Christ, Hercules was a mortal born of a divine father, and he, too, descended into Hell. Book VI of Virgil's *Aeneid* relates how Hercules passes through the gates of the Cumean temple, where Daedalus had placed a representation of his Cretan maze, and into the mouth of Hades. There he shackles the monster Cerberus (representing human envy) with a triple chain, just as the soldiers of Christ bind Satan in the Book of Apocalypse (20:1–2).[46] This infernal descent was Hercules' twelfth and final labor, and from it he ascends.[47] An Italian illustration of the fifteenth century groups three Greek heroes who return from Hades—Orpheus the musician, Hercules, and Theseus (Fig. 7.10).[48] Theseus holds a maze with the satanic Minotaur in the center—perhaps, like the lyre held by Orpheus, a sign of his identity, or perhaps simply a symbol that the three heroes have ascended

FIGURE 7.9 Two views of Hercules at the Crossroads (1497) from two different publications of Sebastian Brant's *Stultifera Navis*. The now-armed warrior must choose either the wide path leading to a life of the flesh (and death), or the higher, rocky road leading to spiritual virtue (and the tree of eternal life).

FIGURE 7.10 Orpheus with lyre, Hercules, and Theseus with maze, three heroes who descend into Hades and return, as depicted by Leonardo da Besozzo in his history of the world (c.1440).

up and out of a hellish labyrinth. Ultimately, Hercules was made fully divine and soared into the heavens to radiate forever as a constellation. There he shines brightly in the March sky, in proximity to the lamb (Aries) and the warrior (Mars).[49]

Jason, Hercules, and the Crusaders

On 29 May 1453 the Christian world suffered a stunning reversal when the Eastern bulwark of the faith, Constantinople, fell to the Turks.[50] The menace of the Saracens was such that not only was the Near East, including the Holy Lands, under Turkish control, but now the infidels also began to push up farther into the Balkans and to threaten Italy by sea as well. Three popes in succession, Nicholas V, Calixtus III, and Pius II, called upon the rulers of the Christian West to embark on a holy war against Sultan Mohammed II (d. 1481), that "monstrous dragon who devours faithful souls."[51] But most Christian rulers greeted these papal pleas with no more than thinly disguised indifference. Only Duke Philip the Good of Burgundy (ruled 1419–

FIGURE 7.11 Duke Philip the Good of Burgundy (ruled 1419–1467) with his collar of the Order of the Golden Fleece.

1467), king in all but rank, professed enthusiasm for a crusade.[52] In February 1454 he summoned his knights and courtiers to the town of Lille. The ducal banquet hall was hung with tapestries honoring the twelve labors of Hercules; in the center, on an elevated stage, the myth of Jason and the Argonauts played out. Riding on the back of an elephant, a man (dressed as a woman to portray the Holy Mother Church) entered to lament the fate of Christendom. Toward the end of this fantastic feast, courtiers and knights submitted their crusading vows to the herald of the Order of the Golden Fleece.[53] Finally, Duke Philip swore, if the occasion permitted, to engage the Grand Turk in single combat.[54] A single warrior could fight for all.

Nearly twenty-five years earlier, in 1430, Duke Philip had founded the Order of the Golden Fleece as a confraternity of twenty-five brave knights. Their mission was to "promote the exaltation of the faith and the Holy Church." Figure 7.11 shows Duke Philip wearing the collar of his Order, with the Golden Fleece of the ram dangling from the bottom. In choosing the emblem of the Golden Fleece as the symbol of his new chivalric order, Philip reached back into classical antiquity, to the mythological story of Jason and his fellow warriors, the Argonauts.[55]

The hero of the Argo is similar to the warrior of the Cretan maze. In his quest for the Golden Fleece, Jason, aided by Medea, daughter of King Athos, defeats sharp-horned bulls and fire-breathing dragons, ultimately returning the fleece of the sacrificial ram to the heavens; so, too, Theseus defeats the horned Minotaur with the help of Ariadne, daughter of King Minos, only later to abandon her, just as Jason did Medea.[56]

Soon the churchmen of the court of Burgundy transformed this earliest of Greek combat myths into a uniquely Burgundian Christian allegory. Christ is both warrior and lamb; Jason is the warrior who redeems the lamb/ram.[57] Jason will restore Christianity by recapturing both Constantinople and the lost city of Jerusalem. Philip is the new Jason and his knights the new Argonauts; they will do battle against the Satan of the East, Sultan Mohammed II.

Or will they? Despite elaborate preparations made in 1454–1456 and again in 1463–1464, the Burgundian crusade never set sail.[58] No sword was raised in battle, no Turk slain. Few princes allied themselves with the Burgundians, and in the end Duke Philip proved more practical than proud. Nevertheless, his crusading spirit stimulated a musical response.[59] Surely it is not a coincidence that the Christian image of the Armed Man, then nearly fifteen hundred years old, was given musical expression for the first time immediately after the fall of Constantinople. So, too, it must not be mere happenstance that the musical tradition of the Armed Man radiated from the lands of the duke of Burgundy.[60] Dufay, Regis, Josquin, and Busnois, four of the earliest musicians to compose an Armed Man Mass, were

FIGURE 7.12 Albrecht Dürer's 1519 portrait of Emperor Maximilian I wearing the collar of the Order of the Golden Fleece. The Golden Fleece can be seen more clearly dangling from the imperial emblem of the double-headed eagle (upper left).

Burgundian subjects and, in some cases, court employees. Philip's son, Charles the Bold, took special delight in the six Naples Armed Man Masses, as we have seen. Indeed, these Masses may have been created expressly for the Order of the Golden Fleece.[61]

. . .

FIGURE 7.13 Emperor Charles V as an Armed Man, painted by Titian in 1548. In his right hand he holds the Holy Lance, once owned by Charlemagne and now a relic in the Hofburg in Vienna. The Holy Lance was intentionally confused with the lance of Longius which pierced the side of Christ, and it was venerated on the Friday of Easter week.

After Charles the Bold's wholly unexpected death at the battle of Nancy (1477), the Burgundian Low Countries and sovereignty of the Order of the Golden Fleece passed to descendants having German-Hapsburg and, ulti-mately, German-Spanish blood. These rulers, too, embraced the signs and symbols that the Burgundian dukes had previously used to elevate their rule to almost kingly status.[62] When Charles the Bold's son-in-law Maximilian I acceded to supremacy of the Order in 1477, he henceforth displayed the Fleece beneath his German eagle (Fig. 7.12). His son Philip the Fair, recently crowned king of Castile, came to be associated with Josquin's Mass in honor of Hercules.[63] In 1516 Philip the Fair's son, the future Emperor Charles V (Fig. 7.13), in turn assumed command of the Order of the Golden Fleece, and a heraldic device was created to commemorate the event.[64] Henceforth Charles's personal emblem would be stamped with the pillars of Hercules surrounded by the motto *Plus Ultra (More Beyond)*, implying that his realm extended far beyond the ancient world of Hercules, from Jerusalem in the Holy Lands to the territories of the New World. Jason, also, was called upon to lend an aura of classical authority. When Emperor Charles entered Milan in 1541 following a series of military successes against the Turks in North Africa, a banner above a triumphal arch read: "I will capture a fleece which will bring back the Golden Age."[65]

Poets, too, saw the warrior Charles preparing a new Christian Age. Ludovico Ariosto (1474–1533) began his *Orlando Furioso*—as did the creator of the sixth Armed Man Mass in the Naples set—by alluding to the first line of Virgil's *Aeneid:* "I sing of arms and a man."[66] Here, however, Ariosto sings not of Aeneas but of Emperor Charles, a new Jason who leads a band of Christian Argonauts. When the Last World Emperor (Charles) has rid the earth of the Antichrist (the sultan) and returned the fleece to Heaven (made the whole world Christian and rendered it to God), then will Christ effect a final gathering of his flock. Simultaneously, the constellation Aries, the primordial cosmic symbol of spiritual renewal, will return to the skies.

> New Argonauts I see and Tiphys new
> Opening, till now an undiscovered way . . .
> To the fifth Charles' triumphant captains bend
> That this way should be hidden was God's will . . .
> Of Aragon and Austria's blood I see a monarch bred . . .
> For such . . . Heaven . . . designs . . .
> And wills that in his time Christ's scattered sheep
> Should be one flock, beneath one Shepherd's keep
> And that this be accomplished with more ease
> Writ in the skies from all eternity.[67]

This Argonautic imagery was not lost on Charles's son, King Philip II of Spain. When in 1571 Philip dispatched his navy to meet the Turks at what would prove to be the decisive Christian victory of Lepanto, the warship leading the vanguard was painted to replicate the imagined Argo.[68]

Charles V and Philip II saw themselves as armed soldiers of Christ. Indeed, Charles had Titian paint him as the *Miles Christianus,* a knight who bears Charlemagne's Holy Lance with the nail from the Cross (Fig. 7.13). Musicians, too, equated these kings with the Armed Man. When Cristóbal de Morales published his four-voice *Missa L'Homme armé* in 1544, he prefaced it with a woodcut depicting Emperor Charles as the Armed Man. Above Charles's head is his emblem framed by the pillars of Hercules; on his neck dangles the collar with the Golden Fleece of Jason.[69] Twenty-six years later, in 1570, Palestrina published his five-voice Armed Man Mass and dedicated it to Charles's son, Philip II of Spain, now commander of the Order of the Golden Fleece.[70] Again the Armed Man Mass is preceded by a woodcut of a warrior, presumably now Philip, surrounded by symbols of Hercules and Jason.[71] The clear implication is that newly Christianized heroes like Hercules and Jason, as well as Christ's kingly knights on earth, Charles and Philip, are worthy companions of the Armed Man.

The hero in the Armed Man Mass is as protean as the warrior in the maze. He is Christ, St. Michael, Aeneas, Hercules, Jason, the knights of the Golden Fleece, as well as all crusaders and all Christians who put on the armor of spiritual virtue. Sometimes the warrior fights in the center of a maze; sometimes he rises up in a polyphonic Mass. His polymorphous nature accounts for the extraordinary popularity of the Armed Man in the pre-modern world. And because *Christus Victor* and potentially every Christian is at the heart of the Armed Man Mass, this religious music enjoyed almost universal liturgical applicability. The Armed Man could step forward at a Mass on the feast of St. Michael, at a votive Mass of the Sword, or at a Mass "contra Turcos."[72] But more important, this was Christian music appropriate for every Mass in every church on every Sunday (a *Missa dominicalis*), a Mass for crusader, king, pope, and commoner alike. As lines three and four of the tune exclaim: "Everywhere the cry has gone out; Everyone should arm himself with a breastplate of iron."

The Armed Man Disappears

The Armed Man dominated the musical landscape during the Middle Ages, when crusading knights tried to establish a new, non-Islamic Jerusalem. But as the Renaissance waxed, this musical signifier waned. Symbolism gave way to more direct mimetic expression. Table B.2 in Appendix B lists in approximate chronological order the composers who wrote Armed Man Masses. It suggests that by the seventeenth century, the Armed Man had all but withdrawn from the spiritual battlefield.

What caused the musical warrior to retreat and, ultimately, disappear? The answer rests, in part, in the changing political landscape brought about by the spread of Protestant theology. From the Middle Ages into the seventeenth century, the crusades and seemingly endless wars against Islam were fought by the papacy and its allies in arms, the Catholic monarchs; after the Reformation, however, the only firmly Catholic countries were those of the Mediterranean world. The geographic base of the Armed Man had been diminished. Similarly, the Armed Man had lost theological force, most notably among the northern Protestants. Protestant theology held that souls did not languish in Purgatory, and thus no hero was needed to rescue them. Although there were exceptions, Protestants generally preferred the image of the dutiful pilgrim to that of the bellicose warrior. When the English Protestants of the nineteenth century resurrected the Armed Man in the hymn *Onward Christian Soldiers* (1865), they did not perpetuate a living tradition, but rather participated in a Gothic revival. The man who penned its text, Sabine Baring-Gould (1834–1924), was also the author of *Curious Myths of the Middle Ages*.[73]

But the most important cause of the disappearance of the Armed Man was the decline of symbolism generally, in religious music as well as in sacred painting. Recall that the principal methods of symbolic communication in music were the meaning-laden *cantus firmus*, number symbolism, and symbolic processes. *Cantus firmus* technique and musical number symbolism all but disappeared in the sixteenth century; the old practice of transforming a tune into a religious symbol was now thought to be too remote, too esoteric, too obscure, and thus not an effective way of expressing the sacred word. Similarly, symbolic processes lost their associations. Retrograde motion, as we have seen, had been used for centuries as a way to signify the round-trip journey of the Lord.[74] But by the time of Haydn and Mozart, it was no more than an abstract contrapuntal procedure, one without spiritual values. When Haydn employs retrograde motion in his Symphony No. 47 (1772), for example, he does so in the Minuet, a light musical genre derived from a courtly dance.[75] Symbol had become pleasurable experience, and the transition began with the humanists of the Renaissance.

Just what a Renaissance humanist thought of medieval musical symbolism can be gleaned from a letter that one reform-minded cleric penned to another on 16 February 1549. Writing to a colleague in Rome, Bernardino Cirillo contrasts the poor state of musical expression in his day with what he perceives to be the far more moving music of the ancient Greeks:

> This much is clear—that the music of today is not the product of theory, but is merely an application of practice. *Kyrie eleison* means "Lord, have mercy upon us." The ancient [Greek] musician would have expressed this affection of asking the Lord's pardon . . . and would have made a contrast between Kyrie and Agnus Dei, between Gloria and Credo, Sanctus and Pleni, psalm and motet. Nowadays they sing these things in any way at all, mixing them in an indifferent and uncertain manner. And then, you see what they invariably do. They say, "Oh, what a fine Mass was sung in chapel!" And what is it, if you please? It is *L'homme armé*, or *Hercules Dux Ferrariae* or *Philomena*. What the devil has the Mass to do with the armed man, or with Philomena, or with the duke of Ferrara?[76]

What indeed? Perhaps we should take Cirillo at his word, that he and his generation had lost touch with the allegorical meaning of the Armed Man, of Hercules, and of the tune *Philomena*. Perhaps, just as Canon Souchet at Chartres would later lose track of the meaning of the maze, Commendatore Cirillo no longer understood the spiritual significance of the Armed Man. Yet more likely, Cirillo's voice is a rhetorical one. He wants the modern composer to abandon the old process of assigning meaning by means of allegorical reinterpretation. Surrounding a symbolic *cantus firmus* with a welter of scholastic counterpoint simply makes a muddle of the sacred text. Toward the end of his letter, Cirillo even suggests doing away with all Gregorian chants as signifiers in polyphonic music. He, too, recognizes that this mode of communication makes all sacred music sound more or less the same, a *Kyrie* like an *Agnus Dei*, a Mass for the dead like a Mass for the Virgin.[77]

Cirillo and his fellow humanists had a point, and it was soon well taken. Sixteenth-century composers increasingly sought to recreate what they perceived to be a means of expression practiced by the ancient Greeks,[78] regardless of the fact that no Greek music actually survived. This was the musical Renaissance, and what was important to the composers of the day was to follow the precepts set forth by the classical Greek philosophers.[79] Music should faithfully reflect the natural spoken rhythm of the text as well as its syntax. Above all, the words should be set to appropriate music—joyful texts to joyful music, mournful ones to sounds of mourning. Henceforth, battle music would be loud, fast, and full of conflicting crashes; pastoral shepherds would move in lilting stepwise motion through a dissonance-free environment. By conveying meaning directly through an array of such mimetic gestures, musicians of the late Renaissance began to create a new language of musical expression. It was the language of music as we know it today. Ultimately, this transition from the symbolic to the mimetic, from the allegorical to the literal, was the single most important development in the history of Western music.[80]

The Armed Man was a symbol of the warrior who defeats evil and thereby rescues all humanity; the maze was a symbol of the zone in which this timeless combat myth unfolds, the arena of life. Both were profoundly affected by the renewed interest in classical antiquity that came with the Renaissance. Recapturing the spirit of Greek music required the dismantling of the symbolic scaffold (the medieval *cantus firmus*) upon which the Armed Man had stood. So, too, reviving the Greco-Roman labyrinth would soon destroy the medieval maze as a monolithic symbol. With the Renaissance came new ways of looking at the labyrinth, as well as new uses for it—in coats of arms, in gardens, and in puzzles and games.

CHAPTER EIGHT

The Maze of Pilgrimage and Pleasure

In the medieval world, the maze had a multitude of meanings. Yet all of these were related, in one way or another, to a single combat myth—a great war between good and evil that brought about spiritual salvation for all humanity. Labyrinthine complexity couched within divinely perfect order, the double-retrograde pattern inherent in the great Gothic pavement mazes, the Easter dance on the maze—all were interpreted as signs of Christ's singular victory. This was the uniformly accepted theology of the maze. So, too, there was a single view of the maze: it had a commonly accepted shape.

Labyrinths, of course, can be formed in an almost endless variety of ways. They can be set within squares, circles, rectangles, triangles, or any other configuration; they can be unicursal or multicursal; they may have one or more centers and one or more points of entry. Yet prior to the High Renaissance, there were remarkably few patterns, and one model in particular was ubiquitous. It developed from the classic seven-circuit Cretan labyrinth known in the ancient Mediterranean world (see Fig. 1.1) to become the eleven-circuit Chartres-type maze stamped with the sign of the cross (see Fig. 1.9). The Chartrain pattern appears in medieval manuscripts and churches from England to Italy. Thus, in pre-modern Europe there was a collective vision of what a labyrinth was and should be: it was unicursal, having a single center as well as a single point of entry and exit; it was highly geometric, often perfectly symmetrical; and it radiated with Christian symbolism.[1]

In the sixteenth century all this began to change. The Reformation brought with it new, more personal forms of devotion, and these altered the meaning of this symbol. Associations of the maze with the Harrowing of Hell and images of soldiers marching in Christ's army began to be replaced by a vision of the solitary pilgrim—not a pilgrim who became a soldier by

207

donning spiritual armor, but one who remained a simple pilgrim. This soul would need divine guidance, but not necessarily that of the established Church of Rome.

Concurrently, the Roman Catholic Church began to lose its claim as sole proprietor of the labyrinth. Mazes now appeared in a wide variety of contexts outside the church: in emblem books, on ceilings, in gardens, within paintings, in embroidery, on board games, and even on clothing. Not surprisingly, as the maze returned to the secular world during the Renaissance, a myriad of new and different patterns began to emerge. The old unicursal labyrinth with its moral imperative to journey to the center and back gave way to a multiplicity of shapes and forms.

Soon even the Catholic Church would begin to lose sight of the maze as a sacred symbol. Like the modern-day tourist visiting the cathedral of Chartres, the priests of the Enlightenment began to wonder: "How did this pagan object come to be placed in the church?" As we shall now see, the maze was cut free of its traditional ties to the Easter liturgy and came to serve as the venue for a miniature pilgrimage to Jerusalem. Yet at the same time the labyrinth also became a place of idle amusement where men, women, and children could frolic, to the annoyance of those trying to conduct religious services nearby. For this and other reasons, the authorities in all but a few churches ultimately had the mazy paving stones torn up and carted away.

Pilgrims on the Maze

Most guidebooks explain the presence of the maze on a cathedral floor in something like the following terms: "In the Middle Ages the labyrinth served as a place where devout souls carried out a vicarious pilgrimage to Jerusalem, praying as they followed the path of the maze on their knees."[2] This line of thought links pilgrimage to the medieval practice of penance; during the First Crusade (1095–1099) the papacy granted to all souls who embarked on a pilgrimage to Jerusalem a plenary indulgence for the remission of all sin.[3] Thus pilgrims could journey to the Holy Land for the redemption of their souls. But as the strength of the Muslims grew, travel to Jerusalem became more difficult, sometimes impossible. Therefore, the theory goes, the bishops of France allowed for substitute pilgrimage routes

FIGURE 8.1 A nineteenth-century sketch of clerics moving through a turf maze near the church of St. Anne at St. Anne's Well, Sneiton, Nottinghamshire, England. The complete maze is shown below.

in the form of pavement mazes to be placed in the church. The twists and turns of the maze replaced the dangers of the pilgrim's road. Is there truth to this claim that the maze entered the church as a site for substitute pilgrimage? None at all.

In fact, the church maze was used as a place of fictive pilgrimages not at the beginning of its history, but at its end. The earliest two documents to refer to the labyrinth as a "path to Jerusalem" date from the late eighteenth century. They refer to the mazes at Reims and at St. Omer, respectively, as a *chemin de Jérusalem.*[4] In the eighteenth century the labyrinths at Chartres and Sens were simply called "la lieue,"[5] possibly because of an etymological connection with the old Gaulish measure of a league (*leuca, leuga,* or *leuva*) of 1500 paces.[6] By the early nineteenth century, however, "pilgrimage fever" seems to have infected the minds of French church historians, affecting interpretations of the mazes at Amiens, Chartres, Bayeux, Poitiers, St. Quentin, and, eventually, turf mazes in England as well.[7]

The image of pious souls chanting prayers as they crept around a maze on bended knee seems to have appealed to the nineteenth-century imagination, which tended to romanticize all that was medieval and Gothic. Figure 8.1 shows a "recreation" of clerics, rosary in hand, moving through a turf maze near the church of St. Anne at St. Anne's Well, Nottinghamshire, England. The illustration was fabricated by a certain "Mrs. Robert Miles" in the mid-nineteenth century, some fifty years after the turf maze there had been destroyed.[8] For French historians, too, this vision of a vicarious pilgrimage had a certain immediacy, for some of them had personally seen, or heard stories about, pilgrims on the maze. Their recollections were correct, for the maze had indeed been the site of a substitute pilgrimage during the eighteenth century.

According to the early nineteenth-century historian Emanuel Wallet, the maze at St. Omer (Fig. 2.11) was called the "path of Jerusalem," and oldtimers in the region recounted how it was used in such a way.[9] At Reims the center of the labyrinth was called "Jérusalem,"[10] and a booklet containing pious prayers to be said along the route was generally available under the title: *Stations on the Path of Jerusalem which is seen in the Church of Our Lady in Reims.*[11] Similarly, at Arras the pious recited prayers on their knees as they made their way around the track of the maze, the journey requiring about an hour.[12] So, too, at Sens, devout souls of the eighteenth century apparently crept around the maze, and here also the full pilgrimage was said to require an hour.[13] Finally, although no document explicitly says as much, there is strong reason to believe that this ritual was performed at Chartres as early as the seventeenth century.

Sometime around 1640 the historian Charles Challine (1596–1678) completed his *Recherches sur Chartres.*[14] It includes a description as well as a re-

LABYRINTHE.

FIGURE 8.2 The labyrinth of the cathedral of Chartres with penitential prayers winding their way to the center.

production of the maze at the cathedral of Chartres (Fig. 8.2). Yet here a succession of spiritual texts now winds its way around the twisting path, starting at the entrance and ending in the center.[15] Undoubtedly these are the Chartrain equivalent of the pious texts published for the pilgrims on the maze at Reims and said by the faithful at Arras and St. Omer as well. Numbers appear at the turning points along the Chartrain route. These perhaps indicate the "stations" of the maze, the points at which the various lines of the text were to be recited as the pilgrims knelt and prayed. Although these verses wind from the outside in, presumably the same or similar texts were appropriate at the same stations during the returning portion of the pilgrimage. By definition, every pilgrimage is a round-trip journey.

What do these Latin verses express? They give voice to the wayward soul crying for assistance from the Lord. The beginning text is Psalm 50, *Have mercy upon me, O God* (*Miserere mei, Deus*), one of the seven Penitential Psalms of David and a psalm integral to the rosary.[16] This is by far the longest text set within the maze, occupying three-fourths of the route; only a few representative verses are given here:

> Have mercy upon me, O God,
> according to thy loving kindness,
> According unto the multitude of
> thy loving kindness, blot out my transgressions. . . .
>
> Cast me not away from thy presence;
> and take not thy holy spirit from me.
> Restore unto me the joy of thy salvation;
> and uphold me with thy free spirit.
> Then will I teach transgressors thy ways;
> and sinners shall be converted unto thee. . . .
>
> Do good in thy good pleasure unto Zion:
> build thou the walls of Jerusalem. . . .

These lines from Psalm 50 are followed by verses extracted and refashioned from Psalm 117 (a song of liberation) and Psalm 68 (prayers of distress). Some of these fragments are repeated continually so as to create a litany-like appeal, a quality typical of church pilgrimages and processions generally.

> Liberate me, O God, from those
> who hate me, and let not the
> depths devour me, nor let the pit
> impel its mouth upon me.
>
> Hear me, O Lord, for your mercy is abundant.
>
> Be attentive to my soul and liberate it,
> Lord God, ruler of all time,
> You alone are merciful.
>
> Hear me, O Lord, for your mercy is abundant.

At the end of the path of the maze, a non-scriptural text spirals around the very center. It is the Introit of the Requiem Mass:

Grant them eternal rest, O Lord,
and may everlasting light shine upon them.
May they rest in peace.
Amen.

The final word, appearing at the epicenter, is "Amen." The questing soul has reached eternal rest in celestial Jerusalem.

During the sixteenth century, as we have seen, the labyrinth lost some of the Christological associations it had acquired during the Middle Ages. It became, as it once was long ago with the patristic fathers, a simple metaphor for the route along which the solitary soul must pass. The texts associated with the labyrinth of Chartres offer further testimony to this transformation, suggesting how the maze evolved from a medieval symbol of noisy Hell and Purgatory to a post-Reformation place of quiet, where a more personal, possibly nonsectarian experience might take place.[17] As the Christological references recede, the words of the Old Testament, particularly those of the Psalter, resonate more loudly. These are verses that could be intoned by Orthodox and Protestant Christians alike. Indeed, one might even go so far as to say that those of the Jewish faith might tread this more ecumenical maze with little doctrinal discomfort, had there been Jews willing and allowed to do so in seventeenth-century Chartres. This maze has no demonic center. There is no implication of a round-trip journey by Christ. There are neither militaristic nor eucharistic overtones. There are no praises to martyrs of the Christian cause. This maze has no special relevance to the season of Easter. The pilgrim may set forth toward Jerusalem at any time.

As he does so, he will find himself alone. In this early-modern maze, the emphasis has shifted from a collective symbol seen from without to an object for individual meditation experienced from within. We should recall that there are no records attesting to, or even suggesting, a personal journey on a church maze prior to the seventeenth century. All earlier accounts speak of clerics dancing on the maze or processing across it on Easter as part of the liturgy of the Roman Catholic Church. Allusions to a meditative experience for laymen begin to appear only in the seventeenth century. Not coincidentally, it is in this period that the "pilgrim on the maze" sets forth in emblem books in the West. Carrying a walking staff and accompanied by his loyal dog (see Fig. 3.6), he follows a life-line of faith toward celestial

FIGURE 8.3 Fashionable citizens of Chartres enjoying the pleasures of the maze, from an engraving of 1696.

Jerusalem. The pilgrim treads across the pages of the Lutheran *Errant Wanderings in the Homeland* (1618), the Moravian *Labyrinth of the World and the Paradise of the Heart* (1631),[18] and the Baptist *Pilgrim's Progress* (1678).[19] Ultimately, the thread followed by the wandering soul leads to the poetic conceit fashioned more than a century later by William Blake:

> *To the Christians:*
> I give you the end of a golden string,
>   Only wind it into a ball,
> It will lead you in at Heaven's Gate,
>   Built in Jerusalem's wall.[20]

Thus by the seventeenth century the shadow of Christ militant had all but withdrawn from the maze, leaving the solitary pilgrim to experience it in a way not originally foreseen by the medieval Roman Catholic Church. What had been an institutional symbol of the Savior's victory over Satan—and an implicit challenge to all to join Christ's army—had become, for Protestant and Catholic alike, a place for prayer and meditation inside a sacred space. Moreover, as the steps of the spiritual pilgrim literally began to efface the tracks of an older ritualistic symbol,[21] the maze became divorced from the liturgical rites of the church.

Proof of this separation of symbol from ritual can be found in words uttered around 1650 by Jean-Baptiste Souchet, historian and canon of Chartres: "In the middle of the nave there is a labyrinth of lead,[22] and I am astonished that they put it there since it is only a crazy amusement at which those who have nothing better to do pass the time running and turning both during and between the hours of the divine service."[23] This offhand remark reveals two things. First, Canon Souchet had no memory that the labyrinth at Chartres had once served as a site of a liturgical dance at Easter; the dance of the maze at Chartres, like those at Auxerre and Sens, must have disappeared during the sixteenth century. Second, the maze at Chartres was being used in Souchet's day for a good deal more than just a surrogate pilgrimage: it satisfied profane desire no less than spiritual yearning.

Just how the maze at Chartres might have become a "crazy amusement" can be seen in Figure 8.3. This nineteenth-century "touch-up" of an engraving originally done in 1696 represents the state of affairs at Chartres around the turn of the eighteenth century.[24] Here we see the wide breadth of the nave (the widest of any French cathedral), the organ on the south wall (where it remains today), and beneath it the pulpit from which the Easter sermon was preached in the Middle Ages. In the distance is the old thirteenth-century rood screen, which would be removed in 1763.[25] Throughout the nave clerics chat amiably with clerics, laymen with laymen, and both with each other. Ladies kneel in prayer before the great pillars on which are sculpted images of the Apostles. A beggar approaches two well-to-do gentlemen. In the center of it all is the maze, and upon it tread six souls: three gentlemen, two ladies, and a girl. The only gestures these maze-walkers make to spiritual solemnity is that the men, like all gentlemen throughout the church, have removed their hats. No one kneels in prayer on the maze, and no one carries a book of pious verse. These are not plaintive pilgrims but rather fashionable pleasure-seekers. They are enjoying the game of the maze.

The Game of the Maze

What had caused the maze to change from sacred symbol to place of pleasure? Or, to put it more accurately, what had caused a lessening of sacred associations and the introduction of pleasurable experience? For the answer, we must return to the Renaissance, for with the Renaissance came, if not an actual rebirth, at least an intensified interest in classical literature, science, medicine, art, architecture, and music. The labyrinth, which during the Middle Ages had been confined exclusively within the church, now resurfaced in civic buildings and private residences, in engravings and woodcuts, and in paintings and enamels, all illustrating classical texts or illuminating scenes from ancient mythology.[26] For example, around 1500 an anonymous Tuscan painter created a beautiful set of tableaux depicting the myth of the labyrinth (Fig. 8.4). At the center of the illustration shown here, Theseus does battle with the Minotaur while Ariadne and her sister Phaedra await the outcome.[27] Yet this reborn Chartres-type maze, with its cruciform design, was intended to decorate the inside of an Italian palazzo, not a church. Outside that villa, quite possibly, there was a garden maze. Certainly geometrical gardens, many in labyrinthine patterns, flourished in Italy, France, and England during the Renaissance. These, too, changed the way the labyrinth was viewed and experienced, for they encouraged the playful soul to see the maze as a place for fun and games.

FIGURE 8.4 Theseus and the Minotaur engage in mortal combat while Ariadne (left) and her sister Phaedra await the outcome. Painting by an anonymous Tuscan artist, sometimes identified as the Master of the Campana Cassoni, c.1500. Here the myth from classical antiquity and the maze from the medieval church are united in a humanistic painting designed purely for worldly enjoyment.

FIGURE 8.5 Court jester fashioned as a maze, from a woodcut in Francesco Segala's
sixteenth-century *Libro de laberinti.*

Every child enjoys the challenge of a maze. This is not new, for ancient
graffiti suggest that the labyrinth has provided youthful amusement for
thousands of years. But the direct ancestor of the maze books, puzzles, and
board games enjoyed by children today are the maze games that emerged
during the Renaissance.[28] Exploring minds created labyrinthine games by
means of anagrams—by rearranging letters, words, or phrases to make a
labyrinthine word puzzle. Sometimes the game of the maze is purely
graphic: a complex pattern invites the eye to find the most direct route from
beginning to end. In Francesco Segala's mid-sixteenth-century court jester,
for example, one enters the maze at the foot and works toward the head
(Fig. 8.5). This is, of course, a multicursal labyrinth wherein choices must

be made and errors—useless deviations from the most direct route—will occur. The eye can easily be fooled.

But the game of the maze need not be a challenge only to the eye; it can be experienced with the entire body. In 1551 Innocentio Ringhieri published his *One Hundred Fanciful and Easy Games (Cento Giuochi Liberali, et d'Ingegno)*, the forty-ninth of which is entitled "The Game of the Labyrinth" *(Giuoco del labirinto)*.[29] The players form a circle, alternating men and women, and hold hands. They surround a labyrinth, one made of other players or of natural materials as in a garden maze. In the center of the labyrinth is the allegorical figure Amore (Cupid), who directs a "School of Love" for six attending maidens; outside the labyrinth wait Theseus, Ariadne, and six gentlemen. As the encircling players raise and lower their arms, a gentleman and then a lady in turn try to find their way out of, and into, the labyrinth. Should they meet along the path of the maze, they are encouraged to kiss and exchange affectionate words, for this is Cupid's desire. When all the gentlemen have moved to the center of the maze and all the ladies to the outside (reversed positions), the game is over and a general dance ensues with Cupid leading the way.[30]

All is not merely amusement, however, for this mid-sixteenth-century game is an allegory for other human experiences. To the rules of the game Ringhieri appends a series of questions of the sort that might be debated in a literary academy during the Renaissance: "Why is the maze called blind? Why does the state of love resemble a labyrinth? Is it appropriate to believe that human life is an inextricable maze? Why is a woman's golden hair, or blond braids, an intricate yet very sweet maze? Should the study of philosophy be called a maze because the inquiring mind never finds a way out?" By posing such diverse points of debate, Ringhieri has taken the traditional spiritual values of the labyrinth and intertwined them with philosophical and amorous issues. The tangled golden locks of the beloved, for example, are like the snares of the labyrinth.[31] These amatory associations are part of a long-standing literary tradition called the "labyrinth of love," one extending from Boccaccio's *Corbaccio o Laberinto d'amore* (1354–1355) to Cervantes's *El laberinto de amor* (1615) and beyond.[32] In this context the maze symbolizes the ambiguities, difficulties, and reversals associated with love and erotic relationships generally. The house of the Minotaur is now occupied by Cupid!

Allegorical love, and death as well, are also at the heart of *The Labyrinth*

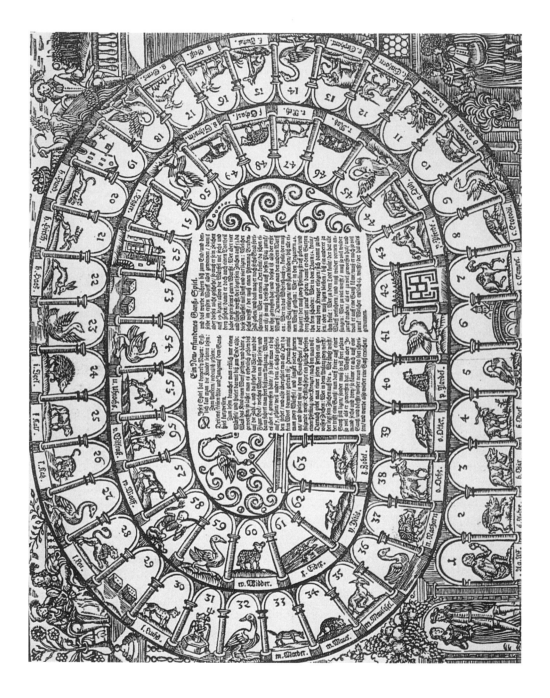

of Arioso: Heroic Game for Gentlemen and Ladies (*Il Laberinto dell'Arioso: Gioco Heroico di Cavalieri e Dame*) invented about 1650 by Thomas François of Carignano (d. 1656), prince of the House of Savoy.[33] This is a board game, though the board is in fact a large, circular table around which as many as a dozen players can be seated. On the table are painted 339 spaces arranged in the form of a labyrinth full of "turns and returns." Eighty-nine of the spaces are painted with scenes and events taken from Ludovico Arioso's epic poem *Orlando Furioso* (1532). Each player chooses a hero portrayed in Arioso's verse (Roland, Roger, Brademant, for example) and moves the wooden or silver marker around the maze by rolling dice. Landing on beneficial spaces such as the Temple of Merlin, the Palace of Alcina, or the House Where Lost Things are Found permits the occupant to collect fines from subsequent visitors. Malevolent spaces, such as St. Patrick's Purgatory, Alcina's Prison, or Hell itself, result in a fine and loss of turn. There are captives (those who are in prison and have lost their turn) and liberators (those who arrive at an occupied space) and, should anyone free all captives from all twelve prisons, a Grand Liberator. Along the path of the labyrinth the players encounter witches, a killer whale, and flesh-eating giants. The person advancing first to the final space of the maze wins the game. Although Arioso's poem *Orlando Furioso* has Christian overtones,[34] the Grand Liberator of the *Heroic Game* can hardly be equated with Christ the Harrower of Hell. This game is purely for pleasure.

A similarly mazy board game, this one coming from seventeenth-century Germany (Fig. 8.6), is called *A Newly Invented Game of Goose (Ein Neu-erfundenes Ganss-Spiel).*[35] Its name suggests a tie to the church pavement maze, for in the eighteenth century the faithful said that the floor of the cathedral of Chartres resembled a "Game of Goose" *(Jeu de l'oie).*[36] Like the *Heroic Game,* this German *Game of Goose* involves players moving by means of the fateful dice from beginning to end. The sixty-three spaces are filled with pictures and names, mostly of animals. Landing on the Goose earns an extra turn, but "He who lands in the maze *(Irrgarten)* at 42 must pay a two-penny fine and move backward three spaces: the maze has no pity."[37] Similar to a unicursal labyrinth, the board winds toward the center,

FIGURE 8.6 A spiraling Game of Goose with an incorrectly designed maze at space 42. According to the directions in the center: He who lands therein must pay a two-penny fine and go back three spaces.

and the first player to arrive there is the victor. The instructions in the center further stipulate that when a player lands on a space he is to read and pronounce the name of the animal depicted there. The animals are arranged on the board in alphabetical order from Aff (monkey) to Zobel (sable). The *Game of Goose* is thus not only an amusement for young and old *(konnen Alte und Junge auf dem Gansspiel kurzweilen)*, but also a child's reading primer *(kan man die Kinter lehren lesen)*.

Children and mazes, a timeless union. Indeed, these seventeenth-century labyrinthine games are not substantively different from many of the serpentine board games played by youngsters today (*Uncle Wiggly, Candyland,* and *Chutes and Ladders,* for example). Players move figures along a winding unicursal route, their fate determined by the blind caprice of the dice; there are rewards and penalties, advances and reversals, friends and enemies along the way. Perhaps it is not going too far to suggest that the path of another important icon of contemporary culture, the Yellow Brick Road in *The Wizard of Oz,* can be traced back to the twisting route of the *Heroic Game* and similar board games of the early seventeenth century.

As these examples of labyrinthine games suggest, during the sixteenth and seventeenth centuries the meaning of the maze became secularized, even trivialized. The older spiritual labyrinth by no means disappeared, but the maze ceased to be solely a sacred symbol as it had been during the Middle Ages. New visions of what a maze might be—visual puzzle, place of amorous adventure, board game, or even musical composition—began to obscure the meaning bestowed upon it by the medieval church. Nowhere, however, is the deconsecration of the labyrinth more in evidence than in the garden maze.

Garden Mazes

Is not a garden maze something of an oxymoron? The maze is a symbol of the hellish terrestrial world, while the garden, ever since creation (Genesis 2:8), represents Paradise on earth. That the maze came to be a part of countless Renaissance and Baroque gardens suggests a blurring of the border separating sacred symbol from earthly Eden. What had been a representation of the sinful world with a unicursal path of righteousness was coming to be seen as a secular diversion offering amusement and little more. Instead of a single path, a multitude of routes might appear in a gar-

FIGURE 8.7 The beginning of Cipriano de Rore's Marian motet *Ave regina celorum,* with the *Hortus conclusus* (Mary as a protected garden) symbolized by a labyrinth at the bottom right. The spiritual theme is medieval, but the form of the maze comes from Roman antiquity.

den maze. Finding the most direct passage to the center provided outdoor sport for the pleasure-seeking courtiers of the period.[38] Equally important, the high hedge maze provided a measure of seclusion where lovers might enjoy a momentary dalliance. Hundreds of garden mazes are known to have been constructed from the sixteenth through eighteenth centuries;[39] here, however, only a few will serve to demonstrate the myriad forms and characteristics of the garden labyrinth.

Although many garden mazes were planted in France during the late Middle Ages, we know nothing about their design.[40] Several went by the name *la maison de Dédalus* and were presumably horticultural versions of similarly named unicursal mazes prominent in French cathedrals at the time.[41] In Italy architects were sketching garden labyrinths as early as 1460, but not until the mid-sixteenth century did the garden maze become established as an outdoor reality. By this time mazes were a favorite part of the gardens at Belriguardo near Ferrara, at the Villa d'Este at Tivoli, at the Palazzo del Te at Mantua, and at the Villa Lante near Viterbo.[42] So commonplace did the garden maze become that it frequently was included in paintings and manuscript illuminations depicting outdoor scenes.

Figure 8.7 shows a superbly illuminated music manuscript compiled for Duke Albrecht V of Bavaria in 1559, specifically, the music of the motet *Ave regina celorum* by Cipriano de Rore (c.1516–1565).[43] The imagery here celebrates the immaculate nature of Mary, the mother of God.[44] Reading from top to bottom, the viewer encounters a host of symbols and faintly written inscriptions, a litany-like collection traditionally associated with the Virgin.[45] The texts are taken mainly from the Song of Songs and allude to the Shulamite Maiden whom the Middle Ages took to be a prefiguration of Mary (2:1–2; 3:12; 4:4; 4:12; 4:15; 6:10).[46] She is as beautiful as the moon *(Pulchra ut luna)*, elect as the sun *(Electa ut sol)*, a mirror without blemish *(Specula sine macula)*, a flowering stem of Jesse *(Virga Jesse florida)*, star of the sea *(Stella maris)*, gate to heaven *(Porta celi)*, tower of David *(Turris David)*, city of God *(Civitas Dei)*, and font of the waters of life *(Puteus aquarium viventium)*. At the bottom of the page is a walled garden within which flourish the traditional floral and arboreal symbols of the Virgin (rose, lily, olive, and cedar). On the right side of the garden is a hedge maze with the central words *Hortus conclusus,* an inscription derived from Song of Songs (3:12): "A garden enclosed is my sister, my spouse; a spring shut up, a fountain sealed."[47]

Once again, the age-old symbol of the maze has been imbued with new meaning. In the context of the Marian garden the labyrinth now signifies a virtue of the Virgin. Its twists and turns suggest that Mary is inviolate, that stain cannot negotiate the tortuous route and penetrate to the center of her womb. This is a maze *in bono,* a protective, sheltering maze, in contrast to the more traditional labyrinth *in malo* with its demonic overtones. In addition, this Marian maze is not the circular, cruciform labyrinth of the church, but a quadratic one derived from the mosaic maze of ancient Rome (see Fig. 1.3). Here in the Renaissance, a classical design has taken root in a garden of medieval Marian imagery.

The observant viewer will have noticed that the maze forming the closed garden of the Virgin in Figure 8.7 is, nevertheless, still unicursal in form. Indeed, until the end of the sixteenth century, garden mazes, as well as representations of such mazes in the visual arts, were predominantly "one-way." Here the unicursal quadratic maze of the Roman villa was simply transplanted outdoors. By the end of the sixteenth century, however, the numerical balance begins to shift decidedly in favor of the multicursal maze. So synonymous did garden maze and multicursal maze become that when the Germans needed to coin a new word to denote a multi-path maze, they began to call it an "error garden" *(Irrgarten),* whether the maze was in a garden or not. By the seventeenth century most new mazes were multicursal.

A hint of labyrinthine patterns to come is contained in Jan Vredeman de Vries's *Forms of Gardens (Hortorum viridariorumque),* printed in Antwerp in 1583. De Vries was an influential architect who worked in Holland, Belgium, Germany, and Bohemia in the service of Emperor Rudolph II.[48] Among the nine topiary mazes found in *Forms of Gardens* is one entitled "Ionica," so-called because of the two Ionic columns that mark the entrance into the labyrinth (Fig. 8.8). Stepping between them, the maze-walker is immediately confronted with a dilemma: to go right or left. Even if the correct choice is made (to the right), soon a similar decision must be made, and then another, and so forth along a lengthy path of decisions. The importance of de Vries's maze rests in the imperative implied by the multicursal design. Blindly following a preordained path is no guarantee of success; the maze-treader must chart his own route. This is the fundamental characteristic of all multicursal mazes, and, from the sixteenth century forward, Western culture would identify the maze principally by this one

FIGURE 8.8 The garden maze entitled "Ionica" from Jan Vredeman de Vries's *Forms of Gardens* (*Hortorum viridariorumque*; Antwerp, 1583).

property—success depends on individual initiative that is not only decisive but correct.

Jan Vredeman de Vries was a native of Holland. During the seventeenth century his Dutch compatriots became as obsessed with gardens and floral mazes as they were infatuated with the newly imported tulip. Landscape architects published handsome folio volumes offering labyrinthine patterns —almost all multicursal—by means of which a garden might be graced.[49] The royals William and Mary enjoyed "his and hers" labyrinths on the west and east sides, respectively, of their palace at Loo near Utrecht.[50] The year after William acceded to the throne of England in 1689 as King William III, he instructed his gardeners George London and Henry Wise to lay out a labyrinth at his newly acquired royal residence at Hampton Court.[51]

Surely the labyrinth at Hampton Court (Fig. 8.9) is the most popular garden maze in the world today—more than a half million visitors walk its paths annually. Not only is it England's most famous maze, but it is also that country's oldest surviving horticultural labyrinth; the earlier outdoor

FIGURE 8.9 The famous hedge maze at the royal residence of Hampton Court.

mazes of Henry VIII and other monarchs simply have not withstood the ravages of time.[52] Consider the multicursal configuration of the Hampton Court maze and the fact that the hedges delineating its paths are now, as intended in the time of King William, seven to eight feet tall. The tops of the trees at the center of the maze can be seen, but not the route thereto. Depending upon the path chosen, the wayfarer may encounter as many as eight crossroads. Choosing the wrong direction will lead to a dead end or, worse, to an earlier spot of decision-making now unrecognizable because it is approached from a new direction. "Have I been here before?" Frustration, a feeling of inadequacy, even a bit of motion-sickness can take hold. This is a seventeenth-century roller coaster on a two-dimensional plane. Although the maze at Hampton Court was designed to rest within a broad park called "the wilderness," this situation has no larger significance.[53] Here there are no biblical allusions to forty years of wandering in a wilderness, no classical inscriptions set along the path. Mastery won't save the soul, only the ego.

. . .

FIGURE 8.10 The maze designed by André Le Nôtre (1613–1678) for King Louis XIV's palace at Versailles.

The final stop on our brief garden tour is *Le labyrinthe* at Louis XIV's palace at Versailles, the most elaborate and expensive horticultural labyrinth ever created. Despite its great size, the maze at Versailles, west of Paris, was just a small patch in the king's woodland madness. Forests were felled, rivers diverted, lakes created, and a colossal palace constructed, all by a work force approaching 36,000.[54] The noted landscape architect André Le Nôtre (1613–1678) designed the gardens at Versailles and therein fashioned a forest labyrinth, for he set his maze within a backdrop of newly planted trees (Fig. 8.10). Of course the labyrinth of the Sun King could be no ordinary thing. It occupied approximately two acres to the southwest of the palace, and its curving paths were almost half a mile (750 meters) in length. At the entrance stood two statues, one of Cupid and the other of Aesop, allegorical figures of Love and Wisdom. Along the paths Le Nôtre placed thirty-nine fountains, each of which contained sculpted creatures that acted out one of Aesop's fables. The gist of each tale was inscribed in gilded letters on a bronze plaque affixed to the fountain. Though courtiers might enter this bower to be instructed in the ways of either pleasure or virtue, the voluptuaries at Versailles surely came more often under the tutelage of Cupid than of Aesop. At every turn fountains dazzled the eye and life-size animals, animated by water pumps, charmed the imagination. The labyrinth at Versailles was less a maze than it was a magical kingdom, less a zone of confusion than a land of enchantment.

At Versailles fanciful display was matched by whimsical form. Notice that the labyrinth's multicursal pattern (Fig. 8.10) has no single center but rather three interconnected clusters of divergent geometric shapes. Although there is a primary entrance on the east, one could also enter by two back gates on the west. Moreover, although the fountains were numbered, it was not necessary to enjoy them in any particular sequence. Indeed, King Louis XIV is known to have "loved to discover the park in several manners,"[55] presumably to demonstrate that its pleasures were nearly inexhaustible. Finally, to follow the fountains in numerical order would require the maze-walker to "double back" over at least two of them—a clumsy arrangement unworthy of a Daedalus. In sum, most of the traditional qualities of the maze are lacking here at Versailles: there is no single entrance, no unicursal path or one direct route couched within a multitude of choices, and no progressive journey culminating in a single mysterious center. At Versailles, conspicuous display supplanted ingenious design.

. . .

Ultimately, the garden labyrinth suffered the same fate as did the church maze: it fell victim to the changing sensibilities of the eighteenth century. Across pre-revolutionary Europe, voices were being raised against extravagance and contrived artificiality. Rousseau urged a simpler, more natural life; Marie Antoinette became a shepherdess and took to a hut in the woods of Versailles. By the end of the century the highly controlled, geometric garden was giving way to the unfettered English landscape in which Nature could express herself freely.[56] Louis XIV's labyrinth was destroyed in 1774. In its place his grandson, Louis XVI, put a simple park with a single statue of Venus.[57] The contrived fantasy-land of the late Baroque garden maze, exemplified by the labyrinth at Versailles, went the way of the courtier's face paint, perfume, and powdered wig.

The Church Maze Disappears

The revival of classical antiquity during the Renaissance had suggested new forms and uses for the maze. The Protestant Reformation, in turn, accelerated the fragmentation of the medieval symbol, encouraging individual interpretation and experience. As Christ and then his knight, the Christian soldier, had once replaced Theseus, now the solitary pilgrim supplanted the warrior of the maze. Soon the pilgrim had to share the mazy path with the pleasure-seeker questing for nothing more than a few moments of fun. The labyrinth had been stripped of most of its sacred associations. At the least, it was no longer exclusively a hallowed symbol. But what became of the now deconsecrated church maze?

The English, of course, had never fashioned mazes on the floor of the church, preferring instead the outdoor turf or topiary maze where a spiritual environment need not exist.[58] Although there were many garden mazes in Germany, the only church maze known there (at St. Severin in Cologne) was destroyed for some unknown reason around 1840.[59] In Italy, the church maze seems not to have been the victim of any organized plan of destruction, but rather a casualty of neglect and random misfortune.[60] The maze at Pavia was in a state of disrepair in the late sixteenth century, as was that at Santa Maria in Trastevere in the early eighteenth. Those at Piacenza and at Santa Maria in Aquiro in Rome disappeared in the nineteenth century, while the small stone maze coming from Pontremoli survives, although the church in which it stood was destroyed by an Allied bombardment in 1945. Of the Italian mazes, only two, those at Lucca and Ravenna, remain in their original state.

Unlike their Italian brethren, the French clergy had long used the maze as a sacred space in which to perform liturgical rites. By the seventeenth century, however, the links between the labyrinth and the liturgy had been broken; the maze no longer had a theological justification. As a result, during a period of little more than a hundred years, from 1690 to 1795, the mazes at Auxerre, Sens, Arras, Reims, and St. Omer were removed. The revolutionary citizenry at Chartres contemplated taking out the labyrinth there as part of a general removal of the entire cathedral, but fortunately the plan died under the enormous weight of the task. In large measure, then, the French church mazes were destroyed not by neglect but by the more literal spirit of the eighteenth century, which had little sympathy for the symbols and superstitions of the Middle Ages. Along with saintly relics and old bishops' bones, the stones of the labyrinth were thrown upon the rubbish pile of Enlightenment disbelief.

Although we do not know all the particulars as to why, when, and how the French church mazes were destroyed, events at the cathedral of Reims may be taken as typical. In August 1778 Jean Jacquemart presented a petition to his fellow canons, which was discussed at a capitular meeting in the following terms:

> Having read the letters of Lord Jean Jacquemart, treasurer, in which is exposed the great indecency that arises owing to the labyrinth in the nave of this church because frequently people are wandering around on it, [and] in which he offers the sum of one thousand *livres* for its removal ... the chapter, gratefully accepting the proposition of said Lord Jacquemart, appoints Lord Senescallos and the master of the fabric, to refer thanks to said Lord [Jacquemart], and asks that the master of the fabric shall confer with him and with Lord Lefebvre, architect, on the subject of the labyrinth and that afterward he shall report back to the chapter.[61]

Once again it seems that pleasure-seekers on the maze were causing trouble. The threat to the maze was made worse by the fact that, true to the spirit of the Enlightenment, the clergy now had begun to brighten and "air out" the church. Darkly colored stained glass was removed in favor of clear panes, and parchment manuscripts were tossed away. Most important for the architecture of the church was the fact that in many cathedrals the late-medieval rood screen (see Fig. 8.3) was torn down. This stone wall, often five meters high and two meters wide, had separated the clergy in the choir from the populace in the nave. In its place was now set a simple wrought-iron grill in hopes of bringing clergy and populace closer together. The rood screens at Reims, Sens, and Chartres disappeared in 1744, 1762, and 1763, respectively.[62] But with intimacy came annoyance. The sights and sounds emanating from the maze now penetrated directly into the choir, as those of noisy tourists today intrude upon the clergy in the now open choir at Notre-Dame of Paris. For this reason the canons of Reims turned an especially sympathetic ear to the petition of Canon Jacquemart in 1778. The next year the black and white labyrinth was removed, replaced by a gleaming white floor. With the maze now gone, Canon Jacquemart could finally read his missal in peace.

CHAPTER NINE

Musical Mazes from Moses to Mozart

Wʜᴀᴛ ᴅᴏᴇs ᴛʜᴇ ᴍᴀᴢᴇ have to do with music? At first glance the two appear to have more differences than similarities. The maze is a physical object, and through it one either walks or follows a path with the eye. Music, on the other hand, is an invisible wonder—sounds and silences passing unseen through time. Do these two seemingly disparate phenomena have anything in common?

It takes time to proceed through a maze, just as time is required for a musical composition to unfold. Time, then, is a dimension common to both. More important, mazes and musical compositions involve a conscious organization of the route along which the maze-treader or the listener must pass. Mazes have paths that are always confusing and sometimes beautifully intricate. The twisting trail creates the shape of the maze. Music, too, has "directionality" in that the composer must lay out a line of progression—a sequence of sonic events—from beginning to end, and this also can create a form. Sometimes the path of a maze and a composition are identical; as we have seen, the retrograding pattern of the church labyrinth was mirrored in retrograde motion in early religious music.

Mazes and musical labyrinths, moreover, can project identical psychological states. A unicursal maze is a circumscribed zone in which a spiritual journey may begin and end. It possesses a traditional set of assumptions about the nature of that journey: the voyage will be a quest, a process that, once started, cannot be broken off; it will begin and end in the same place; the path of the return will reverse exactly the route of the entry; tension will exist within the maze, increasing as the center is approached and diminishing as it is left; and, finally, spiritual enlightenment will attend the pilgrim's progress—the wandering soul will undergo a trial, will be purified by the ordeal, and will depart the maze having risen to a higher realm of spiritual consciousness.

Music can simulate the psychological states experienced during a journey through a labyrinth. Sounds can be made to unfold with a purpose and be directed toward a goal. This goal—a final note, chord, or key—will be the same music as that with which the piece began. Tension can be placed at the center by means of dissonance, tonal conflict, or harmonic instability. Such tension can progressively increase toward the middle of the piece and diminish toward the end. The musical material on either side of the center can be similar or, perhaps, in mirror image (a musical palindrome or retrograde). Finally, a feeling of heightened perception can accompany a journey through the musical maze. Having surmounted some specific technical difficulty or complexity, the musical Daedalus now possesses a better understanding of his abilities, his art, and, by extension, the divine creator of all arts.

There is, of course, a more straightforward way of representing a labyrinth in sound: the story of the maze, or some part of it, can be set to music. Such music will seem labyrinth-like because it retells and amplifies through sound the myth of the maze. Thus, three ways in which musicians through the centuries have created musical mazes are duplicating a labyrinthine pattern, recreating the psychological states of a labyrinth, or setting part of the myth to music.

The Israelites Wander in Tonal Uncertainty

A simple example will explain how music might mirror the experience of the maze. Recall that in many medieval churches in the West, the clergy sang *When Israel went out of Egypt* (*In exitu Israel de Egypto*) on Easter Sunday as they came out of the baptistry and crossed the labyrinth in the nave.[1] Known throughout history as the Pilgrim's Psalm,[2] this chant tells how Moses led the Israelites out of bondage in Egypt, of their passage across the Red Sea, and of their doubt and uncertainty as they wandered in a wilderness for a quarantine of years before reaching the Promised Land. As part of the Book of Psalms, the text dates back, as tradition has it, to the time of King David. The melody to which it was sung may be equally ancient.

Psalm 113 has traditionally been chanted to an unusual melody called the *tonus peregrinus* (the "wandering tone").[3] It is so named either because this melody sets a text about wandering, or because the melody itself wanders

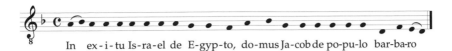

In   ex-i-tu Is-ra-el de E-gyp-to, do-mus Ja-cob de po-pu-lo bar-ba-ro

EXAMPLE 9.1 The wandering tone (*tonus peregrinus*) setting Psalm 113: *When Israel went out of Egypt.* From a tenth-century French manuscript (Paris, Bibliothèque nationale, MS fonds latin 1118, fol. 113v).

in pitch. The origins of the wandering tone can be traced back to the Jews of Yemen, whose musical practices are said to predate the destruction of the Second Temple.[4] In addition, Psalm 113 was sung to the wandering tone as the first psalm in the *Hallel* of the Passover liturgy. Thus it is possible that this melody, or something very much like it, was used by the descendants of David as they sang of their forebears' liberation from Egypt. Later the *tonus peregrinus* passed into the rites of the Byzantine church and into the West. By the ninth century the wandering tone had been added—as something in the nature of a special ornament—to the group of eight standard tones used for singing psalms in the Roman Catholic Church. Each of the standard eight had a reciting tone that was stable and undeviating, but not so the *tonus peregrinus,* which changed from "a" in the first phrase to "g" in the second (see Example 9.1).[5] The absence of a tonal anchor reflects the psychological state of those participating in the Exodus. It suggests the "shaking and quaking" that would occur on Easter Sunday in French cathedrals as the clergy crossed the maze.[6]

A fourteenth-century theologian, speaking of this moment in the Easter liturgy, said: "It is appropriate that the boys rejoice and dance in order to show the joy of the Jews who crossed the Red Sea and our joy at the redemption through the blood of Jesus Christ."[7] Dante, too, envisaged Christ liberating the elect from Purgatory and heard them sing *When Israel went out of Egypt.*

> As more and more toward us came, more bright
> Appear'd the bird of God, nor could the eye
> Endure his splendor near: I mine bent down.
> He drove ashore in a small bark so swift
> And light, that in its course no wave it drank.
> The heavenly steersman at the prow was seen,

Visibly written Blessed in his looks.
Within a hundred spirits and more there sat.
In exitu Israel de Egypto
All with one voice together sang . . .[8]

So, too, Martin Luther spoke of the ecstasy of liberation. Early in his career he preached an Easter sermon "on the psalm [113] in which joyfully all souls are led out."[9] Luther's musical disciples, including Johann Sebastian Bach, set the *tonus peregrinus* as liturgical polyphony into the nineteenth century.[10] Thus since time immemorial have the faithful celebrated the beginning of a spiritual exodus by means of a melody full of tonal uncertainty.

A Medieval Labyrinth of Love

The medieval clergy danced and reveled on the maze at Easter at churches in Auxerre, Sens, and Chartres, as we have seen. But were there others? Hints of such practices survive from the cathedrals of Amiens and Reims. On the afternoon of Easter Sunday, the bishop and younger clerics at medieval Amiens evidently played tennis and enjoyed similar amusements.[11] Later that day, at Easter Vespers, standing before the maze, they sang the hymn *O filii et filiae*,[12] which was danced at other churches into the seventeenth century. To this day it is sung around the world as *O Sons and Daughters, Let us Sing.*[13] Perhaps the spirit of Daedalus inspired the clergy at Amiens to dance on their maze, perhaps not. But it certainly fired the imagination of a poet and canon of the cathedral, Richard de Fournival.

Richard de Fournival (1201–1260) must be numbered among the most remarkable figures of the Middle Ages, the sort of polymath who puts the lie to the notion of "the Renaissance man" as an aborigine of the Renaissance.[14] A native of Amiens, Fournival served as chancellor of the cathedral for the last twenty years of his life, yet this churchman was also a *trouvère* poet, musician, philosopher, theologian, mathematician, astrologer, surgeon, and alchemist. After his death, his library of more than three hundred volumes—one of the largest private book collections of the Middle Ages—became the nucleus of the library of the new Collège de Sorbonne, the historical heart of today's University of Paris.[15]

Among the works of classical poetry owned by Richard de Fournival was

Ta - lent   a - voi - e   d'a - mer,   Mais pau -

our   m'est   pri - se.   Ki   le   m'a   to - lu.

Kar   i'oi   cieus   d'a - mours   blas - mer.   Et

de   son   ser - vi - che.   K'il l'ont   main - te -

nu   s'ai   per - chu,   K'il   n'en   pue - ent   tor - ner.

EXAMPLE 9.2 Richard de Fournival, *Talent avoie d'amer* (Arras, Bibliothèque municipale, MS 139, fols. 132v–133; the rhythm is conjectural).

a copy of Ovid's *Metamorphoses,* the principal source of the myth of
Daedalus and the Cretan labyrinth.[16] So taken with Ovid was Fournival that
he adopted "Ovidius" as his *nom de plume* when he sat down to write his *De
Vetula* (c.1250).[17] It took no less a poet than Petrarch to recognize that this
lengthy poem was, in fact, not a work surviving from classical antiquity but
a clever medieval forgery.[18] Surely a man whose Latin could pass for that of
Ovid and who owned a copy of *Metamorphoses* knew of "the house of
Daedalus," as the maze was called at Amiens.

If the labyrinth at the cathedral of Amiens was a classical symbol overlaid with Christian significance (see Fig. 2.10), in the music and poetry of
Richard de Fournival it becomes a metaphor for the snares of love. Love is
a labyrinth that closes fatally around the unsuspecting: this, at least at first
sight, appears to be the theme of Fournival's *I had the urge to love* (*Talent
avoie d'amer*), one of his twenty-one surviving songs.[19] A single melody carries each of five strophes (Example 9.2). As Fournival's song progresses, the
image of the maze becomes clearer. Strophe four equates the experience of
love with that of the house of Daedalus into which one can always enter at

will but never depart. In strophe five the Lover chooses not to embark on a quest like that of Theseus, because it is impossible to escape without the aid of the thread, presumably that of Ariadne.

But is it Ariadne's thread? Fournival's chanson would seem to be an early example of the literary "labyrinth of love," an allegorical poem in which the maze provides a forum in which the Lover can complain against Amor. Yet all manuscripts that preserve the song replace the key—and original—word "Theseü" with a later emendation, "Jhesu."[20] The poet, no less than the theologian, wishes to Christianize the classical myth here in the thirteenth century.[21] The thread of salvation, in this emended reading, might therefore be the Christian life-line of faith rather than Ariadne's twine. Like the multivalent pavement labyrinth at Amiens, this song by Fournival can be enjoyed for both its Christian and its classical resonances.[22]

I

I had the urge to love,
but fear now restrains me,
because I see how
even those who curse love
cannot escape from that to which
they have become subjugated.

II

I have seen the captured beast,
straining at his chains,
entangle himself all the more,
just as those who try to free
themselves from love are all the
more ensnared as they contemplate
the way by which to exit.

III

And he who feigns an
escape by claiming independence
is hopelessly lost,
because flattery is useless.
Indeed, the more one consumes
the draughts of passion, the more
one drinks the poison of love.

IV
For love is the house of Daedalus,
a construct easy to enter,
yet where all become prisoners,
because no one can find, or
point to, the place where
the entry was.

V
I have no desire to undertake
a great enterprise
as did Jesus [Theseus],
since it is impossible to
escape from love without the
aid of a thread; indeed, there
have been many with more courage
than I who have never returned.

A Canon in a Medieval Labyrinth

On 12 January 1377, a musician working in Paris completed a treatise on music theory to which he appended a musical composition in the form of a labyrinth (Fig. 9.1).[23] We do not know his name—and that may be just as well, for in his treatise he does little more than crib from the writings of other theorists on topics such as counterpoint, tuning, and notation. Our Parisian musician's musical maze has no relevance to his treatise and seems to be merely a decorative afterthought. Yet, like the intricate labyrinth of Daedalus, it challenges our powers to unravel a riddle, indeed two.

Here labyrinthine symbolism radiates on several levels. First, the music of the maze carries a poem, *En la maison Dedalus,* in which the labyrinth serves as a metaphor for the impossible quest: the unhappy, indeed suicidal, Lover cannot penetrate to the heart of his desire. She rests imprisoned at the center of a maze, one without discernible entry or exit. The poetic conceits here are not clever—musicians are rarely great poets. Yet the picture of a maze comes to life in an ingenious way: text and music are shaped to form a maze.

The composer has constructed an eleven-course labyrinth employing

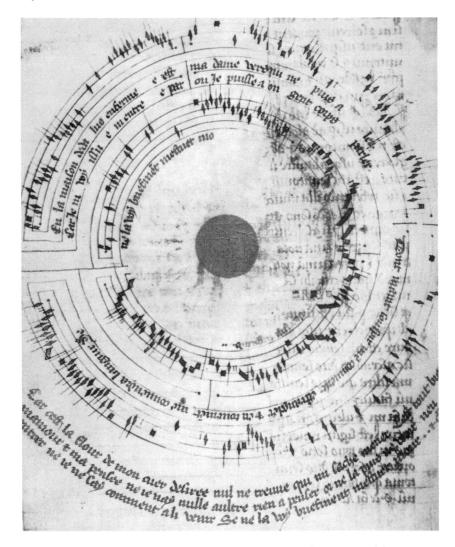

FIGURE 9.1 A fourteenth-century song for three voices, *En la maison Dedalus,* constructed as a maze. The entrance is to the left.

the lines that delineate the tracks as lines of a musical staff; these same lines also carry the first strophe of the poem, a two-strophe ballade. The maze functions as a true, unicursal labyrinth: the eye of the viewer (unlike the Lover) can enter and follow a path to the center. As it does so, the voice must sing what the eye sees, thereby transforming this clever design into a pleasing musical composition.

Starting near the point of entry, an upper voice intones a text and melody situated by means of a "C" clef. The melody proceeds around the outer tracks of the circular maze and then continues and concludes on the innermost tracks. Simultaneously, a lower voice (tenor) begins, notated on the innermost tracks, commencing at "one o'clock" as Figure 9.1 is viewed.

As with most medieval mazes, *En la maison Dedalus* was constructed with a compass, which, along with the line and the square, was one of the principal tools of the medieval architect. Every design for a wheel (*rota*) or a rose window (*rosa*) was made by means of a compass. The builders memorialized in the labyrinths at Reims and Amiens are holding a compass, as is the architect sculpted on the north portal at Chartres. Dante even refers to God, the heavenly architect, as "He who turned His compass round the limit of the world" (see Fig. 1.8).[24] The circle generated by a compass was a sign of divine perfection, in part because the end of the circuitous line merges imperceptibly into the beginning. Indeed, where does a circle begin? *En la maison Dedalus* is the first piece in the history of music to make use of circular notation.

But further ingenuity is hidden in this maze. As we reach the center we see a Latin inscription written beneath the tenor voice (again, at "one o'-clock" in Fig. 9.1). It reads: "The tenor creates the contratenor, one chasing after the other" (*Tenor faciens contratenorem alter alterum fugando*). This means that two voices are to be derived from the single line of the tenor: a voice called the contratenor enters after the tenor and follows its steps exactly, thereby creating a canon at the unison (a simple canon, or round, the voices of which start on the same pitch).

Canons are difficult to create. The composer must invent a melody that can both stand on its own and also generate a pleasing harmony when sung against itself at a staggered interval of time. To write a two-voice canon that will also not be dissonant with yet a third voice, the upper voice of *En la maison Dedalus,* requires even greater cunning. And herein lies the connection to the labyrinth. The maze had traditionally stood as a symbol of complex artistry, an artifact revealing almost super-human craftsmanship. It signified a level of technical accomplishment worthy of a true master, a Daedalus of design, be it in architecture, literature, or poetry. Just as the compass became, and remains, the device of the mason, the canon would come to represent the professional emblem of the musician. Later, when J. S. Bach commissioned his own portrait, he made sure he held in his hands a canon he had crafted.[25] To write a recondite canon signaled that the composer was no less than a musical Daedalus. Musical example A.2, given in Appendix A, shows the melody that is written around the outer tracks of the maze, as well as the tenor and contratenor that form the canon. This music accompanies two strophes of text:

I

My lady is enclosed in
the house of Daedalus where I
cannot go, for I see no exit
or entry by means of which I
may commune with her comely form.
And thus I am compelled to stifle
many a sigh, and languish
in torment;
if I do not see her soon I must die.

II

Though she is the flower of my heart's desire,
I find no one who can lead me there.
She is all good, my love and my obsession.
Though she consumes all my thoughts,
I can neither see nor touch her.
I know not how to get to her;
if I do not see her soon I must die.

Thus *En la maison Dedalus* is ingenious in more ways than one. It possesses the usual tension inherent in the maze, the discord between bewilderment and artful construction; the path of the labyrinth is difficult to follow (as the Lover laments), yet it cleverly leads both to the center and to a successful performance of the music. But this maze is doubly diabolical, for it requires that we not only find the route to the center but that we unlock the riddle of the canon that rests therein. This musical Daedalus has wrapped a puzzle inside an enigma.

Labyrinthine Motets from Renaissance Venice

The invention of printing in the West around 1440 was the most important development in human communication between the appearance of letters in the fourth millennium before Christ and the advent of the computer. Although printers' shops first sprang up along the banks of the Rhine River, the center of the book trade soon shifted to Venice. By the end of the fifteenth century, as many as 150 different Venetian printers had turned out some 4,000 separate titles.[26] Needless to say, this thriving commerce in books was largely a reflection of a general revival of classical Latin literature throughout humanistic Italy.

No book was more revivified in Renaissance Venice than Ovid's *Metamorphoses,* which, as we have seen, was the primary source for the tale of Theseus and the Minotaur. At least seven different editions of it were produced there during the 1490s alone.[27] One of these, a printing of 1497 issued by the firm of Rossa and Giunta, caused something of a sensation: not only was the text translated into Italian for the first time, but also the adventures of the Greek heroes were portrayed by means of woodcuts.[28] Something akin to a fifteenth-century comic book had been created! Ovid's now-illustrated classic was reprinted many times into the sixteenth century as numerous Venetian publishers sought to capitalize on its success. One of these was Girolamo Scotto (c.1505–1572).

During a career spanning more than thirty-five years, Scotto produced 405 different books for humanistic readers.[29] In 1543 he issued a new printing of Ovid's *Heroides,* executed, as was now fashionable, with illustrations. Here the story of Theseus and the Minotaur (Poem 10) was enhanced by means of a newly designed labyrinth. But Scotto was not only a publisher of humanistic texts, he was also one of the principal printers of music in Renaissance Italy. In 1554, no doubt wishing to exploit the success of illustrated editions of Greek mythology, he issued a set of four volumes called *Motets of the Labyrinth: Sacred Songs or Motets* (*Motetti del laberinto: Sacrarum Cantionum sive Motettorum*). Each contained a collection of motets (devotional songs in Latin) for four or five voices, with a total of seventy-one pieces by both major and minor composers.[30]

To create a frontispiece for each of the four collections, the resourceful Scotto simply reused the woodblock he had fashioned a decade earlier for

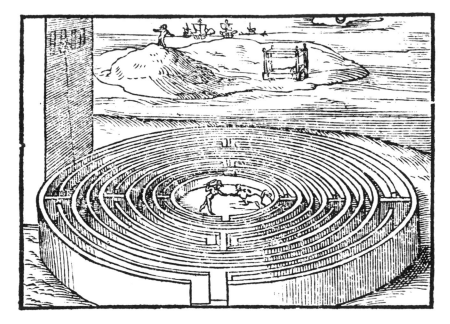

FIGURE 9.2 Frontispiece to Girolamo Scotto's printing of 1554, *Motetti del laberinto.*

his edition of Ovid's *Heroides,* now surrounding it with an appropriate introductory text for each volume (Fig. 9.2). Club in hand, Theseus engages
the Minotaur in combat within an eleven-track maze. In the background
lies the Isle of Naxos. Here the abandoned Ariadne has left the conjugal bed
and climbed to a hill where she laments the betrayal of Theseus, whose ships
disappear in the distance. Thus the chronological events of the myth are to
be taken in by the eye all at once, in what art historians call a simulacrum.

How do Scotto's four sets of motets relate to the labyrinth? Here no musical process duplicates the workings of a maze, but rather a succession of
texts speak to the theological meaning of the labyrinth as it was then understood by the established Church of Rome. In words and music, Christ
girds himself for battle in the infernal regions (I:6);[31] he alone can fight for
all humanity (I:10); the gates of Hell will not stand against his might (I:5);
as Daniel escaped from the den of the lions, so Christ triumphed in Hell
(IV:12); life is a labyrinth, the tracks of which are known only to God (II:11
and III:7); like Saul on the road to Damascus, the pilgrim requires divine
enlightenment (IV:6).[32]

FIGURE 9.3 A recently repaired statue of St. Theodore, presently on display at the Doge's palace and soon to be returned to a place of honor in the Piazzetta San Marco in Venice.

Martyred saints, both male and female, come into view. St. Cecilia is invoked in three motets (III:4, III:13, and III:14), not only because she is the patron saint of music, but also because her suffering was among the longest and most gruesome ordeals experienced by Christian heroines.[33] Succor is also asked of the obscure St. Christina (IV:4), seemingly an odd object of devotion until we remember that Christina herself miraculously descended into Hell and returned to earth to astound her neighbors, thereby gaining the name St. Christina the Astonishing. *Motets of the Labyrinth* concludes with an homage to the Greek warrior St. Theodore, in which the last line reads: "and he [Theodore] squashed the head of the dragon" (IV:16). St. Theodore, whose relics were brought to Venice in 1096, was one of two patron saints of the city, the other being St. Mark.[34] Even today a statue of the Greek hero stands prominently in the Piazzetta San Marco, with a dragon subdued beneath his lance and shield (Fig. 9.3). In the statue, as well as in the final sounds of this labyrinthine collection, yet another warrior has triumphed over the forces of evil.

The *Missa El Laberintho* for King Charles II of Spain

Charles II (1661–1700) was arguably Spain's worst king. But it probably wasn't his fault—at least social theorists attribute his mental and physical deficiencies to 150 years of intense inbreeding within the Spanish Hapsburg royal line. At the age of four Charles still could not stand; at six he could not yet walk.[35] He proudly wore the collar of a knight of the Golden Fleece, as had his father, grandfather, great-grandfather, and so on back through nine generations to Duke Philip the Good of Burgundy, who founded the Order in 1430.[36] Yet he never learned to read, and to write he required an aide to guide his pen. When he died without issue on 1 November 1700, he brought to an end the dynasty of the Hapsburgs in Spain.

But even substandard monarchs receive sovereign flattery. Thus it was that Juan del Vado (c.1625–1691),[37] organist and music master to Charles II, dedicated to him a collection of six *Cánones enigmáticos* and six polyphonic Masses.[38] Canon V is called *The Wandering Hercules* (*El Ercules Peregrino*).[39] The page is bordered by the pillars of Hercules with the epigraph "non plus ultra," the words inscribed by Hercules on the towering rocks at the mouth of the Mediterranean where he stood and could see "nothing more beyond." *The Wandering Hercules* yields an astonishing 64 resolutions; the challenge is to extract 64 compositions (28 duos, 21 trios, 14 quartets, and a quintet) from within del Vado's enigmatic canon.

But just as Christopher Columbus proved Hercules shortsighted, the composer tells us, so the musician can also go farther. As a sixth and final canon, del Vado fabricates an even more ingenious work, one he dedicates to his royal patron by means of the title *El Carlos* (Fig. 9.4) Now connect-

FIGURE 9.4 The circular canon *El Carlos* with the traditional columns of Hercules. The nightingale at the center signifies that Nature is the source of all Art.

ing the pillars of Hercules are the words "plus ultra," a device that Charles II borrowed from his great-great-grandfather, Emperor Charles V (Charles I of Spain), the political force behind the conquest of the New World.[40] So, too, there is more beyond in the music, for from this new *El Carlos* spring no fewer than 82 small compositions, as an accompanying poem suggests:

> This very succinct canon
> Has eighty-two cases.
> View them with care;
> Look for the thread of the labyrinth.
> I paint for you eighteen duos.
> You will see thirty-six trios [and]
> Twenty-eight quartets more.
> In distinct positions,
> Doctrine without opinions,
> What a Master you would prove.[41]

Juan del Vado, musical Daedalus, thus challenges us to become master of the labyrinth. We must find its thread and thereby extract 82 short pieces from the circular music before us. Every contrapuntally correct combination of voices, every interval of delay between voices, and every possible starting pitch must be identified. We must also make sure that the voices go upside down as well as right side up, in mirror image (musical inversion). How do we know? If we look carefully at the columns of Hercules (Fig. 9.4), we can see within them the words *I go and I come* (*Vado et Venio*); one goes up, while the other comes down. Obviously this is a pun on the composer's name, but it is also a reference to the words of Christ at the Last Supper when he announces to the disciples, "I go away and come again unto you" (*vado et venio ad vos;* John 14:28). The recursive prophecy of the Lord provides a clue to the resolution of the puzzle: the melody can go in contrary motion against itself. If we see the music in terms of a mirror, we will master the labyrinth. The feeble-minded king, however, surely could not have solved the complex riddle bearing his name. Thus Juan del Vado, anticipating the crossword puzzle book of today, gives the solution (all 82 pieces) at the end of the manuscript.

But del Vado offers more: for each canon he provides a corresponding Mass. Thus the last Mass, for six voices, he entitles *El Laberintho.* It is so called because it makes use of musical inversion, just as did the enigmatic

EXAMPLE 9.3 The opening of the *Agnus dei* of the *Missa El Laberintho* by Juan del Vado (Madrid, Biblioteca nacional, MS M. 1323, fols. 156v–157).

canon *El Carlos*. At the beginning of the *Agnus dei*, for example, the quintus and sextus voices are inversions of the soprano and tenor (Example 9.3). Musical inversion is contrary motion expressed in terms of pitch, whereas retrograde motion is contrary motion expressed through time. They are both musical analogues of the physical and theological reversals inherent in the unicursal Christian maze. As Christian exalts in Bunyan's *Pilgrim's Progress* (1678): "Rejoyce not against me, O mine enemy! when I fall, I shall arise" (Micah 7:8).

Handel, Theseus, and the Minotaur

Only one operatic work, George Frideric Handel's *Ariadne on Crete* (*Arianna in Creta*, 1734), puts Theseus and the Minotaur at center stage.[42] Yet Handel's libretto radically alters the traditional myth.[43] Theseus arrives on Crete not as a captive Athenian to be sacrificed to the Minotaur but rather as an adventurer, an inter-island flesh trader, who conveys to Crete ever more sacrificial victims; Ariadne is a slave girl at the court of King Minos, unrecognized as his daughter. The power of love draws her to Theseus. Compelled not by necessity or duty, but rather by pride and ambition, Theseus vows to slay the Minotaur. Only when Ariadne's plaintive attempts to dissuade him have failed does she finally offer her hero the magical clew of golden thread. The action moves predictably toward the climactic final act in which Theseus and the Minotaur engage in mortal combat.

EXAMPLE 9.4 Beginning of *A Song of the Labyrinth* (*Un canto del Labirinto*) from the final act of Handel's *Ariadne on Crete*.

The scene is set in a "frightful subterranean cavern" beneath the palace of King Minos. Strains of *A Song of the Labyrinth* (*Un canto del Labirinto*; Example 9.4) emanate from within; these are the cries of the tribute children about to be sacrificed to the monster. Theseus enters and gives voice to their fears as he proceeds through the labyrinth:

> Where am I, oh what horror?
> The hard stones end at every turn of this horrid enclosure.

> What shall I do, where, through this oblique path, shall
> I direct my uncertain steps?
> Here I think I see the footprints of the double-form monster.
> He must not be far.
> I hang the guiding thread to the wall
> and in the center I await the cruel creature.

The accompanying music is slow and stately, with double-dotted rhythms in the style of a regal French overture—Theseus is, after all, the son of an Athenian king. By means of a heroic *da capo* aria (ABA), Handel forces the adventurer to screw up his courage: "Here I challenge you, O infamous monster. Come, you do not scare me!" To create a proper mood, the composer employs a battery of tried-and-true mimetic gestures: rapidly repeated notes signify aggression, running scales suggest fast-paced action, and lengthy passages of vocal bravura demonstrate physical prowess. In the middle section of the aria (section B), Theseus experiences a moment of tenderness as he reflects upon his love for Ariadne: "You [monster] will fall. But if I should become the prey of your desires, spare at least the heart, for that is no longer mine." Appropriately enough, the accompanying music for this B section turns rhythmically flaccid, harmonically passionate at first but subdued at the end.

With the lengthy aria completed, the battle is now joined by means of an interlude entitled *il combattimento* for instruments alone. This background music has the same fighting spirit as Theseus's aria. To these energetic strains the combatants must pantomime a fight to the death.

When the biform monster finally falls, Theseus bursts forth: "I have conquered! Thanks to the gods" (*Ho vinto! Grazie ai Numi*). The warrior of the maze is again victorious—but now he must exit the labyrinth. He does so, surprisingly, to the same instrumental interlude heard during the battle; Handel seems not to have bothered with appropriately bewildering exit music. The stage direction reads: "He returns through the subterranean [maze] where he rejoins Ariadne." Thereafter King Minos recognizes Ariadne as his long-lost daughter and unites the couple in eternally blissful matrimony. No matter that Handel and his librettists have fundamentally changed the story of the maze; the conventions of Baroque *opera seria* require a happy ending.

What goes unnoticed in Handel's *Ariadne on Crete* is the silent presence

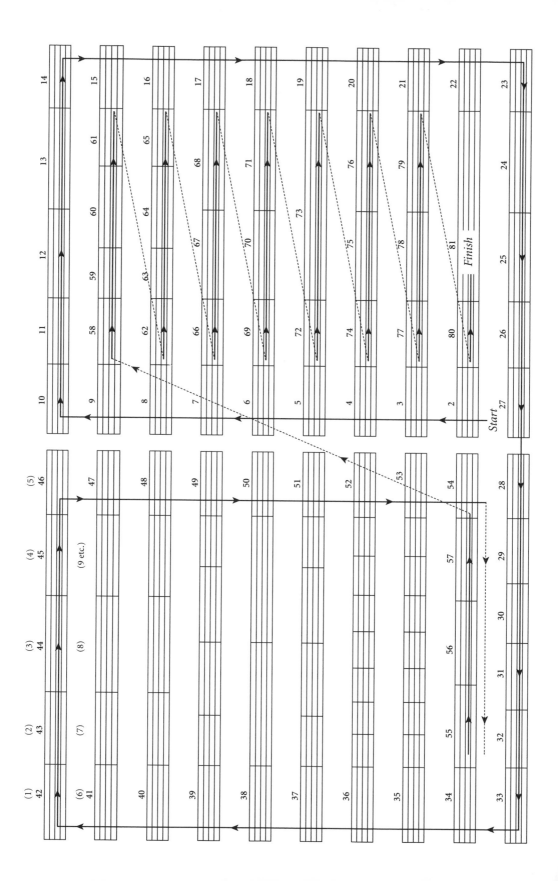

of the Minotaur. Although we see the "double-form monster" during his mortal combat with Theseus, he neither speaks nor sings. Even here in his one moment of glory on the stage, the Minotaur is mute. Thus we are eternally denied, in myth, poetry, and song, his side of the story.

Fiddling through a Baroque Maze

Some musical labyrinths, such as Handel's *Ariadne on Crete,* set the story of the maze to music. Others duplicate the psychological states experienced during a journey through a maze. Still others seek to create a maze-like path by means of musical notation. The route might be circular and constructed with the aid of a compass (see Figs. 9.1 and 9.4), or it might be both rectangular and serpentine, as in the case of the labyrinthine score created by Wolfgang Caspar Printz (1641–1717).

Printz was a German novelist, music theorist, composer, and teacher of composition. When he published an expanded edition of his treatise *The Satirical Composer* (*Phrynis Mitilenaeus oder Satyrischer Componist*), he included a *Musical Labyrinth* (*Labyrinthus Musicus*) to demonstrate the craft of musical invention.[44] In this piece two violinists start simultaneously, Violin I at the beginning of the score (bar 42; see numbers in Fig. 9.5) and Violin II in the middle of the bottom staff (bar 27). As Violin I (called the Ordinary One) proceeds in normal fashion from left to right across the page, Violin II (called the Vagabond or the Errant One) moves rectilinearly and ultimately in a serpentine path, following a sequence of arabic numbers (1–81) written above and below selected measures. Sometimes the violins play measures quite distant from one another, while at other times they play adjacent measures. Thus something akin to a game of Fox and Goose is at work in Printz's *Musical Labyrinth.* Supporting the two voices, but incidental to the game of the labyrinth, is a chordal accompaniment (a *basso continuo* with figured bass). But once again, there is more to this musical labyrinth than first meets the eye.

In Printz's *Musical Labyrinth* it is the Errant One (Violin II) that sets forth as a musical pilgrim. The performer must follow exactly a prescribed succession of measures, an act that requires a certain amount of attention

FIGURE 9.5 The path of the Errant One in Wolfgang Caspar Printz's *Labyrinthus Musicus* (1696).

but no special musical skill. When the Errant One reaches measure 23 in the lower right corner, however, he must perform the notes of eleven consecutive measures backwards, starting with the right-most note of the measure and progressing to the left. Any musician would find this a daunting challenge, just as we would find it extremely difficult to read eleven sentences of this book reflected in a mirror. Finally, toward the center of this labyrinth the two violins come face to face (bars 53 and 54) and tread on the same musical staff at a distance of only one measure apart. The consequence of this moment of "follow the leader" is a short canon at the unison of the sort we saw earlier in *En la maison Dedalus*. Thus Printz's *Musical Labyrinth* possesses two qualities that we have come to associate with the maze: rigorous craftsmanship in the form of a canon at the center, and reverse movement. In the Middle Ages retrograde motion often served to signify the recursive journey of Christ. Here in this Baroque labyrinth, however, there is no symbolism, just process. This maze is a brain-teaser designed to test the powers of concentration of the Errant One.

Baroque Tonal Labyrinths

We have seen how the early Christian fathers employed the labyrinth as a metaphor for the sinful world in which the errant soul must wander. So, too, medieval architects made the maze a symbol of both divine perfection and hellish confusion.[45] Now in the early eighteenth century, musicians gave yet another meaning to the maze. The labyrinth came to symbolize a musical problem that could be solved only with the greatest ingenuity, specifically a problem involving tuning and temperament.

To discuss complicated issues of musical tuning and temperament in a few words is no easy task, but the gist of the matter is this.[46] In music there is a discrepancy between musical intervals derived mathematically through Pythagorean ratios and those produced naturally by means of the harmonic series (vibrating strings and pipes). Because of this, only a few intervals within the scale can be tuned purely, according to mathematical precision; the remaining ones will have to be adjusted around these in one fashion or another. Prior to the time of Bach, musicians usually centered the purest intervals around the chords built on and including the pitch C. Thus pieces could be written and sound perfectly in tune in the key of C, with no sharps or flats, and in closely related keys with just a few of these accidentals (the keys of G, F, D, and B♭ major, as well as A, E, D, and G minor). More distantly related keys, however, such as B♭ minor (five flats) and F♯ major (six sharps) to name two, were avoided because they were wildly out of tune compared to those nearer to C—they contained a "wolf tone," as musicians said. Consequently, although early music was purer in regard to the intonation of a core of chords centering around C, it was also more limited. Composers could not modulate far away from C within a single piece. Nor could they write entire pieces in distant keys without retuning the entire instrument. This "pre-modern" method of tuning was called mean-tone temperament.

To get around the limitations of mean-tone temperament, musicians began to experiment with the idea of tuning the pitches within the octave (the twelve notes of the chromatic scale) in twelve if not equal, at least more equal semitones; they began gradually to replace mean-tone temperament with equal temperament. Although the transition from one system to the other would take nearly two centuries, by the time of Bach many musicians demanded a keyboard in which all the notes were slightly, yet more or less equally, out of tune. But at least now the wolf did not howl quite so ferociously when the performer wandered to distant keys. A tonal journey to all keys could be made, yet it still seemed frightening and bewildering. For that reason the metaphor of the labyrinth was used to describe it.

The German composer Johann Fischer (c.1670–1746) was the first to attempt to explain the challenge of a tonal journey in terms of a labyrinth. In the preface to his *Ariadne Musica* (1702), he calls upon Ariadne, the heroine of the labyrinth, to lead the amazed musician through the dangers of distant keys:

> Arise Ariadne, not that fictitious one honored by the verses of the great poets but another who, though the earlier one appeared to be real, personifies truth itself. For if that Ariadne led Theseus, who was striving for Hercules' bravery, into the dangers of the Cretan labyrinth and through the anfractuous twists and turns of its path, by means of a guiding string, to the threshold so that he might acquire an immortal name by killing the Minotaur, and if then she led him out safe and sound—so this New-Organwork, at the threshold of this art, directs the fearful, endangered wanderer through the labyrinth of many difficulties and the greatest errors by this sweetest thread (its preludes and fugues), and in this way will

teach how to traverse these very same errors of difficulty and cut the throat of the Minotaur.[47]

The twenty pairs of preludes and fugues that follow are the musical equivalent of Ariadne's life-giving thread. By placing them in a carefully ordered sequence of keys, Fischer shows the musician how to progress from one key to the next. He starts with a prelude and fugue in C major, then writes one in C♯ minor, then D minor and D major, and so on, moving by half-steps up the keyboard until the sequence of pieces returns to C; the last prelude and fugue (number 20) is in C minor, just as the first was in C major. However, Fischer has avoided the most distant keys, that of F♯ major with six sharps, for example, and E♭ minor with six flats; he has written only twenty pairs rather than twenty-four. Despite the composer's prefatory promise to lead the courageous musician through the dangerous twists in the maze of harmony, he takes a short cut: he evades those keys that traditionally were the most problematic in terms of tuning. It was left to Johann Sebastian Bach to write a set of pieces that would unwind and recoil fully Ariadne's thread through all twenty-four major and minor keys.

Perhaps taking their musical cue from Fischer, two other musicians fashioned labyrinthine pieces at about this same time. Marin Marais (1656–1728), composer to King Louis XV in Paris, wrote a work entitled *Le labyrinthe* (1717) as part of his *Suite with a Foreign Flavor* (*Suite d'un goût Etranger*).[48] Designed to be played by a solo viola da gamba (a six-string cousin of the cello), *Le labyrinthe* starts with a theme firmly in the key of A major. Marais then pushes the piece through a succession of keys each possessing, in turn, one additional sharp (to E, B, F♯, C♯, and G♯). Finally, he stops on a D♯ major chord, an exceedingly foreign tonality indeed (five sharps and two double sharps)! By means of an enharmonic respelling, D♯ major becomes E♭ major (three flats).[49] From there Marais proceeds along an avenue of keys, each of which has one flat fewer than the preceding, until he reaches C major. After an extended section in C he works his way back to a conclusion in A major, the tonality in which he had begun.

Marais made his labyrinthine tonal journey by departing through the keys with sharps and returning through those with flats. It was also possible to journey the other way, first through the keys with flats and then home through those with sharps. This is the route taken in Friedrich Suppig's *Labyrinthus Musicus* (1722).[50] On the title page of the piece the little-known

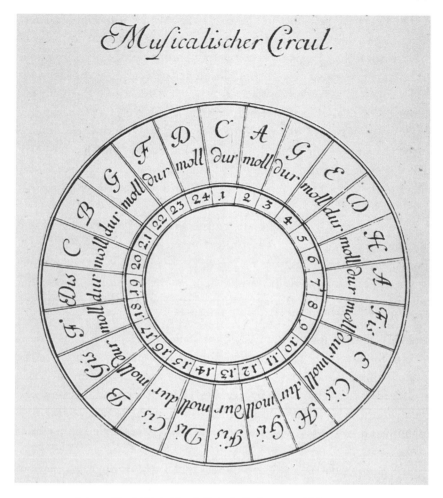

FIGURE 9.6 Johann David Heinichen's "Musicalischer Circul," from his *Der General-Bass in der Composition* (1728), demonstrates a "strange loop," the traditional circle of fifths. Heinichen calls this sequence "the labyrinth of twenty-four keys" (p. 915).

Suppig declares his labyrinth to be "a Fantasia through all keys, namely through 12 major and 12 minor, that is altogether 24 keys, to be played on the harpsichord without pedal or on the organ with pedal." As advertised, Suppig works through all twenty-four keys in this lengthy, one-movement piece, progressing from C major to A minor, F major, D minor, B♭ major, G minor, E♭ major, and so forth, and ultimately passing back through the sharp keys to the starting point of C major.

The operating principle in Marais's *Le labyrinthe* and Suppig's *Laby-rinthus Musicus* is one familiar to all musicians today: modulation around the circle of fifths.[51] Passing, or modulating, through all twenty-four major and minor keys could be verbalized through the metaphor of a labyrinth or visualized as an object, specifically a wheel. Thus music theorists, beginning with Johann David Heinichen (1683–1729), constructed what they called "musical circles" with the familiar key of C major (no sharps or flats) at the top and distant F♯ major (six sharps) at the bottom (Fig. 9.6).[52] In this way it was immediately apparent that the musician could journey either to the right, through the sharp keys, or to the left, through the flat ones.

Yet no matter which direction the musician chooses, the experience will not sit easily upon the ear of the listener if an unequal temperament is used. The farther one proceeds from the key of C, the more dissonant the intervals become. F♯ major was the most distant and dissonant key. It was a tritone away from C. (The tritone consists of three whole tones and thus is a half-step less than a perfect fifth.) Because of its extreme dissonance, that interval had traditionally been called the *diabolus in musica*. Thus a devil lurks in the center of even these musical mazes. To soften the impact of the demonic dissonance, Heinichen urges that the musical pilgrim go slowly and steadily (*gradatim*), step by step, key by key, slowing down now and then.[53] In this way the ear will have time to absorb the impact of each new tonality, and the musical wayfarer will return safely to the beginning point of the journey.

The philosopher Denis Diderot knew that a trip through the maze of harmony could be a frightening experience. Thus in his *Leçons de clavecin et principes d'harmonie,* written with Antoine Bemetzrieder in 1771, he offers a parable of a man who proceeds "through the detours of the labyrinth, led only by the principal harmonies of the twenty four keys." In Diderot's maze there are as many psychic states as there are tonalities.

> Imagine a man awakening at the center of a labyrinth. Immediately he looks to the right and the left for an exit. One moment he believes he has reached the end of his errors; he stops. He follows with an uncertain and trembling step the perhaps misleading route which opens before him. Again he is led astray. He proceeds, and after some turns and returns, the place from which he left is where he again finds himself. There he looks around and perceives a straighter route. He throws himself into it. He

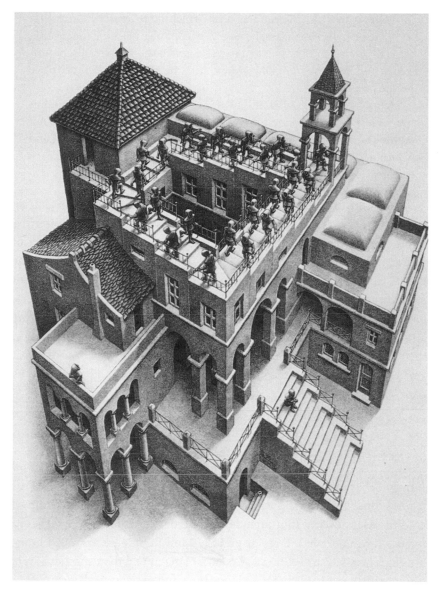

FIGURE 9.7 In M. C. Escher's *Ascending and Descending* (1960) armed men march upward—and downward—without getting higher or lower, thereby creating the sense of an infinite progression having no beginning or end.

imagines a free place beyond a forest which he proposes to cross. He runs; he rests; he runs again; he climbs and climbs, reaching the summit of a hill; he descends; he falls and rises, bruised he falls and refalls; he proceeds; and he arrives. Looking around him, he recognizes the very place where he awoke!

Agitation and pain seize his soul. He laments; his complaint resounds through the places around him. What will become of him? He does not know. He abandons himself to his fate, which promises him an exit and which deceives him. Scarcely has he taken a few steps than he is led back to the place where he began.[54]

Here in the tonal labyrinth, just as in the unicursal maze, the beginning and end are always the same. In a maze one moves away from the starting point while progressing inexorably toward it. Similarly, in the circle of fifths, the farther one pushes straight away from the key of C, the closer one gets to it. This sort of miraculous progression, one in which movement along an apparently straight line ultimately leads back to the beginning, has been called a "strange loop." It occurs not only when one is navigating around a globe or any circle, but also in legal, political, and mathematical theory as well as in the visual arts, best exemplified in the works of M. C. Escher (Fig. 9.7).[55] J. S. Bach knew of the strange loop, and he followed its path on more than one occasion.[56]

Bach's *Little Harmonic Labyrinth*

Johann Sebastian Bach might have called his famous *Well-Tempered Keyboard* a tonal labyrinth. Books I (1722) and II (1742) of this two-volume set each consist of twenty-four preludes and fugues in each of the twenty-four major and minor keys. Pairs of preludes and fugues are arranged in ascending chromatic order, first one pair in C major and then another pair in C minor, then one in C♯ major and C♯ minor, and so on until all twenty-four keys of the chromatic scale have been provisioned, including the devilish F♯ major. At the end, implicitly, the tonality has returned to the initial C major. The *Well-Tempered Keyboard* is no less labyrinthine than the works of Fischer and Suppig. So, too, Bach might have called his *Canon per tonos* from *The Musical Offering* a labyrinth, for it also circles in a miraculous loop, moving progressively through the keys of C, D, E, F♯, G♯, B♭, and safely

FIGURE 9.8 "A German maze" of uncertain date associated with the region of Anhalt.

back to C. What Bach did call a labyrinth, however, was his short piece for organ: *Little Harmonic Labyrinth* (*Kleines harmonisches Labyrinth*).[57]

As is appropriate for a maze, Bach divides his *Little Harmonic Labyrinth* into three sections: *Introitus, Centrum,* and *Exitus* (the music is given as Example A.3 in Appendix A). Instead of moving slowly around the circle of fifths in the *Introitus,* Bach accelerates rapidly—so fast, in fact, that by measure 11 (the exact midpoint of the *Introitus*) he has already moved from the initial key of C major to F♯ major, thereby traversing the diabolical tritone. Along the way the listener is forced to endure some of the most unsettling harmonic shifts anywhere in the Bach repertoire, changes that would have sounded all the more painful in Bach's day on an instrument using an unequal tuning. From F♯ major the performer works his way back to C, this time C minor, the auditory pain subsiding along the way. The *Centrum* of Bach's labyrinth is a three-voice fugue of twelve measures, a very short fugue indeed by Bach's standards. At the exact midpoint (measure 7), Bach applies retrograde motion to the pairs of notes that form the fugal subject. Toward the end he inscribes his own name using the German spelling of the notes B♭-A-C-H(=B♮) most prominently in the soprano line. The *Exitus* is much like the *Introitus,* moving quickly from C to distant keys, and then, with sometimes bizarre harmonic shifts, returning to the initial key of C major. The highly orthodox final cadence in C serves to reinforce the feeling that this harrowing tonal journey has come safely to an end.

Taken as a whole, Bach's *Little Harmonic Labyrinth* is something of a palindrome. It consists of two tonally recursive movements surrounding a brief fugue. The framing prelude (*Introitus*) and postlude (*Exitus*) contain the most distant harmonies and, accordingly, painful dissonances. Bach's center, however, is tonally rock solid, sitting squarely in C minor at beginning and end. It has none of the disconcerting dissonance experienced within the two flanking sections, those which lead directly into and out of the center.

Bach's labyrinth is also highly symmetrical. The *Introitus* consists of eighty beats, the *Centrum* forty-eight, and the *Exitus* also eighty.[58] The retrograde in the *Centrum* begins exactly where the second half commences. Thus the formal plan created by the path of Bach's labyrinth is rather similar to the one found in a labyrinth from Anhalt, Germany, an area in which Bach once worked (Fig. 9.8).[59] The two halves of this German maze are almost mirror images of each other. Confusion is rampant on the left and the right, but the center is secure and strong. Bach's maze is therefore a maze *in bono*—the harmonic Devil skulks on the sides, but not in the center.

More than the other harmonic mazes of the period, Bach's *Little Harmonic Labyrinth* is faithful to the spirit of a true labyrinth. The pieces by Fischer, Marais, and Suppig simply move through difficult keys and back to the beginning. Bach's labyrinth, however, with its tonal progression C-F♯-C, C minor, C-F♯-C, mirrors the double retrograding progress inherent in many mazes. It also has a distinct and substantive center, one that encompasses both retrograde motion and canon (or at least fugue, a less strict form of canon). Canons, as we have seen, can be found at the heart of musical mazes from the fourteenth through the seventeenth centuries. If the *Little Harmonic Labyrinth* seems strange or bewildering compared with more conventional organ works of Bach, that is precisely the point. It is a true maze, and its intent is to confuse and confound the listener.

Where did Bach get the idea for his musical labyrinth? Surely he knew of Fischer's *Ariadne Musica* of 1702, for he later borrowed fugue subjects from it. Surely, too, the devout Bach knew of the traditional theological meaning

FIGURE 9.9 The labyrinth at the court of Anhalt-Cöthen (upper right) in an engraving by Matthaeus Merian in *Topographia Superioris Saxoniae* (1650), displayed today at the castle of Cöthen. Bach worked at this court between 1717 and 1723.

of the maze from Lutheran emblem books.[60] But he may have found inspiration closer at hand: there was a large garden maze on the palace grounds of his employer. Between 1717 and 1723 Bach served the music-loving Prince Leopold of Anhalt-Cöthen (ruled 1704–1728) at the prince's residence in Cöthen. Figure 9.9 shows the castle and gardens at Cöthen as they were in the mid-seventeenth century. In the southeast corner (upper right) is a large, complex maze of the multicursal type.[61] In the center rests a mysterious circular stone chamber with at least one visible door, a *sanctum sanctorum,* perhaps a Temple of Venus of the sort found in other mazes in the region of Anhalt. The existence of this maze, together with other purely musical evidence, suggests that Bach composed his *Little Harmonic Labyrinth* while in Cöthen, specifically sometime between 1717 and 1723. Bach may also have known other mazes, among them the one in the garden of the castle at fashionable Carlsbad (Karlovy Vary), now part of the Czech Republic, where he journeyed with his patron, Prince Leopold, in 1718 and 1720.[62] It is also likely that he knew the labyrinth put in place about 1690 adjacent to the castle of the prince of Anhalt-Dessau in Oranienbaum, a few kilometers to the northeast of Cöthen. Gardens and garden mazes, some built on designs imported from England and Holland, were and remain today an important part of the lush landscape of the region of Anhalt. Thus Bach knew the maze as a musical metaphor for a difficult tonal journey, as a theological topos of the errant soul wandering in the maze of life, and as a horticultural reality.

Strains of Mozart in *The Labyrinth*

Among the list of books appearing in the probate of Wolfgang Amadeus Mozart (1756–1791) is the following entry: "No. 59, Labyrinthe, klein harmonisches von Bach."[63] Obviously Mozart owned a copy of Bach's little musical conceit. Perhaps it is just a coincidence that item number 63 in Mozart's artistic estate is a cantata for solo voice and piano by his friend Joseph Haydn entitled *Ariadne auf Naxos.* Most likely, though, Mozart's interest in mazy music reflects his lifelong fascination with puzzles, riddles, numerology, hieroglyphs, ciphers, and codes.

Mozart probably came to possess Bach's *Little Harmonic Labyrinth* around 1782 when, by his own account, he had his first intense exposure to the music of Bach.[64] It was also at this time, soon after he had moved permanently to Vienna, that Mozart came under the sway of the Freemasons. The Freemasons are important to the history of the maze because their professional ancestors had designed the great pavement labyrinths of the medieval church. They are important with regard to Mozart because Masonic initiation rites influenced the plot of Mozart's *The Magic Flute,* which, in turn, was the inspiration for the opera *The Labyrinth* (*Das Labyrinth*).

The Freemasons were a secret fraternal organization that came to prominence during the early eighteenth century, first in England, then in France, Germany, and Austria.[65] Tracing their lineage back to the cathedral builders of the Middle Ages, the Freemasons placed special emphasis on geometry and the symbolic meaning of geometric figures.[66] Because the father of geometry was Euclid, who resided in Egypt, the Masons took their secret initiation rites from ancient Egyptian religious rituals. In Mozart's day the one tool used pointedly in the initiation rites of the Masons was the compass, the same compass that was employed to design the medieval cathedral as well as the medieval church labyrinth. God, the first Freemason in their eyes, created with a compass, as we have seen (Fig. 1.8). (Even today the emblem of the Masons is a letter G [geometry = God] framed by a compass above and a square below.) Mozart joined the Masonic lodge Beneficence (*Zur Wohltätigkeit*) in 1784, and his father, Leopold, became an honorary member in 1785. Emanuel Schikaneder became a brother as well in 1788. It was with Schikaneder that Mozart would create his "Masonic" opera *The Magic Flute* (*Die Zauberflöte*) in 1791.

Like the myth of the maze, Mozart's *The Magic Flute* is a wanderdrama —the tale of a hero's perilous journey into danger and darkness. The warrior here is Tamino, a young prince who must demonstrate that he possesses courage, faith, and a true heart, and thus is worthy of a higher kingly realm. Around Tamino swirl the forces of good, personified in the lordly Sarastro, and those of evil, as seen in the Queen of the Night and her minions. In his last, most arduous ordeal Tamino enters the Temple of Trial, guarded by two Armed Men who sing:

> Whoever walks along this path so full of troubles
> Is purified by fire, water, air, and earth.
> If he can conquer the fear of death,
> He will soar from earth up to heaven!

So Tamino presses forward through raging fires and rushing waters, shielded only by the sounds of his flute. No thread of Ariadne or life-line of Christian faith here—now the instrument of salvation is a magical instrument! And though there are Armed Men in this hell, these warriors are not soldiers of Christ. This is no Christian allegory. Rather, *The Magic Flute* mimics key elements in the secret rituals of the Freemasons.

Secret though they may have been, much is known about the initiation rites of the Masons.[67] The candidate, or Seeker as he is called, arrives at the door of the lodge and knocks three times. He is admitted, blindfolded, and interrogated as to his purpose. A sword-carrying Terrorizing Brother (*Fürchterlicher Bruder*) leads the Seeker astray as if in a maze—first to the right, next to the left, then upstairs, now downstairs. The aspirant is left alone in a dark chamber, later in a coffin. Throughout it all he must remain courageous and find the path of virtue, which leads to a sacred altar. There he places his right hand on a sword and touches the point of a compass to his bare left breast, swearing to be faithful and guard the secrets of the brotherhood. Finally, when he has proved his worth, the aspirant moves to a higher realm, from darkness to light. He is admitted as a Freemason knight (*Freymaurer Ritter*).

Clearly, the Freemasons were drawing upon the initiation rites of ancient Eastern cults.[68] But there is also here an affinity to Christ's Harrowing of Hell, the Greek myth of Theseus and the Cretan labyrinth, and the epic of the Babylonian hero Gilgamesh as well. Essential to all these renderings of the combat myth is the figure of the warrior: a hero descends into darkness and is purged by trial and ordeal; he engages in single combat to overcome the forces of evil; he ascends to rule in a higher kingdom; his courageous and sacrificial act saves humanity. All Freemasons underwent the Masonic version of this ancient rite of passage, Mozart and Schikaneder included.

When *The Magic Flute* opened in October 1791 it was a wild success, a rare blend of high art and popular entertainment. During the 1790s it was performed nearly 300 times in Vienna, far more than any other opera.[69] The enterprising Emanuel Schikaneder, librettist and producer of the Mozart-Schikaneder team, sought to exploit this popularity by creating a sequel. But Mozart had died only two months after the premiere. Who would write the music of the successor opera? Schikaneder turned to a succession of musicians in Mozart's circle: first Mozart's pupil Franz Xavier Süssmayr (*Der Spiegel von Arkadien*, 1794), then his friend and colleague Franz Anton

Hoffmeister (*Der Königssohn aus Ithaka*, 1795), and finally his acquaintance Johann Mederitsch (*Bibilons Piramiden*, 1797). But none of these new projects generated any enthusiasm among the Viennese public. In the end, Schikaneder determined simply to reuse the plot and characters of *The Magic Flute*, and he hired the pliant Peter Winter to compose the music for what Schikaneder called *The Labyrinth* (1798).

Mozart was dead, but much of his music lived on in *The Labyrinth*.[70] Winter's overture begins with the same sort of three-chord fanfare— thought to mimic the secret knock of the Masons—that had graced the opening of Mozart's overture (Example 9.5). Many of the main characters appear with the same genre of music and in the same key as they had in *The Magic Flute*. The folksy bird-catcher Papageno, for example, enters in G major with the well-known pastoral sounds and even with the identical rising flute motive (Example 9.6). Perhaps most telling is Winter's "revenge" aria for the Queen of the Night ("Ha! bald nahet sich die Stunde"). This is nothing other than a quick "knock-off" of Mozart's famous Queen of the Night aria ("Der hölle Rache kocht in meinem Herzen"), with its racing roulades and jagged arpeggios (Example 9.7).

For a musical impersonation such as this to work, the plot of *The Labyrinth* needed to be virtually identical to that of *The Magic Flute*—and so it is.[71] Again, the force of good (Sarastro) is pitted against evil (the Queen of the Night), though now the latter is aided by the wicked Tipheus, a character modeled on a mythical Egyptian king named Typhon, who lusted for Isis, wife of Osiris.[72] And again the hero Tamino must prove his worth to gain a higher realm and the hand of his beloved Pamina. But this time, instead of wandering through a Temple of Trial, Tamino proceeds through The Labyrinth. Pamina will accompany him. This is a labyrinth of equal opportunity.

> *Sarastro:*
> Now must you wander
> through the anfractuous labyrinth
> as every princely pair.
>
> *Pamina:*
> Through the labyrinth?
> Woe is me!
> I am lost!

Mozart

Winter

EXAMPLE 9.5 A reduction for piano of the opening of Mozart's *The Magic Flute* and the beginning of Peter Winter's *The Labyrinth*.

Mozart

Winter

EXAMPLE 9.6 Mozart's music for Papageno from *The Magic Flute* and Winter's music for Papageno from *The Labyrinth*.

EXAMPLE 9.7 Mozart's music for the Queen of the Night from *The Magic Flute* and Winter's music for the Queen of the Night from *The Labyrinth*.

Tamino:
Hold fast Pamina,
Tamino will find you again.
Come, lead us into the dark paths
of the labyrinth . . .[73]

Once more Tamino passes through torrents and flames, protected only by his magic flute. Finally, he must confront the evil Tipheus in hand-to-hand combat. The hero will fight alone, for as Sarastro says: "Brothers, listen carefully. Why should you spill your innocent blood? One will fight for all." And so the opera concludes: Tamino defeats Tipheus and, as Christ did to Satan at the end of the Book of Apocalypse, casts him down into a fiery pit.

The outcome of *The Labyrinth* is, of course, entirely foreseeable, just as the dialogue is predictable and the characters stereotypical. Mozart's music can return in *The Labyrinth* because it underscores the Manichean contrasts between black and white, light and dark, hero and villain. Yet as George Lucas has demonstrated through his modern-day series *Star Wars*, simplicities, universalities, and stereotyping are necessary preconditions for any successful sequel, especially one dealing with myth.

Successful *The Labyrinth* was. It ran at a suburban Viennese theater, the same one in which *The Magic Flute* had premiered, for six months at raised ticket prices (*Erhöhte Preise*).[74] When public interest began to wane, Schikaneder coupled the ever-popular *Magic Flute* to *The Labyrinth* and performed them on alternate nights. He now called the sequel *The Second Part of the Magic Flute under the title The Labyrinth* (*Der Zweyte Theil der Zauberflöte unter dem Titel Das Labyrinth*).[75] By pairing the two operas, Schikaneder hoped to capitalize on the growing fame of Mozart. To be sure, *The Labyrinth* was still a Mozartian affair, not only in regard to plot and music, but also the cast. Three roles in *The Labyrinth*, including those of Sarastro and the Queen of the Night, were sung by members of the deceased composer's immediate family.[76]

Ultimately, although performances of *The Labyrinth* continued into the nineteenth century,[77] no new labyrinthine operas were created in Vienna or elsewhere. Just as the maze disappeared from the garden and the pavement maze from the church during the Enlightenment, so, too, the story of the labyrinth departed the operatic stage at the end of the eighteenth century. Interest in the maze had run its course.

Epilogue: The Maze Reborn in an Ecumenical Age

By the 1790s, the maze had ceased to be a radiant symbol. No longer did it provide spiritual guidance or artistic inspiration. The skepticism of the Enlightenment and the destruction of the Revolution, among other forces, had destroyed it. During the nineteenth century the labyrinth served merely as an object of archaeological research. Scholars tried to reconstruct the fragments that remained and puzzled over its meaning in earlier epochs. Then, in the last quarter of the twentieth century, the maze arose again as if from the dead, resuscitated by a breath from a "new age" of religious spirituality, ecumenical fellowship, and popular curiosity.[1]

As the millennium approached, Americans in need of spiritual succor set down their anchor of faith along a shore of beliefs, ranging from scriptural fundamentalism to a vaguely defined approach called New Age spiritualism. Today a renewed interest in the maze is expressed by a group that might best be called the "ecumenicalists" of the New Age. These individuals sincerely seek spiritual guidance but do not rigidly follow the teachings of any established religion or church. Some are Catholics, some are Jews, some Buddhists, and some Protestants. Lacking almost all formal theology, doctrine, and ritual, they have seized upon the ancient symbol of the labyrinth and made it serve as a locus on which to center their quest for spiritual well-being. Their one article of faith is that this special geometric form can change one's state of mind for the better.

The maze as a spiritual tool in America was born among the clergy and parishioners at Grace Episcopal Cathedral in San Francisco. Late in 1991 a nearly-to-scale replica of the maze at Chartres was placed in the nave of the church, with the Chartrain pattern painted in purple on six 42-foot pieces of canvas stuck together by Velcro. Recently, the canvas reproduction was replaced by a more permanent carpet made of wool. So far, more than

50,000 people have walked the labyrinth at Grace.[2] In addition, the original canvas labyrinth has been made to travel; the six sections have been packed into duffel bags and transported to other churches. Grace Cathedral has now become something of a corporate headquarters for the expanding world of the maze. To encourage maze-walking in the local community, Grace's World-Wide Labyrinth Project makes available the Labyrinth Seed Kit (at a cost of $130), which contains instructions for designing a unicursal maze. It is also possible to purchase a large canvas replica directly. By attending a two-day training session, one can become a certified Labyrinth Facilitator. This is one way in which labyrinths, labyrinth workshops, and labyrinth walks have spread across the country.

Although labyrinth walks can be experienced in a myriad of ways, let us try to recreate a walk on a maze purchased from Grace Cathedral. A nearly-full-scale canvas replica of the maze at Chartres is spread out on the floor of a church or gymnasium, normally at twilight, and all are encouraged to enter therein. Before the walkers step forth, a maze steward may offer them an American Indian feather blessing "intended to smooth your energy field" and to do honor to the individual who has chosen to engage the maze. Maze-walkers proceed slowly and in silence. Some read scripture to themselves; others stop from time to time to pray or meditate. Some bend at the waist and hold their palms to the floor, trying to sense an energy field within the labyrinth; others hold their palms upward as if reaching to God.

Music enhances the spiritual ambiance of these maze walks. Sometimes the music is newly composed and "live," but most often it is pre-recorded. New Age music of the sort produced by the California company Windham Hill can be heard, but so too can ancient Gregorian chant. More recently, a new type of chant, Taizé music, has been married to the maze. It first came to life at Taizé in southern France among a community of ecumenical brethren. Not surprisingly, all three styles—New Age music, Gregorian chant, and Taizé chant—are characterized by a mellifluous, floating sound devoid of dissonance. None imposes a strong beat or insistent rhythm. This is non-confrontational music intended to soothe the soul and facilitate a "transformative" experience upon the labyrinth.

The modern maze is also noncommittal in terms of its visual imagery and seasonal events. There are no pictures of saints or other Christian symbols. Many would even claim that the cross stamped upon the Chartrain maze is not exclusively a Christian sign, since, like the maze itself, it predates Christianity. Granted, the abstract pattern and emphasis on personal introspection have special appeal to those experienced in meditation-based Eastern religions. But the new maze privileges no race or creed. There are no conditions for membership, and people can come and go at any time.

Similarly, maze-walking is appropriate at any moment. Ancient mazes, both pagan and Christian, came into play with events marking the vernal equinox, be it a spiraling dance to signal the season of agricultural rebirth or a Christian one to commemorate the death and rebirth of a savior. The modern maze, however, is for all seasons and no particular day.

The faithful of the Middle Ages believed that saints provided specific services for the needy. St. Genevieve was said to drive away mice and rats; St. Wilgefort helped women rid themselves of violent husbands; Saint Apollonia took care of toothaches; and St. Fiacre did the same for hemorrhoids. But what tangible benefit does the maze provide for the faithful of today? Those who have walked the maze, and done so repeatedly, testify to a host of beneficial results. The labyrinth deepens self-awareness, releases creativity, increases concentration, and quiets the mind. Following the path to the end aids those who need to bring closure to unfinished tasks. Putting one foot in front of another, with no end in sight, teaches perseverance. Sometimes the path of the labyrinth can mimic experiences in life. But maze-walkers can speak (anonymously) for themselves:[3]

> At first, I thought it was silly. But people don't know anymore what it means to just pray. . . . The labyrinth makes us use our bodies. It put us back in a meditation that uses the body, mind, and spirit.

> One young child walked the labyrinth here and said, "I felt like I was a pencil and God was drawing with me." One older Yankee who walked it said: "It's not for me. I don't understand what the fuss is about. Nothing happened."

> I take it one step at a time. The wrong turns I take are often symbolic of the blind alleys I end up on in life.

> Recently I had an occasion to walk the labyrinth along with a close friend of mine. We both later commented on how the coming close and then departing from each other has always been the basis of our relationship as friends.

We held a workshop for a group from our local AIDS project. We specifically downplayed the religious aspect of the labyrinth in order to make the experiences as devoid of preconceived notions as possible. The purpose of the event was to challenge the pilgrims to come face to face with themselves so as to confront blockades to their healing process.

Only twenty-six percent of the world's population is Christian. At our labyrinth here on Maui we have Hindus, and Taoists, and Episcopalians, and Jews, and Buddhists, and even some New Age folks all walking together. I love this place!

As an engineer, spiritual person, and recovering Catholic I have to say that walking the Chartres labyrinth or the Cretan labyrinth has two functions. One, to calm the spirit and the other to balance the brain. If you look at the Cretan labyrinth, it looks like a cross-section of the brain. By walking it as well as the Chartrain one, you balance all quadrants, hence institute healing on many levels.

Yet, a skeptical voice might ask, if balance and relaxation are needed, why not play a game of chess and go for a swim, or do a crossword puzzle and take a walk in the woods? Indeed, what are the special curative properties of the labyrinth? Personal testimony suggests that the healing powers of the labyrinth rest in its peculiar configuration: the all-inclusive circular design encourages a feeling of unity and community; the boundary of the labyrinth sets limits of human behavior, just as do the walls of a monastic community; the complicated path forces concentration; and the center, reached after much labor, provides the perfect place to "center" one's personality and be closer to God, all within a protected space. Can any of this be proved? Proving causality in matters of faith and mental heath, it would seem, is impossible.

Carl Jung has defined an archetype as a figure, design, or process that continually recurs in human history.[4] Both the maze and the warrior are archetypes belonging to an ancient myth. But now, with the modern ecumenical maze, the traditional Christian warrior has departed, leaving the symbol to stand by itself. Why has the warrior withdrawn—indeed been driven away?

Perhaps a desire to remove religious and ethnic barriers has brought this about. Perhaps the image of a male leader is now less appealing in an age which views masculine authority figures with skepticism. Certainly the majority of maze-walkers are women, and so are the officers of The Labyrinth Society. Removing the warrior from the maze makes it gender-neutral, a symbol of inclusion and universality.

A warrior, by definition, is a figure engaged in combat. In the traditional theology of the maze, the savior is a participant in the battle of good against evil. Those walking the maze today do not seek confrontation. On the contrary, they seek to avoid it; they seek not victory but inner peace. Similarly, combat requires at least two combatants. But when the hero of the labyrinth retired, so, perforce, did the villain. Neither the Minotaur nor Satan lurks in the center of the New Age maze. Today the maze-walker is herself both the villain and the heroine, and she is wholly on her own.

Humans have always believed in the power of symbols, and it is their capacity to do so that separates traditional faith from modern scientific inquiry. Though the warrior and his sparring partner have disappeared from the labyrinth, the symbol endures. As it has for more than four thousand years, the maze today continues to provide enjoyment, comfort, instruction, and nourishment for yet another age. It remains a sign of a timeless human search for guidance in this world and a rational path to the next.

MUSICAL EXAMPLES

EXAMPLE A.1 Guillaume de Machaut, *Ma fin est mon commencement et mon commencement ma fin*, from *Polyphonic Music of the Fourteenth Century*, vol. 3 (Monaco, 1956), pp. 156–157.

EXAMPLE A.2 Anonymous, *En la maison Dedalus,* from *Acta Musicologica,* 39 (1967), 169–170.

EXAMPLE A.2 *(continued)*

EXAMPLE A.3 Johann Sebastian Bach, *Kleines harmonisches Labyrinth*, from *Johann Sebastian Bachs Werke*, vol. 38 (Leipzig, 1891), pp. 225–226.

EXAMPLE A.3 *(continued)*

Appendix B

TABLES

Table B.1 Naples Armed Man Masses

MASS I

Cantus firmus excerpt:

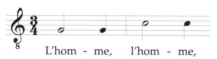

L'hom - me,   l'hom - me,

Canon: Bis vicibus gradatim *vir* in ordine scandit
        Ut prius incessit, ipse retrograditur.
(Twice times two the *man* climbs up stepwise in order.
As before he marched forth, [now] he goes backward.)

Kyrie, plasmator *hominis*	Lord, maker of man
mundique creator,	and creator of the world,
eleyson.	have mercy upon us.
Ut precellat *homo,*	You who give all energy,
qui das vivencia cuncta,	that man may excel,
eleyson.	have mercy on us.
Protegat atque regat *hominem*	May your grace always
tua gratia semper,	Protect and direct man,
eleyson.	have mercy upon us.
Christe, deus qui factus *homo*	Christ, God who was made man,
de virgine natus,	born of the Virgin,
eleyson.	have mercy upon us.
Qui cruce transfixus	Who, transfixed by the Cross,
homini vitam reparasti,	restored life to man,
eleyson.	have mercy upon us.
Salvificet pietas *hominem*	May your mercy
tua nunc et in evum,	save man now and forever,
eleyson.	have mercy upon us.
Kyrie, lux *hominis* venie	Lord, light of man, fount
fons pneumaque sacrum,	of forgiveness and Holy Spirit,
eleyson.	have mercy upon us.
Purificans *hominem*	Purifying mankind,
vitam dans crimina delens,	giving life, removing sins,
eleyson.	have mercy upon us.
Inspires *hominem*	May you inspire and
sacro quoque munere dites,	enrich man with the sacred gift,
eleyson.	have mercy upon us.

MASS II

Cantus firmus excerpt:

L'hom-me_ar - mé, l'hom-me_ar-mé,   l'hom-me_ar - mé

Canon: Ambulat hic **armatus** homo verso quoque vultu
        Arma rapit dextram sequitur sic ut vice versa
        Ad levam scandat vultus sumendo priores
        Ipse retrograditur: repondent ultima primis.
(Here the armed man walks and with face turned takes up arms. He pursues to
the right so, as if turned around, he might climb to the left. Assuming his original
countenance, he goes backward: the end corresponds to the beginning.)

Kyrie, virtutis auctor	Lord, author of virtue, creator of
virique creator	man, and maker of the heaven
celi terre ponthique sator,	earth, and the sea,
eleyson.	have mercy upon us.
Kyrie, fidei miro	Lord, giving arms to man by the
arma donans viro	miracle of faith wherewith he may fight
quis cum hoste dimicet diro,	with the obstinate enemy,
eleyson.	have mercy upon us.
Kyrie, cuius virtute	Lord, by whose virtue the armed man
vir ***armatus*** tute	conquers the enemy in safety and
hostem vincit gaudet salute,	rejoices in salvation,
eleyson.	have mercy upon us.
Christe, salvator	Christ, savior,
viri potens ***armator***	potent armorer of man
armorum dator	giver of arms by which
quibus hostis fit vir triumphator	man is made victor over the enemy
effugatus abit temptator,	and the Devil retires chased away,
eleyson.	have mercy upon us.
Kyrie, spiritus alme	Lord, gracious spirit
viro donans arma palme	giving to man the arms of the palm
dono septemplice	by the sevenfold gift,
patris nati nexus unice,	unique link of the father and son,
eleyson.	have mercy on us.

MASS III

Cantus firmus excerpt:

Doibt   on   doub - ter,   doibt on doub - ter.

Canon: Sic **metuendus** eat gressum repedendo ne pausat
        Demum scandendo per dyatessaron it.
        Ast ubi concendit vice mox versa remeabit
        Descensus finem per dyapente facit.
(So let the one to be feared go forth, repeating the step lest he pause. Then he goes
by climbing up a fourth. Yet where he climbed up then he will remain in reverse.
At the end he makes a descent by a fifth.)

Kyrie, summe pater,	Lord, highest father,
timuit te spiritus ater	you whom the dark spirit feared,
Israel in pelago salvato	the Pharaoh feared you when
pertimuit te	Israel was saved in the sea,
Pharao gente mala;	save thy fearful faithful from
timida salvato fideles,	an evil people,
eleyson.	have mercy upon us.
Christe, **timende** deus	Christ, God to be feared, by your
sola moriturus iniquos	voice alone at the hour of death
voce subegisti presenti	you subjugated the wicked ones,
parce caterve,	spare the living army,
eleyson.	have mercy upon us.
Kyrie, vivificum	Lord, revivifying spirit
da sacri pneuma **timoris**	give the fear of God
quem dudum sanctis electis	which you once freely gave
sponte dedisti,	the elected saints,
eleyson.	have mercy upon us.

MASS IV

Cantus firmus excerpt:

On a fait par - tout cri - er   que chas - cun se viegne ar - mer

Canon: ***Buccina clangorem*** voces vertendo reflectit
              Subque gradu reboat iterum ***clamando*** quaterno.
(The trumpet reflects the sound, turning around the pitches, and echoes again,
crying out a fourth below.)

Kyrie, *altitonans* genitor,	Lord, creator resonating from on high,
deus orbis conditor alme,	God, gracious founder of the earth,
eleyson.	have mercy upon us.
Qui Moysem revocare *tuba*	You who wished Moses to gather
populum voluisti,	his people with the trumpet,
eleyson.	have mercy upon us.
Te *tuba* cuncta *canat*	Let every trumpet sing to you
nostra quoque suscipe vota,	and hear also our prayers,
eleyson.	have mercy upon us.
Christe, deus homoque judex,	Christ, God, man, and judge,
ultor viciorum,	avenger of sins,
eleyson.	have mercy upon us.
Cuius judicium *tuba*	Whose future judgment
precinet alta futurum,	the trumpet shall sound on high,
eleyson.	have mercy upon us.
Voce *tube* populis	Upon the sound of the trumpet
indulge vivificandis,	be merciful to the awakening
eleyson.	populace, have mercy upon us.
Kyrie, spiritus immense,	Lord, immense spirit,
patri natoque coeve,	at one with the father and son,
eleyson.	have mercy upon us.
Qui *sonitu* magno	You who, coming with a great
veniens tua dona dedisti,	sound, gave your gifts,
eleyson.	have mercy upon us.
Ultima soleris nos	May you console us when the last
cum *tuba* fine *sonabit,*	trumpet shall sound at the end,
eleyson.	have mercy upon us.

MASS V

Cantus firmus excerpt:

D'ung   hau - bre - gon de   fer

Canon: Per dyapente sonat subter remeando *lorica*
         Post ubi finierit gressum renovando resumit
         Tuque gradu sursum cantando revertere quinto
         Principio finem da qui modularis eundem.
(The breastplate, going back, sounds a fifth below. Afterward it resumes its step by
recommencing where it finished. And you must revert singing a fifth above. You
who are singing, give an ending that is the same as the beginning.)

[Kyrie], O deus excelse,
   lorica caside tali
protege christicolas
   famulosque tuos velud olim
David Goliam vicit
   et Israel hostem,
   eleyson.
Christe, spei galea
   scuto fideique salutis
contritis tenebris
   nos indue lucis et armis,
   eleyson.
[Kyrie], spiritus optime,
   da *loricam* dulcis amoris
obstantem jaculis nos
   quis ferit imundus hostis,
   eleyson.

Lord, oh God towering aloft,
with such remarkable armor and helmet
protect Christians
and your servants, just as once
David conquered Goliath
and Israel the enemy,
have mercy upon us.
Christ, clothe us with the helmet
of hope, with the shield of faith of
salvation from the sorrowful shadows
and with the arms of light,
have mercy upon us.
Lord, perfect spirit,
give the breastplate of sweet love
that repels the arrows with which
the unclean enemy strikes us,
have mercy upon us.

MASS VI

Cantus firmus: Entire Song; see Musical Example 6.1

Canon: Arma virumque cano vincorque per arma virumque
            Alterni gradimur; hic, ubi signo, tacet.
            Sub lychanos hypaton oritur sic undique pergit
            Visceribus propriis conditur ille meis.
(I sing of arms and a man and am conquered by arms and by a man. We proceed in
alternation; where I have a sign, he is silent. He arises under the lichanos hypaton
and so forth proceeds. He himself is founded from my own inner flesh.)

[Kyrie], alme pater summeque deus	Lord, gracious father and highest God
celi quoque rector,	and also rector of heaven,
eleyson.	have mercy upon us.
Principium finis	Beginning, end,
immensi conditor orbis,	and founder of the immense world,
eleyson.	have mercy upon us.
Ne pereat, da plasma tuum	Grant that thy creature
sed pace fruatur,	may not perish but enjoy peace,
eleyson.	have mercy upon us.
Christe, coeterne splendor	Christ, coequal splendor
sapiencia virtus,	wisdom and virtue,
eleyson.	have mercy upon us.
Lumen ymago patris	Radiance, image of the father,
lux verbum nate redemptor,	light, word incarnate, redemptor,
eleyson.	have mercy upon us.
Sanguine perfuso proprio	Having spilled your own blood
tu parce redemptis,	you spare the redeemed,
eleyson.	have mercy upon us.
[Kyrie], spiritus une dei	Lord, one God,
nexus spiramen amorque,	unifier, breath and love,
eleyson.	have mercy upon us.
Igne sono linguis	By fire, by sound and by tongues,
qui missus dona dedisti,	you who were sent gave gifts,
eleyson.	have mercy upon us.
Munere tu nostra septemplice	With your sevenfold gift
complue corda	rain on our heart,
eleyson.	have mercy upon us.

Table B.2 Composers of Armed Man Masses

1450s–1480s	1480s–1520s	1520s–1550s	1550s–1600s	Seventeenth Century
Philippe Basiron	Juan de Anchieta	Robert Carver	Francisco Guerrero	Giacomo Carissimi*
Antoine Busnois	Antoine Brumel	Andreas de Silva	Palestrina (2)	
(Philippe?) Caron	Loyset Compère	Cristóbal de Morales (2)		
Guillaume Dufay	Josquin Desprez (2)	Francisco de Peñalosa		
Guillaume Faugues	Pierre de la Rue (2)	Ludwig Senfl		
Johannes Ockeghem	Jean Mouton			
Johannes Regis (2)	Jacob Obrecht			
Johannes Tinctoris	Marbriano de Orto			
Six Anonymous Naples	Mattheus Pipelare			
Masses (by Busnois?)	Bertrandus Vaqueras			

*The Missa L'Homme armé attributed to Giacomo Carissimi (1605–1674) survives, in various guises, in six sources, most of which date from the nineteenth century, and only one of them attributes the Mass to Carissimi. The style and authenticity of this work have yet to be fully examined. On the sources, see Claudio Sartori, Carissimi: Catalogo delle opere attribuite (Milan, 1975), p.109; and Iva M. Buff, A Thematic Catalog of the Sacred Works of Giacomo Carissimi, No. 15 of Music Indexes and Bibliographies (Clifton, 1979), p. 81.

Abbreviations

AH	*Analecta Hymnica Medii Aevi*
CCCM	*Corpus Christianorum Continuo Medievalis*
CCEL	*Corpus Christianorum Ecclesiasticorum Latinorum*
CCMSPM	*Census-Catalogue of Manuscript Sources of Polyphonic Music 1400–1550*
CCSL	*Corpus Christianorum Series Latina*
CE	*The Catholic Encyclopedia* (1927)
DALC	*Dictionnaire d'archéologie et de liturgie chrétienne*
DHGE	*Dictionnaire d'histoire et de géographie ecclésiastiques*
DTC	*Dictionnaire de théologie catholique*
JAMS	*Journal of the American Musicological Society*
LU	*The Liber Usualis* (1934)
NCE	*New Catholic Encyclopedia*
NG	*The New Grove Dictionary of Music and Musicians*
OCD	*Oxford Classical Dictionary* (1996)
PG	*Patrologia Cursus Completus . . . Series Graeca*
PL	*Patrologia Cursus Completus . . . Series Latina*
PM	*Polyphonic Music of the Fourteenth Century*
RISM	*Répertoire internationale des sources musicales*

Works Cited

Allendy, René. *Le Symbolism des nombres,* Paris, 1921.

Amé, Emile. *Les Carrelages émaillés du moyen âge et de la Renaissance,* Paris, 1859.

Anderson, Gordon. *Notre Dame and Related Conductus: Opera Omnia,* vol. 8, Henryville, Ottawa, Binningen, n.d.

Andrieu, Michel. *Ordines Romani du haut moyen âge,* 5 vols., Louvain, 1931–1958.

Artress, Lauren. *Walking a Sacred Path: Rediscovering the Labyrinth as a Spiritual Tool,* New York, 1995.

Avril, François. "Interprétations symboliques du combat de Saint-Michel et du dragon," in *Millénaire monastique du Mont Saint-Michel,* 3 vols., Paris, 1971, III, 39–64.

Backman, E. Louis. *Religious Dances in the Christian Church and in Popular Medicine,* London, 1952.

Baltzer, Rebecca A. "Thirteenth-century Illuminated Miniatures and the Date of the Florence Manuscript," *JAMS,* 25 (1972), 1–28.

Batschelet-Massini, Werner. "Labyrinthzeichnungen in Handschriften," in *Codices Manuscripti: Zeitschrift für Handschriftenkunde,* 4 (1978), 33–65.

Beleth, Johannes. *Summa de Ecclesiasticis Officiis,* ed. Herbert Douteil, vols. 41 and 41a of *CCCM,* Turnholt, 1976.

Bente, Martin, Marie Louise Göllner, Helmut Hell, and Bettina Wackernagel. *Bayerische Staatsbibliothek: Katalog der Musikhandschriften,* 3 vols., Munich, 1989.

Bernstein, Jane. *Music Printing in Renaissance Venice: The Scotto Press (1539–1572),* Oxford, 1998.

Blackburn, Bonnie J. "The Virgin in the Sun: Music and Image for a Prayer Attributed to Sixtus IV," *Journal of the Royal Musical Association,* 124 (1999), 157–195.

Blackburn, Bonnie, and Leofranc Holford-Strevens. *The Oxford Companion to the Year,* Oxford, 1999.

Bord, Janet. *Mazes and Labyrinths of the World,* London, 1976.

Borgeaud, Philippe. "The Open Entrance to the Closed Palace of the King: The Greek Labyrinth in Context," *History of Religions,* 14 (1974), 1–27.

Bouché-Leclercq, Auguste. *L'Astrologie grecque,* Paris, 1899.

Bradshaw, Paul. *The Search for the Origins of Christian Worship,* New York and Oxford, 1992.

—— "'Diem baptismo sollemniorem': Initiation and Easter in Christian Antiquity," in *Eulogema: Studies in Honor of Robert Taft, S.J.,* ed. E. Carr, Rome, 1992, pp. 41–51.

Branner, Robert. "The Labyrinth of Reims Cathedral," *Journal of the Society of Architectural Historians,* 21 (1962), 18–25.

—— *Chartres Cathedral,* New York, 1969.

Bucher, François. *Architector: The Lodge Books and Sketchbooks of Medieval Architects,* New York, 1979.

Bulteau, Marcel-J. *Monographie de la cathédrale de Chartres*, 3 vols., Chartres, 1887–1901.

Cailleaux, Denis. *La Cathédrale St. Étienne de Sens*, Paris, n.d.

Camille, Michael. *Image on the Edge: The Margins of Medieval Art*, Cambridge, Mass., 1992.

Campbell, Jackson J. "To Hell and Back: Latin Tradition and Literary Use of the 'Descensus ad Inferos' in Old English," *Viator*, 13 (1982), 107–158.

Carboni, Stefano. *Following the Stars: Images of the Zodiac in Islamic Art*, New York, 1997.

Carpeggiani, Paolo. "Labyrinths in the Gardens of the Renaissance," in *The Architecture of Western Gardens*, ed. Monique Mosser and Georges Teyssot, Cambridge, Mass., 1991, pp. 84–87.

Castleden, Rodney. *The Knossos Labyrinth*, London and New York, 1990.

Caumont, Arcisse de. "Le Labyrinthe de Chartres," *Bulletin monumental*, 13 (1847), 202–203.

Cerf, Charles. *Histoire et description de Notre-Dame de Reims*, 2 vols., Reims, 1861.

Chailley, Jacques. "La Danse religieuse au moyen-âge," in *Arts libéraux et philosophie au moyen-âge: Actes du quatrième congrès international de philosophie médiévale*, Montreal and Paris, 1969, pp. 357–380.

Challine, Charles. *Recherches sur Chartres, transcrites et annotées par un arrière-neveu de l'auteur*, ed. Roger Durand, Chartres, 1918.

Chambers, E. K. *The Mediaeval Stage*, 2 vols., Oxford, 1903.

Chance, Jane. *Medieval Mythography from Roman North Africa to the School of Chartres*, A.D. 433–1177, Gainesville, 1994.

Charpentier, Louis. *Les Mystères de la cathédrale de Chartres*, Paris, 1966.

Chauveau, Abbé. "Origine de la Métropole de Sens et diverses époques de sa construction," *Congrès archéologique de France, Séances générales tenues à Sens, Tours, Angoulême, Limoges, en 1847*, Paris, 1848, pp. 170–218.

Chevalier, C. Ulysse. *Sacramentaire et martyrologie . . . de la Métropole de Reims*, Paris, 1900.

Chevalier, Jacques M. *A Postmodern Revelation: Signs of Astrology and Apocalypse*, Toronto, 1997.

Chevard, Vincent. *Histoire de Chartres*, 2 vols., Chartres, 1800–1802.

Ciampini, Giovanni Giustino. *Vetera Monimenta*, 2 vols., Rome, 1690–1699.

Cipolla, Gaetano. *Labyrinth: Studies on an Archetype*, New York, 1989.

Clasby, Eugene. *Guillaume de Deguileville: The Pilgrimage of Human Life (Le Pèlerinage de la vie humaine)*, New York, 1992.

Cohen, Judith. *The Six Anonymous L'Homme Armé Masses in Naples, Biblioteca Nazionale, MS. VI E 40*, vol. 21 of *Musicological Studies and Documents*, Rome, 1968.

Collins, Adela Yarbro. *The Combat Myth in the Book of Revelation*, Missoula, 1976.

Comenius (Komensky), John Amos. *The Labyrinth of the World and the Paradise of the Heart*, trans. Count Lützow, New York, 1901.

—— *The Labyrinth of the World and the Paradise of the Heart*, trans. Matthew Spinka, Chicago, 1942.

Connolly, Thomas. *Mourning into Joy: Music, Raphael, and Saint Cecilia*, New Haven, 1994.

Cowen, Painton. *Rose Windows,* San Francisco, 1979.

Crisp, Frank. *Medieval Gardens,* London, 1924, rpt. 1966.

Critchlow, Keith, Jane Carroll, and Llewylyn Vaughn Lee. "Chartres Maze, a Model of the Universe?", *Architectural Association Quarterly,* 5 (1973), 11–23.

Crocker, Richard L. "A New Source for Medieval Music Theory," *Acta Musicologica,* 39 (1967), 161–171.

Daniélou, Jean. *The Bible and the Liturgy,* Ann Arbor, 1979.

David, Hans T., Arthur Mendel, and Christoph Wolff, eds. *The New Bach Reader: A Life of Johann Sebastian Bach in Letters and Documents,* New York, 1998.

Davidson, Clifford, and Thomas H. Seiler, eds. *The Iconography of Hell,* Kalamazoo, 1992.

Deedes, C. N. "The Labyrinth," in *The Labyrinth: Further Studies in the Relation of Myth and Ritual in the Ancient World,* ed. S. H. Hooke, London, 1935, pp. 3–42.

Delaporte, Yves. *L'Ordinaire chartrain du XIIIe siècle,* vol. 19 of *Mémoires de la Société archéologique d'Eure-et-Loir,* Chartres, 1953.

Delaporte, Yves, and Étienne Houvet. *Les Vitraux de la cathédrale de Chartres: Histoire et description,* 3 vols., Chartres, 1926.

Delisle, Léopold. *Le Cabinet des manuscrits de la Bibliothèque impériale,* 3 vols., Paris, 1868–1881.

Demaison, Louis. "Les Architectes de la cathédrale de Reims," in *Bulletin archéologique du Comité des travaux historiques et scientifiques,* Paris, 1894, pp. 1–40.

—— "Communication" to the *Bulletin de la Société nationale des antiquaires de France,* Paris, 1931, pp. 150–153.

—— "Nouveau Renseignement sur Bernard de Soissons, maître de l'oeuvre de la cathédrale de Reims," *Nouvelle revue de Champagne et de Brie,* 9 (1931), 186–187.

—— *La Cathédrale de Reims,* Paris, 1935.

Demaray, John G. *Dante and the Book of the Cosmos,* Philadelphia, 1987.

Demouy, Patrick. *Notre-Dame de Reims: Sanctuaire de la monarchie sacrée,* Paris, 1995.

Deschamps des Pas, Louis. "Essai sur le pavage des églises antérieurement au quinzième siècle, *Annales archéologiques,* 10 (1850), 233–241 and 305–311, 11 (1851), 16–23 and 65–71, and 12 (1852), 137–152.

Diehl, Huston. "Graven Images: Protestant Emblem Books in England," *Renaissance Quarterly,* 39 (1986), 49–66.

—— "Into the Maze of Self: The Protestant Transformation of the Image of the Labyrinth," *The Journal of Medieval and Renaissance Studies,* 16 (1986), 281–301.

Doob, Penelope Reed. "The Auxerre Labyrinth Dance," *Proceedings of the Eighth Annual Conference [of the] Society of Dance History Scholars, 15–17 February 1985,* pp. 132–142.

—— *The Idea of the Labyrinth from Classical Antiquity through the Middle Ages,* Ithaca and London, 1990.

Doren, A. *Fortuna im Mittelalter und in der Renaissance,* in *Vorträge der Bibliothek Warburg 1922/23,* Leipzig and Berlin, 1924.

Doublet de Boisthibault, François-Jules. "Notice sur le labyrinthe de la cathédrale de Chartres," *Revue archéologique,* 8 (1852), 437–447.

Du Cange, Charles du Fresne. *Glossarium Mediae et Infimae Latinitatis*, 10 vols., Niort, 1883–1887, rpt. 1954.

Duffy, Kathryn Pohlmann. "The Jena Choirbooks: Music and Liturgy at the Castle Church of Wittenberg under Frederick the Wise, Elector of Saxony," Ph.D. diss., University of Chicago, 1995.

Durand, Georges. *Monographie de l'église Notre-Dame, cathédrale d'Amiens*, 3 vols., Amiens and Paris, 1901–1903.

Durand, Julien. "Les Pavés-mosaïques en Italie et en France," *Annales archéologiques*, 15 (1855), 223–231, and 17 (1857), 119–127.

Dykmans, Marc. *L'Oeuvre de Patrizi Piccolomini ou Le cérémonial papal de la première renaissance*, 2 vols., Vatican, 1980–1982.

Earp, Lawrence. *Guillaume de Machaut: A Guide to Research*, New York, 1995.

Eggebrecht, Hans, ed. *Handwörterbuch der musikalishen Terminologie*, Wiesbaden, 1972–.

Elders, Willem. *Studien zur Symbolik in der Musik der alten Niederländer*, Bilthoven, 1968.

—— *Composers of the Low Countries*, trans. Graham Dixon, Oxford and New York, 1991.

—— *Symbolic Scores: Studies in the Music of the Renaissance*, Leiden and New York, 1994.

Eliade, Mircea. *Le Mythe de l'éternel retour: archétypes et répétition*, rev. ed., Paris, 1969.

Ellsworth, Oliver B. *The Berkeley Manuscript, University of California Music Library, MS. 744 (olim Phillipps 4450)*, Lincoln and London, 1984.

Emmerson, Richard K. *Antichrist in the Middle Ages*, Seattle, 1981.

Emmerson, Richard K., and Ronald B. Herzman. *The Apocalyptic Imagination in Medieval Literature*, Philadelphia, 1992.

Erasmus of Rotterdam. *Enchiridion: Handbüchlein eines christlichen Streiters*, ed. Werner Welzig, Graz and Cologne, 1961.

—— *Enchiridion*, trans. and ed. Raymond Himelick, Bloomington, 1963.

—— *Handbook of the Militant Christian*, trans. John P. Dolan, Notre Dame, Ind., 1962.

Erbacher, Rhabanus. *Tonus Peregrinus: Aus der Geschichte eines Psalmtons*, Münsterschwarzach, 1971.

Evans, Arthur J. *The Palace of Minos: A Comparative Account of the Successive Stages of the early Cretan Civilization as Illustrated by the Discoveries at Knossos*, 4 vols., London, 1921–1935.

Fallows, David. "The Life of Johannes Regis, ca. 1425 to 1496," *Revue belge de musicologie*, 43 (1989), 143–172.

Fanelli, Maria Cristina. *Labirinti: Storia, geografia et interpretazione di un simbolo millenario*, Rimini, 1997.

Faulkner, Ann. "The Harrowing of Hell at Barking Abbey and in Modern Production," in *The Iconography of Hell*, ed. Clifford Davidson and Thomas H. Seiler, Kalamazoo, 1992, pp. 141–157.

Favier, Jean. *Dictionnaire de la France médiévale*, Paris, 1993.

Ferguson, George. *Signs and Symbols in Christian Art,* Oxford, 1961.

Fleury, E. *Antiquités et monuments du département de l'Aisne,* 4 vols., Paris, 1877–1882.

Fourrey, René. *Dans la Cathédrale Saint-Étienne d'Auxerre: Notes et d'histoire,* Auxerre, 1934.

Freeman, Rosemary. *English Emblem Books,* London, 1948.

French, Dorothea R. "Journeys to the Center of the Earth: Medieval and Renaissance Pilgrimages to Mount Calvary," in *Journeys toward God: Pilgrimage and Crusade,* ed. Barbara N. Sargent-Baur, Kalamazoo, 1992, pp. 45–81.

Fresson, Gilles. "A propos du labyrinthe [de la cathédrale de Chartres]," in *Notre-Dame de Chartres,* 21 (1990), 16–18.

Friedman, John Block. "The Architect's Compass in Creation Miniatures of the Later Middle Ages," *Traditio,* 30 (1974), 419–429.

Gaignebet, Claude, and Jean-Dominique Lajoux, *Art profane et religion populaire au moyen âge,* Paris, 1985.

Garde, Judith N. *Old English Poetry in Medieval Christian Perspective,* Suffolk, 1991.

Gardiner, Eileen, ed. *Visions of Heaven and Hell Before Dante,* New York, 1989.

Géruzez, Jean Baptiste François. *Description historique et statistique de la ville de Reims,* 2 vols., Reims, 1817.

Gimpel, Jean. *The Cathedral Builders,* trans. Teresa Waugh, New York, 1983.

Gleadow, Rupert. *The Origin of the Zodiac,* London, 1968.

Gobillot, René, and Joseph Lemarie. "Le Labyrinthe de la cathédrale," *Notre-Dame de Chartres,* 3 (1972), 6–9.

Gomart, Charles. "Notes historiques sur la Maîtrise de Saint-Quentin et sur les célébrités musicales de cette ville," *Mémoires de la Société académique de Saint Quentin,* VII (1850), 212–279.

—— *Extraits originaux d'un manuscrit de Quentin de la Fons, intitulé Histoire particulière de l'Église Saint-Quentin,* 3 vols., St. Quentin and Paris, 1854–1856.

Gougaud, Louis. "La Danse dans les églises," *Revue d'histoire ecclésiastique,* 15 (1914), 5–22 and 229–245.

Graham, John Walter. *The Palaces of Crete,* 2nd ed., Princeton, 1987.

Gundersheimer, Werner L., ed. *Art and Life at the Court of Ercole I d'Este: The 'De triumphis religionis' of Giovanni Sabadino degli Arienti,* vol. 127 of *Travaux d'humanisme et renaissance,* Geneva, 1972.

Haass, Walter. *Studien zu den "L'homme armé"-Messen des 15. und 16. Jahrhunderts,* vol. 136 of *Kölner Beiträge zur Musikforschung,* ed. Heinrich Hüschen, Regensburg, 1984.

Haft, Adele J. "Maps, Mazes, and Monsters: The Iconography of the Library in Umberto Eco's *The Name of the Rose,*" *Studies in Iconography,* 14 (1995), 9–50.

Haggh, Barbara. "The Archives of the Order of the Golden Fleece and Music," *Journal of the Royal Musical Association,* 120 (1995), 1–43.

Hahnloser, Hans R. *Villard de Honnecourt: Kritische Gesamtausgabe des Bauhüttenbuches ms. fr. 19093 der Pariser Nationalbibliothek,* 2nd ed., Graz, 1972.

Hall, James. *Dictionary of Subjects and Symbols in Art,* rev. ed., New York, 1974.

Hamann-Mac Lean, Richard. *Die Kathedrale von Reims,* 3 vols., Stuttgart, 1993–1996.

Hamilton, Edith. *Mythology: Timeless Tales of Gods and Heroes,* Boston, 1940.

Haubrichs, Wolfgang. "*Error inextricabilis.* Form und Function der Labyrinthabbildung in mittelalterlichen Handschriften," in *Text und Bild: Aspekte des Zusammenwirkens zweier Künste in Mittelalter und früher Neuzeit,* ed. Christel Meier and Uwe Ruberg, Wiesbaden, 1980, pp. 63–174.

Heilbron, J. L. *The Sun in the Church: Cathedrals as Solar Observatories,* Cambridge, Mass., 1999.

Héliot, Pierre. "Chronologie de la basilique de Saint-Quentin," *Bulletin monumental,* 107 (1959), 7–50.

—— *La Basilique de Saint-Quentin,* Paris, 1967.

Heller, John L. "Labyrinth or Troy Town?", *Classical Journal,* 42 (1946), 123–139.

Hennecke, Edgar. *New Testament Apocrypha,* ed. Wilhelm Schneemelcher, trans. R. McL. Wilson, 2 vols., Philadelphia, 1963.

Higgins, Paula. "A Priest, A Pope, A Poet and His Penance," paper read at the annual meeting of the American Musicological Society, Phoenix, November 1997.

Hooke, Samuel Henry. *The Labyrinth: Further Studies in the Relation between Myth and Ritual in the Ancient World,* London, 1935.

Hopper, Vincent F. *Medieval Number Symbolism: Its Sources, Meaning, and Influence on Thought and Expression,* rev. ed., New York, 1969.

Houdoy, Jules. *Histoire artistique de la cathédrale de Cambrai,* Lille, 1880, rpt. 1972.

Hubert, Jean. "Les 'Cathédrales doubles' de la Gaule," in *Genava,* 2nd series, 11 (1963), 114–119.

Hübner, Wolfgang. *Zodiacus Christianus: Jüdisch-christliche Adaptationen des Tierkreises von der Antike bis zur Gegenwart,* Königstein, 1983.

Huizinga, Johan. *The Autumn of the Middle Ages,* trans. Rodney J. Payton and Ulrich Mammitzsch, Chicago, 1996.

Hulme, William Henry. *The Middle-English Harrowing of Hell and Gospel of Nicodemus,* Oxford, 1907, rpt. 1978.

Hutton, Ronald. *The Stations of the Sun,* Oxford and New York, 1997.

Irmen, Hans-Josef. *Mozart's Masonry and the Magic Flute,* trans. Ruth Ohm and Chantal Spenke, Essen, 1996.

Irtenkauf, Wolfgang. "Der Computus ecclesiasticus in der Einstimmigkeit des Mittelalters," *Archiv für Musikwissenschaft,* 14 (1957), 1–15.

Jacobsson, Ritva. "The Conception of Easter in the Liturgical Celebration, Reflected in the Poetry of the Medieval Church," in *Feste und Feiern im Mittelalter,* ed. Detlef Altenburg et al., Sigmaringen, 1991, pp. 283–307.

Jahrmärker, Manuela, and Till Gerrit Waidelich, eds. *Der Zauberfloete zweyter Theil unter dem Titel: Das Labyrinth,* Tutzing, 1992.

James, John. *The Contractors of Chartres,* 2 vols., Wyong, New South Wales, 1979–1981.

Johnson, Glenn Pier. "Aspects of Late Medieval Music at the Cathedral of Amiens," Ph.D. diss., Yale University, 1991.

Julian, John. *A Dictionary of Hymnology,* 2nd rev. ed., London, 1907, rpt. 1957.

Jungmann, Joseph A. *The Mass of the Roman Rite: Its Origins and Development,* trans. Francis A. Brunner, 2 vols., New York, 1951–1954.

Kämper, Dietrich. "Fortunae rota volvitur": Das Symbol des Schicksalrades in der spätmittelalterlichen Musik," *Miscellanea medievalia: Veröffentlichungen des Thomas-Instituts der Universität Köln,* 8 (1971), 357–371.

Katzenellenbogen, Adolf. *The Sculptural Programs of Chartres Cathedral,* Baltimore, 1959.

Kellman, Herbert. "Josquin and the Courts of the Netherlands and France," in *Josquin des Prez: Proceedings of the International Josquin Festival-Conference, New York, 1971,* ed. Edward Lowinsky, Oxford, 1976, pp. 181–216.

Kerényi, Karl. "Labyrinth-Studien: Labyrinthos als Linienreflex einer mythologischern Idee," in Kerényi, *Humanistische Seelenforschung,* Munich and Vienna, 1966, pp. 226–273.

—— *Nel labirinto,* Turin, 1983.

Kern, Hermann. *Labyrinthe: Erscheinungsformen und Deutungen 5000 Jahre Gegenwart eines Urbilds,* Munich, 1982.

Ketley-Laporte, John and Odette. *Chartres: Le Labyrinthe déchiffré,* Chartres, 1992.

Kirkendale, Warren. "Circulatio-Tradition, *Maria Lactans,* and Josquin as Musical Orator," *Acta Musicologica,* 56 (1984), 69–92.

Knight, W. F. Jackson. *Cumean Gates: A Reference of the Sixth Aeneid to the Initiation Pattern,* Oxford, 1936.

Koerner, Joseph Leo. *Die Suche nach dem Labyrinth: Der Mythos von Dädalus und Ikarus,* Frankfurt am Main, 1983.

Komensky, John Amos. *See* Comenius, John Amos

Kroll, Josef. *Gott und Hölle: Der Mythos vom Descensuskampfe,* vol. 20 of *Studien der Bibliothek Warburg,* Leipzig and Berlin, 1932.

Lablaude, Pierre-André. *The Gardens of Versailles,* trans. Fiona Biddulph, London, 1995.

Lane, Barbara. *The Altar and the Altarpiece: Sacramental Themes in Early Netherlandish Painting,* New York, 1984.

Langdon-Davies, John. *Carlos: The King Who Would Not Die,* Englewood Cliffs, N.J., 1963.

Lawler, Lillian. "The Geranos Dance—a New Interpretation," *Transactions of the American Philological Association,* 77 (1946), 112–130.

—— *The Dance in Ancient Greece,* Middletown, 1965.

Lebeuf, Jean. *Mémoires concernant l'histoire civile et ecclésiastique d'Auxerre et de son ancien diocèse,* ed. A. Challe and M. Quantin, 4 vols., Auxerre, 1848–1855, rpt. 1978.

Le Goff, Jacques. *The Birth of Purgatory,* trans. Arthur Goldhammer, Chicago, 1984.

Lesser, George. *Chartres,* vol. 3 of *Gothic Cathedrals and Sacred Geometry,* London, 1964.

Lethaby, William R. *Architecture, Mysticism, and Myth,* London, 1891, rpt. 1974.

Lockwood, Lewis. "Aspects of the 'L'Homme armé' Tradition," *Proceedings of the Royal Musical Association,* 100 (1973–1974), 97–122.

—— *Palestrina: Pope Marcellus Mass,* New York, 1975.

—— *Music in Renaissance Ferrara, 1400–1505,* Cambridge, Mass., 1984.

Lonegren, Sig. *Labyrinths: Ancient Myths and Modern Uses,* Glastonbury, 1991.

Long, Michael P. "*Arma virumque cano:* Echoes of a Golden Age," in *Antoine Busnoys: Method, Meaning, and Context in Late Medieval Music,* ed. Paula Higgins, Oxford, 1999, pp. 135–156.

Lowinsky, Edward. "The Goddess Fortuna and Music," *The Musical Quarterly,* 29 (1943), 45–74.

Lütteken, Lauren. "Ritual und Krise: Die neapolitanischen 'L'homme armé'-Zyklen und die Semantik der Cantus firmus-Messe," in *Musik als Text: Bericht über den Internationalen Kongress der Gesellschaft für Musikforschung Freiburg im Breisgau 1993,* ed. Hermann Danuser and Tobias Plebuch, Kassel, 1998, pp. 207–218.

MacCulloch, John Arnott. *The Harrowing of Hell, a Comparative Study of an early Christian Doctrine,* Edinburgh, 1930.

MacDougall, Elisabeth, and Naomi Miller. *Fons Sapientiae: Garden Fountains in Illustrated Books, Sixteenth–Eighteenth Centuries,* Washington, D.C., 1977.

Machabey, Armand. *Guillaume de Machaut,* 2 vols., Paris, 1955.

Macrez, Jean. *Le Labyrinthe de la cathédrale d'Amiens,* Amiens, 1990.

Mâle, Emile. *The Gothic Image: Religious Art in France of the Thirteenth Century,* trans. Dora Nussey, New York, 1958.

Mancini, Sylvia. "Le Rituel du labyrinthe dans l'idéologie de la mort en Corse," *Revue de l'histoire des religions,* 209, fas. 1 (1992), 24–53.

Matthews, William Henry. *Mazes and Labyrinths,* London, 1922, rpt. 1970.

Maunder, E. Walter. *The Astronomy of the Bible,* New York, 1908[?].

Mehl, Erwin. "Der Ausweg aus dem Laybrinth," in *Volkskunde: Fakten und Analysen. Festgabe für Leopold Schmidt zum 60. Geburstag,* ed. Klaus Beitl, Vienna, 1972, pp. 402–428.

Ménestrier, Claude-François. *Des Ballets anciens et modernes selon les règles du Théâtre,* Paris, 1682, rpt. 1972.

Merkley, Paul, and Laura Matthews. "Iudochus de Picardia and Jossequin Lebloitte dit Desprez: The Names of the Singer(s)," *The Journal of Musicology,* 16 (1998), 200–226.

Meyer, Heinz. *Die Zahlenallegorese im Mittelalter: Methode und Gebrauch,* Munich, 1975.

Meyer, Wilhelm. *Fragmenta Burana,* Berlin, 1901.

Miller, Clarence H. "Hercules and His Labors as Allegories of Christ and His Victory over Sin in Dante's *Inferno,*" *Quaderni d'italianistica,* 5 (1984), 1–17.

Miller, James. *Measures of Wisdom: The Cosmic Dance in Classical and Christian Antiquity,* Toronto, 1986.

Monnier, Jean. *La Descente aux enfers,* Paris, 1904.

Murray, Stephen. *Notre-Dame Cathedral of Amiens: The Power of Change in Gothic,* Cambridge, 1996.

Naert, Dominique. *Le Labyrinthe de la cathédrale de Reims,* Fontenay-sous-Bois, 1996.

Owens, Jesse Ann. "An Illuminated Manuscript of Motets by Cipriano de Rore (München, Bayerische Staatsbibliothek, Mus. Ms. B)," Ph.D. diss., Princeton University, 1979.

Padoan, Giorgio. "Il mito di Teseo e il cristianesimo di Stazio," *Lettere Italiane*, 11 (1959), 432–457.

Palisca, Claude V. *Humanism in Italian Renaissance Musical Thought*, New Haven and London, 1985.

—— "Bernardino Cirillo's Critique of Polyphonic Church Music of 1549: Its Background and Resonance," in *Music in Renaissance Cities and Courts: Studies in Honor of Lewis Lockwood*, ed. Jessie Ann Owens and Anthony M. Cummings, Warren, Mich., 1997, pp. 281–292.

Palmer, Leonard R. *A New Guide to the Palace of Knossos*, London, 1969.

—— *The Penultimate Palace of Knossos*, vol. 33 of *Incunabula Graeca*, Rome, 1969.

Panofsky, Erwin. *Hercules am Scheidewege*, vol. 18 of *Studien der Bibliothek Warburg*, Berlin, 1930, rpt. 1997.

—— *The Life and Art of Albrecht Dürer*, Princeton, 1943.

—— *Renaissance and Renascences in Western Art*, Stockholm, 1960.

Paris, Louis. "Notice sur Le Dédale ou labyrinthe de église de Reims," *Bulletin monumental*, 22 (1856), 540–551.

Pelikan, Jaroslav. *Christianity and Classical Culture*, New Haven and London, 1993.

—— *Mary Through the Centuries: Her Place in the History of Culture*, New Haven and London, 1996.

Pennick, Nigel. *Labyrinths: Their Geomancy and Symbolism*, Runestaff, 1984.

—— *Mazes and Labyrinths*, London, 1990.

Perkins, Leeman, and Howard Garey, eds. *The Mellon Chansonnier*, 2 vols., New Haven and London, 1979.

Peroni, Adriano. "Il mosaico pavimentale di San Michele Maggiore a Pavia: materiali per un'edizione," *Studi Medievali*, 3rd series, 18 (1977), 705–743.

Perrault, Charles. *Le Labyrinthe de Versailles*, Paris, 1677, rpt. 1982.

Pieper, Jan. *Das Labyrinthische: über die Idee des Verborgen, Rätselhaften, Schwierigen in der Geschichte der Architectur*, Braunschweig/Wiesbaden, 1987.

Planchart, Alejandro. "Guillaume Du Fay's Benefices and his Relationship to the Court of Burgundy," *Early Music History*, 8 (1988), 117–171.

Prache, Anne. *Chartres Cathedral: Image of the Heavenly Jerusalem*, trans. Janice Abbott, Paris, 1993.

Prévost, F. "Notice sur le labyrinthe de l'église de Reparatus," *Revue archéologique*, 8, 2nd part (1851–1852), 566–571.

Prizer, William. "Music and Ceremonial in the Low Countries: Philip the Fair and the Order of the Golden Fleece," *Early Music History*, 5 (1985), 113–153.

Rasch, Rudolf, ed. *Friedrich Suppig: Labyrinthus Musicus: Calculus Musicus*, Utrecht, 1990.

Rastall, Richard. "The Sounds of Hell," in *The Iconography of Hell*, ed. Clifford Davidson and Thomas H. Seiler, Kalamazoo, Mich., 1992, pp. 102–131.

Réau, Louis. *Iconographie de l'art chrétien*, 3 vols., Paris, 1955–1959.

Reese, Gustave. *Music in the Renaissance*, New York, 1959.

Reinhardt, Hans. *La Cathédrale de Reims*, Paris, 1963.

Reynolds, Christopher. "The Origins of San Pietro B 80 and the Development of a Roman Sacred Repertory," *Early Music History*, 1 (1981), 257–304.

—— *Papal Patronage and the Music of St. Peter's, 1380–1513*, Berkeley and Los Angeles, 1995.

Robertson, Anne. "The Mass of Guillaume de Machaut in the Cathedral of Reims," in *Plainsong in the Age of Polyphony*, ed. Thomas F. Kelly, Cambridge, 1992, pp. 100–139.

Rohloff, Ernest, ed. *Der Musiktraktat des Johannes de Grocheo nach den Quellen neu herausgegeben*, Leipzig, 1943.

Rokseth, Yvonne. "Danses cléricales du XIIIe siècle," *Mélanges 1945, III: Études Historiques*, Paris, 1947, pp. 93–126.

Roth, Adalbert. "*L'homme armé, le doubté turcq, l'ordre de la toison d'or*: Zur 'Begleitmusik' der letzten grossen Kreuzzugsbewegung nach dem Fall von Konstantinopel," *Feste und Feiern im Mittelalter*, ed. Detlef Altenburg et al., Sigmaringen, 1991, pp. 469–479.

Rouillard, Sébastien. *Parthénie ou Histoire de la très auguste et très dévote Église de Chartres*, Paris, 1609.

Rouse, Richard. "The Early Library of the Sorbonne," *Scriptorium*, 21 (1967), 42–71 and 227–251.

—— "Manuscripts belonging to Richard de Fournival," *Revue d'histoire des textes*, 3 (1973), 253–269.

Sahlin, Margit. *Étude sur la carole médiévale: L'origine du mot et ses rapports avec l'Église*, Uppsala, 1940.

Saint-Hilaire, Paul. *L'Univers secret du labyrinthe*, Paris, 1992.

Salet, Francis. "Chronologie de la cathédrale [de Reims]," *Bulletin monumental*, 125 (1967), 347–394.

Santarcangeli, Paolo. *Il libro dei labirinti: storia di un mito e di un simbolo*, Florence, 1967.

—— *Le Livre des labyrinthes: Histoire d'un mythe et d'un symbole*, Paris, 1974.

Schiller, Gertrud. *Iconography of Christian Art*, trans. Janet Seligman, 2 vols., Greenwich, Conn., 1971.

Schnapper, Edith B. "Labyrinths and Labyrinth Dances in Christian Churches," in *Festschrift Otto Erich Deutsch*, ed. Walter Gerstenberg et al., Kassel, 1963, pp. 352–360.

Smits van Waesberghe, Joseph. *Musikerziehung*, in *Musikgeschichte in Bildern*, vol. III/3, Leipzig, 1969.

Soyez, Edmond. *Les Labyrinthes d'églises. Labyrinthe de la cathédrale d'Amiens*, Amiens, 1896.

Starr, Pamela. "Southern Exposure: Roman Light on Johannes Regis," *Revue belge de musicologie*, 49 (1995), 27–38.

Strohm, Reinhard. *Music in Medieval Bruges*, Oxford, 1985.

—— *The Rise of European Music: 1380–1500*, Cambridge, 1993.

Talley, Thomas J. *The Origins of the Liturgical Year*, New York, 1986.

Tanner, Marie. *The Last Descendant of Aeneas: The Hapsburgs and the Mythic Image of the Emperor*, New Haven and London, 1993.

Taruskin, Richard. "Antoine Busnoys and the *L'homme armé* Tradition," *JAMS*, 39 (1986), 255–293.

Taylor, Margaret Fisk. *A Time to Dance: Symbolic Movement in Worship*, n.p., 1981.

Tester, S. J. *A History of Western Astrology*, Woodbridge, 1987.

Trollope, Edward. "Notices of Ancient and Mediaeval Labyrinths," *The Archaeological Journal*, 15 (1858), 216–235.

Turmel, J. *La Descente du Christ aux enfers*, Paris, 1908.

Turner, Ralph V. "*Descendit ad Inferos:* Medieval Views on Christ's Descent into Hell and the Salvation of the Ancient Just," *Journal of the History of Ideas*, 27 (1966), 173–194.

Vallery-Radot, Jean. "Auxerre: La cathédrale Saint-Étienne. Les principaux textes de l'histoire de la construction," *Congrès archéologique*, 116 (1958), 40–50.

Van Der Meulen, Jan, with Rüdiger Hoyer and Deborah Cole. *Chartres: Sources and Literary Interpretation, a Critical Bibliography*, Boston, 1989.

Vaughan, Richard. *Philip the Good: The Apogee of Burgundy*, London, 1970.

—— *Charles the Bold: Last Valois Duke of Burgundy*, London, 1973.

Verbrugge, Armand-Raymond. "Les Labyrinthes: Autour de ceux de Compiègne et Pierrefonds," *Bulletin de la Société historique de Compiègne*, 31 (1990), 135–145.

Vidal, G. *Un Témoin d'une date célèbre. La Basilique chrétienne d'Orléansville (324)*, Algiers, n.d.

Villers, Georges. "Mémoire de M. G. Villers sur le labryinthe de Bayeux," in *Congrès archéologique de France, Séances générales tenues à Lille, en 1845*, Paris, 1846, pp. 83–96.

Villetard, Henri. "La Danse ecclésiastique à la Métropole de Sens," *Bulletin de la Société archéologique de Sens*, 26 (1911), 105–122.

Villette, Jean. "Quand Thésée et le Minotaure ont-ils disparu du labyrinthe de la cathédrale de Chartres?", *Mémoires de la Société archéologique d'Eure-et-Loir*, 25 (1969–1972), 265–270.

—— "L'Enigme du labyrinthe," *Notre-Dame de Chartres*, 15 (1984), 4–14.

—— *Guide des vitraux de Chartres*, Rennes, 1987.

—— *Le Plan de la cathédrale de Chartres: Hasard ou stricte Géométrie?*, Chartres, 1991.

Vivell, Célestine. "Le 'Tonus peregrinus,'" *Revue du chant Grégorien*, 18 (1909–1910), 147–153 and 187–192, and 19 (1910–1911), 18–22.

Vovelle, Michel. *Les Âmes du purgatoire*, Paris, 1996.

Wallet, Emanuel. *Description d'une crypte et d'un pavé mosaïque de l'ancienne église St-Bertin, à Saint-Omer, découverts lors des fouilles faites en 1831*, Douai, 1843.

Walther, Hans. *Initia Carminum Ac Versuum Medii Aevi Posterioris Latinorum*, Göttingen, 1959.

Warmington, Flynn. "The Ceremony of the Armed Man: The Sword, the Altar, and the *L'homme armé* Mass," in *Antoine Busnoys: Method, Meaning, and Context in Late Medieval Music*, ed. Paula Higgins, Oxford, 1999, pp. 89–130.

Wegman, Rob C. "Guillaume Faughes and the Anonymous Masses *Au chant de l'alouette* and *Vinnus vina*," *Tijdschrift van de Vereniging voor Nederlandse Muziekgeschiedenis*, 41 (1991), 27–64.

—— *Born for the Muses: The Life and Masses of Jacob Obrecht*, Oxford, 1994.

Welch, Evelyn. *Art and Society in Italy 1350–1500,* Oxford and New York, 1997.

Werner, Eric. "The Common Ground in the Chant of Church and Synagogue," in *Atti del congresso internazionale di musica sacra organizzato dal Pontificio Istituto di Musica Sacra e dalla Commissione di Musica Sacra per l'Anno Santo (Roma, 25–30 Maggio 1950),* Tournai, 1952, pp. 134–148.

Whitrow, G. J. *Time in History: The Evolution of Our General Awareness of Time and Temporal Perspective,* Oxford, 1988.

Wieck, Roger. *Time Sanctified: The Book of Hours in Medieval Art and Life,* New York, 1988.

Wild, Robert A. "The Warrior and the Prisoner: Some Reflections on Ephesians 6:10–20," in *The Catholic Biblical Quarterly,* 46 (1984), 284–298.

Wolff, Christoph. *Johann Sebastian Bach: The Learned Musician,* New York, 2000.

Wood, Chauncey. *Chaucer and the Country of the Stars: Poetic Images of Astrological Imagery,* Princeton, 1970.

Woodward, Kathryn Christine. "*Error labyrinthi:* An Iconographic Study of Labyrinths as Symbolic of Submission and Deliverance in Manuscripts and on Pavements Dating from Late Antiquity through the High Middle Ages," Ph.D. diss., Bryn Mawr College, 1981.

Wright, Craig. "Dufay at Cambrai: Discoveries and Revisions," *JAMS,* 28 (1975), 175–229.

—— *Music and Ceremony at Notre Dame of Paris: 500–1550,* Cambridge, 1989.

—— "Dufay's *Nuper rosarum flores,* King Solomon's Temple, and the Veneration of the Virgin," *JAMS,* 47 (1994), 395–441.

—— "Bachs Kleines harmonisches Labyrinth (BWV 591): Echtheitsfragen und theologisches Hintergrund," *Bach-Jahrbuch,* 86 (2000), 51–64.

Wunderlich, Hans Georg. *The Secret of Crete,* London, 1975.

Young, Karl. "The Harrowing of Hell," in *Transactions of the Wisconsin Academy of Sciences, Arts, and Letters,* 16, part II (1909), 889–947.

—— *The Drama of the Medieval Church,* 2 vols., Oxford, 1933.

Notes

Prologue: Maze Mania

1. This and the following examples are drawn from Pennick, *Mazes,* chap. 5.
2. For other labyrinthine operas of the second half of the twentieth century by Berio, Bosseur, and Menotti, see Kern, *Labyrinthe,* p. 344.
3. Pennick, *Mazes,* p. 176.
4. Santarcangeli, *Labyrinthes,* p. 394.
5. Paul Webster, "Lost and found in the world's largest maze," *Guardian Weekly,* 27 July 1997.

1. The Ancient and Early Christian Maze

1. The following paragraph draws mainly on Ovid, *Metamorphoses,* book viii, lines 136–183; Virgil, *Aeneid,* book vi, lines 22–30; and especially Plutarch, *Lives,* book i (The Loeb Classical Library), "Theseus," pp. xv–xxii.
2. The following draws on Evans, *Palace;* Palmer, *Palace;* Wunderlich, *Secret;* Graham, *Palaces;* and Castleden, *Labyrinth.* Evans and Graham view the remains at Knossos as a palace, Wunderlich as a necropolis, and Castleden as a temple.
3. Evans, *Palace,* I, 433–447.
4. Ibid., III, 282–284. Castleden's *Labyrinth* simply uses the word "labyrinth" as an alluring synonym for temple.
5. Matthews, *Mazes,* p. 35.
6. The difficulty of identifying the maze as "a tangible 'fact' to which the system of mythical representations could be anchored" is discussed in Borgeaud, "Labyrinth."
7. Pieper, *Architectur,* pp. 20–21.
8. These coins are discussed and photographic reproductions of them are given, among other places, in Matthews, *Mazes,* figs. 26–31; and Kern, *Labyrinthe,* p. 49 and figs. 39–58.
9. There appears to be here a divergence between the poetic and pictorial, or architectural, evidence: if Theseus could go only one way, why did he need Ariadne's clew? The Hellenic poets created multicursal mazes, but the architects did not.
10. The Trojan ride is discussed, among other places, in Carl Diem, *Das Trojanische Reiterspiel* (Berlin, 1942); Heller, "Labyrinth," pp. 123–139; Kern, *Labyrinthe,* pp. 99–111; and Doob, *Labyrinth,* pp. 26–33.
11. *The Aeneid of Virgil,* book v, lines 583–591; trans. C. Day Lewis (Garden City, 1952), p. 121.

12. On the Tragliatella pitcher, see the discussion and the sources cited in Kern, *Labyrinthe*, pp. 101–107, as well as Doob, *Labyrinth*, p. 27.

13. Fanelli, *Labirinti*, p. 43.

14. See Trollope, "Labyrinths," pp. 216–235; Heller, "Labyrinth," pp. 123–139; Santarcangeli, *Labyrinthes*, p. 154; and Doob, *Labyrinth*, pp. 115–116.

15. On the maze as a representation of Jericho, see Haubrichs, "*Error*," pp. 142–146; Kern, *Labyrinthe*, pp. 182–198; Pennick, *Labyrinths*, p. 14; and Pennick, *Mazes*, p. 36.

16. Roman floor mazes are discussed in Matthews, *Mazes*, pp. 45–51; and in greater depth in Santarcangeli, *Labyrinthes*, pp. 258–266, and in Kern, *Labyrinthe*, pp. 112–137.

17. Kern, *Labyrinthe*, p. 112, provides a map that situates the floor mazes that survive from the Roman world.

18. Haubrichs, "*Error*," pp. 99–100.

19. Santarcangeli, *Labyrinthes*, p. 260.

20. Reproduced in Matthews, *Mazes*, p. 46.

21. Doob, *Labyrinths*, p. 40.

22. Haubrichs, "*Error*," p. 100; and Kern, *Labyrinthe*, p. 207.

23. On the Algerian maze, see Prévost, "Labyrinthe"; Soyez, *Labyrinthe*, p. 2; Matthews, *Mazes*, p. 54; Vidal, *Témoin*; Santarcangeli, *Labyrinthes*, p. 285; and Kern, *Labyrinthe*, pp. 119 and 232.

24. The church subsequently fell into disrepair after the invasion of the Vandals. Soldiers in the French army corps of engineers discovered the labyrinth beneath layers of dust in 1843. During the 1920s it was removed from the floor and encased to prevent destruction. Sometime thereafter the encased labyrinth was removed to the present cathedral of Algiers. Santarcangeli, *Labyrinthes*, p. 286 (citing Vidal); and Kern, *Labyrinthe*, p. 119.

25. Kern, *Labyrinthe*, p. 119.

26. Ibid., p. 142; and Haft, "Maps," pp. 16–19.

27. For an introduction to medieval cartography as it relates to spiritual pilgrimage, see French, "Journeys."

28. See, for example, Paris, Bibliothèque nationale, MS fonds latin 5371, fols. 240–240v.

29. Hildegard of Bingen, *Scivias*, as translated by Sabina Flanagan in *Hildegard of Bingen, 1098–1179: A Visionary Life* (London and New York, 1989), p. 35.

30. On the symbolism of west and east, see Backman, *Dances*, p. 71.

31. Daniélou, *Bible*, pp. 30–32.

32. Hutton, *Stations*, p. 180.

33. Batschelet-Massini, "Labyrinthzeichnungen," p. 41; and Kern, *Labyrinthe*, pp. 135–136.

34. This void and the possible causes of it are discussed in Haubrichs, "*Error*," pp. 100–101.

35. The development of the maze in Carolingian and post-Carolingian manuscripts is chronicled in Haubrichs, "*Error*"; Batschelet-Massini, "Labyrinthzeichnungen"; and Kern, *Labyrinthe*, chap. VII.

36. See Allendy, *Symbolism*, pp. 321–322; Kern, *Labyrinthe*, p. 141; and Van Der Meulen, *Chartres*, p. 378.

37. Several early Chartres-type mazes originated at the monastery of St. Germain in Auxerre or at its filiated Benedictine house, St. Germain in Paris (see Kern, *Labyrinthe*, figs. 174–175, 177, 182, and 192). The development of the Chartrain pattern is discussed in Haubrichs, "*Error*"; Batschelet-Massini, "Labyrinthzeichnungen"; and Van Der Meulen, *Chartres*, p. 378.

38. The Byzantine Church, by contrast, continued to embrace the Cretan-pagan maze form, eschewing any attempt to invest it with Christian number symbolism or stamp it with the cross (see Kern, *Labyrinthe*, figs. 222 and 227).

39. On the contexts of this important manuscript, see Haubrichs, "*Error*," pp. 85–86.

40. The text comes from the ninth-century *Liber glossarum* (Haubrichs, "*Error*," pp. 85–86).

2. THE MAZE AS SYMBOL IN THE CHURCH

1. Haubrichs, "*Error*," pp. 80 and 103; Kern, *Labyrinthe*, p. 229.

2. Kern, *Labyrinthe*, pp. 219, 222, and 228.

3. On English turf mazes, see Trollope, "Labyrinths"; Matthews, *Mazes*, chap. X; Bord, *Mazes*, pp. 46–58; and Kern, *Labyrinthe*, pp. 243–254.

4. For discussions of church mazes in Italy, see Santarcangeli, *Labyrinthes*, pp. 288–290; Haubrichs, "*Error*," pp. 102–104; and especially Kern, *Labyrinthe*, pp. 206–257.

5. The following is drawn primarily from Peroni, "Mosaico"; see also Kern, *Labyrinthe*, pp. 232–233, and the sources he lists in connection with his figs. 270–272.

6. Rome, Biblioteca Apostolica Vaticana, MS Barb. lat. 4426, fol. 35.

7. On the theme of the wildman in the Middle Ages, see Richard Bernheimer, *The Wildman in the Middle Ages* (Cambridge, Mass., 1952) and Timothy Husband, *The Wildman, Medieval Myth and Symbolism* (New York, 1980).

8. This reversal of fortune is anticipated, of course, in the Canticle of Mary, the Magnificat: "He hath put down the mighty from their seats; and exalted them of low degree" *(Deposuit potentes de sede, et exaltavit humiles)* (Luke 1:52).

9. Mâle, *Image*, p. 136, citing Augustine, *Sermo* XXXII, 83–84 and 138–139, vol. 41 of *CCSL*, 400–401. David's encounter with Goliath was equated to Christ's descent into Limbo throughout the Middle Ages, particularly in the *Biblia Pauperum* (see Mâle, *Image*, pp. 172–173).

10. See Matthews, *Mazes*, p. 57; Santarcangeli, *Labyrinthes*, p. 289; Haubrichs, "*Error*," p. 102; and Kern, *Labyrinthe*, p. 234.

11. I, 241.

12. I am grateful to Tova Choate for pointing out this passage to me.

13. Matthews, *Mazes*, p. 57; Santarcangeli, *Labyrinthes*, p. 288; Haubrichs, "*Error*," p. 104; and Kern, *Labyrinthe*, p. 238.

14. Durand, "Pavés-mosaïques," p. 119.

15. Ibid., p. 127, n. 3; and Xavier Barbier de Montault, "Labyrinthes," in his *Oeuvres complètes*, 16 vols. (Poitiers, 1889–1902), VIII, 5.

16. On the history of this church see Dale Kinney, *Santa Maria in Trastevere from its Founding to 1215* (New York, 1975); Carlo Cecchelli, *Santa Maria in Trastevere* (Rome, 1933); and Roberto Luciani, *Santa Maria in Trastevere* (Rome, 1987).

17. Ciampini, *Vetera Monimenta*, II, 5: "Animadversione dignum est, labyrinthum hunc admodum varijs viarum ambagibus implicatum esse, ac similem integrum in presentiarum cerni hac in Urbe Roma, in Ecclesia S. Mariae trans Tyberim, pariter tessellati operis in pavimento, prope sacrarij Ianuam, quod a negligente plebe minime observatur."

18. This is the figure reproduced in Durand, "Pavés-mosaïques," 17 (1857), opposite p. 11, and discussed on p. 127, n. 3.

19. The maze is reproduced in Kern, *Labyrinthe*, fig. 235.

20. Ubaldo Formentini, "Il laberinto di Pontremoli ed il 'Troiae lusus,'" in *Archivio Storico per le Province Parmensi*, 2, 4th series (1949/50), 125–132; and Patricia Villiers-Stuart, "The Pontremoli Labyrinth," in *RILKO [Research Into Lost Knowledge Organization] Newsletter* (London, 1982), pp. 24ff. I have been unable to see the latter publication.

21. On the Trojan ride, see Chapter 1.

22. Durand, "Pavées-mosaïques," p. 125; Matthews, *Mazes*, p. 56; Santarcangeli, *Labyrinthes*, p. 288; Haubrichs, "*Error*," p. 104; and Kern, *Labyrinthe*, pp. 230–231.

23. Durand, "Pavées mosaïques," p. 125.

24. A useful introduction to the history and art of Ravenna is Gianfranco Bustacchini, *Ravenna, Capital of Mosaic* (Ravenna, 1988).

25. Wiktor A. Daszewski, *La Mosaïque de Thésée: Études sur les mosaïques avec représentations du labyrinthe, de Thésée et du Minotaure*, vol. II of *Nea Paphos* (Varsovie, 1977), p. 117.

26. Friedrich Wilhelm Deichmann, *Ravenna: Hauptstadt des spätantiken Abendlandes*, Kommentar, 2. Teil (Wiesbaden, 1976), pp. 54–55.

27. See above, p. 18.

28. In a remarkable way the status of the twelfth-century Italian church maze as cultural artifact is identical to that of the Gregorian chant of twelfth-century Italy. Roman chant was imported into Gaul in the eighth century, overlaid with French forms and styles, and exported back to Italy around 1000 A.D. in a state generally resembling what we call today Gregorian chant. Similarly, the classical maze was brought to Gaul by the Romans; its design was eventually given a new configuration; and this amalgam of classical tradition and Carolingian innovation was dispatched back to Italian churches during the eleventh century.

29. Among these are a maze on a stone-relief in the parish church in the village of Genainville, a tile labyrinth at a now-destroyed monastery at Châlons-sur-Marne, two other tile labyrinths in side chapels in the cathedrals of Mirepoix and Toulouse in the south of France, and a maze graffito at the cathedral of Poitiers. Although brief descriptions of these mazes can be found in Saint-Hilaire, *Labyrinthe*,

pp. 165ff, far better are those given in Kern, *Labyrinthe,* pp. 219ff. Churches in Bayeux and Caen in Normandy possessed what might be called "mid-size" labyrinths; on these, see Villers, "Labyrinthe," p. 86; and Amé, *Carrelages,* p. 52.

30. *DHGE,* s.v. "Chartres."

31. See above, Chapter 1.

32. The bibliography of the architectural history of Chartres is enormous, but its extent can be accurately gauged in Van Der Meulen, *Chartres,* chap. V. The most recent and straightforward account is given in Prache, *Chartres.*

33. Branner, *Chartres,* p. 80; and Prache, *Chartres,* pp. 50–64.

34. The widths of naves in the principal Gothic churches of France, measuring mid-pillar to mid-pillar, are as follows: Chartres, 16.40 m., Strasbourg, 16.20 m., Beauvais, 15.90 m., Sens, 15.25 m., Reims, 14.65 m., Amiens, 14.60 m., Bourges, 14.50 m., Paris, 13.80 m., and Auxerre, 13 m. (Villette, "Labyrinthe," p. 5, n. 1).

35. Villette, "Labyrinth," p. 7.

36. Bulteau, *Monographie,* III, 49–50; and Gobillot and Lemarie, "Labyrinthe," pp. 6–9.

37. Charles Challine, *Histoire de Chartres,* Chartres, Bibliothèque municipale, MS 1140, p. 159: "Il se voit au milieu de la nef devant et audessous de la chaire ou l'on preche un fort beau labyrinth, ou dédale de marbre noir figuré sur le pavé, au centre duquel on voit dans un cercle la figure de Thésée et du Minotaure. Ce dédale est vulgairement appelé la *lieue,* parce qu'on estime qu'en suivant tous ses méandres on fait une lieue." There are four other manuscripts of Challine's work at Chartres (MSS 1074, 1076, 1318, and 1518), as well as one in Paris at the Bibliothèque nationale (fonds français 14583), and they do not always agree in content. On the subsequent emendations of this source, see Van Der Meulen, *Chartres,* p. 407. Ultimately, using MS 1318 as the basic source, Challine's work was published as *Recherches sur Chartres* (Chartres, 1918).

38. Janvier de Flainville quotes a description of the labyrinth as "artistement fait de pierre noire entaillée vers le pavé, et ajoute-t-il, l'on voit dans la figure qui est au centre la figure de Thésée et du Minotaure" and adds: "Nota: les figures qui étaient au milieu du labyrinthe sont fort effacées; il est impossible d'y rien reconnaître" (in Chartres, Bibliothèque municipale, MS 1011, cited by Doublet de Boisthibault, "Labyrinthe," p. 9); Villette, "Labyrinthe," p. 6; and Villette, "Thésée," pp. 267–268.

39. Chevard, *Chartres,* II, 63; cited in Villette, "Labyrinthe," p. 6; and Villette, "Thésée," p. 270.

40. Walter Horn and Ernest Born, *The Plan of St. Gall,* 3 vols. (Berkeley, 1979), I, 131.

41. Villette, *Guide,* p. 13; and especially Prache, *Chartres,* pp. 50–58.

42. Villette, "Labyrinthe," pp. 4–14, especially p. 12.

43. Ketley-Laporte, *Labyrinthe,* p. 53.

44. On this point, see Cowen, *Windows,* pp. 98–99; and Demaray, *Dante,* pp. 22–23.

45. See the drawing given in Ketley-Laporte, *Labyrinthe,* p. 53.

46. Bulteau, *Monographie,* III, 221; Delaporte, *Vitraux,* I, 519–521; and Villette, *Guide,* pp. 13–15.

47. Among the better treatments of the design and measurements of Chartres are

James, *Contractors;* Villette, *Plan;* and Lesser, *Chartres.* Far less reliable are Charpentier, *Mystères;* and Saint-Hilaire, *Labyrinthe.*

48. See below under "Reims" and "Amiens."

49. Bulteau, *Monographie,* III, 46; and Branner, *Chartres,* p. 69.

50. It is found in Auxerre, Bibliothèque municipale, MS 215, fol. 33v. The volume is entitled *Recueil des épitaphes et des inscriptions de la ville de Sens; levées et copiées avec soin dans la cathédrale, les églises paroissiales, les monastères, et les édifices publics et particuliers: Avant la Révolution de l'Année 1789* and constitutes a miscellany collected by the publisher and antiquarian of Sens, Théodore Tarbé, around the turn of the nineteenth century. All previous authors had published a bogus drawing first printed by Abbé Chauveau in 1848, without inquiring as to its source or questioning its reliability. Curiously, MS 215 must have been known to Chauveau, because he reports much of the information found at the bottom of folio 33v, but he cites no source and produces a "quisse [*sic*] du labyrinthe de la cathédrale de Sens" that is not the one given in MS 215 ("Sens," pp. 170–218; see especially p. 217).

51. See below, n. 62.

52. Auxerre, Bibliothèque municipale, MS 215, fol. 33v: "Ce labyrinthe existoit autrefois dans la nef de l'Eglise Métropolitaine de Sens, sous la tribune des orgues; cet ouvrage, qui n'etoit point sans mérite, etoit de plomb incrusté fort avant dans le tombes de pierre dont l'eglise etoit pavé. Messieurs du chapitre le firent détroire [*sic*] en 1768 lorsqu'ils firent paver regulièrement leur Eglise."

53. Ibid.: "Ce Labyrinthe avoit trente pieds de diametre. Il fallait, dit-on, une heure entiere pour en parcourir les circuits; et l'on faisait 2,000 pas en suivant tout les détours sans repasser par le meme endroit. Il occupait toute la largeur de la nef. Le dessin en est tres ingénieusement combiné. [Une] lettre de 1758 dit qu'il en ignore la destination."

54. Auxerre, Archives départementales de l'Yonne, G. 1203, liasse, no folio. It is unlikely that the dividers separating the circuits of the maze were made of lead—lead and the more usual blue-black dividing stones were easily confused (see Kern, *Labyrinthe,* p. 240).

55. Favier, *Dictionnaire,* s.v. "pied."

56. Wallet, *Description,* p. 99.

57. This information derives from a capitular act discovered by Wolfgang Krönig in Auxerre, Archives départementales de l'Yonne ("Osterfreude und liturgisches Spiel," in *Quatember: Vierteljahreshefte für Erneuerung und Einheit der Kirche,* 43 [1979], 115–116), and discussed by Heinz Ladendorf ("Kafka und die Kunstgeschichte," *Wallraf-Richartz Jahrbuch,* 25 [1963], 250) and Kern (*Labyrinthe,* p. 240). The wording of this notice and the nature of the document ring true, but I was not able to locate it during a search of the Archives départementales de l'Yonne in July 1996.

58. The maze at Sens may actually predate the one at Chartres by some fifty years because the central vessel and pavement of this church were completed around 1160. In 1268, however, disaster literally befell the clergy of Sens: the twelfth-century south tower began to crumble and within three days had fully imploded into the west end of the church, destroying much of the southwest portion of the building

and possibly the floor at the west end as well. Perhaps there was no maze at Sens before this event, and the labyrinth was inserted as part of a repaving of the church. If so, it dated only from the end of the thirteenth century, some sixty years after the maze at Chartres. On the history of the church, see Chauveau, "Sens," pp. 170–171; and Cailleaux, *Sens*, pp. 2–3.

59. Much material from the cathedral of Sens is now preserved in Auxerre. Liturgical books of the usage of Sens are found in the Bibliothèque municipale, and the bulk of the extant archives of the cathedral of Sens, including a valuable run of fabric accounts, are housed in the Archives départementales de l'Yonne, again in Auxerre.

60. On the locations of the cathedral and baptistry at Sens and Auxerre, see Hubert, "Cathédrales."

61. On the history of the present Gothic cathedral of Auxerre, see Lebeuf, *Mémoires*, I, 30; and Vallery-Radot, "Auxerre," pp. 40–50.

62. *Mercure de France*, May 1726, p. 923: "Cet instrument [the organ] étoit à la portée des Acteurs, puisqu'ils exerçoient leur personnage presque au-dessous du buffet, dans l'endroit de la Nef, où avant l'an 1690 on voyoit sur le pavé une espece de labyrinthe en forme de plusieurs cercles entrelacez, de la même manière qu'il y en a encore un dans la Nef de l'Eglise de Sens."

63. Claude Hohl, *Guide des Archives de l'Yonne* (Auxerre, 1974), p. 96.

64. Fourrey, *Auxerre*, p. 159.

65. Lebeuf, *Mémoires*, II, 252.

66. Recently, in September 1996, Pope John Paul II journeyed to Reims to commemorate the fifteen-hundredth anniversary of this event.

67. Hamann-Mac Lean, *Reims*, I, 344; and Demouy, *Reims*, p. 114.

68. Hopper, *Symbolism*, p. 77; Meyer, *Zahlenallegorese*, pp. 139–141; Mâle, *Image*, p. 14; *Glossa ordinaria* on 1 Kings 17:14 in *PL*, CXIII, 556; and Santarcangeli, *Labyrinthes*, p. 219.

69. Demouy, *Reims*, p. 23.

70. See, for example, Demaison, "Architects," p. 23; and Reinhardt, *Reims*, p. 81.

71. Reinhardt, *Reims*, p. 82; and Demouy, *Reims*, p. 17.

72. For the particulars on the removal of the labyrinth at Reims, see the end of Chapter 8.

73. Of the four verbal descriptions, the earliest and the most valuable is that of Pierre Cocquault. All four texts are given in Branner, "Labyrinth," p. 19; as well as Salet, "Chronologie," p. 350.

74. Cellier's drawings of the cathedral of Reims not only include the maze but sketches of the interior, the jubé, the organ, and a general floor plan as well. They are preserved today in Paris, Bibliothèque nationale, MS fonds français 9152.

75. Reims, Bibliothèque municipale, MS 1609, III, fol. 26: "Un peu plus bas vers le grand portail, entre six pilliers du milieu de ladicte nef sur le pavé dicelle, est un compartiment ou dedalle faict de marbre noir et a douze lignes ou traict distant de tous costes, distant egalement lun de lautre douze poulces de largeur. Le tout a en quarre xxxiiij pieds."

76. See below, n. 79.

77. "Upper stories of the chevet" is derived from "coiffre." On the translation of this ambiguous word, see Branner, "Labyrinth," pp. 18–20.

78. The various theories are summarized by Salet in "Chronologie," pp. 391–394. To this list should be added Hamann-Mac Lean, *Reims*, I, Band 1, 343–349. Only Salet and Branner doubt that the maze holds any information relevant to the chronology of the cathedral.

79. He is not a prelate, as Saint-Paul and Reinhardt have suggested. He is dressed precisely as the other four architects are, and, as Cellier says, all the figures, implicitly including the center one, were architects. Moreover, this master must be responsible for the plan of the labyrinth: Cocquault says that this was the effigy of "celuy qui l'a faict," referring to either the masculine maze *(labyrinthe)* or Daedalus *(dédale)*, but not the feminine church *(église)* or cathedral *(cathédrale)*. Reims, Bibliothèque municipale, MS 1609, III, fol. 26: "Au milieu dudict dedale y a un rond large de six pieds et demy, dans lequel est insculpee la representation de celuy qui l'a faict avec quelque escriture a lentour laquelle ne se peult cognoistre."

80. On this document, see Demaison, "Communication"; and his "Renseignement."

81. I am grateful to Dr. Nancy Wu for sharing her recent analysis of the cathedral of Reims with me ("Uncovering the Hidden Codes: The Geometry of the East End of Reims Cathedral," Ph.D. diss., Columbia University, 1996). A less satisfactory explanation of the geometry inherent in the church is given in Naert, *Labyrinthe*, pp. 62–70.

82. The altar of the Holy Cross apparently was at one time co-dedicated to Mary Magdalene, a fact kindly brought to my attention by Prof. Anne W. Robertson (see also Cerf, *Reims*, I, 117).

83. On the theology of baptism, see Hooke, *Labyrinth*, p. 242; Bradshaw, *Worship*, pp. 173–178; and Bradshaw, "Initiation."

84. Allendy, *Symbolism*, p. 253.

85. See Le Goff, *Purgatory*, p. 124; Allendy, *Symbolism*, pp. 252–256; Hopper, *Symbolism*, p. 77; and Meyer, *Zahlenallegorese*, pp. 139–141.

86. Jean Chevalier and Alain Gheerbrant, *A Dictionary of Symbols*, trans. John Buchanan-Brown (London, 1996), p. 343.

87. On these ceremonies at Reims see Chevalier, *Sacramentaire*, pp. 132–133; Reims, Bibliothèque municipale, MS 330, fols. 40 and 41v; MS 331, fol. 30; as well as *Processionale secundum usum insignis ac Metropolis Ecclesiae Rhemensis, par Antoine Colard* (Reims, 1571), p. 102.

88. On this song, see Chapter 9.

89. The labyrinth is called a "maison Daedalus" in a fourteenth-century martyrology and register of the cathedral preserved in Amiens, Archives départementales de la Somme, MS 2975, fol. 247.

90. The central medallion is today preserved in the Musée de Picardie in Amiens. The plaque presently on the floor of the church is a replica placed there at the end of the nineteenth century. It is reproduced on the cover of Macrez, *Labyrinthe*.

91. The original French of this document, preserved in Amiens, Archives départementales de la Somme, MS 2975, fol. 247, is reproduced, among other places, in Stephen

Murray's excellent *Amiens*, p. 129; as well as in Soyez, *Labyrinthe*, p. 33; and Kern, *Labyrinthe*, p. 220.

92. John Ruskin, *The Bible of Amiens*, cited in Pennick, *Mazes*, p. 118. The later history of the labyrinth at Amiens is told succinctly by Murray in *Amiens*, pp. 129 and 165, making use of documents cited in Durand, *Amiens*, I, 459–465.

93. Héliot, *Saint-Quentin*, p. 78.

94. On the history of this institution, see Héliot, "Chronologie," pp. 7–19.

95. The other, of course, is at Chartres (see Fig. 2.4).

96. Gomart, *Extraits*, I, 70; Héliot, "Chronologie," pp. 17–18; and Héliot, *Saint-Quentin*, pp. 76 and 89–90.

97. Fleury, *Antiquités*, III, 257–258, and IV, 228.

98. Wallet, *Description*, pp. 99–102.

99. In 1533 the pattern of the maze at St. Omer was duplicated in the town hall in Ghent, Belgium. This does not represent an exception to the rule that medieval pavement mazes were religious in spirit. The Ghent maze rested on the floor of a antechamber of a muncipal chapel (Kern, *Labyrinthe*, p. 228).

100. The reconstructed maze at St. Omer can be see in Saint-Hilaire, *Labyrinthe*, opposite p. 68.

101. Fanelli, *Labirinti*, p. 63. See also Mâle, *Image*, p. 153; and Welch, *Art*, p. 152.

102. MacCulloch, *Harrowing*, pp. 168–169.

103. There is no mention of a labyrinth in the voluminous cartularies and capitular acts of Notre Dame of Paris preserved in the Archives nationales and the Bibliothèque nationale, documents from which formed the basis of Wright, *Paris*.

104. For an introduction to the subject of symmetry, see Ian Stewart and Martin Golubitsky, *Fearful Symmetry* (Oxford, 1992).

105. Honnecourt's notebook is reproduced and discussed in Hahnloser, *Honnecourt;* and Bucher, *Architects*.

106. Joseph L. Blau, *The Christian Interpretation of the Cabala in the Renaissance* (New York, 1944), pp. 7–8 and 58.

107. Plato had spoken of the supreme truth resting behind the worldly object (*Timaeus*, 28B–C and 51A), and St. Paul explained to the Romans that "the invisible things of God are clearly seen, being understood by the things that are made" (1:20).

108. To name just a few: *Speculum majus* (by Vincent of Beauvais) consisting of a *Speculum naturale* and *Speculum historiale, Speculum ecclesiae* (Honorius Augustudunensis), *Speculum morale* (Thomas Aquinas), and *Speculum musicae* (Jacques de Liège).

109. See Santarcangeli, *Labyrinthes*, pp. 56–57; and Kern, *Labyrinthe*, figs. 5–6 and 56–58.

110. Evans, *Palace*, I, 423–427; Castleden, *Labyrinth*, pp. 48, 57–58, 98–99, and 130–131; Pieper, *Architectur*, p. 23; and Santarcangeli, *Labyrinthes*, p. 237.

111. This is an almost literal borrowing from Arthur C. McGiffert, *A History of Christian Thought*, 2 vols. (New York, 1932), II, 253–254.

3. THE THEOLOGY OF THE MAZE

1. See the beginning of Chapter 1.

2. Hippolytus, *Philosophumena* (*Refutation of All Heresies*), book v, chap. 10; trans. F. Legge, *Philosophumena or the Refutation of All Heresies,* 2 vols. (New York, 1921), I, 145; and Haubrichs, "*Error,*" p. 120.

3. *Sancti Ambrosii Opera: Pars Quinta: Expositio Psalmi CXVIII,* vol. 62 of *CCEL,* pp. 167–168; see also Doob, *Labyrinth,* p. 75. References to psalms in this book follow the numeration of the Vulgate.

4. Ambrose's friend and colleague Augustine invokes the image of the Christian labyrinth in everything but name when he says: "Let us therefore keep to the straight path, which is Christ, and with Him as our Guide and Saviour, let us turn away in heart and mind from the unreal and futile cycles of the godless" (*City of God,* trans. Marcus Dods [New York, 1950], p. 404).

5. *Apotheosis,* lines 203–205; trans. H. J. Thomson, *Prudentius: Works,* 3 vols. (Cambridge, Mass., and London, 1949), I, 134–135.

6. *Apotheosis,* preface, lines 5–13; trans. H. J. Thomson, *Prudentius: Works,* I, 117–119.

7. Kern's fig. 240 (*Labyrinthe,* p. 203), executed c.1450, is one of the earliest datable representations of a multicursal labyrinth.

8. The multicursal maze as literary construct is treated at length in Doob, *Labyrinth.*

9. Prudentius, *Contra Orationem Symmachi, Liber II,* lines 882–904; trans. H. J. Thomson, *Prudentius: Works,* II, 79.

10. Prudentius, *Apotheosis,* preface, lines 33–45; trans. H. J. Thomson, *Prudentius: Works,* I, 119–121.

11. Translating from the French given in *Grégoire de Nysse: La catéchèse de la foi,* trans. Annette Maignan (Paris, 1978), p. 90.

12. Ibid., p. 94; see also p. 89: "On the triple baptismal immersion."

13. Jerome, *Commentariorum in Zachariam Liber Secundus,* in *PL,* XXV, 1453.

14. See also Padoan, "Teseo."

15. A bibliography of important studies on this subject can be found in Haubrichs, "*Error,*" p. 65, n. 5. See also Pelikan, *Christianity;* and Panofsky, *Renaissance,* chap. 2.

16. Munich, Bayerische Staatsbibliothek, MS Clm 6394, fol. 164v. The somewhat corrupt poem is edited and discussed by Haubrichs, "*Error,*" pp. 70–71; the labyrinth with enveloped poem is reproduced and discussed in Kern, *Labyrinthe,* fig. 231.

17. An earlier Christian version of Ovid's *Metamorphoses* in French, called *Ovide moralisé,* is ascribed, perhaps wrongly, to the poet and musician Philippe de Vitry (Paris, Bibliothèque nationale, MS fonds latin 24306: "Liber in gallico et rithmice editus a magistro Philippo de Vitriaco, quondam Meldensi episcopo, ad restam domine Johanne quondam regine Francie"). The authorship of *Ovide moralisé* is discussed by C. de Boer in *Verhandelingen der Koninklijke Nederlandse Akademie van Wetenschappen, afd. Letterkunde,* New Series, XV (1915), 10. On the sources of both the French *Ovide moralisé* and the Latin *Ovidius Moralizatus,* see Panofsky, *Renaissance,* pp. 78–79, n. 2.

18. The text used here is found in Milan, Biblioteca Ambrosiana, MS D.66 as reproduced in Haubrichs, "*Error*," pp. 135–136. I am indebted to Dr. Robert Babcock for assistance in translating this text. A slightly different version of it appears in the edition of 1509, as can be seen in the facsimile edition *Metamorphosis Ovidiana Moraliter . . . Explanata: Paris 1509: Pierre Bersuire*, with introductory notes by Stephen Orgel (New York and London, 1979), Liber VII, fols. LXII–LXIII.

19. The most recent and thorough treatment of the development of the doctrine of Purgatory is Le Goff, *Purgatory*. Also useful, especially with regard to the visual arts, is Vovelle, *Purgatoire*.

20. These and other visions are conveniently gathered in Gardiner, *Visions*.

21. Ibid., pp. 129–130.

22. The following draws heavily on Le Goff, *Purgatory*, chaps. 5 and 7.

23. See Chapter 1.

24. Hulme, *Harrowing*, p. lxiii.

25. Hennecke, *Apocrypha*, I, 471–475. A useful edition of the Latin text of the Gospel of Nicodemus can be found in H. C. Kim, *The Gospel of Nicodemus* (Toronto, 1973), in which the account of the *Descensus* can be found on pp. 35–50. The interpretation of this text in the Middle Ages is discussed in Zbigniew Izydorczyk, *The Medieval Gospel of Nicodemus* (Tempe, 1997).

26. Hulme, *Harrowing*, p. lxii; and MacCulloch, *Harrowing*, chaps. 1–4. On this point, see also Le Goff, *Purgatory*, pp. 1–14.

27. See Kroll, *Gott*.

28. The enduring influence of this theme, from Bede to Voragine, is the topic of Monnier, *Descente*, as well as Turmel, *Descente*. It is also treated in Kroll, *Gott*, pp. 126–182; MacCulloch, *Harrowing*, p. 156; Hulme, *Harrowing*, pp. lx–lxx; Turner, "*Descendit*"; Campbell, "Hell"; and Garde, *Poetry*, chap. 5.

29. See, for example, *The Glory of Byzantium: Art and Culture of the Middle Byzantine Era A.D. 843–1261*, ed. Helen C. Evans and William D. Wixom (New York, 1997), figs. 34, 60, 63, 68B, 74, 91, 93, 98, 115, 230, 235, 254, 308, 317, and 319.

30. Renderings in the visual arts of Christ's descent are listed in Hulme, *Harrowing*, pp. lxiv–lxv; Monnier, *Descente*, chap. 10; and Réau, *Iconographie*, II, 535–537.

31. Dürer's composition served, in turn, as the model for a great mosaic on the west front of Saint Mark's Basilica in Venice, one accompanied by antiquated leonines top and bottom: "Having left the sinful ancient world, Christ visits Hell so as to proffer the heavenly kingdom" (*Visitat infernum regnum pro dando supernum partibus antiquis dimissis Christus iniquis*), and "He is the mighty one who breaks down the doors and carries me off as spoil" (*Quis fractis portis spoliat me campio fortis*).

32. The following draws on Meyer, *Fragmenta*, pp. 98–101; Chambers, *Stage*, II, 74–76; Monnier, *Descente*, chap. XI; Young, "Harrowing"; Young, *Drama*, chap. V; and Faulkner, "Harrowing."

33. The antiphon was well known in Ireland, England, and Germany, but less so in France (see Meyer, *Fragmenta*, p. 100; Monnier, *Descente*, p. 226; and Young, "Harrowing," pp. 918 and 928).

34. Young, "Harrowing," p. 928.

35. Monnier, *Descente,* pp. 241–242.

36. Rastall, "Sounds." See also the section on the "Zerschlagen des Janustores durch die Discordia," in Kroll, *Gott,* pp. 512–522; as well as the discussion of cries and chaos in Mancini, "Labyrinthe," p. 25.

37. A particularly full exchange is recorded in the York Plays; see Lucy Toulmin Smith, ed., *York Plays: The Plays Performed by the Crafts or Mysteries of York* (New York, 1885, rpt. 1963), pp. 385–392.

38. See Rastall, "Sounds," p. 112; and especially Chambers, *Stage,* II, 74.

39. See Du Cange, *Glossarium,* s.v. "Verberare."

40. Chartres, Archives départementales d'Eure et Loir, Supplément à la série G, MS 169, p. 22.

41. See Bernard of Clairvaux's second and fourth sermons for Ascension (*PL,* CLXXXIII, 301–304 and 309–316); and Guillaume Deguileville, *Pèlerinage de l'âme;* Paris, Bibliothèque nationale, MS fonds français 12466, lines 10,378ff, ed. J. J. Stürzinger (London, 1895), p. 336. I am grateful to Prof. Bernard McGinn for having brought the former source to my attention.

42. See, for example, John Van Engen, *Devotio Moderna: Basic Writings* (New York, 1988).

43. This is the translation of the title *Enchiridion Militis Christiani* given in *The Oxford Illustrated History of Christianity,* ed. John McManners (Oxford and New York, 1996), p. 252.

44. This paragraph draws on the introductory essay in *Handbook of the Militant Christian,* trans. Dolan, esp. p. 58.

45. *The Enchiridion of Erasmus,* trans. and ed. Himelick, p. 83.

46. See Erasmus's *Handbüchlein,* ed. Welzig.

47. Panofsky, *Dürer,* p. 151.

48. Ibid., p. 154.

49. For more on this point, see the final section of this chapter.

50. Originally written in Czech in 1623 but not published until 1631, Comenius's strikingly inventive work appeared in a new expanded edition in Antwerp in 1663. An abridged German edition was printed in Potsdam in 1781 and the first English translation, by Franz Lützow, in 1901 with the title *The Labyrinth of the World and the Paradise of the Heart.* Lützow's introduction offers a useful history of the work. See also the exhibition catalogue edited by Peter Spielmann, *Labyrinth der Welt und Lusthaus des Herzens: Johann Amos Comenius/Jan Amos Komenský (1592–1670)* (Bochum, n.d.).

51. Comenius, *Labyrinth,* trans. Spinka, p. 124.

52. Ibid., p. 125.

53. Ibid., p. 126.

54. See, for example, Kern, *Labyrinthe,* p. 302.

55. Diehl, "Images," p. 49.

56. Facsimile reproduction available in Guillaume de La Perrière, *Le theatre des bons engins: La morosophie,* introduction by Alison Saunders (Aldershot, 1993).

57. Facsimile reproduction available in Thomas Combe, *Theater of Fine Devices*, introduction by Mary V. Silcox (Aldershot, 1990).

58. On Hugo, see *Dictionnaire de spiritualité* (Paris, 1968), s.v. "Hugo (Herman)."

59. Bibliographic information on *Pia Desideria Emblematis* is given in Mario Praz, *Studies in Seventeenth-Century Imagery*, 2nd ed. (Rome, 1964), pp. 376–380. The following commentary is based on an exemplar of the original 1624 edition (Yale University, Beinecke Library, Beckford 266, pp. 134–144).

60. *Confessiones*, VI, 16, line 21.

61. *Enarrationes in Psalmos*, XXXIX, 6, line 3.

62. See Kern, *Labyrinthe*, figs. 379, 384, 385, and 414.

63. "O dass meine Wege gerichtet würden / zu halten deine Rechte / In dem verwirrten Irregarten / Der so von Krümmen zugerichte / Geh ich und will ohn Furcht erwarten / Die Hülffe die dein Wort verspricht.... / Diezz Leben ist ein Irregarten / Auff dass der Wandel sicher sey / Du ohn Falsch auf Gott im blinden / Glauben warten / In reiner Liebe ohne Heucheley" (Kern, *Labyrinthe*, p. 300).

64. See Kern, *Labyrinthe*, p. 302.

65. On Quarles and the English emblem book generally, see Freeman, *Books*; Ernest B. Gilman, "Word and Image in Quarles' *Emblemes*," in *The Language of Images*, ed. W. J. T. Mitchell (Chicago, 1980), pp. 59–84, rpt. from *Critical Inquiry*, VI (1980), 385–410; and Diehl, "Images."

66. Freeman, *Books*, p. 117. Hugo's *Pia Desideria* was not only received in England in Quarles's adaptation, but in what purported to be a more faithful translation by Ed. Arwalker, *Pia desideria or Divine addresses* (London, 1690). Ironically, the labyrinth emblem offered there is not the original of the Hugo print, but the reverse-image one of Quarles!

67. On the purely Protestant overtones of Quarles's poetic rendition of the maze, see Diehl, "Maze," p. 287.

68. Freeman, *Books*, p. 233.

69. Francis Quarles, *Emblems, Divine and Moral* (New York, 1816), pp. 205–208.

4. THE WARRIOR, THE LAMB, AND ASTROLOGY

1. The following draws heavily on the articles "Agneau de Dieu" in *DTC* and "Agneau" in *DALC*. Useful discussions in English can be found in Schiller, *Iconography*, II, 117–121; *CE*, s.v. "Lamb"; and *NCE*, s.v. "Lamb of God."

2. Paris, Bibliothèque nationale, MS fonds latin 8878, fol. 193v. A facsimile of this manuscript has been published by Emile-A. van Moé, *L'Apocalypse de Saint-Sever* (Paris, 1943).

3. Paris, Bibliothèque nationale, MS neerlandais 3, fol. 22.

4. See Chapter 5.

5. *Antiphonale monasticum* (Tournai, 1934), p. 459.

6. Kroll, *Gott,* p. 134. The Latin text, attributed to the sixth-century poet Fortunatus, can be found, among other places, in Andrieu, *Ordines,* V, 300.

7. Louis Duchesne, ed., *Le Liber Pontificalis,* 3 vols. (Paris, 1955–1957), I, 381, n. 42. On the *Agnus dei* generally, see Jungmann, *Mass,* II, 332–340.

8. The work is found in a collection of polyphony compiled in Paris c.1250 and now preserved in Florence, Biblioteca Medicea Laurenziana, MS Pluteus 29.1, fol. 150v.

9. *Nusmido* appears within a collection of substitutes for the organum of the Mass. *Dominus* would have been sung first and then *Nusmido.*

10. For a fascinating description of the manufacture of the waxen Agnus dei figures and their distribution in 1731, see Blackburn and Holford-Strevens, *Year,* pp. 626–627.

11. Dykmans, *Patrizi,* I, 138. Although Dykmans publishes this text as part of Patrizi's ceremonial, he notes (p. 138, n. 1) that it was already included in the papal ceremonial at the time of Benedict XIII, that is, in the early fifteenth century.

12. See Chapter 2 under "Sens."

13. On this subject, see Jacobsson, "Easter," pp. 283–307.

14. Whitrow, *Time,* pp. 190–191; and Blackburn and Holford-Strevens, *Year,* p. 792.

15. Cesare Ripa, *Iconologia* (Padua, 1611), cited in Tanner, *Aeneas,* p. 287, n. 16; Hulme, *Harrowing,* p. lvii; Talley, *Year,* pp. 90–96; and Blackburn and Holford-Strevens, *Year,* p. 130.

16. Beleth, *Summa,* vol. 41a of *CCCM,* pp. 209–210.

17. Drawn from the sequence *Salve, sancta Christi parens,* the text of which is given in *AH,* LIV, 427.

18. For a discussion of Christ's descent and the Harrowing of Hell, see above, pp. 80–86.

19. Many such words are found in the sermon "De paschali die" of Honorius Augustudunensis (c.1080–c.1155) edited in *PL,* CLXXII, 928–934. See also Jacobsson, "Easter," pp. 290–293; Kroll, *Gott,* pp. 134–135 and 140; and Woodward, "Labyrinths," pp. 140–143.

20. Reims, Bibliothèque municipale, MS 330 (dated 1356), fol. 40.

21. The full text with music is found in *Processionale secundum usum insignis ac Metropolitane Ecclesiae Remensis* (Reims, 1624), p. 117.

22. Although Machaut received his canonicate in expectation in 1333, he may not have taken up residence at Reims until 1340. The most thorough biography of Guillaume de Machaut remains that of Machabey, *Machaut.* A recent useful synthesis of his life is Earp, *Machaut,* chap. 1.

23. Paris, Bibliothèque nationale, MS fonds français 403, fol. 43. On this source, see L. Delisle et P. Meyer, *L'Apocalypse en français (Bibl. nat. fr. 403)* (Paris, 1901). Strictly speaking, this translation seems to have fashioned something of an amalgam of Apocalypse 7:14 and 22:14.

24. For a list of authors treating the subject matter of this piece, see Earp, *Machaut,* p. 340.

25. See above, pp. 64–70.

26. For a penetrating discussion of labyrinthine metaphors in *The Consolation of Philosophy*, see Doob, *Labyrinth*, chap. 9.

27. From the seventeenth-century English translation of the unidentified "I.T" as given in William Anderson, *The Consolation of Philosophy by Anicius Manlius Severinus Boethius* (Carbondale, 1963), p. 81.

28. Ibid., p. 64.

29. Ibid., p. 15.

30. Cambridge, Trinity Hall, MS 12, fol. 50v, reproduced in Kern, *Labyrinthe*, fig. 211.

31. A partial manuscript of Boethius's tract in Latin (Reims, Bibliothèque municipale, MS 409) as well as a French translation (loc. cit., MS 879) once were stored in the vestry of the cathedral. I am grateful to Prof. Anne Robertson for this information.

32. *Le Jugement du roy de Behaigne and Remede de Fortune*, ed. James I. Wimsatt and William W. Kibler (Athens, 1988), p. 37.

33. C. De Boer, "Guillaume de Machaut et *l'Ovide moralisé*," *Romania*, 43 (1914), 335–352.

34. Johnson, "Amiens," p. 253; Machabey, *Machaut*, I, 30; and Earp, *Machaut*, p. 18.

35. Both Beleth (*Summa*, vol. 41a of *CCCM*, p. 223) and, a century later, Guillaume Durand (*Rationale diviorum officorium*, IV, 86, 9) mention the playing of "ludus pilae" at Reims and other major churches on Easter Sunday, but admonish that it would be more appropriate to eliminate such frivolities. On Easter processions at Reims, see Chapter 2 under "Reims."

36. On the location of Machaut's place of burial, see Robertson, "Machaut," pp. 100–101 and 131.

37. Antonia Fraser, *Mary Queen of Scots* (New York, 1969), p. 413.

38. See Maurice Baring's biography of Mary Queen of Scots, *In My End Is My Beginning* (London, 1931), p. vii.

39. Fraser, *Mary Queen of Scots*, p. 413.

40. The poem is printed, among other places, in Helen Gardner, *The Composition of Four Quartets* (London and Boston, 1978). The musical quality of *East Coker* undoubtedly rests in its formal affinities to a musical rondeau.

41. Jacobsson, "Easter," p. 284.

42. Canon of the Mass to be found, among other places, *LU*, pp. 4–5.

43. This paragraph draws entirely on Philip V. Bohlman, "The Akedah and the Embodiment of Music: On the Origins of Music in Jewish Thought," *Sources: The Chicago Journal of Jewish Studies* (Spring 1996), pp. 52–58.

44. Ibid., p. 54.

45. See Chapter 2 under "Sens" and "Reims."

46. See Chapter 8.

47. An excellent introduction to the pilgrimage festival of the Hajj is F. E. Peters, *The Hajj: The Muslim Pilgrimage to Mecca and the Holy Places* (Princeton, 1994). On the issue of sacrificial sheep, see especially pp. 254 and 307–308.

48. *CE*, s.v. "Passover," p. 1069.

49. Among the authors who convey parts of the tale are Apollonius of Rhodes, Pindar, Euripides, and Ovid. A convenient synthesis of their accounts can be found in Hamilton, *Mythology*, chap. 7.

50. Ovid, *Fasti*, III, 876.

51. Medea and Ariadne are not only analogous, they were cousins—the daughters respectively of Helios's son Aetes and daughter Pasiphaë.

52. A rational treatment of the cosmological significance of the maze can be found in Kern, *Labyrinthe*, pp. 30–33 and figs. 13–20.

53. Critchlow, "Maze."

54. Charpentier, *Mystères*, pp. 34 and 40–44. For similarly absurd astronomical assertions regarding the placement of the maze at Chartres, see Saint-Hilaire, *Labyrinthe*, chap. 12.

55. Macrez, *Labyrinthe*, p. 7. Several nineteenth-century authors claim that the eastern-most branch of the central plaque at Amiens points to the spot of the rising sun on 15 August, day of the Assumption and patronal feast at Amiens (Soyez, *Labyrinthes*, p. 32).

56. Some of the more fanciful assertions of this sort are found in Lonegren, *Labyrinths*, pp. 19–22.

57. See Heilbron, *Sun*.

58. Hutton, *Stations*, p. 179. For a discussion of the methods used to reckon the date of Easter, see Heilbron, *Sun*, chap. 1, "The Science of Easter."

59. Quoting from the Talmud as cited in Talley, *Year*, p. 81; see also Chevalier, *Astrology*, p. 249.

60. There was also, of course, a prolonged coexistence of an autumn and a spring new year in the Jewish tradition (see Blackburn and Holford-Strevens, *Year*, p. 722).

61. Needless to say, the bibliography of astrology is enormous. A useful introduction to the subject is Tester's *Astrology*. All serious discussions of astrology during the last hundred years have benefited from the magisterial study of Bouché-Leclercq, *L'Astrologie grecque*.

62. Gleadow, *Zodiac*, p. 206.

63. See the opening lines of the Prologue to *Canterbury Tales*.

64. For an introduction to this topic, see Maunder, *Astronomy*; and Hübner, *Zodiacus*, pp. 9–36 and 101–119.

65. Maunder, *Astronomy*, p. 245; and Tester, *Astrology*, pp. 14, 71, and 180.

66. On the Babylonian, Greek, and Roman terms, see Bouché-Leclercq, *L'Astrologie grecque*, pp. xix and 56–57; on the Egyptian and Hebrew terms, see Chevalier, *Astrology*, p. 250; on the signs of the zodiac in the synagogues of Palestine, see Tamsyn Barton, *Ancient Astrology* (London and New York, 1994), p. 70 and fig. 9; on the Arabic term *al-hamal*, see Carboni, *Stars*, p. 25.

67. Chevalier, *Astrology*, p. 249–250.

68. Manilius, *Astronomica*, I, lines 263–274, translated in Tester, *Astrology*, p. 31. The Latin and a somewhat different translation can be found in the edition of G. P. Goold, The Loeb Classical Library (Cambridge, Mass., 1977), pp. 24–27.

69. *The Nun's Priest's Tale,* line 3188, cited in Wood, *Chaucer,* p. 163.

70. On this point, see the excellent discussion of the symbolism of Aries during the late Middle Ages and Renaissance in Tanner, *Aeneas,* chap. VIII.

71. Robert Holkot, *Super sapientiam Salomonis* (Speyer, 1483), chap. 61, cited in Hübner, *Zodiacus,* p. 128.

72. Wood, *Chaucer,* pp. 272–297; and Hübner, *Zodiacus,* p. 95.

73. *Zenonis Veronensis Tractatus,* ed. B. Löfstedt, vol. 22 of *CCEL,* col. 1.38.

74. Ibid., 1.38,7; and Hübner, *Zodiacus,* pp. 63 and 134.

75. From Hirenicus's *De Ratione Duodecim Signorum,* in *Monumenta Germania Historica, Poetarum Latinarum Medii Aevi* (Berlin, 1923), IV_2, 693. The editor Karl Strecker cites similar passages from Bede and Isidore of Seville.

76. Hübner, *Zodiacus,* p. 204.

77. Ibid., p. 200.

78. For an example of a poet exploiting the image of Aries "writ in the skies for all eternity," see Chapter 7.

79. See James Snyder, *Northern Renaissance Art* (New York, 1985), p. 109 and fig. 103.

80. For an edition of this Mass see *Jacob Obrecht: Collected Works,* ed. Chris Mass, vol. 5 (Utrecht, 1985), and especially the critical commentary, pp. xi–xv. I owe my knowledge of this inscription to the kindness of Prof. Michael Long of the University of Buffalo.

81. Tester, *Astrology,* p. 4.

82. On this point, see "Retrogradations and Progressions" in Miller, *Dance,* pp. 449–465.

83. For a collection of such remarks, see Du Cange, *Glossarium,* s.v. "Retrogradus"; see also Maunder, *Astronomy,* p. 246.

84. *OCD,* p. 929.

85. Carboni, *Zodiac,* p. 25.

86. For a useful compendium of medieval citations of Mars, see Chance, *Mythography,* s.v. "Mars" in the index.

87. *The Divine Comedy of Dante Alighieri,* trans. Henry F. Cary (New York, 1909), pp. 346–347.

88. Ibid., p. 362.

89. See the beginning of Chapter 2 under "Pavia" and "Piacenza."

90. See also above, Figure 1.7, a maze found in a collection of poems relating to the seven planets, the months and days of the year, and the stars. A similar seven-track labyrinth is found in an eleventh-century manuscript from Lucca, now in the Pierpont Morgan Library in New York (MS 925, fol. 11v); here the labyrinth is surrounded by a computational book of Bede, Gregory of Tours's *De Cursu Stellarum,* and two zodiacal charts.

91. Paris, Bibliothèque nationale, MS fonds latin 5371, fol. 240v. I owe my knowledge of this source, a heroic transcription of the faint text, and a preliminary bibliography to the generosity of Barbara Haggh and Michel Huglo.

92. Even with the aid of an ultraviolet lamp, this text is difficult to decipher. Moreover,

where a firm text exists, ambiguities persist ("*horis*," for example, can be taken to be a reverse-spelling for "*oris*," and could be translated "from our shores"). Thus neither the construction of the Latin nor the translation offered here is entirely certain.

93. On this poem, see Walther, *Initia*, No. 310. It also appears in conjunction with the mazes reproduced earlier in Figures 1.7 and 1.10.

94. See Irtenkauf, "Computus"; and Smits van Waesberghe, *Musikerziehung*, p. 178.

95. The source is briefly discussed in Jean Leclercq, "Formes anciennes de l'office marial," *Ephemerides liturgicae*, 74 (1960), 97.

96. On this, see Wieck, *Time Sanctified*, p. 45; Harry Bober, "The Zodiacal Miniature of the Très Riches Heures . . . —its Sources and Meaning," *Journal of the Warburg and Courtauld Institutes*, 11 (1948), 1–34; and A. Katzenellenbogen, *Chartres*, s.v. "Zodiac" in the index.

5. THE DANCE OF THE MAZE

1. *Iliad*, book XVIII, lines 678–694.

2. Miller, *Dance*, pp. 24–25; and Kern, *Labyrinthe*, pp. 50–51.

3. A complete list of sources discussing Theseus's dance on Delos is given by Miller, *Dance*, p. 550.

4. Ibid., p. 351.

5. The term "Crane dance" may be a misreading of the Greek words meaning "winding dance"; see Lawler, "Dance"; and her *Dance*, p. 47; as well as *OCD*, s.v. "Dancing."

6. *Plutarch's Lives: Dryden Edition Revised* (London, 1948), p. 14.

7. *Onomasticon*, IV, 101, ed. Ericus Bethe (Leipzig, 1900), pp. 230–231, here translated from the German translation of W. Batschelet-Massini given in Kern, *Labyrinthe*, p. 52.

8. Santarcangeli, *Labyrinthes*, p. 223.

9. Kern, *Labyrinthe*, p. 53. A dance of this sort could still be seen in southern France in 1838 (see the end of this chapter).

10. See Chapter 1.

11. *Aeneid*, book V, lines 546–591.

12. Santarcangeli, *Labyrinthes*, pp. 227 and 256–257; and Doob, *Labyrinth*, p. 27.

13. See Kerényi, "Labyrinth-Studien," p. 251; Kerényi, *Labirinto*, p. 56; Pieper, *Architectur*, pp. 28–30; Sanctarcangeli, *Labyrinthes*, p. 37; and Kern, *Labyrinthe*, pp. 50–54.

14. See pp. 148–154.

15. The translation here is that of Miller (*Dance*, pp. 81–83), who also includes the original Greek of the salient passages.

16. Backman, *Dances*, p. 15; and Miller, *Dance*, p. 88.

17. Acts of St. Thomas 6, as translated in Backman, *Dances*, p. 16.

18. Acts of St. Thomas 6, as translated by Miller in *Dance*, p. 119.

19. Gregory of Nazianzus, *Oratio* 24:19, translated in Miller, *Dance*, p. 398, with the salient passages given in the original Greek.

20. See the end of Chapter 4.

21. Honorius Augustodunensis, *Gemma animae*, I, 139, in *PL*, CLXXII, 587.

22. *Paradise Lost*, book V, lines 618–627. I am indebted to Prof. Thomas Greene for bringing this passage to my attention.

23. *New Oxford Book of Carols*, ed. Hugh Keyte and Andrew Parrott (Oxford, 1992), pp. 464–466.

24. From the diaries of the Reverened Francis Kilvert, as quoted in Blackburn and Holford-Strevens, *Year*, p. 624.

25. *Four Sermons*, I, in *PG*, X, 1146; trans. in Taylor, *Dance*, p. 74.

26. Backman, *Dances*, p. 27.

27. *Homilia in Ebriosos*, XIV, in *PG*, XVI, 446; the relevant passage is translated in Backman, *Dances*, p. 25.

28. See below, "The Dance of the Maze at the Cathedral of Sens."

29. See the list of admonitions against such "pagan" activities given in Gougaud, "Danse," pp. 11–14.

30. See his *Image*, chap. 1.

31. See the end of Chapter 1.

32. Gougaud, "Danse," p. 11.

33. The document is given in the original Latin by Abbé Jean Lebeuf, "Remarques sur les anciennes Réjouissances Ecclesiastiques," *Mercure de France*, May 1726, pp. 921–922. I am greatly indebted to Dr. Robert Babcock for his thoughts on this text.

34. See Chapter 2 under "Auxerre."

35. See, for example, Auxerre, Archives départementales de l'Yonne, G. 1798, no folio (15 March 1410); G. 1798, no folio (16 March 1411); G. 1798, fol. 285 (19 April 1412); and G. 1798, fol. 285 (23 April 1412). The chapter act of 18 April 1396, apparently now lost, is cited by Lebeuf in *Mercure de France*, May 1726, pp. 915–916.

36. Auxerre, Archives départementales de l'Yonne, G. 1798, fol. 285. The full Latin is given by Lebeuf in *Mémoires*, IV, 322.

37. The complete Latin is given in Lebeuf, *Mémoires*, IV, 322.

38. For more on Guillaume Durand's remarks, see p. 317 n. 35.

39. Lebeuf, *Mémoires*, IV, 322; and *Mercure de France*, May 1726, pp. 918–921.

40. Lebeuf, *Mémoires*, IV, pp. 321–322. A useful interpretation of these events can be found in Fourrey, *Auxerre*, pp. 161–162.

41. The best of these is to be found in Doob, "Dance"; and Doob, *Labyrinth*, pp. 123–127.

42. In the French rendition of Ovid's *Metamorphoses*, the popular fourteenth-century *Ovide moralisé*, the ball of pitch is called *un poleton*, the French equivalent of the Latin *pilota*: "Un poleton compost li baille/De glus, de saïn et de cole/Quant il vous baera la gole/Por vous destruire et devorer/Jetez li ens sans demorer/Si l'es-tranglerois sans arreste." Book VIII, lines 1308–1313, ed. C. De Boer, in *Verhan-*

delingen der koninklijke Akademie van Wetenschappen, new series, 30 (1931), 140. See also Doob, "Dance."

43. Chambers, *Stage,* I, 128–129 and n. 4. See also Backman, *Dances,* pp. 71–72; Schnapper, "Dances," p. 358; Kern, *Labyrinthe,* pp. 191–192; Hutton, *Sun,* p. 204; and Blackburn and Holford-Strevens, *Year,* p. 624.

44. Garde, *Poetry,* p. 74; and Hübner, *Christianus,* pp. 144–147. See also Dürer's famous engraving *Sol Justitiae* as discussed in Panofsky, *Dürer,* p. 78 and fig. 101.

45. See Batschelet-Massini, "Labyrinthzeichnungen," pp. 59–60.

46. See the beginning of this chapter.

47. *Ars grammatica,* in *Grammatici latini,* ed. Heinrich Keil (Hildesheim, 1961), p. 60. On this passage see the excellent discussion in Doob, *Labyrinth,* p. 68.

48. Paris, Bibliothèque nationale, Réserve B.2950, fol. lxxvi^v.

49. Paris, Bibliothèque nationale, MS fonds latin 1055, first part, fols. 212–213; and ibid., Réserve B.6231, fol. Mii^v.

50. Paris, Bibliothèque nationale, Réserve B.2950, fol. lxxix.

51. Ibid., fol. lxxvi^v.

52. On this document, see Chapter 2, n. 57.

53. See Chapter 2 under "Sens."

54. Poitiers, Bibliothèque municipale, MS 336, fols. 90–90v, cited in Villetard, "Danse," pp. 113–114.

55. Remark of canon Leriche, dated 1709, preserved in Auxerre, Bibliothèque municipale, MS 207, fol. 24; also cited in Villetard, "Danse," p. 112.

56. Letter of canon Fenel to Abbé Jean Lebeuf, dated 6 December 1740, and published in Jean Lebeuf, *Lettres,* ed. Quantin et Cheresy, 2 vols. (Auxerre, 1866–1867), II, 289; also cited in Villetard, "Danse," p. 113.

57. Paris, 1682, rpt. 1972, fol. eij^v.

58. Sens, Bibliothèque municipale, MS 62, pp. 37–38.

59. These and other mentions of women dancing in the church are given by Gougaud in "Danse," pp. 11–13.

60. See Rokseth, "Danses," p. 97.

61. On this point see ibid., pp. 94–95; and Woodward, "Labyrinths," pp. 85–90. See also the discussions of Christmas and Easter in Hutton, *Sun.*

62. See, for example, Guillaume Durand, *Rationale divinorum officiorum,* IV, 86 at 9; and Jean-Baptiste Thiers, *Traité des jeux et des divertissemens* (Paris, 1686), p. 403.

63. Chartres, Archives départementales d'Eure-et-Loir, Supplément à la série G, MS 169, pp. 21 and 28; and MS G 435, liasse, no folio (extract of chapter act of 1354).

64. See p. 133. For additional discussions of the term *chorea* see Du Cange, *Glossarium,* s.v. "Chorea"; Gougaud, "Danse," passim; Chailley, "Danse," pp. 363–365; Sahlin, *Carole,* chaps. 1–3; and Delaporte, *Ordinaire,* pp. 256–257. Sometimes the dean and sometimes the Devil was at the center of the *chorea.* Jacques Chailley ("Danse," p. 364) cites a fifteenth-century sermon that condemns dances by means of the following syllogism: "The ring-dance is circular. The journey of the Devil is circular. Therefore the ring-dance is the movement of the Devil" (*Chorea est iter circulare.*

Diaboli iter est circulare. Ergo chorea est motus diaboli). As late as the seventeenth century the *chorea* was still being defined as "a circular dance in the center of which is the Devil" (Kirkendale, "Circulatio-Tradition," p. 78).

65. Rome, Biblioteca Apostolica Vaticana, MS Reg. Lat. 4756, fol. 194; and Delaporte, *Ordinaire*, p. 113.

66. As described in the *Ordo veridicus* for the feast of Easter. Sometime before the Second World War Yves Delaporte made a copy of this ordinal of Chartrain usage, and the original was subsequently lost. The passage relating to Easter Sunday can be found on p. 36 of Delaporte's copy, which is today preserved in the Archives du diocèse de Chartres. I am grateful to Abbé Pierre Bizeau and to Prof. Margot Fassler for making this document available to me.

67. See Chapter 2 under "Chartres."

68. Chartres, Archives départementales d'Eure-et-Loir, Supplément à la série G, MS 169, p. 22: Du chapitre generale de Purification 1452, fol. 66: Deffence de faire dance ni debattre aucun le jour et la semaine de pasque. "Capitulum declaravit prout declaraverat alias quod a caetero nulli capellanorum aut aliorum de choro et panis ecclesie carnotensis liceat pendente servicio faciendo in chorea quae consuevit fieri in festo Sancte Paschae et per ebdomadam ejusdem festi aliquem tam in navi quam in choro vel alibi verberare propter insolentias et opprobria quae continue possent et possunt in futurum."

69. See above, p. 85.

70. Rouillard, *Parthénie*, fols. 168v–170v.

71. The clerical dancing master Thoinot Arbeau [Jehan Tabourot], canon of the cathedral of Langres, describes in his *Orchésographie* (Langres, 1588, rpt. 1970), fols. 68v–93, no fewer than twenty-five different types of *bransles*.

72. Challine, *Chartres*, p. 193.

73. See the decree of 1517 discussed above under "The Dance of the Maze at the Cathedral of Sens."

74. Florence, Biblioteca Medicea Laurenziana, MS Pluteus 29.1. On this source, see Baltzer, "Manuscript."

75. The music and texts of these dances are edited in exemplary fashion in Anderson, *Conductus*. The texts can also be found in *AH*, XXI, 37–47.

76. Tours, Bibliothèque municipale, MS 927. The Tours manuscript is described in *RISM*, BIV, 449–450, and its texts are edited in Victor Luzarche, *Office de Pâques ou de la Résurrection* (Tours, 1856). See also Eduard Krieg, *Das Lateinische Osterspiel von Tours* (Würzburg, 1956).

77. *Der Musiktraktat des Johannes de Grocheo nach den Quellen neu herausgegeben*, ed. Ernst Rohloff (Leipzig, 1943), pp. 50–51. For a related description from Italy at this time see Eggebrecht, *Handwörterbuch*, s.v. "Rondellus/rondeau, rota."

78. Eggebrecht, *Handwörterbuch*, s.v. "Rondellus/rondeau, rota."

79. Rokseth, "Danses," p. 108, has observed that the Easter dances are the ones that most consistently make use of the circular form of the *cantilena rotunda*, and that dances for other times of the liturgical year do not.

80. See p. 142.

81. M5 in the aforementioned Anderson, *Conductus.*

82. M7 in Anderson, *Conductus.*

83. N4 in Anderson, *Conductus.*

84. M11 in Anderson, *Conductus.*

85. M22 in Anderson, *Conductus.*

86. On this point, see p. 80–85.

87. M4 in Anderson, *Conductus.*

88. See the following paragraph.

89. M3 in Anderson, *Conductus.*

90. For Spanish, English, and Scottish manuscripts preserving these dances, see the "Critical Notes" in Anderson, *Conductus.*

91. *Luto carens,* for example, is found in three-voice polyphony in the Scottish source Wolfenbüttel, Herzog-August Bibliothek, MS 628, fol. 73.

92. [Constant] Leber, *Collection des meilleurs dissertations, notices et traités particuliers* (Paris, 1838), IX, 428–429.

93. Ibid., IX, 436.

94. "Sumpto prandio, et finito sermone, Domini canonici et capellani, manibus se tenentes, choream agunt in claustro, vel in medio navis ecclesiae, si tempus sit pluviosum" (ibid., IX, 426).

95. At Comberton, Cambridgeshire, as reported in Trollope, "Labyrinths," p. 232.

96. *Sumer is icumen in* is a rota, or round, composed c.1250 probably in the area of Reading. The sole copy is preserved in a monastic manuscript (London, British Library, MS Harley 978, fol. 11). For bibliography on this piece, see *NG,* s.v. "Sumer is icumen in."

97. The original Latin text reads: "Observe Christians, what condescension! The heavenly Husbandman, for the fault of the vine, spared not His Son, but offered Him to the fate of death. He restores the half-perished prisoners from punishment to life, and crowns them with Him on the throne of heaven" (translation given in Jamieson B. Hurry, *Sumer is icumen in* [London, 1914], p. 13).

98. The first five notes of the *pes* (bass) are identical to the opening of *Regina caeli laetare,* a chant sung in Franciscan and Dominican houses and elsewhere at Compline after Vespers, from Easter Sunday until Pentecost (see *LU,* p. 275).

99. See Mancini, "Labyrinthe."

100. The name likely derives from the Cretan port city of Candia (Iráklion) located only a few kilometers from the remains of Knossus. Prior to the wars for Greek independence, the French and other Europeans referred to Crete as *Candia* (Amé, *Carrelages,* p. 33).

101. Anonymous, "La Danse candiote," *Magazin pittoresque,* 6 (1838), 216.

102. A similar dance, though with fewer classical resonances, was still to be seen in Cornwall, England, in the nineteenth century and is described in W. G. Wade, *The Antiquary* of April 1881 (quoted in Pennick, *Mazes,* p. 60). Other dances with possible connections to the labyrinth are discussed in Kern, *Labyrinthe,* pp. 391–395.

103. Moreau de Saint-Méry in his *Della Danza* (Venice, 1817) says that "the Greek dance

representing the history of Ariadne and Theseus was called *Candiotta*" and that it had been carried as far as present-day Haiti and the Dominican Republic (cited in Santarcangeli, *Labyrinthes*, p. 224). Is there a connection between the West Indian dance called "the Limbo" and this European dance of liberation?

6. Symbolizing the Christian Warrior

1. Willem Elders has devoted much of his life to the subject of musical symbolism. See his *Studien, Composers*, and *Scores*.

2. On this subject, see Tilman Seebas, "The Visualization of Music through Pictorial Imagery and Notation in Late Mediaeval France," in *Studies in the Performance of Late Mediaeval Music*, ed. Stanley Boorman (Cambridge, 1983), pp. 19–34.

3. See Chapter 9.

4. Wulf Arlt, "'Triginta denariis'—Musik und Text in einer Motette des *Roman de Fauvel* über dem Tenor *Victime paschali laudes*," in *Pax et Sapientia: Studies in Text and Music of Liturgical Tropes and Sequences in Memory of Gordon Anderson*, vol. 29 of *Acta Universitatis Stockhomiensis* (Stockholm, 1985), pp. 97–113.

5. Wright, "Temple."

6. Marcus Van Crevel, ed., *Jacobus Obrecht: Opera Omnia: Missae: VI: Sub tuum presidium* (Amsterdam, 1959), pp. xvii–xxv; and Wegman, *Obrecht*, pp. 337–340.

7. See pp. 23 and 57.

8. For examples of this sort of symbolism, see Elders, *Scores*, pp. 189–195.

9. See Lowinsky, "Fortuna."

10. See pp. 85 and 111.

11. I am grateful to Peter Lefferts for kindly bringing this motet to my attention. Prof. Lefferts edits and discusses this motet in vol. 17 of *PM*, pp. 142–148, 183, and 221.

12. See Hans-Erich Keller and Alison Stones, *La Vie de Sainte-Marguerite* (Tübingen, 1990).

13. Dr. Bonnie Blackburn has kindly brought to my attention that the anonymous early sixteenth-century motet *Celebremus conversionem sancti Paul*, preserved in Padua, Biblioteca capitolare, MS A 17, has a retrograde presentation of the chant commencing the *secunda pars*, thereby symbolizing Paul's conversion.

14. For a basic bibliography of the Armed Man tune, see Lockwood, "Tradition"; as well as Roth, "*L'homme*"; and Lütteken, "Ritual."

15. Strohm, *Rise*, p. 466.

16. Among them, Johann Nepomuk David, *Fantasie super "L'homme armé" für Orgel* (1959); Peter Maxwell Davies, *Missa Super L'homme armé* (1971); Fisher Tull, *Fantasy on L'homme armé for Oboe and Piano* (1976); Thomas C. Duffy, *The Philosopher's Stone* (1996); and Thierry Pécou, *L'Homme armé* (1996).

17. The verb "doubter" might equally well be translated as "respected" in the sense that the Armed Man is a "redoubtable" figure. On this point, see Haass, *Studien*, p. 16, n. 4.

18. Among other translations of the text are those offered by Reese in *Renaissance,* p. 73; and Garey in Perkins and Garey, *Mellon,* II, 334.

19. The version of the tune that appears in the Mellon Chansonnier (New Haven, Yale University, Beinecke Library, MS 92), fol. 45, adds the text "A l'assault, a l'assault" at this point.

20. An overview of discussions regarding the origins of the Armed Man tune is given in Lockwood, "Tradition," pp. 99–107.

21. See Strohm's *Bruges,* p. 130; and his *Rise,* pp. 465–466.

22. The earliest appearance of the tune within a purely secular context, one outside of the Mass, is the well-known setting of the melody as a three-voice song in the Mellon Chansonnier, compiled in Naples around 1475–1476 (see Perkins and Garey, *Mellon,* I, 31–32). The earliest Armed Man Masses, on the other hand, appear at least a decade earlier: a *Missa L'Homme armé* by Regis was copied at Cambrai in 1462–1463 (Houdoy, *Histoire,* p. 84) and one by Caron was copied in Rome, Biblioteca Apostolica Vaticana, MS San Pietro B 80 around 1463 (Reynolds, "Origins," pp. 286–292; and his *Patronage,* p. 102; as well as *CCMSPM,* I/4, 66–67), and finally the *Missa L'Homme armé* by Dufay was entered into a manuscript prepared in Bruges in 1469–1470 (Strohm, *Bruges,* pp. 192 and 195).

23. Lists of the various musical arrangements in which *The Armed Man* tune appears are found in Cohen, *Masses,* pp. 72–77; and Haass, *Studien,* pp. 20–21. See also *NG,* s.v. "L'homme armé."

24. For a list of these Masses, see Table B.2 in Appendix B.

25. See Carla Casagrande and Silvana Vecchio, "Clercs et jongleurs dans la société médiévale (XII et XIIIe siècles)," *Annales: économies, sociétés, civilisations,* XXIV/5 (1979), 913–928; John W. Baldwin, "The Image of the Jongleur in Northern France around 1200," *Speculum,* 72 (1997), 639; and David M. Music, *Instruments in Church: A Collection of Source Documents,* vol. 7 of *Studies in Liturgical Musicology* (Lanham, Md., and London, 1998).

26. The following paragraph draws on Johan Huizinga's classic study *Autumn,* chap. 12.

27. Striking examples of symbolism of this sort appear in the so-called Merode Altarpiece attributed to Robert Campin and preserved at the Cloisters of the Metropolitan Museum of Art in New York. Among the many discussions of this work is Lane, *Altarpiece,* pp. 40–43 and 74, n. 5.

28. Augustine, *Sermo,* CXXX, 2, in *PL,* XXXVIII, 726: "Et quid fecit Redemptor noster captivatori nostro? Ad pretium tetendit muscipulum crucem suam: posuit ibi quasi escam sanguinem suum."

29. See chap. 12, "Art in Life," in his *Autumn.* See also Janet Wolff, *The Social Production of Art,* 2nd ed. (London, 1983).

30. A *L'Homme armé* Mass of Josquin Desprez was deemed appropriate for the feast of St. Michael at the court of Wittenberg in 1543 (Duffy, "Wittenberg," pp. 255 and 266; I am grateful to Anne Robertson for providing me with extracts from this dissertation). The association with St. Michael had earlier been posited by Lockwood in "Tradition."

31. Munich, Bayerische Staatsbibliothek, Mus. MS 37, fols. 146v–190. The manuscript is described in *CCMSPM,* I/2, 200–201; and Bente, *Staatsbibliothek,* I, 150–153.

32. Mâle, *Image*, pp. 121–122.

33. *De Anima*, ascribed to Hugh of St. Victor, in *PL*, CLXXVII, 186.

34. For theological sources discussing this passage, see Wild, "Warrior." Similar allusions to the "armor of God" can be found in Isaiah (59:17), the Wisdom of Solomon (5:18–21), 2 Corinthians (10:3–4), and Thessalonians (5:8).

35. See Adolf Harnack, *Die christliche Religion und der Soldatenstand in den ersten drei Jahrhunderten* (Tübingen, 1905); and Hilarius Emonds, "Geistlicher Kriegsdienst. Der Topos der militia spiritualis in der antiken Philosophie," in *Heilige Überlieferung, Festschrift für I. Herwegen* (Münster, 1938), 21–50; as well as Dolan's translation of Erasmus's *Militant Christian*, p. 36.

36. *Grégoire de Nysse: La catéchèse de la foi*, trans. Annette Maignan (Paris, 1978), p. 90, n. 75.

37. Garde, *Poetry*, p. 126.

38. Version B, passus XVIII, lines 22–23, cited and discussed in Philippa Tristram, *Figures of Life and Death in Medieval English Literature* (London, 1976), p. 198.

39. Henri Suso, *Wisdom's Watch Upon the Hours*, trans. E. Colledge, vol. 4 of *The Fathers of the Church—Medieval Continuation* (Washington, D.C., 1994), p. 82.

40. *Henry Suso The Exemplar, with Two German Sermons*, trans. Frank Tobin (New York, 1989), p. 214. Once again, I am indebted to Anne Robertson for bringing this passage to my attention.

41. There are no fewer than twenty-nine copies of *Le Pèlerinage de la vie humaine* surviving today in Paris in the Bibliothèque nationale. It has been edited by J. J. Sturzinger (London, 1893) and translated by Eugene Clasby (New York, 1992). All known manuscripts of this work are listed by Clasby (*Deguileville*, pp. xxx–xlv).

42. This and what follows draw from Clasby, *Deguileville*, p. 52.

43. It is thus perhaps not merely a homonymic accident that one source calls the *Missa L'Homme armé super voces musicales* of Josquin Desprez *Missa L'Ame armé super voces musicales* ("The armed soul Mass on different musical pitches"). See *Missae tredecim quatuor vocum* (Nuremberg, 1539), cited in *Werken van Josquin des Prés*, ed. A. Smijers, *Missen* (Amsterdam, 1926), part 1, p. vii.

44. See Clasby, *Deguileville*, p. xxx, and the sources he cites.

45. This text and what follows are taken from the first edition of *Pilgrim's Progress* (London, 1678), pp. 84–85. I have modernized the spelling and punctuation.

46. Ibid., pp. 94–95.

47. Ibid., p. 96.

7. Sounds and Symbols of an Armed Man

1. For the possibility that Johannes Ockeghem was the first to write a *Missa L'Homme armé*, see Fabrice Fitch, *Johannes Ockeghem: Masses and Models* (Paris, 1997), p. 62; that Antoine Busnois may have composed the first, see Taruskin, "Busnoys," p. 260.

2. See Chapter 2 under "Rome."

3. The list of books in Dufay's library is published in Wright, "Dufay," p. 216.

4. See above, pp. 170–171.

5. The fourteenth-century Flemish mystic Jan Ruysbroec explains the imputation of the sign of Cancer to Christ in the following terms: "When the sun rises as high as possible in the heavens, that is, when it enters the sign of Cancer (which means the Crab, because the sun cannot rise any higher but begins to move backwards, like a crab) . . . In the same way, when Christ, the divine sun, has risen as high as possible in our hearts . . ." (*The Spiritual Espousals and Other Works,* trans. James A. Wiseman [New York, 1985], p. 84). I am grateful to Prof. Anne Robertson for drawing my attention to this passage.

6. Deguileville borrows this notion of Christ's life as a triple journey from the discussion of the Resurrection in Jacobus de Voragine's widely popular *Golden Legend.*

7. Paris, Bibliothèque nationale, MS fonds français 12466, lines 10,375–10,395, edited by J. J. Stürzinger (*Pèlerinage de l'âme,* London, 1895), p. 336.

8. On the Book of Apocalypse as a primordial combat myth, see Collins, *Combat Myth,* chap. II.

9. Lille, Archives départementales du Nord, 4G 4670, cited in Houdoy, *Histoire,* p. 194.

10. Regis may have written two Armed Man Masses, judging from a remark of Johannes Tinctoris (see Wegman, "Faughes," pp. 61, n. 56, and 78; and Fallows, "Regis," p. 168). If that is the case, it is impossible to know which of the two was copied at Cambrai in 1462–1463. The surviving Mass is edited by Cornelis Lindenburg, *Johannes Regis: Opera Omnia,* vol. 9 of *Corpus Mensurabilis Musicae* (Rome, 1956), I, 1–24; and by Laurence Feininger, *Missae super L'homme armé, Monumenta Polyphoniae Liturgicae Sanctae Ecclesiae Romanae* (Rome, 1948), 2nd series, fascicle 5. For a bibliography of discussions of the work, see Starr, "Regis," p. 36, n. 53.

11. This paragraph draws on an article by Jean Fournée and two by Marcel Baudot that appear in vol. 3 of *Millénaire monastique du Mont Saint-Michel,* 3 vols. (Paris, 1971).

12. The Index of Christian Art at Princeton University contains more than 900 references to representations of Michael in the visual arts before 1400.

13. The following draws on Avril, "Interprétations."

14. From a liturgical calendar in the *Liber floridus* of canon Lambert of St. Omer (Ghent, University Library, MS 1125, fol. 2; cited in Avril, "Interprétations," p. 52).

15. The antiphon *Pueri Hebreorum portantes* is almost identical musically to *Pueri Hebreorum vestimenta,* a similar processional antiphon for Palm Sunday (see *LU,* pp. 581–582). In truth, it is impossible to tell which of these two melodies Regis is quoting, and it matters not at all—undoubtedly the double resonance resulting from the ambiguity was intended by the composer.

16. A similar invocation of the image of the triumphant entry of Christ into Jerusalem appears in the "Hosanna in excelsis" of Johannes Tinctoris's *Missa L'Homme armé.*

17. The definitive study of this ruler remains Vaughan's *Charles the Bold.*

18. Naples, Biblioteca nazionale, MS VI.E.40. The colophon of the manuscript attests to the duke's interest in these Masses. It is reproduced in Cohen, *Masses,* opposite p. 63, and edited and translated on pp. 62–63.

19. Cohen, *Masses,* pp. 62–67; Taruskin, "Busnoys," pp. 275–285; and Strohm, *Rise,* p. 468.

20. On the structural organization of these Masses, see Taruskin, "Busnoys," pp. 275–278.

21. "Arma virumque cano" becomes "Arma virumque cano vincorque per arma virumque," literally: "I sing of arms and a man, and am conquered by arms and a man."

22. Chance, *Mythography,* p. 3.

23. Ibid.

24. See Tanner, *Aeneas,* passim; and Long, "Age," p. 145.

25. For connections, both real and imagined, between Aeneas and the hero of the Naples Armed Man Masses, see Lütteken, "Ritual."

26. See above, p. 111.

27. The biography of Josquin Lebloitte dit Desprez is presently being rewritten on the basis of new archival data. The most recent efforts in this regard can be found in Merkley and Matthews, "Jossequin."

28. Rome, Biblioteca Apostolica Vaticana, MS Capella Sistina 154, fol. 24v, and MS Capella Sistina 197, fol. 10v. I am grateful to Prof. Michell Brauner for drawing my attention to these historiated initials.

29. See, for example, the opening folio of Rome, Biblioteca Apostolica Vatican, MS Capella Sistina 23, where a representation of St. Michael slaying a dragon appears at the beginning of the Kyrie of Prioris's *Missa de angelis.*

30. The sources for Josquin's two *Missae L'Homme armé* are given in A. Smijers, ed., *Werken van Josquin des Prés: Missen 1* (Amsterdam and Leipzig, 1926), pp. vi–vii, and *Missen V* (Leipzig, 1931), pp. v–vii.

31. In his canon BWV 1072 Bach likewise has a canon moving forward in some voices while others sing the theme in retrograde motion (see Wolff, *Bach,* pp. 336–337).

32. In the year in which Josquin entered René's service (1477), a payment was made to "reffaire le Dédalus qui est és jardins dudit lieu de Baugé" (Matthews, *Mazes,* p. 112).

33. At Belriguardo, twelve kilometers southeast of Ferrara, Duke Ercole d'Este maintained a sumptuous palace and gardens, including two garden mazes, one unicursal of the Roman mosaic type, the other multicursal (see Gundersheimer, *Art,* fig. 4).

34. Claude Hémeré, *Augusta Viromanduorum* (Paris, 1643), cited in Gomart, "Notes," p. 244, n. 2. See also Herbert Kellman, "Josquin's Career in the Absence of Judochus de Picardia: A Hypothetical Narrative," response presented at the annual meeting of the American Musicological Society, Phoenix, November 1997.

35. Héliot, *Saint-Quentin,* pp. 45 and 78.

36. See Chapter 2 under "St. Quentin."

37. On Josquin's visit to Condé-sur-l'Escaut in 1483, see Kellman, "Josquin," pp. 207–209.

38. Gomart, *Extraits,* I, 78.

39. On this subject generally, see R. G. de Witt, *Hercules at the Crossroads: The Life, Works and Thought of Coluccio Salutati*, vol. 6 of Duke Monographs in Medieval and Renaissance Studies (Durham, 1983); Lockwood, *Ferrara*, p. 281; Werner Gundersheimer, *Ferrara, the Style of Renaissance Despotism* (Princeton, 1973), pp. 210–211; and Gundersheimer, *Art*, pp. 19 and 59. The most recent and complete discussion of Ercole's reign is Thomas Tuohy, *Herculean Ferrara: Ercole d'Este, 1471–1505, and the Invention of a Ducal Capital* (Cambridge and New York, 1996).

40. The coin is reproduced in Charles M. Rosenberg, *The Este Monuments and Urban Development in Renaissance Ferrara* (Cambridge, 1997), p. 164. I owe my knowledge of this source to the kindness of Prof. Lewis Lockwood.

41. The *cantus firmus* is not the Armed Man tune but rather a melody fashioned from the vowels of "Hercules dux Ferrarie." On the method by which the *cantus firmus* was created, see Reese, *Renaissance*, p. 236.

42. Lockwood, *Ferrara*, p. 243.

43. Chance, *Mythography*, pp. 33, 233–240, and 259–262.

44. See Miller, "Hercules."

45. The theme of Hercules at the Crossroads is the subject of Panofsky's *Hercules*. When J. S. Bach set the text of his cantata *Hercules at the Crossroads* (1733), he constructed at its center a bass of only two notes, C - F♯—the devilish tritone—thereby symbolizing that the two paths of Vice and Virtue were not compatible (Wolff, *Bach*, p. 351).

46. Chance, *Mythography*, p. 237.

47. Hamilton, *Mythology*, pp. 155–156.

48. Ibid.

49. The syzygy of Aries, Mars, and Hercules appears, among other places, on the astrological ceiling of the Sala della Ragione in Padua in association with the first month (March) of the celestial cycle.

50. On the fall of Constantinople generally, see Steven Runciman, *Fall of Constantinople, 1453* (Cambridge, 1965). The effect of this loss on the papacy and the Burgundian court is discussed, among other places, in Vaughan, *Philip the Good*, pp. 296–298; Long, "Age"; and Higgins, "Priest."

51. "Suasere ut arma sumerent: defensionem catholicae fidei subirent, furentibus bestijs obviam irent, nec sinerent immanem draconem Mahometem fideles devorare animas": from a *Bulla de profectione in Turcos* (22 October 1463) of Pope Pius II, as given in Higgins, "Priest," example 3.

52. Vaughan, *Philip the Good*, pp. 296–297 and 358–367.

53. Ibid., pp. 144–145.

54. Ibid., pp. 145 and 297.

55. Vaughan, *Charles the Bold*, p. 191; and Georges Doutrepont, "Jason et Gédéon, patrons de la Toison d'Or," *Mélanges Godefroid Kurth*, Université de Liège: Bibliothèque de la Faculté de Philosophie et lettres: II: Mémoires littéraires, philologiques et archéologiques (Liège, 1908), II, 193–194.

56. Hamilton, *Mythology*, p. 117.

57. Guillaume Fillastre, *Le premier volume de la toison d'or* (Paris, 1517), fols. iiii–iiii^v.

The clerics of the court of Burgundy also embraced the warrior Gideon of the Old Testament as a model for the knights of the Order of the Golden Fleece; see Vaughan, *Philip the Good*, p. 162; and especially Haggh, "Fleece," pp. 15–20.

58. A succinct account of Philip the Good's vacillations regarding a crusade is given in Vaughan, *Philip the Good*, pp. 385–372.

59. Ruth Hannas was the first to draw a connection between the planned crusade of the fifteenth century and the Armed Man tradition ("Concerning Deletions in the Polyphonic Mass Credo," *JAMS*, 5 [1952], 168). Other writers to do similarly are Roth, "*L'homme*"; Long, "Age"; and Higgins, "Priest."

60. The association of the Armed Man Masses with the Burgundian Order of the Golden Fleece was first strongly made by William Prizer ("Fleece"). Prizer's initial thoughts were extended by Alejandro Planchart ("Burgundy"). See also Lockwood, "Tradition," p. 109; and Haggh, "Fleece," pp. 30–38.

61. Planchart, "Burgundy," pp. 159–160 and 164–165; and Roth, "L'homme," pp. 477–478.

62. What follows draws heavily upon Tanner, *Aeneas*.

63. Lockwood, *Ferrara*, p. 249. For later resonances of Josquin's Mass along the Spain-Hapsburg line, see Anthony Fiumara, "Escobedo's *Missa Philippus Rex Hispanie:* a Spanish descendant of Josquin's *Hercules* Mass," *Early Music*, 28 (2000), 50–62, and especially n. 18.

64. Tanner, *Aeneas*, chap. VIII. On the heraldic device, see also Earl E. Rosenthal, "Plus Ultra: Non Plus Ultra, and the Columnar Device of Emperor Charles V," *Journal of the Warburg and Courtauld Institute*, 34 (1971), 204–228; and Rosenthal, "The Invention of the Columnar Device of Emperor Charles V at the Court of Burgundy in Flanders in 1516," *Journal of the Warburg and Courtauld Institute*, 36 (1973), 198–230.

65. Tanner, *Aeneas*, p. 156.

66. Ibid., p. 289, n. 43.

67. Ariosto, *Orlando Furioso*, canto 15, stanzas 21f, quoted in Tanner, *Aeneas*, p. 157.

68. Tanner, *Aeneas*, p. 158.

69. *Missarum liber secundus* (Rome, 1544); see *RISM*, A/I/6, 18.

70. *Missarum liber tertius* (Rome, 1570); see *RISM*, A/I/6, 397.

71. In fact, the woodcut that prefaces the Armed Man Mass of Palestrina is identical to that appearing before the Mass of Morales. Both Morales's Second Book of Masses and Palestrina's Third Book were issued by the firm of Valerio and Luigi Dorico in Rome. For the Mass of Palestrina the printer simply reused the earlier woodcut—not the only instance of this firm cutting such a corner. The famous woodcut "Palestrina presents a book of Masses to Pope Julius III" (reproduced in *NG*, XIV, 119) is a recycling of the earlier "Morales presents a book of Masses to Pope Paul III" (1544).

72. On the Mass of the Sword, see Warmington, "Sword." On processions and Masses against the Turks, see Amiens, Bibliothèque municipale, MS 517, fol. 65; and Reims, Bibliothèque municipale, MS 1148, fol. 295.

73. On Baring-Gould, see Julian, *Dictionary*, s.v. "Baring-Gould"; and *NG*, s.v. "Baring-Gould."

74. In addition to the aforementioned sacred works using retrograde motion to symbolize Christ and the Mystical Lamb in the *Agnus dei,* other fifteenth-century works to do so include Caron's *Missa Jesus autem transiens,* Busnois's *Missa L'Homme armé* (retrograde inversion), Heyns's *Missa Pour quelque paine,* and Obrecht's *Missa Grecorum, Missa Petrus Apostolus,* and *Missa L'Homme armé* (retrograde inversion). This symbolic process can also be found in the early sixteenth century in the *Agnus dei* of Masses by Forestier, Gascogne, Benedictus, and Brumel, as well as two anonymous works, one in Brussels, Bibliothèque royale, MS 215–216 (a Mass for the Seven Sorrows of the Blessed Virgin Mary, possibly by Pierre de la Rue) and the other in Siena, Biblioteca comunale degli Intronati, MS K.I.2. Several of these identifications were made for me by Dr. Bonnie Blackburn and Prof. Marica Tacconi.

75. I am grateful to Prof. Robert Morgan for bringing this piece to my attention. The two other works of the period using exact retrograde motion in all parts are also minuets. Full bibliographical information about them can be found in Prof. Morgan's "Symmetrical Form and Common-Practice Tonality," *Music Theory Spectrum,* 20 (1998), 27.

76. Lockwood, *Mass,* pp. 10–16; and Palisca, "Critique."

77. See above, p. 160.

78. What follows draws heavily on the work of Claude V. Palisca; see, in particular, chapters 1 and 13 of his important *Humanism.*

79. Specifically, Plato's *Laws* (Books II and III) and *Republic* (Book I) as well as Aristotle's *Poetics* (Books I and II) and *Politics* (Book VIII). These passages discuss music and were known to Renaissance humanists.

80. Karol Berger has constructed a related, but by no means identical, formulation around the antipodes of abstract and mimetic music; see his *A Theory of Art* (New York and Oxford, 2000), pp. 120–139.

8. The Maze of Pilgrimage and Pleasure

1. On the more or less uniform conception of the pre-modern labyrinth, see also Lethaby, *Architecture,* pp. 149–153.

2. For example, Demouy, *Reims,* p. 16; Macrez, *Labyrinthe,* p. 6; Artress, *Path,* p. 32; Santarcangeli, *Labyrinthes,* pp. 73–74; Crisp, *Gardens,* p. 70; and the list of authors cited by Doob (*Labyrinth,* p. 119, n. 34). Only Doob (*Labyrinth*) and Kern (*Labyrinthe*) seriously question whether a substitute pilgrimage on the maze was actually a medieval practice.

3. Villers, "Labyrinthe," p. 87.

4. Géruzez, *Reims,* I, 315–316; and Wallet, *Description,* p. 99.

5. For Chartres: "Ce dédale est vulgairement appelé *la lieue,* parce qu'on estime qu'en suivant tous ses Méandres on fait une lieue" (Challine, *Histoire,* pp. 143–144); for Sens: "Labyrinthe qui etoit incruté dans le carreau de l'iglise [*sic*] de Sens vulgairement appellé la lieue" (Auxerre, Bibliothèque municipale, MS 215, fol. 35).

6. Doublet de Boisthibault, "Labyrinthe," p. 439. In actuality, the length of the route at Chartres, for example, is only 261.5 meters one way (Villette, "Labyrinthe," p. 9).

7. See, for example, Villers, "Labyrinthe"; Caumont, "Labyrinthe"; and Doublet de Boisthibault, "Labyrinthe."

8. Trollope, "Labyrinths," p. 229; and Kern, *Labyrinthe*, pp. 303–304.

9. Wallet, *Description*, p. 99.

10. Géruzez, *Reims*, I, 315–316; see also Santarcangeli, *Labyrinthes*, p. 283.

11. *Stations au chemin de Jérusalem qui se voit en l'église de Notre-Dame de Reims* (cited in Cerf, *Reims*, I, 78). I have been unable to locate surviving copies of this pamphlet in Reims or elsewhere.

12. Wallet, *Description*, p. 99.

13. See Chapter 2 under "Sens."

14. The volume was not published until more than two hundred and fifty years later; see Challine, *Chartres*. The complicated history of Challine's *Chartres* is discussed in Van Der Meulen, *Chartres*, pp. 406–407. Not all manuscript copies of the work surviving in the Bibliothèque municipale in Chartres include the texted maze discussed here. The illustration of the maze may have been among the additions to the text made by Challine's grandnephew and daughter in the latter half of the seventeenth century or early eighteenth century. Although the text in this labyrinth is in a more modern hand, the tradition it represents is likely that of the time of the elder Challine.

15. Spiritual texts spiraling around the path of a maze began to appear in Germany in the late sixteenth century and continued to appear in Germany and France until the late eighteenth century (see Kern, *Labyrinthe*, figs. 387–389 and 391–398).

16. Kern (*Labyrinthe*, pp. 329–331) discusses Renaissance paintings which show that David must do penance in this world, as symbolized by a labyrinth, for his lust for Bathsheba and betrayal of Uriah (2 Samuel 11:1–27).

17. For example: the text inscribed toward the end of the Chartrain path, "God sent forth a propitiation through faith for the remission of sins," is a severe truncation of the original "Christ Jesus whom God hath set forth to be a propitiation through faith in his blood, to declare his righteousness for the remission of sins that are past . . ." (Romans 3:24–25).

18. The former work is by John Valentine Andrea (1586–1654) and the latter by John Amos Comenius. On Comenius's work, see above, p. 90.

19. On Bunyan's *Pilgrim's Progress*, see above, p. 173.

20. Blake, *Jerusalem*, end of chapter 3, plate 77.

21. At Chartres the figures in the center medallion were barely visible by 1750 (see Chapter 2 under "Chartres").

22. Lead can easily be confused with the blue-black stone that outlines the shape of the maze at Chartres.

23. Written between 1650 and 1654 by Jean-Baptiste Souchet in his *Histoire du diocèse et de la ville de Chartres*, 4 vols. (Chartres, 1866–1873), I, 220: "Dans le milieu de la nef, il y a un labyrinth de plomb que je m'étonne qu'on y aie mis n'étant qu'un amusement fol, auquel ceux qui n'ont guères à faire perdent le temps à tourner et

courir durant et hors le service divin." This sense of ignorance is similar to that of an anonymous cleric writing about the maze at the cathedral of Sens in 1752, who said that "he had no idea of the purpose of it [the maze]" ("il en ignore la destination") (Auxerre, Bibliothèque municipale, MS 215, fol. 33v).

24. It appears as the frontispiece to vol. III of Bulteau's *Monographie*.

25. On the *jubé* (rood screen) at Chartres, see the sources cited in Van Der Meulen, *Chartres*, pp. 357–362.

26. The best discussion of the labyrinth in the midst of the humanistic Renaissance is found in Kern's chapters, "Widergeburt der Antike" and "Labyrinthisches Selbstverständnis," in his *Labyrinth*, pp. 255–294.

27. As to why Phaedra is here, see Leofranc Holford-Strevens, "'Her eyes became two spounts'; Classical Antecedents of Renaissance Laments," *Early Music*, 27 (1999), 386.

28. For more detailed discussions of maze games, see Kern, *Labyrinthe*, pp. 343–358; and Santarcangeli, *Labyrinthes*, pp. 352–396.

29. The discussion of the *Giuoco del labirinto* is found on fols. 74–76 of the edition of 1551.

30. I am indebted to Prof. Mauro Calcagno for his help in translating this passage of sixteenth-century Italian as well as comparing various editions of Ringhieri's *Cento Giuochi Liberali*.

31. Ringhieri was making use of a popular poetic conceit often connected to the "labyrinth of love." The composer Claudio Monteverdi would later do likewise in his madrigal *Se i languidi miei squardi* (Venice, 1619), which speaks of "My beloved golden forest, your precious locks, love wove that labyrinth in which you, my soul, will never be able to leave." I am grateful to Tova Choate for bringing this text to my attention.

32. On the maze as a metaphor for the snares of love, see Kern, *Labyrinthe*, pp. 328–329. To the literary works cited there may be added Petrarch's sonnet *S'una fede amorosa*, in which love is compared to "un lungo error in cieco laberinto."

33. This description of *The Labyrinth of Ariosto* is based on an account preserved in Ménestrier's *Ballets*, pp. 308–319. It is possible that the rules of this game were published in a "game book" long before this.

34. See above, p. 201.

35. For relevant bibliography on *Ein Neu-erfundenes Ganss-Spiel*, see Kern, *Labyrinthe*, p. 356.

36. Doublet de Boisthibault, "Labyrinthe," p. 445; and Villette, "Labyrinthe," p. 5.

37. For a discussion of the significance of the number 42 as an ancient symbol of life in continual flux and, ultimately, death, see Santarcangeli, *Labyrinthes*, pp. 352–354.

38. Carpeggiani, "Labyrinths," p. 84.

39. Even the exhaustive catalogue of Kern *(Labyrinthe)* makes no claim of completeness when it comes to garden mazes (pp. 359–360).

40. For a list of late-medieval garden mazes and the documents relevant to them, see Crisp, *Gardens*, pp. 70–72; and Kern, *Labyrinthe*, pp. 359–360.

41. Kern, *Labyrinthe*, pp. 329 and 360.

42. On the labyrinths at Ferrara, see above, p. 190; and on those at Tivoli, Mantua, and Viterbo, see Kern, *Labyrinthe,* pp. 279–284 and 388; and Carpeggiani, "Labyrinths," p. 84.

43. Munich, Bayerische Staatsbibliothek, Mus. MS B, fol. 136. See Bente, *Staatsbibliothek,* I, 56–58. The manuscript and its contents are treated in Owens, "Manuscript." I am grateful to Prof. Owens for drawing my attention to this labyrinth. Another maze can be seen in Mus. MS A, vol. II, fol. 67.

44. On the various doctrinal views of the immaculate nature of the Virgin in this period, see Blackburn, "Virgin," pp. 173–180.

45. In the visual arts this aggregate of Marian symbols had appeared in liturgical books by the fifteenth century and continued to be valued as a theological topos by Catholics well into the seventeenth (see Henry Hawkins, *Parthenia Sacra or the Mysterious and Delicious Garden of the Sacred Parthenes* [n.p., 1633]). It is also briefly discussed in Hall, *Dictionary,* p. 327.

46. In 1564 the German humanist Samuel Quickelberg compiled an explanation of the verbal and visual imagery contained in this manuscript and identified the scriptural citations for each text. This commentary volume to Munich B is reproduced in Owens, "Manuscript," where the discussion of the symbols surrounding Rore's *Ave regina celorum* is found on fols. 85v–87v.

47. On Mary as an enclosed garden, see, among other sources, Pelikan, *Mary,* pp. 29–30.

48. MacDougall and Miller, *Fountains,* p. 70.

49. Typical of these is H. Cause, *De Koninglijcke hovenier* (Amsterdam, 1676), which contains drawings for five mazes.

50. The mazes in the gardens at Loo are called "labyrinths" and "wildernesses" interchangeably in Walter Harris's *A Description of the King's Royal Palace and Gardens at Loo* (London, 1699), pp. 13–17. Harris provides an engraving of the palace and gardens at Loo as well as a detailed description of both. The engraving is reproduced in Matthews, *Mazes,* fig. 109.

51. The maze at Hampton Court is discussed, among other places, in Matthews, *Mazes,* pp. 128–130; Santarcangeli, *Labyrinthes,* p. 338; and Pennick, *Mazes,* pp. 145–147.

52. Pennick, *Mazes,* p. 142.

53. Matthews, *Mazes,* pp. 128–130.

54. This and the following paragraph are drawn primarily from Lablaude, *Gardens,* as well as Perrault, *Labyrinthe.* The latter volume was reprinted in 1982 with a useful but unpaginated "Postface" by Michel Conan.

55. See the above-mentioned, unpaginated "Postface" of Michel Conan.

56. Santarcangeli, *Labyrinthes,* p. 333; and Pennick, *Mazes,* pp. 148–149.

57. Conan, "Postface" to Perrault, *Labyrinthe,* n.p.

58. On outdoor mazes in England, see Trollope, "Labyrinths"; and Pennick, *Mazes,* pp. 61–74.

59. Only the center medallion is preserved today (Kern, *Labyrinthe,* p. 229).

60. See Chapter 2 under "Italian Church Mazes."

61. Paris, "Labyrinthe," p. 550.

62. Demouy, *Reims,* p. 30; Chauveau, "Sens," p. 208; and Van Der Meulen, *Chartres,* p. 360.

9. MUSICAL MAZES FROM MOSES TO MOZART

1. Of the great Gothic churches possessing mazes, only Chartres did not use *In exitu Israel de Egypto* at this moment in the service. For documentation on this point for Amiens, see Amiens, Bibliothèque municipale, MS Réserve 21 D, fol. Alxxix^v; for Reims, see Reims, Bibliothèque municipale, MS 331, fol. 30; for St. Quentin, see Paris, Bibliothèque nationale, MS fonds latin 1267, fol. 141v; for Auxerre, see Bibliothèque nationale, MS fonds latin 1029, fol. 154v; and for Sens, see Bibliothèque nationale, MS fonds latin 1028, fol. 120v.

2. Psalm 113 for Catholics, 114 for Jews and Protestants.

3. On the *tonus peregrinus,* see the following: H. Gaisser, "L'Origine du tonus peregrinus," in *Congrès d'histoire de la musique, 1900* (Combarieu, [1901]), pp. 127–133; Vivell, "Tonus"; Werner, "Ground," p. 141; *NG,* s.v. "Tonus peregrinus"; and especially Erbacher, *Tonus.*

4. Werner, "Ground," p. 141; and Erbacher, *Tonus,* pp. 62–64.

5. Like all chants, the *tonus peregrinus* varied slightly from epoch to epoch and region to region. A comparison of eight versions of the basic melodic type is given in Vivell, "Tonus," pp. 190–191.

6. See above, p. 150.

7. Erbacher, *Tonus,* p. 29.

8. *Purgatory,* Canto II, *The Divine Comedy of Dante Alighieri,* trans. Henry F. Cary (New York, 1908), p. 150.

9. Erbacher, *Tonus,* p. 29, n. 8.

10. Ibid., pp. 130–148.

11. Jean Beleth, writing about 1160, says that the game of tennis (*ad ludum pile*) was played at Reims and at other cathedrals (*Summa,* chap. 120a, vol. 41a of *CCCM,* p. 223). Since Beleth was believed to have been a dignitary at Amiens (see, for example, Soyez, *Laybrinthes,* p. 29; and Chailley, "Danse," p. 370), it is thought that he was referring to practices at this cathedral as well. In the eighteenth century, it was said that "that profane ceremony was abolished long ago at the church of Amiens" (Pierre Grenier, *Introduction à l'histoire générale de la province de Picardie* [Amiens, 1856], p. 49).

12. *O filii et filiae* was sung in the nave, at the west end of the church, with the clergy facing eastward. The responsory verse *Dicant nunc Judei* came immediately before it, and the sequence *Victimae paschali laudes* immediately after. At Amiens as at Auxerre (see Chapter 5 under "The Dance of the Maze at the Cathedral of Auxerre"), the latter chant was sung with organ accompaniment (Amiens, Archives départementales de la Somme, série G, MS 2974, fol. 274).

13. In 1682 Claude-François Ménestrier reported that he had seen this dance, with "its bouncy triple meter character in the style of a popular round dance," executed on Easter Sunday in many churches in France (*Ballets*, cited in Gougaud, "Danse," p. 236; and Rokseth, "Danses," p. 98). On the history of this hymn, see Julian, *Dictionary*, pp. 828–829.

14. The best recent treatment of the life of Fournival, with relevant bibliography, can be found in Johnson, *Amiens*, pp. 282–308.

15. A description of many of Fournival's manuscripts is given in his *Biblionomia* and is reproduced in Delisle, *Cabinet*, II, 518–535. See also Rouse, "Library"; and Rouse, "Fournival."

16. Described as the "[Ovidii] liber Metamorphoseos" in Richard's *Biblionomia*; see Delisle, *Cabinet*, II, 531.

17. See Dorothy M. Robathan, *The Pseudo-Ovidian de Vetula* (Amsterdam, 1968).

18. Ibid., pp. 1–2.

19. The text is edited and analyzed, among other places, in Yvan G. Lepage, *L'Oeuvre lyrique de Richard de Fournival* (Ottawa, 1981), pp. 92–95.

20. "Jhesu" is clearly an emendation to the poet's original intent because it destroys the five-syllable line which had hitherto ruled in the strophe. All modern editors (Zarifopol, Gennrich, Dragonetti, and Lepage) have changed "Jhesu" back to the original "Theseü."

21. On the *interpretatio christiana* given to the myth by medieval theologians, see Chapter 3 under "The Maze Made Christian."

22. The translation offered here of Fournival's chanson seeks to render the spirit, if not the letter, of the original poem. It has been prepared from Arras, Bibliothèque municipale, MS 139, reproduced in Alfred Jeanroy, *Le Chansonnier d'Arras* (Paris, 1925), fols. 132v–133. The musical rhythm shown in Example 9.2 is somewhat arbitrary because fully texted musical notation of the thirteenth century did not convey precise rhythmic durations. For a recording, see Hyperion CD A6619.

23. The treatise is called the "Berkeley Manuscript" because of its present location (see Ellsworth, *Manuscript*). An initial description of the manuscript can be found in Crocker, "Source." The musical maze, *En la maison Dedalus*, is situated on the last page of the manuscript (p. 62) and was first transcribed by the late Thomas Walker. The piece is also edited, with a somewhat better reading of the text, in Willi Apel, *French Secular Compositions of the Fourteenth Century*, 3 vols. (Rome, 1970–1972), II, piece no. 140. A concordance for *En la maison Dedalus*, but without the labyrinthine notation, is found in Florence, Biblioteca Medicea Laurenziana, MS San Lorenzo 2211, fol. x (modern 49 recto). I am grateful to Prof. John Nádas for helping me track down this latter version of the piece.

24. *Paradise*, 19:39. On the image of God with compass, see Friedman, "Compass."

25. The portrait that Bach commissioned from Elias Gottlieb Haussmann in 1746, the only surviving authenticated likeness of the composer made during his lifetime, is often reproduced; see, for example, the cover of Christoph Wolff's *Bach: Essays on His Life and Music*, first paperback edition (Cambridge, Mass., 1993).

26. Martin Lowry, *The World of Aldus Manutius* (Ithaca, 1979), p. 6.

27. See E. Valenziani and E. Cerulli, *Indice generale degli incunaboli delle biblioteche d'Italia* (Rome, 1965), pp. 179–180.

28. For the present study, a 1522 reprint of the original 1497 *Ovidio Metamorphoseos vulgare novamente stampato in Venetia* was used.

29. See the prize-winning study of Bernstein, *Music Printing*, where details on the life of Scotto can be found in her Chapter 2. I am grateful to Prof. Bernstein for generously providing me with materials and ideas.

30. In this same year Scotto also issued a set of madrigals by Ippolito Ciera (*Madrigali del Laberinto a quatro voci libro primo*), of which only the soprano, tenor, and bass part-books survive (see item 121 in the catalogue of Bernstein, *Music Printing*). Appropriately enough, this volume was dedicated to Filippo Mocenigo, archbishop of Crete.

31. Roman numerals refer to a specific volume within the four sets comprising *Motetti del laberinto*, while Arabic numerals indicate the motet within each set. I have adopted the numbering of motets used in Bernstein, *Music Printing*.

32. The first volume of *Motetti del laberinto* has been edited by Richard Sherr in *Girolamo Carli: Motetti del Laberinto*, vol. 24 of *Sixteenth-Century Motet* (New York and London, 1995). For a complete bibliographical description of it, see item 120 in Bernstein, *Music Printing*. Volumes two, three, and four have not appeared in a modern edition.

33. On St. Cecilia, see *Butler's Lives of the Saints*, IV, 402–405. For a more detailed treatment of her life and significance, see Connolly, *Cecilia*.

34. On St. Theodore tiro (not to be confused with St. Theodore stratelates), see *Butler's Lives of the Saints*, I, 269; Antonio Niero, "I santi patroni," in S. Tramontin et al., eds., *Culto dei Santi a Venezia*, vol. 2, no. 7, of *Collana Storica dello Studium cattolico Veneziano* (Venice, 1965), pp. 75–98; and Brian Pullan, *Le Scuole di Venezia* (Milan, 1981), pp. 218–219. I owe my knowledge of the latter sources to the kindness of Prof. Mauro Calcagno.

35. Langdon-Davies, *Carlos*, chap. 8.

36. Ibid., p. 60.

37. On del Vado, see *NG*, s.v. "Vado, Juan del"; as well as Luis Robledo, "Los Cánones Enigmáticos de Juan del Vado (?Madrid?, ca. 1625–Madrid, 1691): Noticias Sobre su Vida," *Revista de Musicologiá*, 3 (1980), 129–196.

38. The canons and six Masses, dedicated to Charles II, are found in Madrid, Biblioteca Nacional, MSS M. 1323 and M. 1324. The manuscript and a copy (M. 1325 and M. 1326) are inventoried in Higinio Anglés and José Subira, *Catálogo Musical de la Biblioteca Nacional de Madrid*, 3 vols. (Barcelona, 1946), I, 221–228. This source was kindly brought to my attention by Lorenzo Francisco Candelaria. The content of the following paragraphs I owe to his labors and generosity.

39. It may have been inspired by a contemporary work likewise dedicated to Charles II, *Trabajos y afanes de Hércules*, by Juan Francisco Fernández de Heredia.

40. On the words "Plus ultra" and the pillars of Hercules in the device of Charles V, see above, p. 201.

41. Madrid, Biblioteca Nacional, MS M. 1323, fol. 6.

42. The only modern edition of the opera appears in *Georg Friedrich Händels Werke,* vol. 83 (Leipzig, 1881). It has never been recorded.

43. The libretto is based on a text by Pietro Pariati with emendations by Francis Colman and apparently Handel himself. See Albert Scheibler, *Sämtliche 53 Bühnenwerke des Georg Friedrich Händel* (Cologne, 1995), p. 151.

44. Wolfgang Caspar Printz, *Phrynis Mitilenaeus oder Satyrischer Componist* (Dresden and Leipzig, 1696). His *Musical Labyrinth* is an insertion to part three. It is discussed on pp. 217–220.

45. See above, Chapters 2 and 3.

46. An extensive treatment of the subject can be found under "Temperament" in *NG.* I am grateful to my colleague Kerry Snyder for her time and patience in discussing issues of eighteenth-century temperament with me.

47. Fischer issued a second edition of *Ariadne Musica* in 1715. A facsimile of it has recently appeared in the Performers' Facsimiles series (New York, 1997). The music is edited in *Johann Kaspar Ferdinand Fischer: Sämtliche Werke für Klavier und Orgel* (Wiesbaden, 1901, rpt. 1965).

48. This suite appears in *Pieces a une et a trois violes composées par M. Marais* [Book IV], Paris, 1717, pp. 71–78. A copy is preserved in New Haven, Yale University, Irving Gilmore Music Library, Rare M239 V54 M299+ v.4.

49. Enharmonic notes are those that, in the system of equal temperament, have the same pitch but are spelled with different letter names: C♯ and D♭, D♯ and E♭, F♯ and G♭, for example. They have traditionally been used by composers as a convenient place to shift from the sharp to the flat keys, or vice versa, simply by changing the spelling of the note and then continuing with sharp or flat keys.

50. Suppig's manuscript, which today resides in the music division of the Bibliothèque nationale in Paris (MS Réserve F 211–212), has never appeared in a modern edition, though Rasch (*Suppig*) offers an excellent facsimile.

51. The circle of fifths is an arrangement of keys in which the home pitches (tonics) of all the major keys are taken in order beginning with C and proceeding in turn to keys a distance of a perfect fifth away. By moving in this fashion, each additional key will have one more sharp or one less flat. A sequence of keys arranged in this way produces a closed, palindromic circle: C-G-D-A-E-B-F♯=G♭-D♭-A♭-E♭-B♭-F-C.

52. First published as *Anweisung . . . General-Basses* (Hamburg, 1711), Heinichen's treatise was reissued in a greatly expanded version entitled *Der General-Bass in der Composition* (Dresden, 1728, rpt. 1994). In the revised edition questions of temperament are discussed on pp. 837–916.

53. *Der General-Bass in der Composition* (1728), pp. 840, 855–856, and 868.

54. The original French can be found in *Leçons de clavecin et principes d'harmonie, par M. Bemetzrieder,* ed. Jean Mayer and Pierre Citron, in vol. 19 of the Hermann edition of *Denis Diderot: Oeuvres complètes* (Paris, 1983), pp. 353–354. I owe my knowledge of this passage to Prof. Thomas Christensen.

55. See Douglas R. Hofstadter, *Gödel, Escher, Bach: An Eternal Golden Braid* (New York, 1979), p. 10.

56. One further "harmonic labyrinth" should be mentioned: Pietro Locatelli's "Labir-

into armonico" (Caprice 23 of his *L'arte del violino,* 1733). Although it begins with an inscription reading "easy to enter but difficult to exit" *(facilis aditus, difficilis exitus)* reminiscent of the maze at Piacenza (see Chapter 2 under "Piacenza"), in fact this is not a "harmonic" labyrinth at all, but rather a "harmonious" one. The performer improves his technique by progressing through a succession of passages requiring ever greater skill in fingering and positioning on the violin. The labyrinth sometimes ascribed to Antonio Caldara (e.g., Kern, *Labyrinthe,* p. 344), as nearly as I can determine, is a phantom.

57. BWV 591. The work is published in *Johann Sebastian Bachs Werke,* vol. 38 (Leipzig, 1891, rpt. 1947), pp. 225–226; and in the *Edition Peters* of Bach's organ music, vol. 9 (Leipzig, 1940), pp. 34–35. Although this piece is often ascribed to Johann David Heinichen, a source-critical study demonstrates that it is by Bach and suggests why it came to be attributed to Heinichen (see Wright, "Labyrinth").

58. As explained in Wright, "Labyrinth," the symmetry of the piece only becomes apparent when it is correctly barred.

59. See the *London Daily Mail,* Saturday, 23 September, 1899, p. 7.

60. A list of devotional and theological books owned by Bach is printed in David, Mendel, and Wolff, *Reader,* pp. 253–254.

61. The maze at Cöthen was undoubtedly still in place in Bach's day; see Johann Christophe Beckmann, *Historie des Fürstenthums Anhalt in Sieben Theilen verfasset* (Zerbst, 1710, rpt. 1993), part II, chap. II, sec. VI, p. 36: "Der Nachlass dieses schönen Wercks ist annoch umb der Fürstlichen Residence zu Köthen gleich wie auch die ehemalig Anstalt zu einem Italiänischen Garten noch vor dem Thore daselbst zu sehen." On the gardens at Cöthen generally at this time, see *Acta Inventarium der Fürstlichen Schlossgarten übergen von Zacharias Gottshalch [1707–1732],* manuscript at the Landesarchiv at Oranienbaum. On the labyrinth specifically, see Albert Haase, "Der Schlossgarten von Köthen," in *Askania,* 20 (1931–1932), 78–79, and 21 (1931–1932), 82–83.

62. The court garden, with labyrinth, is reproduced in Kern, *Labyrinthe,* p. 339. On Bach's visits to Carlsbad, see David, Mendel, and Wolff, *Reader,* pp. 6 and 82; and Christoph Wolff, *Johann Sebastian Bach* (New York, 2000), p. 210.

63. Otto E. Deutsch, *Mozart: Die Dokumente seines Lebens* (Kassel and Basel, 1961), p. 499.

64. Letter to his father of 10 April 1782 (*The Letters of Mozart and His Family,* ed. Emily Anderson, 3 vols. [London, 1938], III, 1191–1192).

65. What follows draws on Irmen, *Masonry,* some of which is highly speculative.

66. On the historical links between the master stone masons and the Freemasons, see Gimpel, *Builders,* pp. 90–91.

67. Irmen, *Masonry,* pp. 87–97 and 110–115.

68. These sources are named and discussed in ibid., pp. 33–49.

69. Otto Erich Deutsch, "Das Freihaus-Theater auf der Wieden," in *Mitteilungen des Vereines für Geschichte der Stadt Wien,* 16 (1937), 73; and Anton Bauer, "Der 'Zauberflöte zweiter Teil': Eine heroische Opera von Emanuel Schikaneder und Peter Winter," in *Österreichische Musikzeitschrift,* 4 (1949), 180 and 184.

70. The sources of *Das Labyrinth* are carefully listed in Jahrmärker and Waidelich, *Labyrinth*, pp. 117–120. For the present study the following were consulted: piano vocal score prepared by J. Henneberg and published by André in Offenbach am Main in 1798 or 1799 (Yale University, Irving Gilmore Music Library, Rare M1503 W789 L12+); full score in manuscript preserved from the 1803 Berlin production (Berlin, Deutsche Staatsbibliothek, Mus. MS 23153).

71. The libretto of *Das Labyrinth* is published in full in Jahrmärker and Waidelich, *Labyrinth*, pp. 7–83.

72. Collins, *Combat Myth*, p. 63. Compare the Greek mythological monster Typhoeus (see *OCD*, s.v. "Typhon").

73. Jahrmärker and Waidelich, *Labyrinth*, p. 29.

74. Ibid., p. 87.

75. Ibid.

76. Ibid., p. 88.

77. For a list of these performances as well as reviews, see ibid., pp. 88–93.

Epilogue: The Maze Reborn in an Ecumenical Age

1. For general discussions of the maze among modern spiritualists, see Jill Purce, *The Mystical Spiral: Journey of the Soul* (London, 1974), pp. 28–31; Lonegren, *Labyrinths*, pp. 134–141; and especially Artress, *Path*.

2. Artress, *Path*, p. xi.

3. I collected some of these quotations myself, and others were kindly brought to my attention by Claud Brown of the Yale Divinity School.

4. See, for example, his essays collected in *Four Archetypes: Mother, Rebirth, Spirit, Trickster*, ed. R. F. C. Hull (Princeton, 1970).

Illustration Credits

1.1 Vienna, Kunsthistorisches Museum, Inv. No. MK 14559.

1.2 Comune di Roma, Musei Capitolini, Sovraintendenza ai Beni Culturali.

1.3 Cremona, Civico museo, Ala Ponzone, no. 5 (644) 3.

1.4 Paul Gauckler, *Inventaire des mosaïques de la Gaule et de l'Afrique* (Paris, 1910), vol. 2, no. 187.

1.5 *Revue archéologique*, 8 (1851–1852), 566–571.

1.6 Stephan Braun, "Die Basilika des Reparatus," in *Christliche Kunstblätter* (Freiburg, 1870), p. 103.

1.7 Rome, Biblioteca Apostolica Vaticana, MS Reg. Lat. 438, fol. 35v.

1.8 Vienna, Österreichische Nationalbibliothek, Cod. 2554, fol. 1v.

1.9 Blois, Editions Valoire.

1.10. Paris, Bibliothèque nationale, MS fonds latin 13013, fol. 1v.

2.1. Spoleto, Centro Italiano di Studi sull'Alto Medioevo, from Adriano Peroni, "Il mosaico pavimentale di San Michele Maggiore a Pavia," *Studi Medievali*, 3rd series 18 (1977), figures 3 and 4.

2.2 *Annales archéologiques*, 17 (1857), opposite p. 11.

2.3 Cartography by Philip Schwartzberg, Meridian Mapping, Minneapolis.

2.4 *Notre-Dame de Chartres, Revue trimestrielle*, March 1984, p. 13.

2.5 George Lesser, *Gothic Cathedrals and Sacred Geometry* (London, 1964), vol. 2, end piece.

2.6 Auxerre, Bibliothèque municipale, MS 215, fol. 35v; author's photograph.

2.7 Paris, Bibliothèque nationale, MS fonds français 9152, fol. 77.

2.8 Louis Demaison, *La Cathédrale de Reims* (Paris, 1935), frontispiece.

2.9 Based on Paris, Bibliothèque nationale, MS fonds français 9152, fol. 77.

2.10 Amiens, Centre régional de documentation pédagogique.

2.11 Edmond Soyez, *Les Labyrinthes d'églises: Labyrinthe de la Cathédrale d'Amiens* (Amiens, 1896), plate 2.

2.12 Paris, Bibliothèque nationale, MS fonds français 19093, fol. 7v.

2.13 Chantilly, Musée Condé, MS 724/1596, fol. 21 (Cliché PE 10353).

2.14 Arthur Evans, *The Palace of Minos* (London, 1921–1935), I, 435.

3.2 Rotterdam, Gemeentebibliotheek, 2H22, fol. XVI.

3.4 From the 1907 Jena edition of Comenius's *Labyrinth of the World;* Bochum, Germany, Museum Bochum.

3.5 New Haven, Yale University, Beinecke Rare Book and Manuscript Library, Hd29 L312 T4.

3.6 New Haven, Yale University, Beinecke Rare Book and Manuscript Library, Beckford 266.

3.7 Württemberg, Landesbildstelle Württemberg, Nr. 52705.

4.1 Paris, Bibliothèque nationale, MS fonds latin 8878, fol. 193v.

4.2 Paris, Bibliothèque nationale, MS fonds neerlandais 3, fol. 22.

4.3 Paris, Bibliothèque nationale, MS fonds latin 5371, fol. 240v.

5.1 Florence, Museo Archeologico.

5.2 Florence, Museo del Duomo.

5.3 Florence, Biblioteca Medicea Laurenziana, MS Pluteus 29.1, fol. 463.

5.4 *Magasin pittoresque,* 6 [1838], 216.

6.1 Jakob Bellaert's edition of *The Pilgrimage of Human Life* (Haarlem, 1486); courtesy of The Boston Athenaeum.

6.2 New Haven, Yale University, Beinecke Rare Book and Manuscript Library, Ij B886 678Pbg.

7.1 Oxford, Oxford University, Bodleian Library, Douce 180, fol. 9.

7.2 Paris, Bibliothèque nationale, MS fonds latin 9471, fol. 159.

7.3 Avignon, Musée du Petit Palais.

7.4 Bruges, Hôpital Saint-Jean.

7.5 Florence, Biblioteca Medicea, Laurenziana, MS Edili 148, fol. 66.

7.6 Rome, Biblioteca Apostolica Vaticana, MS Capella Sistina 154, fol. 23v.

7.7 Robert Laffont editions, Paris.

7.8 Modena, Galleria Estense; courtesy of Soprintendenza per i beni artistici e storici di Modena e Reggio Emilia.

7.9 New Haven, Yale University, Beinecke Rare Book and Manuscript Library, Zi 7776; and *idem,* 1972 165.

7.10 Milan, Collection Vittorio Crespi.

7.11 Dijon, Musée des Beaux Arts.

7.12 Vienna, Kunsthistorisches Museum.

7.13 Madrid, Museo del Prado.

8.1 *The Archaeological Journal,* 15 [1858], 229.

8.2 Charles Challine, *Recherches sur Chartres* (c.1640; Chartres, 1918), p. 144.

8.3 Marcel Bulteau, *Monographie de la cathédrale de Chartres* (Chartres, 1887–1901), vol. 3, frontispiece.

8.4 Avignon, Musée du Petit Palais.

8.5 Rome, Biblioteca Apostola Vaticana.

8.6 Munich, Bayerisches Nationalmuseum, Inv. No. 47/21, 1813.

8.7 Munich, Bayerische Staatsbibliothek, Mus. MS B, fol. 136.

8.8 Amsterdam, Rijksmuseum, Rijksprentenkabinet, 309-B-13.

8.9 Historic Royal Palaces and the Controller of Her Majesty's Stationary Office.

8.10 New Haven, Yale University, Beinecke Rare Book and Manuscript Library, Jay45 679L.

9.1 Berkeley, University of California, Music Library, MS 744 [olim Phillipps 4450], p. 62.

9.2   Rome, Biblioteca Apostolica Vaticana.

9.3   Author's photograph.

9.4   Madrid, Biblioteca Nacional, MS M. 1323, fol. 6.

9.5   Derived from New Haven, Yale University, Irving Gilmore Music Library, Rare MT40 R957 1677.

9.6   New Haven, Yale University, Irving Gilmore Music Library, Rare MT H468 G32.

9.7   Cordon Art B.V.-Baarn-Holland. All rights reserved.

9.8   *Daily Mail,* London, Saturday, 23 September 1899.

9.9   Author's photograph.